CW01024461

HARRIER

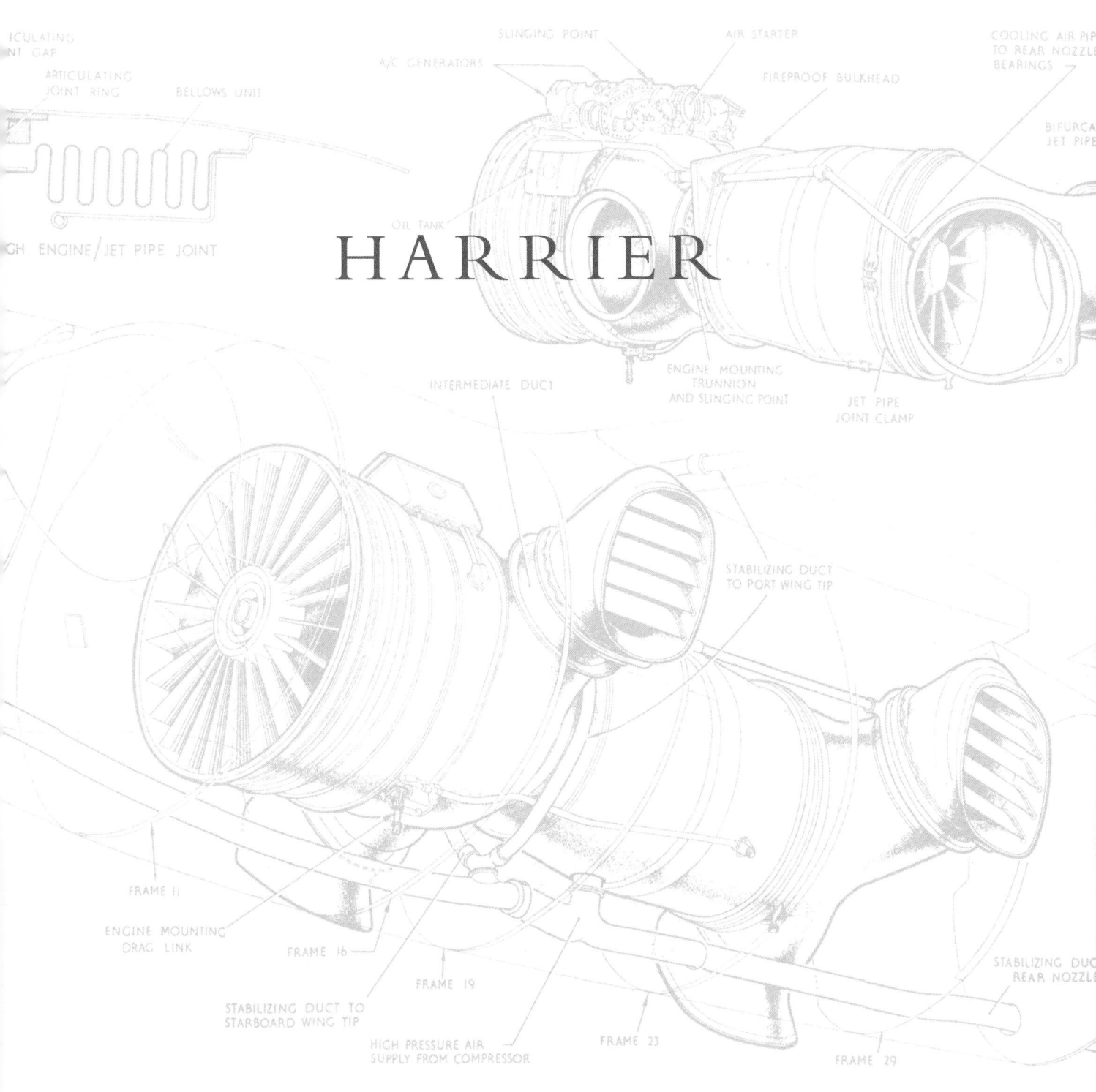

ICULATING
NT GAP

ARTICULATING
JOINT RING   BELLOWS UNIT

GH ENGINE/JET PIPE JOINT

SLINGING POINT   AIR STARTER   COOLING AIR PIP
TO REAR NOZZLE
BEARINGS

A/C GENERATORS   FIREPROOF BULKHEAD

BIFURCA
JET PIPE

OIL TANK

INTERMEDIATE DUCT   ENGINE MOUNTING
TRUNNION
AND SLINGING POINT   JET PIPE
JOINT CLAMP

STABILIZING DUCT
TO PORT WING TIP

FRAME 11

ENGINE MOUNTING
DRAG LINK

FRAME 16

FRAME 19

STABILIZING DUCT TO
STARBOARD WING TIP

HIGH PRESSURE AIR
SUPPLY FROM COMPRESSOR   FRAME 23

STABILIZING DUC
REAR NOZZLE

FRAME 29

Engine installation

Harrier

Tim McLelland

CLASSIC

An imprint of
Ian Allan Publishing

THE AUTHOR

Tim McLelland is an established aviation writer and photographer with an interest in all aspects of aerospace, specialising primarily in post-war military subjects. He has authored a wide range of books on a variety of subjects. He has also produced numerous features for many aerospace magazines and journals and has been a contributor to *Aircraft Illustrated, Air Extra, Armed Forces, Air Forces Monthly, Flypast, Aviation News* and others. Tim also edited *Air Forces International* magazine, and *Scale Models* magazine, in addition to the house magazine of the International Plastic Modellers Society (UK).

As part of his photography and writing work, Tim counts himself fortunate to have been afforded a great deal of direct access to military units around the world. He has talked to serving air crew and staff officers on all aspects of operational and training activities. He has also been given many opportunities to fly as passenger in a wide range of combat aircraft, enabling him to see first-hand what military flying is all about. His 'log book' includes types such as the Jaguar, Lightning, Harrier, Tornado fighter and bomber, Hawk, Hunter, F-4 Phantom (both in US and British service), Buccaneer, Nimrod, Canberra, Hercules, VC10, Chinook, and many others, as well as historical types such as the Lancaster and Shackleton and a number of flights with the world-famous Red Arrows, and the US Navy's Blue Angels team.

Away from the world of military operations, Tim McLelland has also worked with Channel 4 Television, as a stills photographer.

His published works include *Buccaneer, Vulcan – A Complete History, The RAF Manual, Fighter Pilot, Tiger Meet, Flying Tankers, Hunter – A Complete History, Avro Vulcan, Fight's On*, and *C-130 Hercules*. He is also the author of the acclaimed *English Electric Lightning – Britain's First and Last Supersonic Interceptor* (2009) and *TSR2 – Britain's Lost Cold-War Strike Aircraft* (2010) for Classic Publications.

ACKNOWLEDGEMENTS

Assembling a book on the Harrier is, as one might imagine, not the kind of task which can be achieved in splendid isolation, and in order to gather photographs and information on the magnificent 'beast', the author was duly obliged to rely upon the support of many individuals, all of whom were keen to share in this timely celebration of the aircraft. As author, I must extend my thanks to everyone who took the time to supply me with photographs, drawings, snippets of information, and much more. Naturally, not everything could be directly translated into printed pages and a great deal of material simply cannot be fitted within the available space, but the efforts of everyone towards this book are, of course, greatly appreciated. It would be unfair to single out contributors for particular thanks, suffice to say that I am extremely grateful to all who have supported this project, and I am particularly indebted to some individuals who went the proverbial 'extra mile' to provide so many fascinating first-hand accounts of their experiences with the Harrier. Although I cannot claim that the resulting book covers every imaginable aspect of the Harrier's long and fascinating history, I hope that together we have created a colourful and entertaining look back at what has been, by any standards, a truly remarkable aircraft, worthy of recognition. To the following people, however, I must extend (in no particular order) my sincere gratitude for all their help: Gareth Brown (lowflyingphotography.com), Andy Townsend, Chris Sandham-Bailey (inkworm.co.uk), Andre Jans, Francesco Checuz, Richard Caruana, John Adams, Steve Bond, Paul Tomlin, James Blackmore, Morley Lester, Rich Pittman (vlnphotography.co.uk), Philip Stevens (targeta.co.uk), Paul Tremelling, Nicholas Dimitruk, Parminder Ubhi, Andrew Lawson, Y.Nisho, Peter Lee, Peter Collins, Dennis Jenkins, Mick Roth, Terry Panopalis, Simon Watson (aviation-bookshop.com), Zachary Falzon (fencecheck.com), Lance Pawlik (fencecheck.com), Peter Mitrovich, Andy Robinson, RAF Cottesmore, MoD Defence Image Library, Thomas Cheney, Martin Thorn, Chris Parker (fourfax.co.uk), Pete Mears, Anthony Thornborough, Stuart Skelton, and Mark Rourke.

CONTENTS

'SITTING ON TOP OF JET POWER'

An Introduction

IT probably goes without saying that for any aircraft enthusiast, the opportunity to take to the skies in any aeroplane is one which is seized with eagerness and enthusiasm. Big or small, fast or slow, the quirks and characteristics of every imaginable aircraft type make flying a fascinating and unforgettable experience. But one particular aeroplane exhibits unique qualities which no other aircraft can replicate with reliability or flair, and when I was presented with the chance to fly in a Harrier, I could scarcely believe my luck. My excitement and eagerness was tempered somewhat by a long day of preparations at the Royal Navy's sprawling base at Yeovilton in Somerset, the Fleet Air Arm's 'home' and the shore base for the Navy's Harrier fleet. After first satisfying a doctor that I was capable of surviving the experience (something which brings a touch of sobriety to the joyous prospect of going flying), the flying clothing people then took charge, issuing the regulation thermal (and fire-retardant) underwear, flying overalls, gloves, boots, and the bizarre 'g-suit' which Harrier pilots routinely wear for every sortie. In fact it's hardly a suit at all. It resembles something akin to fetish wear, in the form of lace-festooned trousers which fit (with some difficulty) over one's thighs, calves and stomach, aided by long, tight zip fasteners. Once attached (and even this is quite a feat), the suit is laced-up to fit snugly. Of course the term 'snugly' is subjective, as once the g-suit is plugged into the Harrier's pneumatic system, the entire garment can (and will) inflate automatically when any g-force is applied to the aircraft, squeezing the wearer's body with a surprisingly firm grip. The aim is to restrict the flow of blood to one's extremities so that one's brain isn't starved of oxygen under the application of g-force – something which would quickly lead to blackout and potential disaster. In practice the g-suit doesn't quite work in this way and it is the responsibility of the wearer to use the suit's firm embrace to physically squeeze and clench one's muscles against it as the g-force is applied, grunting and gasping until the effects of gravity finally release their powerful grip on one's body. It all begins to sound rather brutal, but then flying a Harrier has never been about gentility.

The ubiquitous fast jet flying helmet (the 'bone dome') is then fitted. The flying clothing folks wryly comment that the wearer's head is generally adjusted to fit the helmet rather than vice versa and it does feel as if the screw fittings are reshaping one's head rather than the proportions of the helmet's inner core. But the bulky and absurdly heavy helmet serves a vital purpose, protecting the wearer not only from injury inside the aircraft but (most importantly) from injury should he be obliged to abandon the aircraft in flight. Leaving the Harrier in a hurry is a relatively simple task and something which can be achieved very quickly. It has to be this way as things can go wrong in a fast jet at any time, but in a Harrier things can go very wrong very quickly, often with no time to even think about the situation. Abandonment has to be instantaneous and instinctive, and the Martin Baker ejection seat enables the pilot to make a rapid exit from the Harrier, simply by pulling the seat's operating handle attached to the seat pan. In most circumstances, regardless of height, speed or attitude, the seat will extract the occupant from the Harrier and place him under a parachute canopy in less time that it takes to read these words, capable of compensating for a descent rate of up to 100 feet per second. But of course this ability comes at a price and the ejection seat is not some clumsy spring-powered prop from a James Bond movie. It's a tough, heavy, rocket-powered missile which makes no concessions for the comfort of its occupant, who must ensure that his limbs are clear of the aircraft structure (or they will be broken) and that he is properly positioned at the time of the ejection. Poor posture is not a matter of etiquette in the Harrier; it's the only way to avoid spinal injury. The clumsy bone dome might seem unnecessary but should the ejection seat be used, its protection might be crucial. Attached to the helmet is an oxygen mask which (like all flying clothing) seems to be tailored to create as much discomfort as possible for the wearer. Hooked and adjusted with screw fittings, the mask incorporates a small flip switch which opens a microphone for communication. Another clip forces the mask firmly onto the wearer's face with a vice-like grip making any attempt to speak quite an effort. This pseudo-torture is thankfully only necessary should the Harrier de-pressurise in flight or if fumes should enter the cockpit, the snug fit of the mask enabling oxygen to be supplied directly to the wearer. With the clear and tinted visors pulled down to touch the outer edges of the oxygen mask, one's face is entirely obscured by this bizarre arrangement of 'furniture'. Intentionally so of course, as this ensures that the wearer's face is protected, particularly during the ejection sequence when the Harrier's canopy is shattered by an internal explosive cord. Fragments of Perspex and molten lead droplets are obviously not the sort of thing that one would like embedded in one's face.

Having survived the attentions of the medical team and the flying clothing specialists, the Harrier flight line still seemed very distant, particularly as I sat in a gloomy hall while a survival specialist explained the various support equipment which would be available to me, should I find myself on the ground or in the sea without my Harrier to protect me. The inflatable dinghy, flares, food and distress beacon are common to most fast jets, but the Navy's safety briefings have a uniquely hands-on approach. Not only is a dinghy actually inflated for my information (and amusement), but I am also obliged to attach myself to a parachute harness before being suspended in mid-air, blindfolded. This might seem like a slightly grotesque party trick but after having been spun for a few seconds whilst still blindfolded (to create even more disorientation), I am asked to unfasten my parachute harness by touch, allowing me to tumble onto the (padded) floor. It's a good way to ensure that the survival theories have been understood and digested.

At long last the preparations are over and I am declared ready to go flying. The next morning I join No.899 Naval Air

Squadron. This unit was responsible for the training of new Sea Harrier pilots and the retraining of pilots returning from other duties. With an average of eight instructors and a similar number of students, 899 NAS was a relatively small unit, equipped with a handful of Sea Harriers and twin-seat T4N Harriers, together with a pair of Hunter T8M trainer aircraft. Students usually came to the squadron directly from the RAF's No.233 Operational Conversion Unit at Wittering, where they would have first spent thirty hours learning to fly the Harrier. At Yeovilton the students would then be taught to fly the 'navalised' Sea Harrier, using 899's mixed fleet of aircraft. The unit's Hunters were something of an oddity, being somewhat aged twin-seat examples of the classic aircraft, equipped with rather ugly nose cone fairings which housed the Sea Harrier's Blue Fox radar. Fitting the radar into the dual-control Harrier T4 (which retains the early-production Harrier's thin nose contours) would have required major redesign work and the Hunters provided a more cost-effective solution. No.899 NAS' twin-seat T4N Harriers were therefore used mostly for instrument rating check flights, initial conversion flying and for teaching students the basics of launching from the famous 'ski jump' (commonly referred to on the squadron as 'the ramp') which equipped the Navy's 'Through deck Cruiser' fleet. The T4N would also provide a suitable free seat from which I would be able to observe the Harrier's operation at first-hand. In order to show me what Harrier flying was all about, Charlie Cantan (a Falklands Sea Harrier veteran) was tasked with flying me as passenger on a combined training and demonstration sortie. After briefing the planned sortie and getting myself kitted-up again in my flying clothing, it was finally time to 'walk' and once Charlie had completed signing-off our aircraft, he escorted me out onto the flight line at Yeovilton where a gaggle of assorted single and twin-seat Harriers was assembled and prepared for the day's flying schedule.

Although I had spent many years as a photographer staring at countless Harriers, the aircraft takes on a rather different appearance when one is about to go flying in it. Up close, the Harrier isn't quite as sleek and slippery as it looks when it races past the crowds at an air show. In fact, the Harrier is quite a portly aircraft – essentially a pair of huge, gaping air intakes accompanied by a sharply downward-raked wing (itself covered by flat-plated vortex generators) and a strangely-contoured fuselage featuring all manner of ugly bumps and protuberances. The Harrier is also surprisingly small and even at close range the aircraft gives an impression of compactness, particularly when the aircraft's wings taper down to almost waist level. It's not often that you can stand on the ground and look down at an aircraft's wing tip. Even the twin-seat T4N seems quite small when compared to other combat aircraft, but the raised rear cockpit, longer fuselage and extended tail fin somehow make the 'twin-sticker' seem substantially larger than the diminutive Sea Harrier, even though they are essentially the same aircraft. The Navy's T4N was in effect identical to the RAF's T4 trainer, but without the add-on laser rangefinder nose fairing. Our designated aircraft was already prepared for our arrival and while Charlie conducted a careful walk-round visual inspection of the aircraft (to ensure that no obvious faults had been overlooked and that locks and covers were all removed), I clambered carefully up the rather tall and shaky step-ladder which was positioned beside the aircraft's rear cockpit. Small though the Harrier may be, climbing into the rear cockpit gives one the impression of being perilously high but after stepping over onto the ejection seat (whilst holding onto the windscreen

frame), I carefully routed my boot-clad feet into the tiny floor space ahead of the seat pan, and gingerly sat down. The sensation of being perched high above the aircraft was now gone, replaced by an impression of clutter, metalwork, Perspex, dials, switches and pipes which festoon the tiny cockpit interior. My first task after sitting down was to lean forward and route the ejection seat's leg restraint cables through the buckles attached to my calves before clipping them into place on the seat's base. These cables serve no purpose during normal flight, but if the seat's ejection sequence is initiated, they instantly draw themselves into the seat, pulling the occupant's legs firmly into place before the seat begins its rapid and violent departure from the aircraft. The main seat and parachute straps came next and with the aid of the ever-helpful ground crew, I was soon firmly attached to my seat and ready to attach the PEC (Personal Equipment Connector) which links the oxygen supply and radio link between the aircraft and its occupant, followed by the PSP (Personal Survival Pack) clip which ensures that the dinghy and survival pack stay with you, should you need to eject. It also sets off a distress beacon which alerts the Search and Rescue force. Helmet on, radio link plugged in, oxygen mask clipped on, visor down, gloves on, straps tightened and everything is done apart from a few adjustments of the radio communications switches, to ensure that I can hear both the pilot and the air traffic broadcasts.

Once satisfied that everything looks 'good to go', Charlie climbed into the front cockpit and started his careful setting-up of the aircraft's switches prior to engine start. With the huge Perspex canopy pulled over my cockpit the surroundings became even more claustrophobic, and even though the rear seat is positioned higher than the pilot's position, the forward view in the Harrier isn't great, not least because there's a blast screen positioned between the two cockpits (in effect a duplicate of the pilot's external windscreen) and the associated framework gives an impression of clutter and a typical 1960s feel which is also apparent from the cockpit's internal layout. No fancy CRT screens here, just a very traditional collection of dials and switches which look little different from those found in the Harrier's predecessor – the immortal Hunter. With a buzz of audio static and a crackle through my helmet's speakers, Charlie said hello from the front cockpit and informed me that if I was ready, he could now start-up the Pegasus engine. I was more than ready of course and a few seconds later a gentle vibration felt under my seat confirmed that the engine was slowly spooling-up and even though my tight-fitting bone dome was keeping out most of the noise, the distinctive whine of the Harrier's Pegasus was soon ringing through my ears. Unlike most jet engines, which can barely be distinguished audibly from each other, the Pegasus exhibits a noise which is unique to the Harrier and even with the massive air intakes just inches away from my shoulders, the familiar Harrier 'wail' sounded much the same as it always had – just considerably louder. But with the canopies closed the noise is greatly diminished and after confirming that my canopy was locked closed, I removed the remaining safety pins to arm the canopy detonation chord and the ejection seat. Settled in the small (almost cramped) cockpit with a set of flickering instruments in front of me, my preparations were now complete and I could sit back and enjoy the ride.

With the wheel chocks pulled away and a signal from the ground marshalled, the Harrier rolls forward, stopping smartly as Charlie stabs the brakes to check their effectiveness before turning left and off round the perimeter taxiway towards the runway. The journey is slow but comfortable, the Harrier's tough undercarriage demonstrating a smooth 'spongy' feel as the wheels ride over the taxiway's expansion joints. Ahead of us the Harrier's older cousins can be seen, a pair of Hunters setting off on their take-off run, embarking on another simulated attack mission over the English Channel. Once they are clear of the runway we are given permission to line up for our own take-off. It might be imagined that any Harrier flight might begin with a demonstration of the aircraft's unique vertical take-off abilities but, with a full fuel load (around 6,500 lb), the aircraft is too heavy to be supported by the Pegasus engine's thrust and we are therefore required to use Yeovilton's very ample main runway to get airborne. A change in engine tone is the signal that we are about to go and as the brakes are released the aircraft lurches smartly forward with a rattle and roar of engine power, almost like a dog being released from a leash. Full power is applied and this is the moment when the Harrier gives a passenger their first surprise. With some previous experience of flying in fast jets (including those with powerful, afterburning engines) I had assumed that the Harrier's non-afterburning engine would provide the aircraft with a fairly pedestrian take-off performance. Of course I was forgetting that the Pegasus is a very powerful engine and that the Harrier is small and comparatively light. This combination of power-versus-weight is the key to the Harrier's unusual performance. Denied the opportunity to get us airborne vertically, the brutal power of the Pegasus engine is vectored away behind us, pushing the Harrier forwards at a truly breathtaking rate of acceleration. Rushing forward, we hurtle along the runway and in a matter of seconds Charlie is deflecting the engine's nozzles downwards and we immediately leap up off the runway into the air. Vertical it wasn't, but still very impressive.

In a matter of seconds we were comfortably airborne, the landing gear tucked away (without so much as a perceptible clunk) and flaps up, and by the time we swiftly skimmed over Yeovilton's perimeter road (where the hardy enthusiasts were busy pointing their cameras in our direction), there was little to indicate that we were flying in anything other than a pretty conventional jet. Indeed the initial climb-out seemed indistinguishable from a similar experience I'd had at Yeovilton in a Hunter which (by pure chance) had been one of the Hunters assigned to the Harrier Conversion Unit back in 1970, when the RAF first took delivery of the revolutionary aircraft. There is no doubt though that the rush of the Harrier's initial take-off acceleration is quite something when compared to the Hunter, but then with nearly twice as much thrust I suppose this shouldn't be a surprise. Climbing gently as we departed to the south-west, we quickly popped into a layer of milky, grey gloom but just a matter of seconds later we were out over the top of the cloud cover in glorious sunshine. With little to do or see for the time being, I had the opportunity to examine the Harrier's interior more carefully, and with everything running, the hood closed and helmet on, the Harrier's 'office' is a cosy place. It is small by any standards and the instrument panel is correspondingly modest, with flight instruments to both sides of a large central display screen which dominates the panel. Above it, the HUD clutters up what is already a fairly restricted forward view (through an internal windscreen and then the forward cockpit), but looking to the left and right, the view of the outside world is commendably good. Panels on either side

of the ejection seat contain yet more switchery but the most obvious item here is the combined throttle and nozzle selector which sits by my left hand on the console. It's a small cockpit but the elevated position above the front cockpit and nose tends to compensate for this, and high above Cornwall the view of the outside world is spectacular.

We are soon gently climbing through 20,000 feet and ahead of us we have a rendezvous with a refuelling tanker. The tiny speck on the horizon eventually grows larger and as Charlie brings us in closer, we find that we are not the only 'customers' visiting the not-so-solitary VC10 tanker. Assembled in its wake is another VC10, two Buccaneers and our 'playmates' from Yeovilton in the shape of two Sea Harriers. Aerial refuelling was a regular part of Harrier operations for both the RAF and FAA although the 'first generation' Harriers did not have the luxury of a more permanent (and retractable) refuelling probe. Instead, a large 'bolt-on' probe was attached to the aircraft when required, fixed above the port air intake and projecting forwards and outwards to the side of the canopy. It looked every inch an afterthought (which it was, as a refuelling probe was not built into the P.1127's original design) but it worked well and didn't affect the aircraft's handling in any way. The key to successful refuelling was for the pilot to concentrate on the tanker aircraft, taking visual cues from the tanker position (and alignment markings painted on its undersides), and to use only peripheral vision to nudge the Harrier's probe into the refuelling basket. Looking directly at the probe created a tendency to overcompensate and the result could be a slightly comical period of last-second frantic control column juggling which often ended in failure (and could result in a snapped probe nozzle or even a detached basket). More experienced Harrier pilots had an ability to conduct the potentially hazardous task without any care for stipulated procedures, and managed to make the art of 'tanking' look far easier than it actually was.

With our time with the tanker completed, Charlie slowly edged our aircraft away from the VC10 and the attendant gaggle of customers, and radioed the air traffic control authority to request permission to descend. I assumed that the descent would be as gentle and uneventful as our climb up to the tanker had been, but Charlie had other ideas, and although I didn't know it, he was about to demonstrate what an agile and manoeuvrable aircraft the Harrier is. With a call of 'Let's go down – are you ready?' over the intercom, I confirmed that I was happy and suddenly the world literally turned upside down. The Harrier flicked over with astonishing speed and as the horizon whirled round to a position above my head, we pulled smartly downwards, the carpet of cloud below us suddenly filling the view ahead of me. We were heading down and down vertically like a brick, the altimeter 'clock' visibly spinning like something from a cartoon. In a matter of seconds we were slowly recovering to a more civilised attitude. As the cloud cover came up to meet us, we re-entered the gloom and continued a more gentle descent, emerging above a patchwork-quilted Devon countryside, speckled with patches of sunlight as we headed northwards and out of the miserable weather front. By the time we had settled at lower altitude the cloud cover had almost gone and I was able to enjoy a few minutes of sightseeing as we continued our journey back to Somerset in bright sunlight. But this was no time for joyriding, as Charlie wanted to demonstrate what combat flying looked and felt like. As a Falklands veteran, he was no stranger to the art of low-level flying and as we turned to head north-east, he eased the

Harrier's nose downwards slightly and gently descended through 2,000 ft, then 1,000 ft and still down until I noticed that we were still edging towards the earth through 500 ft. The gentle ride was just about over. The fields below were starting to grow significantly closer and gave the impression that they were about to come up and wrap themselves around the cockpit, and as Charlie announced that we were now settled into the low-level leg of our sortie, the instruments confirmed that we were just 250 ft above the Somerset countryside, with trees, roads, farmhouses and streams flashing by either side of the cockpit, seemingly within touching distance. The sensation of speed was very obvious, but by looking directly forward through the HUD, the world seemed less disorientating. Looking out to the side at any passing object was almost pointless as by the time I had turned to look at it, we'd gone past it in a dizzying 480-knot hurry. The key to gaining any spatial awareness was to keep looking forward. Things then got even more exciting, as Charlie added another touch of power and began a series of representative evasive manoeuvres, combined with an astonishing demonstration of knap-of-the-Earth flying. As the speed pushed through 500kt, the g-forces came on, squeezing me forcibly into the ejection seat, making my arms almost too heavy to move and my head feeling as if it was made of lead. The g-suit inflated, squeezing my legs and guts, the horizon rolled left and right and as I'd been briefed, I concentrated on squeezing my muscles to try and maintain consciousness while the g-force kept coming. I'd been warned to expect this but it's still a surprise when it starts to happen, and all of one's attention is consumed by the simple act of staying awake and alert; quite how Charlie managed to fly the aircraft is hard to imagine. Even more difficult to grasp is how the tactics of warfare can be entertained when the world is rolling left and right, the wings are streaming clouds of vapour and the cockpit seems to be a tight, claustrophobic, sweaty hell-hole. Still down in the proverbial weeds and still manoeuvring, we approach a looming hillside and as the forward view seems suddenly to fill with grass, the g-force comes on and we bang, rattle and thunder up the side of the hill, the g-force suddenly easing as the aircraft flicks over onto its back. We pull smartly over the brow of the hill – I look upwards through the top of the canopy and to my amazement a Land Rover flashes by, its occupant stood nearby staring straight up at us, seemingly just a few feet away. The g-force comes on again and – still inverted – we pull down the other side of the hill, snapping into a sharp roll which brings us wings level, and on comes the g-force once more as we bottom-out back in the weeds on the other side. Never was the term 'gob-smacking' more appropriate.

Charlie announces that he's finished with the manoeuvring (much to my relief) and we settle onto a direct heading for Yeovilton. Once back in the airfield circuit we nudge down for a low run across the airfield and a sprightly break to port, winding down the speed as the g-force comes back for the last time, until we are comfortably settled on the downwind leg of the circuit with wings level, speed knocked-off and the undercarriage coming down. The steady roar of air speed is gone now, and the Harrier seems like a very different machine as we lumber around onto final approach, the engine tone now very evident. Crossing the runway threshold looks and feels entirely normal, but it is only now that Charlie demonstrates the uniqueness of Harrier flying. The air speed continues to decay and as I look out and downwards, I can see that we're passing a speed at which any normal jet aircraft would have

shuddered and stalled. But we're not stalling – the aircraft is slowing still further, down through 80kt, 40kt… until, amazingly, we seem to be at little more than walking speed but we are still comfortably airborne, fifty feet above the ground. And then it finally happens – the unique Harrier experience… we come to a complete stop. It is at this point that your senses defy your logic. The noise of engine thrust roars around you even through the thick cockpit canopy and your sturdy helmet and ear cushioning. But we are stationary, hanging in mid-air, supported only by a column of pure power. The sensation is remarkable, and even more so because there is no feeling of 'artificiality' to detract from the very real feeling of jet thrust. The aircraft edges slightly forward, left and right, never entirely motionless, and the cockpit rattles with vibration, while the odour of hot kerosene drifts into the oxygen mask and up your nose. You really are left in no doubt that you are sitting on top of jet power. We start to move forwards again, and the rudder pedals occasionally shudder, reminding me that the aircraft's air stream detection system is warning Charlie to keep the aircraft straight ahead, otherwise catastrophe would ensue and our flight would – at best – be ended courtesy of Martin Baker's seats. But in Charlie's expert hands we are soon above the landing pad and as the grass begins to come even closer, we make a gentle vertical descent until, with a last-second thud, we drop (almost bounce, in fact: the undercarriage is surprisingly springy) onto the concrete pad as the roar of the Pegasus simultaneously winds down.

Back on the flight line and with the canopy swung open, I'm able to gather my thoughts and clamber carefully back onto the concrete, soaked in sweat, tired, my head still spinning. The sheer rush of a fast jet mission is enough to thrill anyone, but to end the flight in such a remarkable and unique fashion is something that can – or at least could – only be achieved courtesy of the Harrier. By any standards, it was quite a ride.

It is some fifty years since the Harrier emerged as the world's first fully-operational vertical take-off and landing jet aircraft. Astonishingly, it is still the only aircraft which routinely combines the functions of a combat-capable warplane with the unique ability to hover, take off and land vertically. It is true that the Harrier might not enjoy this unique place in the history of aviation for too much longer, now that Boeing's F-35 is nearing the end of its design and development story, but the story of the F-35 has been a long and complicated one, fraught with politics and cost escalations. Even now there is no guarantee that it will ever enter service with the United States Marine Corps or indeed any other potential customer. It may well be that the F-35 emerges as a 'conventional' aircraft without the vertical take-off capability which has been at the heart of the aircraft's design since it was first conceived. What is now certain is that the United Kingdom's Royal Air Force and Royal Navy look set to buy the aircraft as a non-VTOL machine, and the USMC may well (if cost increases and delays continue) follow the same path.

Sadly, the all-new F-35 has effectively ended the long and fascinating history of the remarkable Harrier for good. The Harrier will remain in service with the USMC, Italy and Spain for a few years, with India too for a while, and in Thailand, where the last examples of the original 'first generation' Harrier remain in use. It is perhaps particularly ironic that the first nation to abandon the Harrier is the very country where it was designed and built. But the Harrier has always enjoyed a unique position in Britain's military capability and even from the outset its future was never entirely certain. Created in response to a revolutionary concept proposed by a French designer, it took the expertise of a famous British aircraft manufacturer to turn the idea into a viable warplane. It also required the brilliant technical abilities of a British engine manufacturer to produce a truly unique power plant which could turn the bizarre French proposal into a working engineering concept. The result was a relatively small and simple aircraft, powered by a big – and incredibly bold – jet engine which combined the usual effects of horizontal thrust with a unique ability to vector its output downwards, thereby keeping the aircraft airborne without any aerodynamic lift at all. The idea was ambitious but the result was a huge success.

Today, it might seem obvious that a combat aircraft that has no need for a long runway is a truly significant asset for any military air arm. Reliance on runways is acceptable if there is no risk of the runway disappearing, but through the dark years of the Cold War it was readily apparent that airfields (and particularly their huge runways) would be irresistible targets for an advancing enemy. No matter how effective a force of bomber or fighter aircraft might be, without a runway from which to operate they are of course useless, and it was this unavoidable fact which led to the search for VTOL ability. Freed from the runway requirement, a VTOL combat aircraft could operate from any site almost at will, be it a simple grass field, a woodland clearing, or a service station forecourt. The Harrier – designed to support ground forces – was an ideal solution, able to operate literally at the 'front line' of any action, ready to support an army no matter where it might roam.

It was also abundantly clear that the Harrier's abilities would be of significant value to naval forces, especially those that cannot rely upon the support of huge, expensive aircraft carriers. Operating combat aircraft at sea traditionally required a big deck, a steam catapult and arrester cables, but the Harrier needed none of these. The creation of the famous 'Ski Jump' expanded the Harrier's abilities still further, making even smaller vessels capable of becoming viable 'mini-carriers' that were far less expensive to operate, but still carried a mighty punch. But despite the Harrier's seemingly supreme capabilities, the aircraft was not embraced by all of the world's air arms. Even a relatively small naval air wing must be maintained at some size if it is to remain operationally effective, and so the once popular prediction that even small nations might embrace the Harrier's abilities proved to be unfounded. But for the aircraft's key customers (Britain and America) the Harrier proved itself to be an immensely valuable asset, and it was only the prospect of an all-new (and much more advanced) VTOL aircraft which finally brought the Harrier's long history towards its conclusion.

Britain's decision to abandon VTOL capability might seem somewhat strange, given the country's reliance upon the Harrier for so many years. It is undoubtedly true that without the Harrier the UK could not have successfully recaptured the Falkland Islands in 1982. It could also be argued that without the RAF's Harrier, Britain would not have had a truly effective force with which to fight the Soviet Union, had the much-feared war ever broken out across the German plains. But it is important to understand that the world is very different to the days of the Cold War. There is no realistic risk of a major conflict between East and West, and the prospect of a long and ugly battle being fought across Europe now seems to be nothing more than a distant (and distinctly horrifying) memory.

It was for this very scenario that the Harrier was created, and now that it is gone, the Harrier's role has also gone too. The need to escape from reliance upon runways was once almost essential but now it is no longer an issue. The RAF's modern combat aircraft are not faced with the prospect of their primary airfield sites being destroyed, therefore there is no longer any need to retain any ability to disperse forces out into the surrounding landscape. Likewise, Britain's Royal Navy has successfully fought for the construction of two new aircraft carriers which are in effect 'full scale' designs, which will rely on conventional launch and recovery systems, and so VTOL is no longer a necessity. Thus, even though the Harrier's abilities were once almost vital, they are now in effect redundant.

But to suggest that the Harrier is no longer regarded as a necessity might also suggest that the aircraft was in some way deficient. In fact, nothing could be further from the truth. The Harrier was a brilliant example of technology and engineering at its very best and for decades it was a vitally important part of the RAF's inventory (and – for many years – the Navy's too). But the Cold War is now gone, and with it must also go one of its most famous and successful creations.

In this book I have endeavoured to trace the Harrier's fascinating and colourful history, tracing the story from its very beginnings through to the present day. For a subject such as this, it would probably require the space of numerous volumes to fully explore every aspect of such a versatile aircraft which has been around for so long. But of course a great deal of excellent material has already been published which examines specific parts of the Harrier's story, either in terms of variants, the countries which operate the aircraft, or some of the many conflicts in which the aircraft has been involved. This book forms a more comprehensive look at the whole story – a celebration of a magnificent aircraft which combines the story of the Harrier's design and operational life with stories from just some of the people who have flown, maintained or worked with the aircraft. I hope that the resulting book is an entertaining and enjoyable look at one of the most revolutionary and significant aircraft ever to have been produced.

GLOSSARY

AAA - Anti-Aircraft Artillery

ACE - Allied Command Europe

ACM - Air Combat Manoeuvring

ADD - Air Direction Detector

AFB - Air Force Base

AMRAAM - Advanced Medium Range Air-to-Air Missile

ATC - Air Training Corps

AWACS - Airborne Warning And Control System

BAC - British Aircraft Corporation

BAe - British Aerospace

BVR - Beyond Visual Range

CAP - Combat Air Patrol

CAS - Close Air Support

CRT - Cathode Ray Tube

CVS - Aircraft Carrier

ECM - Electronic Counter Measures

FAA - Fleet Air Arm

FAC - Forward Air Controller

FLIR - Forward-Looking Infra Red

FOD - Foreign Object Danger

FSD - Full-Scale Development

GPS - Global Positioning System

HAS - Hawker Siddeley Aviation

HCT - Harrier Conversion Team

HUD - Head Up Display

HDD - Head Down Display

HOTAS - Hands-On Throttle And Stick

INAS - Inertial Navigation System

LERX - Leading Edge Root Extensions

LGB - Laser-Guided Bomb

LRMTS - Laser Rangefinder and Marked Target Seeker

MFD - Multi-Function Display

MLU - Mid-Life Update

MoA - Ministry of Aviation

MoD - Ministry of Defence

MoS - Ministry of Supply

MWDP - Mutual Weapons Development Programme

NAS - Naval Air Squadron

NATO - North Atlantic Treaty Organisation

NVG - Night Vision Goggles

OCU - Operational Conversion Unit

PCB - Plenum Chamber Burning

PDR - Pilot's Display Recorder

PEC - Personal Equipment Connector

PSP - Personal Survival Pack

QFI - Qualified Flying Instructor

QWI - Qualified Weapons Instructor

RAE - Royal Aircraft Establishment

RAFG - Royal Air Force Germany

RAT - Ram Air Turbine

RCV - Reaction Control Valve

RIC - Reconnaissance Interpretation Centre

ROE - Rules of Engagement

RR - Rolls Royce

RWR - Radar Warning Receiver

SA - Situational Awareness

SACEUR - Supreme Allied Commander Europe

SAM - Surface-to-Air Missile

SBAC - Society of British Aerospace

SDR - Strategic Defence Review

SNEB - Societe Nouvelle des Etablissements Edgar Brandt

STO - Short Take-Off

STOVL - Short Take-Off and Vertical Landing

STOL - Short Take-Off and Landing

TES - Tripartite Evaluation Squadron

TIALD - Thermal Imaging and Laser Designation

USAF - United States Air Force

USMC - United States Marine Corps

VIFF - Vector In Forward Flight

VSTOL - Vertical or Short Take-Off and Landing

VTOL - Vertical Take-Off and Landing

WWII - World War Two

The Fleet Air Arm's Harrier T8 fleet adopted the RAF's all-black 'high visibility' paint scheme, although national insignia were applied in a 'toned down' red and blue style. (Photo: Rich Pittman/VInphotography.co.uk)

An aerial view of RNAS Yeovilton. The Harrier 'ski jump' ramp and VTOL landing pads adjacent to the main runway are clearly visible. No.899 NAS at Yeovilton took responsibility for all naval Harrier training from January 1989. (Photo: RNAS Yeovilton)

CHAPTER ONE

Vertical Dreams

al blower   Gear boxes   8,000hp Bristol Orion

AN aircraft's ability to take off or land vertically was once the stuff of dreams. It was the introduction of the helicopter which finally demonstrated that not all aircraft needed to rely on long strips of concrete or grass in order to become airborne. But helicopters are slow and cumbersome. Versatile and valuable they may be, but helicopters are not fighters or bombers. Creating a combat aircraft which can combine the abilities of a fast and agile fighter with the versatility of a helicopter is a challenge which might seem to have been met only relatively recently. But the concept is, in fact, far from new. It was during the dark days of the Second World War that Nazi Germany first explored the possibility of creating a combat aircraft which could operate independently of fixed runways, safe from the risk of destruction by enemy forces. Erich Bachem was credited with the design of the Ba 349 'Natter', an inventive rocket-powered interceptor which was intended to give the *Luftwaffe* a means of successfully defending the *Reich* from relentless Allied bombing. Conventional fixed-wing fighter aircraft were, of course, already available to the *Luftwaffe* in huge numbers as the Second World War progressed, but by late 1943 the Allied air offensive was already challenging Germany's air superiority over its own territory. Although the *Luftwaffe's* fighter pilots were capable of defending German airspace and proved a tough adversary for the Allied bombers and their escort fighters, German aircraft were inevitably vulnerable whilst on the ground, tied to the confines of easily-located airfields which could be

destroyed (or at least severely damaged) almost at will. Even the new Messerschmitt Me 163 *Komet* rocket-powered interceptor with its phenomenal speed and manoeuvrability still needed an airfield from which to operate and no matter how impressive the aircraft might have been once in the air, it was just as vulnerable as any other aircraft whilst on the ground. Airfields were sitting targets. The radical design of the *Natter* was to have given Germany an interceptor which would be completely mobile, capable of being launched from any suitable clearing amongst the safety of woodland camouflage where the chances of locating and destroying it prior to launch were almost nil. Various ingenious ideas to counter enemy bombers had already been proposed to *Luftwaffe* chiefs, including rail-launched fighters and surface-to-air missiles (SAMs) but the *Natter* (which was, in effect, almost a manned missile) offered the most promising solution. Launched vertically under radio control, the diminutive wooden-built interceptor would rocket upwards from its support tower and head directly towards its target, at which stage the pilot would resume

The revolutionary German Bachem 'Natter' of 1944-45 - in effect a 'manned missile' intended as in interceptor, but also the first practical application of VTOL technology. (Photo: Brian Stanley collection)

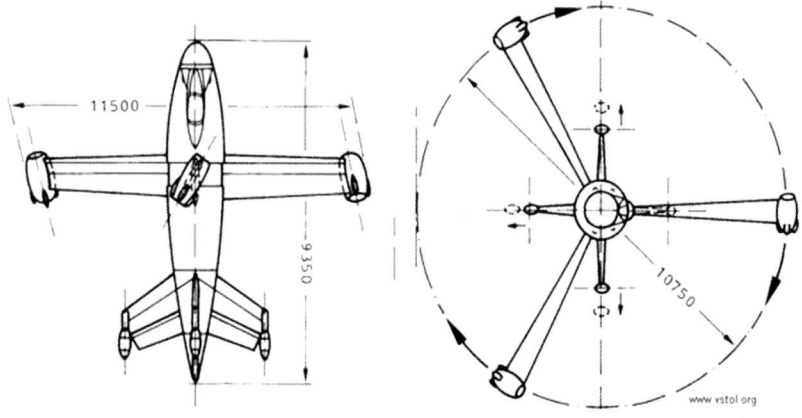

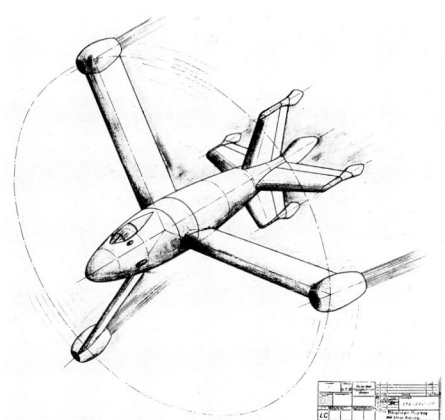

Above and below: The Focke-Wulf Triebflügel never progressed beyond the design stage, but like other concepts which emerged at the same time, it demonstrated Germany's fervent interest in the concept of VTOL. (Courtesy Vstol.org)

direct control and fire a salvo of rockets at his target after which, if necessary, he would use his fuel-starved aircraft to ram an enemy bomber before ejecting to return to the ground by parachute. It was not the most practical of concepts, not least because it was inevitably a one-shot weapon, and the prospect of ending every mission under a parachute could hardly have been the most inspiring prospect for *Luftwaffe* pilots. However the *Natter's* ability to lurk far beyond any risk of enemy detection prior to launch promised to make the interceptor invulnerable, and with sufficient development it could have become a vital asset which had the potential to contribute greatly towards German air defence. Luckily for the Allies, the *Natter's* development was far from trouble-free and although the concept clearly worked, it was still a long way from attaining operational status by 1945. But despite the fact that the *Natter* failed to reach its full potential, it was clear that both Allied and German forces were only too well aware of the vulnerability of their airfields. For example, during one orchestrated attack mounted against enemy airfields by the *Luftwaffe* on 1 January 1945, nearly 400 Allied aircraft were destroyed or damaged. Airfields (and the aircraft situated on them) were easy and valuable targets. The Bachem *Natter* certainly demonstrated that the ability to operate independently of fixed airfields could – at least in theory – provide a pivotal advantage over the enemy. Vertical take-off made good sense.

The *Natter* was not the only vertical take-off concept which Germany pursued. Amongst a variety of radical design proposals, one of the more unusual was the Focke-Achgelis Fa 269, a piston-powered fighter which was to have been operated from Germany's merchant vessels. Unlike the *Natter*, the Fa 269 did not rely on rocket power to achieve vertical take-off, but took advantage of another revolutionary idea which had emerged from many months of scientific research – thrust

vectoring. The aircraft's two propellers fixed aft of the wing could power the aircraft for conventional flight, but thanks to some ingenious engineering work they could also be pivoted downwards, giving the aircraft an ability to take off vertically from the confines of a ship's deck. In contrast to the *Natter*, the Fa 269 could also reverse this process and after completing a mission the aircraft could slow to a hover and return vertically to the ship. Like the *Natter*, it was a project which showed great promise but it never proceeded beyond the design stage, and the manufacturer's drawings and partially-completed mock-up were eventually destroyed by Allied bombing. In some respects the Fa 269 was a hybrid design which combined the abilities of a fixed-wing aircraft and a helicopter, whereas the *Natter* was essentially a missile, capable only of being operated as an aircraft during the terminal attack phase. Together they represented two very different means of achieving vertical take-off and both concepts would re-emerge elsewhere in post-war years. Other ambitious proposals were also being considered, such as the Focke-Wulf *Triebflügel*, a particularly bizarre design which comprised three small jet engines fixed to wings which rotated about the aircraft's fuselage, combining the properties of jet thrust with the vertical lift of helicopter blades. Whether the concept would ever have worked is open to question but the *Triebflügel*, like all of the *Luftwaffe's* colourful concepts, illustrated that Germany was eager to get into the vertical take-off business as soon as it possibly could.

After the end of the Second World War it was in America that interest in vertical take-off and landing (VTOL) began to develop during the late 1940s. Having learned many vital lessons during the war, the US military clearly understood the concept's potential, and the evidence and influence of Germany's still-born VTOL projects inevitably spread amongst America's aircraft design teams, not least through the digestion of so much research material (and manpower) which eventually found its way to the US from Germany. It was almost inevitable that (like so many innovative ideas which emerged during World War Two) the concept of VTOL would be explored in some detail and in 1951 the US Navy issued (with surprising boldness) a requirement for a fleet fighter with VTOL capabilities which would be operated from the Navy's surface vessels. Precisely how much influence the wartime German designs might have had on the Navy's thinking is open to question but instead of pursuing the concept of a 'flat rising' aircraft like the Fa 269 (an aircraft which can take-off vertically whist remaining horizontal), the Navy's interest was geared towards a tail-sitter design which would literally hang under its propeller and after having clawed its way into the air, the aircraft would then rotate through ninety degrees into forward flight. Of course the reverse operation would be required to bring the aircraft back to the ground vertically but the perils of this complicated and risky transition do not seem to have been regarded as significant by either the designers or the potential customer. Eventually a pair of designs emerged, these being the Lockheed XFV-1 (two prototypes) and the Convair XFY-1 (three prototypes), both powered by an Allison T40-a-14 turboprop engine driving huge contra-rotating propellers. The first of these took to the air in August 1954 and although the test programme was regarded as successful, the Navy abandoned its interest in the concept just two years later. It seems likely that the difficulties of the complicated (and potentially dangerous) transition to and from vertical flight were eventually sufficient to convince the Navy that an operational aircraft would be troublesome (possibly even a disaster) and, of course, the basic design of the aircraft (geared exclusively towards the VTOL performance rather than flying capability) did not offer any obvious means of easy development into a viable combat aircraft. But regardless of the difficulties of VTOL operations (or at least those connected with tail-sitter designs) the US Navy's dismissal of the concept was not simply due to its complexity. The US Navy was (and still is) firmly entrenched in the aircraft carrier business, believing that 'might is right' and that bigger and better carriers would always be the way forward. The development of VTOL aircraft was an interesting avenue which promised to give the Navy a useful and versatile asset, but it would also have represented a completely contradictory concept to the notion of conventional carrier operations. Developing aircraft which patently did not need huge carriers ran the risk of rendering carrier power obsolete, and no-one within the Navy had any interest in advocating that kind of thinking. It is this consideration which undoubtedly persuaded the Navy to shift its attention to other concepts and it was this same mindset which undoubtedly affected Britain's Royal Navy a decade later.

In order to understand the history of VTOL development, one must appreciate that with the exception of the *Natter*, the Fa 269 and both the Lockheed and Convair designs were all driven by propellers. It was the Ryan Aeronautical Company which first explored the possibility of utilising jet thrust for VTOL and by 1947 the San Diego company was busy developing a 'test rig' (powered by an Allison J33 turbojet) capable of hovering and manoeuvring with the aid of reaction controls (jet thrust bled from the engine and expelled through small outlets placed at the rig's extremities) and a two-axis auto stabiliser. Although the test rig could not transition to vertical flight (indeed it could not 'fly' at all, being merely an engine with supporting structure – and the jet engine was permanently fixed downwards), it did successfully demonstrate that jet thrust (if greater than the all-up weight of the aircraft) could provide sufficient power to achieve VTOL capability. The Ryan test rig led to the receipt of a USAF contract for a 'proof-of-

concept' aircraft and on 10 December 1955 the Ryan X-13 made its first (conventional) flight. The X-13 was a small and rather squat delta-winged jet design with an all-up weight of around 7,500 lb. Its single Rolls-Royce Avon turbojet delivered a thrust of 9,100 lb and with a full fuel load the X-13 was capable of operating for up to a maximum of just twelve minutes. Not much flying time, but sufficient for the aircraft to make transitions to and from vertical flight (in effect this was all that the aircraft was designed to do) and this was first achieved in May 1956. Unlike the Navy's VTOL aircraft the X-13 did not operate directly from the ground, and without any fixed landing gear it was attached to an hydraulically-operated ramp which raised the aircraft to its vertical launch position prior to release. In some respects this made the X-13 even more difficult to handle than the Convair and Lockheed designs, as each landing required the aircraft to be slowed from horizontal flight, manoeuvred in the vertical hover position and finally hooked onto a nylon rope suspended between two steel towers. Not surprisingly, slowing a jet aircraft to stalling speed, tipping it onto its tail and nudging it into recovery position with just a few minutes of fuel to spare was a perilous procedure and certainly not something that any regular service pilot could be expected to perform. Clearly the X-13 had no potential as an operational aircraft – but then it had not been designed for this purpose. The X-13 was intended only to demonstrate the viability of jet lift and the practicality of creating an operational aircraft which could be powered by a jet engine providing

The remarkable Convair XFY-1 represented one of the more obvious means of achieving VTOL but it did not address the equally obvious difficulties of transitioning to and from vertical flight. Experience soon demonstrated that the tricky manoeuvre was barely within the skills of test pilots and could not be applied to an operational design. (Photos: US Navy).

Bell's X-14A was the first aircraft to fly with vectored thrust. Although a pure research vehicle, it enabled the concept of jet-powered lift deflection to be explored extensively. (Photo: Nasa)

Ryan's X-13 was a successful jet-powered VTOL aircraft, but like the earlier propeller-driven XFV-1 and XFY-1, it suffered from the same difficulties in transitioning to and from vertical flight, making the concept impractical for operational development. (Photo: Teledyne-Ryan)

sufficient thrust for VTOL. In these respects the X-13 achieved its aims but in much the same way as the Navy eventually lost interest in the concept, the USAF also shifted its attention to other projects. Without any interest in preserving carrier power it is more difficult to understand why the USAF saw no potential for VTOL. However, like the Navy with its huge fleet, the Air Force presided over an almost countless number of vast airfields spread across the continental US and far beyond, and did not regard any of these facilities in any way vulnerable. Therefore it seems likely that although VTOL was an interesting concept, there was no obvious need for an aircraft with such abilities. However, across the Atlantic, in Europe, VTOL's potential was already understood.

The post-war European environment was undoubtedly very different to that of the United States, but after the formation of the North Atlantic Treaty Organisation (NATO) in 1949, America began to develop a more active interest in European military thinking and ploughed huge amounts of money into NATO at the start of what would become the Cold War. Key to the defence of Europe from the emerging Soviet threat, was the creation of new combat aircraft and airfields from where American and NATO fighters, bombers,

reconnaissance and army support aircraft could operate within range of the East-West border. Many long-established wartime airfields were already scattered across West Germany and were undoubtedly suitable for modernisation, but their proximity to the Soviet border made them less than ideal locations. Although they were certainly within easy reach of the border, it did not take much imagination to accept that if a conflict began, these airfields would be overrun by Soviet forces in just a matter of hours. Alternative sites had to be created further west, and with funding supplied by America, huge new airfields began to appear from where American and NATO forces could bring in fast and capable aircraft to the new front line. These airfields were all designed in keeping with American thinking and assumed that combat aircraft would require almost an over-abundance of space from which to get airborne or recover. Massive concrete runways were laid, their gleaming white surfaces visible for many miles (most were subsequently 'toned down' in order to camouflage them partially), while some airfields were built just a matter of miles from each other, their respective air traffic zones often conflicting with each other in a vast complex of inter-operational activity. This was NATO at its mightiest. Vast hangars, tall control towers and huge support complexes all became familiar sights across the region and although these magnificent new air bases were undoubtedly impressive, few military observers were willing to acknowledge that these brilliant examples of engineering were also fundamentally flawed. They were big and they were permanent and if a conflict should ever occur they would undoubtedly be hit – and be hit very hard. Destroying these sites would be the Soviets' primary aim, and even at some distance from the East-West border, sufficient enemy air assets could be directed against them to quickly render them useless – probably on the very first day of any confrontation. All of America's investment and effort had been geared towards the creation of these key assets even though it was reluctantly (but certainly not overtly) accepted that they would be destroyed – inevitably – before they were ever properly used. But America and NATO really did not have any other options at their disposal. Combat aircraft (particularly new jet fighters and bombers) had been designed with their flight capabilities and weapon-carrying abilities in mind, but no concessions had been made as to their airfield performance. They all required runways – long runways in fact, and nobody was willing to grapple with the question of how NATO could continue to operate its fighter and attack aircraft if these runways were disabled or destroyed. For example, by 1956 the USAF's first supersonic F-100 jets were arriving in Germany and although the gleaming Super Sabres which now thundered through the skies over Bitburg (the aircraft's first European base) were probably impressive enough to convince any potential aggressor that NATO meant business, it was also true that without Bitburg's mile-long stretch of concrete, these Sabres could never be rattled. It was a flaw that few people were willing to accept openly. However, during the same month that the Sabres arrived, one man – a Frenchman – was addressing this very issue.

Michel Wibault was – by 1956 – a respected and established aviation designer, having been responsible for the creation of many pre-war metal-built monoplanes and the production of many unusual and imaginative design concepts. Having formed his own company near Paris, he had become a consultant for the Vickers company in the UK before

Michael Wibault, the respected French designer who first proposed the revolutionary concept of vectored jet thrust. (Photo: Brian Stanley collection)

moving to the US where he worked for various aerospace companies, including Republic. His enthusiasm for innovative designs led to some very unusual projects, not least the 'Gyroptère', a strange fixed-wing and helicopter hybrid featuring an enclosed rotor design. Little is known about this aircraft and it never proceeded beyond the preliminary design stage, but the Gyroptère (together with later 'flying winged disc' designs revealed by Republic which presumably benefited from Wibault's input) illustrated his long-standing fascination with VTOL aircraft. During February 1956 Wibault approached the French Air Ministry in Paris with yet another revolutionary design, this time a small swept-winged aircraft powered by a single jet engine which he believed would be suitable as the basis for a new aircraft to eventually replace (or supplement) NATO's Fiat G-91 light attack aircraft. Unusually, instead of featuring a conventional exhaust emerging from the rear of the aircraft, Wibault's 'Ground-Attack Gyroptère' design embraced the new concept of vectored jet thrust, using an 8,000 hp Bristol BE.25 Orion turboprop engine to power four centrifugal blower units positioned at right angles to the aircraft's fore-and-aft datum line. By shifting (vectoring) the position of these blowers from horizontal to vertical, the aircraft would be capable of taking off and landing vertically as a simple 'flat riser' aircraft. Wibault was unclear as to precisely what function the aircraft would perform but he believed that the basic concept had merit and could be translated into a useful combat aircraft that might meet NATO's longer-term plans for a small, light strike fighter which would replace the Fiat G-91. The French Air Ministry was somewhat bemused by this revolutionary design and was at` first inclined to dismiss it as impractical; but given Wibault's background and reputation, he could hardly be regarded as a crank. By this stage, the concept (if not the practicality) of VTOL was certainly established: in France there was already evidence of some serious interest in the idea with engine

manufacturer SNECMA busy testing its own experimental machine comprising an Atar turbojet which had been mounted vertically on a castoring base, with a pilot seated precariously on top of the power plant. This preliminary French research eventually led to the annular-winged *Coleoptère* – a truly bizarre 'flying engine' – which was ultimately abandoned, doomed to suffer from the same flight-transition difficulties (and lack of development potential) encountered by the American tail-sitter VTOL designs. By comparison, Wibault's 'flat riser' aircraft design was surprisingly orthodox, even if its propulsion system was not and the Air Ministry officials did recognise that amongst the many VTOL designs that were emerging, Wibault's Gyroptère did at least seem to possess some practical potential. But despite this, and in the absence of any obvious requirement for a small VTOL aircraft which, ultimately, would be no more advanced than the G.91 (and possibly inferior), the French Ministry officials were distinctly lukewarm towards the proposal, even though everyone understood just how valuable a VTOL capability could be. Despite the revolutionary nature of Wibault's concept, nobody seriously believed that the Gyroptère could be developed into a useful fighting machine.

However, Wibault's enthusiasm for the Gyroptère sustained him through a series of presentations and meetings with a variety of officials, and eventually he was advised to approach the MWDP – the Mutual Weapons Development Program (which was being funded by the United States) and also to approach NATO's AGARD (Advisory Group for Aeronautical Research and Development). The MWDP's Colonel Willis 'Bill' Chapman studied the proposal with interest and instructed a team of experts to thoroughly investigate Wibault's idea

France pursued the VTOL concept through a variety of experimental designs, including these rather bizarre SNECMA Atar test rigs. The vertical jet lift engine concept eventually proved to be too troublesome and expensive to pursue and France abandoned its interest in the idea. However it was a French designer (Wibault) who first proposed the concept of vectored jet thrust. (Photo: SNECMA)

Wibault's engine proposal described the use of four fans, driven by a Bristol Orion engine. Although the fan system was immediately dismissed as being complex and inefficient, the overall concept of vectoring the engine's thrust output provided the basis for further development. (courtesy BAE Systems)

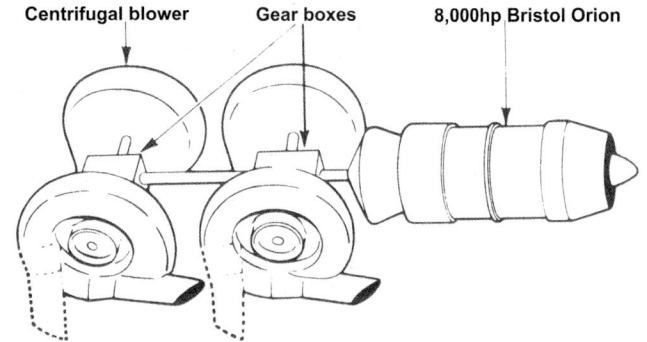

Centrifugal blower   **Gear boxes**   **8,000hp Bristol Orion**

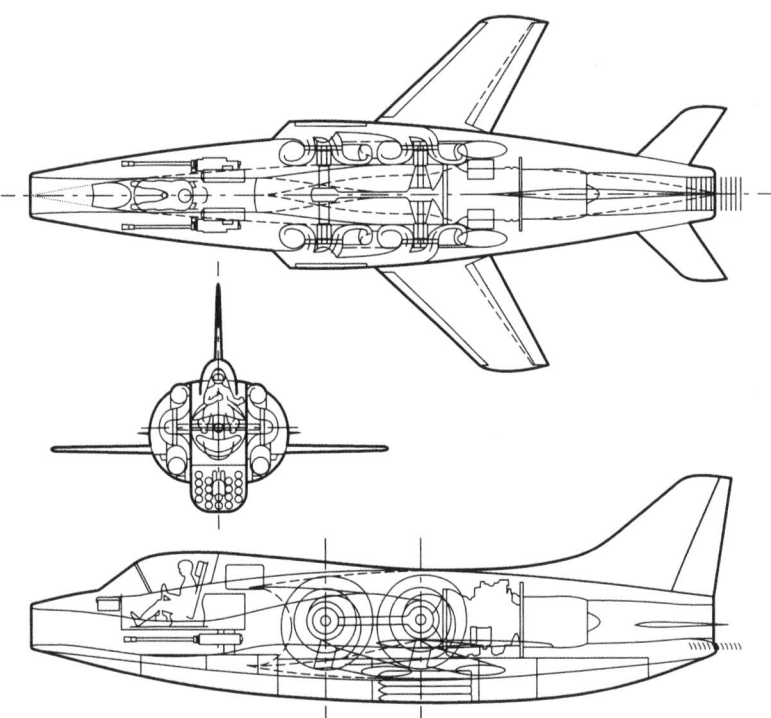

Michael Wibault's Gyroptère design as originally proposed. The fan drive was quickly regarded as inefficient, but the basic concept of vectoring jet thrust had been identified and it was this key aspect which was fundamental to the subsequent development of the Harrier. (courtesy BAE Systems)

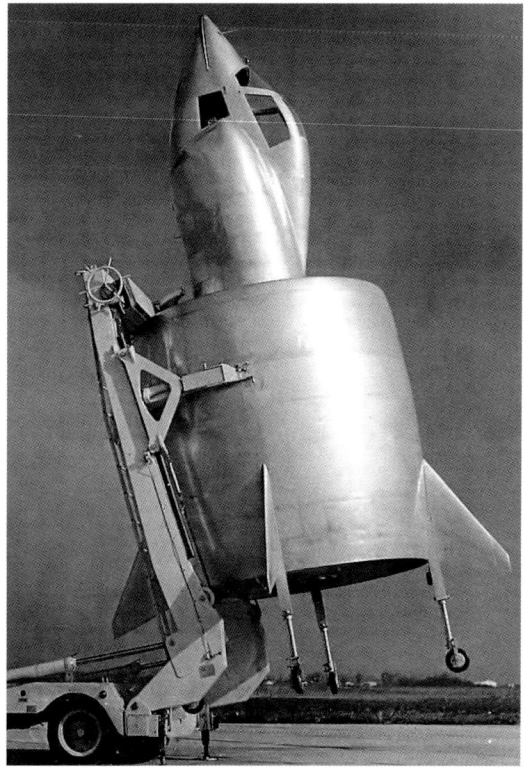

The magnificent Coleoptère – a truly remarkable concept (essentially a 'flying engine'), but one which was ultimately dogged by the difficulties of transitioning to and from vertical flight which made the concept impractical (and potentially lethal) for routine use. (Photo: Brian Stanley collection)

while the wider NATO organisation pursued a similar study. AGARD's Theo von Karman stated that he was already familiar with the concept of vectored thrust but that he was excited by the proposal of achieving this with a jet engine, making the now-famous comment '... *ah – vectored thrust with a jet*', thereby encapsulating the very essence of future VTOL design. Both teams concluded that the concept was a good one and that there was undoubtedly a need for an aircraft with VTOL capability, but they also expressed doubts as to the practicality of the engineering aspects inherent in the design. In essence, they felt that the idea was sound but that Wibault had perhaps not 'thought it through' quite as much as was necessary in order to translate the concept into a viable design. However, Chapman believed that the idea should be pursued and as the MWDP was already working with Bristol Engines in the UK (developing the Orpheus turbojet for the projected NATO light strike fighter which eventually became the aforementioned Fiat G-91), it seemed logical to refer the matter to that company, and in particular the company's Technical Director, Sir Stanley Hooker.

Sir Stanley had come to Bristol Engines from Rolls-Royce where he had become a very well-respected expert on engine design and development. Rolls-Royce had already taken a great interest in VTOL engine concepts and in 1953 the company had produced the Thrust Measuring Rig – a cumbersome and rather comical looking device similar in concept to Ryan's research machine. It comprised two 5,000 lb thrust Rolls-Royce Nene turbojets positioned at each end of a metal framework onto which the hapless pilot was obliged to be seated, controlling the machine by means of long arm pipes through which high pressure air was tapped from the engines to provide roll and pitch stability. The TMR was better known as the 'Flying Bedstead' and as it hopped and skipped precariously around the company's airfield at Hucknall, it demonstrated clearly the viability of the jet lift concept which had been proposed by Rolls-Royce's Dr. A.A. Griffith, its Chief Scientist. However, Griffith did not foresee any projected use for jet lift in combat aircraft. His interest was primarily in civil aviation and his belief that the development of a small and powerful vertical lift jet engine would enable designers to create new airliners which could combine long range and high cruising speeds (powered by conventional rearwards-directed engines) with an ability to take off and land vertically (through the use of vertical jet lift engines). This eventually led to the development of the Rolls-Royce RB.108, a small lightweight turbojet intended almost exclusively for the provision of vertical jet lift, with a thrust-to-weight ratio of around 8-to-1 (which compared very favourably to the 3-to-1 ratio of the company's conventional Avon engine). Of course, history records that the concept of VTOL airliners was one which ultimately had little potential, civil aviation having been developed around the use of huge, sprawling airports and the creation of mass-produced (and therefore relatively inexpensive) conventional aircraft which did not have – and did not actually need – any VTOL ability. The prospect of airliners climbing vertically from small runway-free sites was a romantic idea but the cost of developing aircraft which would rely on a whole battery of vertical lift jet engines (which were very

Left: The diminutive Shorts SC.1 was designed as a research platform, achieving VTOL through the use of vertically-fixed lift engines. Although successful, the programme was intended only as a research project and did not have any direct impact upon Britain's defence thinking in terms of VSTOL capability. (Photo: Shorts)

Right: XG905 illustrating the large intake area (covered by mesh) atop the fuselage, with the Rolls-Royce lift engines buried directly below. The downward-flowing intake achieved good stability in the hover and did not suffer from the Harrier's yaw vulnerability, caused by the horizontal flow into the intakes either side of the fuselage. (Photo: Shorts)

Above: The two SC.1 aircraft demonstrated that vertical lift engines provided an effective means of achieving VTOL, but when compared to vectored-thrust, the system was less efficient and far less reliable. Rolls-Royce maintained an active interest in the concept, but ultimately it was Bristol's vectored-thrust engine which held far more potential. (Photo: Shorts)

efficient but which would also have to be carried in conventional forward flight as 'deadweight' on long intercontinental routes) was not practical. But despite this increasingly obvious fact, Britain's Ministry of Supply recognised the potential of the basic concept of jet lift, and issued Specification ER.143 for a small flat-rising VTOL aircraft which could investigate the potential of Rolls-Royce's RB.108 engines, and demonstrate how the power plant could be incorporated into a fixed-wing aircraft with conventional aerofoil surfaces, propelled by a conventional rearwards-directed turbojet. With no serious commercial or military application in mind, the MoS simply proposed to investigate the concept in order to establish whether it was worthy of further study. Belfast-based Short Brothers submitted a proposal to meet the specification and this was eventually accepted, resulting in two prototypes of their diminutive SC.1 being ordered in August 1954.

Despite the SC.1's relatively simple and uncluttered exterior, the aircraft was surprisingly complex. The basic design was based around four RB.108 engines stacked vertically in the aircraft's fuselage with a further engine arranged to emerge

horizontally from the rear of the fuselage (it was, in fact, positioned at an angle as the engine's oil system was designed for near-vertical operation). It might be imagined that the provision of four jet lift engines would have given the SC.1 a very respectable safety margin should one of the engines fail whilst in the critical jet lift-supported 'flight' regime, but with the engines stacked in pairs either side of the aircraft's centre line, the failure of any single engine would immediately impart a very severe asymmetric lift force on the aircraft (and also reduce overall lift thrust by 25 per cent), requiring an immediate compensatory input from the aircraft's reaction controls. The SC.1 was therefore equipped with a very capable three-axis auto stabilisation system which required a great deal of preliminary design work and even the aircraft's

Tom Brooke-Smith brings the diminutive SC.1 into the hover for a vertical landing during handling trials at RAE Bedford. After initial trials both SC.1s were assigned to research flying at Bedford until retirement. (Photo: Shorts)

The bizarre Rolls-Royce Thrust Measuring Rig (TMR) pictured during one off its 'hops' at Hucknall. Although clumsy and cumbersome the TMR did demonstrate successfully that a vehicle could be controlled in the hover purely through the use of jet lift, aided by reaction control vents with which to achieve roll, pitch and yaw. (Photo: Rolls Royce)

Trials of the TMR were largely successful although one 'hop' ended in disaster when the machine struck a gantry and overturned, killing the test pilot, Wing Commander H.G.F. Larson. The TMR did however demonstrate the viability of jet thrust as a means of achieving VTOL and ultimately led to the creation of Rolls Royce's RB.108 vertical lift jet engine. (Photo: Rolls Royce)

landing gear was rather less simple that it appeared. Fixed in the extended position, the main gear legs could be manually raked forward for conventional take-off and landings (giving the aircraft an optimum aerodynamic angle), or moved rearwards for VTOL operations (it was felt that the forward-raked position might encourage the aircraft to tip onto its tail), thanks to the incorporation of a two-position hydraulic jack. Thus, the SC.1 presented its pilots with a variety of challenges, all of which had to be mastered. The first aircraft (XG900) made its first conventional flight on 2 April 1957 from Boscombe Down, powered only by a single rearwards-facing engine. On 23 May of the following year the second aircraft (XG905) made its first tethered hover with the lift engines installed. These initial hover trials were all performed over a metal grid platform so that the lift engine's exhaust could immediately be directed away from the aircraft. It was already understood that as jet engine thrust inevitably diminishes in relation to a rise in ambient air temperature, the hot air expelled from the RB.108 engines would be deflected upwards from a normal airfield surface and would be re-ingested by the engines, severely degrading the amount of available thrust which was theoretically little more than 500 lb above the SC.1's all-up weight. It was not until November 1958 that test pilot Tom Brooke-Smith achieved a vertical landing on concrete. By September 1959 Shorts and Rolls-Royce were eager to demonstrate the SC.1's abilities to both the media and public, and XG905 was dispatched to Farnborough to demonstrate the novel concept of jet-powered hovering at the SBAC show. Unfortunately, Brooke-Smith's first demonstration ended abruptly after he experienced

a sudden and rather worrying loss of lift power. After making a hurried landing it was discovered that the landing area's grass surface had been carefully mown in anticipation of the SC.1's arrival, but the grass clippings had not been cleared away. When the aircraft became airborne the clippings were blasted skywards and immediately sucked back into the RB.108's air intake stream, fouling and eventually almost entirely blocking the air intake grilles. XG905's colourful carpet of grass was removed and a very public demonstration had been made of just how unpredictable and potentially hazardous jet lift could be.

In April 1960 the SC.1 made its first transition to and from vertical and conventional flight regimes and during the SBAC show in September, Tom Brooke-Smith demonstrated the aircraft's full capabilities to the public. Testing continued and XG905 was refitted with an improved auto stabilisation system which was expected to be more capable of coping with sudden external loads on the aircraft, particularly gusts of wind. Sadly, on 2 October 1963 the aircraft's system failed despite the inbuilt triple redundancy system, and the test pilot (J.R. Green) was unable to assume manual control before the aircraft hit the ground and overturned, killing him. This was, in fact, the second British jet VTOL fatality as Rolls-Royce's second Thrust Measuring Rig (XK426) had collided with a support gantry and had overturned at Hucknall on 27 November 1957, resulting in the death of its pilot (Wing Commander H.G.F. Larson). The SC.1 was eventually repaired and both airframes continued to provide valuable research data for many years, but with no practical application for jet lift technology in sight (the airliner concept never progressed beyond very basic design proposals), the SC.1 represented an interesting, but ultimately fruitless, episode in the story of VTOL development.

However, the development of Rolls-Royce's RB.108 had been watched with great interest by Bristol's Stanley Hooker. Unfortunately (and rather frustratingly) for him, Rolls-Royce had patented the engine design and had effectively precluded any possibility of the concept being developed elsewhere. Although Hooker remained interested in VTOL he was therefore unable to pursue the concept with Bristol Engines, but when he was invited to Paris by Chapman in July 1956 he was eager to learn more of Michel Wibault's proposal. In principle, Wibault's *Gyroptère* design was certainly an exciting one and appeared to offer great potential. Instead of reliance upon vertically-mounted jet lift engines (which, despite their excellent power-to-weight ratio, had to be carried as a very significant 'deadweight' in conventional flight) combined with an additional horizontally-mounted engine, the *Gyroptère's* single engine could provide both horizontal propulsion and jet lift. It would also enable the aircraft (a 'flat riser') to be controlled relatively easily through the tricky transition from both flight regimes, and the engine's four exhaust nozzles could be positioned at optimum positions at the aircraft's centre of gravity. On the other hand, Wibault's system (built around a Bristol Orion engine) promised to be extremely heavy, cumbersome and complicated, thanks to the arrangement of gearboxes, shafting and rotating scrolls. Hooker liked the idea but the proposal as it stood seemed unlikely to offer any practical means of creating a useful VTOL aircraft. Despite this, Hooker was mindful of the support given to Bristol Engines by the MWDP during development of its Orpheus engine, and he agreed to give Wibault's idea a more detailed appraisal. After only two weeks, Bristol had already identified ways in which the concept could be revised and refined. Most importantly, Wibault's centrifugal blower system was abandoned in favour of a less complicated (and more efficient) means of directing flow from a central axial compressor through two rotating pipes (one of which would emerge on each side of the aircraft fuselage), which were cranked downwards at their extremities. The remainder of the engine layout would function conventionally, with a standard horizontal exhaust at the rear. This meant inevitably that there would

be insufficient (vertical) thrust to enable the aircraft to take off and land vertically, but it would give an aircraft a very useful short take-off capability. It was Bristol's Gordon Lewis who proposed linking the Orion engine to drive a large frontal fan (from the forward stages of the company's Olympus engine) from which high pressure air could be directed to left and right rotating nozzles, to provide both vertical lift and/or horizontal thrust. This design (the BE.48) was the first in a series of developments which translated Wibault's idea into a viable propulsion system. Further studies suggested that additional improvements could be made by replacing the Orion engine with the new Orpheus power plant. The Orpheus was a lighter (and potentially cheaper) engine which still delivered a similar amount of thrust and it was established that by adding a turbine to the rear of this engine, the front (high pressure) turbine could be powered through a linking shaft that could run through the existing high pressure shaft inside the Orpheus. This would enable the complicated reduction gearbox to be eliminated. The result was the more advanced Bristol BE.53 engine with an estimated vectored thrust of some 8,000 lb. Clearly, this was a far more practical proposition than Wibault's basic concept, and it was envisaged that two of these engines could be used to power a new combat aircraft design. Nobody ventured to suggest what kind of combat aircraft this might actually be, but everyone was aware of NATO's established plans for a three-stage procurement programme for the G-91, followed by a more advanced strike fighter and, ultimately, an even more ambitious aircraft which would ideally have STOVL (Short Take-Off and Vertical Landing) capability.

It was at this stage that another significant development occurred – almost by accident. Hawker Aircraft's Chief Designer, the legendary Sir

The BE.48 engine featured rotatable nozzles to deflected air from the forward compressor, while conventional jet thrust emerged from the rear of the power plant. It was in effect a 'half way' stage between a conventional engine and the four-nozzle Pegasus. (courtesy Rolls Royce).

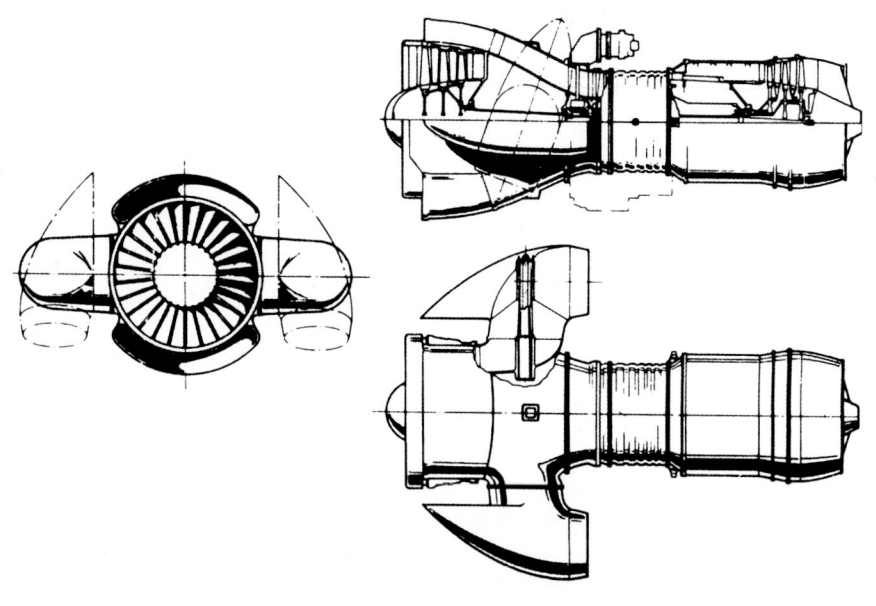

Sydney Camm, attended the 1957 Paris Air Show and during his visit he was escorted by Major Gerard Morel, a French representative of both Hawker Aircraft and Bristol Engines. Whilst observing a demonstration of SNECMA's unwieldy 'flying Atar' test rig, Morel asked Camm whether he was aware of Bristol's work on the BE.53 engine and its possible applications for future combat aircraft design. Camm replied that he knew nothing about the project but expressed some interest in the idea, and just a few days later a full descriptive brochure arrived at Hawker's headquarters at Kingston-upon-Thames. There is no doubt that 1957 was not a good time for Hawker Aircraft. Having become well established as a reputable company which specialised in fighter aircraft design (creators of the Hurricane and Hunter, amongst many other significant aircraft), the 1957 Defence White Paper threatened to destroy the company's future prospects. Minister Duncan Sandys claimed that manned fighter aircraft would no longer be necessary thanks to the projected development of surface-to-air missiles and that the continuing development of English Electric's Lightning (which had progressed too far to be cancelled economically) would represent the end of the manned fighter concept. This notion was, of course, nonsense but Sandys had been advised that missile technology would soon make manned aircraft almost completely redundant and with the Treasury's pressure for cost savings firmly in mind, he abandoned the manned fighter concept at a stroke. Hawker had been busy working on development (financed by itself without any Government support) of a supersonic air superiority fighter design which had been created as a private venture project, ultimately intended to replace Hawker's magnificent Hunter. With no Government backing, the company's spending on the project was cut back during October 1957 and subsequently dwindled to zero when efforts were redirected towards a wider project (embraced by the whole Hawker Siddeley combine) to produce a design with which to meet the RAF's requirement for a Canberra replacement. Eventually, this requirement was met by the ill-fated BAC TSR2 and it left Hawker with no major design programme with which to survive. It was therefore fortuitous that the possibility of a revolutionary new project emerged, but when Sydney Camm had first studied the BE.53 proposal, he was less than enthusiastic. He doubted seriously Bristol's claim that a developed engine might produce up to 11,000 lb of thrust, but he accepted that the engine did (at least in theory) offer the possibility of creating an aircraft with STOL (Short Take-Off and Landing) abilities. He instructed one of his senior design engineers, Ralph Hooper, to investigate the engine more thoroughly and consider what kind of aircraft might take advantage of the engine's unique properties. Hooper quickly concluded that the estimated thrust of the engine

would be insufficient to enable any significant weapons load to be carried and he therefore proposed that the engine could power a small three-seat STOL battlefield liaison aircraft. It was not the most ambitious of ideas, but given the relative lack of thrust which the BE.53 was likely to deliver (and a pervasive belief within Hawkers that any suggestion of new fighter designs would be pointless in any case), a simple Army Support aircraft seemed to be the most practical application. The first design drawing for this aircraft was dated 28 June and specified as the Hawker P.1127.

Both Hooper and his design engineering colleague, John Fozard, were not particularly enthusiastic about the P.1127, chiefly because of the BE.53 engine's limitations. Although the vectored thrust promised to deliver STOL performance, the two nozzles had to be deflected through 100 degrees (i.e., partially forward) in order to cancel out the rearwards thrust and this reduced the already limited amount of jet lift still further. The long nozzle arms were clumsy and as the aircraft accelerated to forward speed, they would have to remain deflected, contributing nothing to rearwards thrust. A subsequent design for a two-man aircraft (with revised intakes) offered the prospect of a slightly more practical aircraft, but it was agreed that developmental increases in weight would inevitably overtake engine performance, and in essence it was only Hawker's increasingly desperate need for a future project which kept the design alive, rather than any real enthusiasm for the design. A high-speed battlefield liaison aircraft was no Hurricane or Hunter, and in many respects P.1127 was an abstract design concept in need of a practical application, rather than vice versa. But everything changed drastically when Hooper suddenly realised that Hawker had already created a neat solution to the BE.53's limitations. Its Sea Hawk fighter had been powered by a single Rolls-Royce Nene engine, but through the application of an ingenious engineering solution (patented by Hawker) the engine's exhaust had been bifurcated to emerge as separate flows either side of the aircraft's fuselage, thereby enabling the engine's thrust to be maintained instead of decreasing significantly through the employment of a more traditional long fuselage jet pipe to the tail. Hooper concluded that the same bifurcated exhaust arrangement could be incorporated into the BE.53 jet lift engine, so that the 'hot end' of the Orpheus exhaust was split into a second pair of exhaust nozzles. This would enable the engine to deliver all of its thrust either in the vertical or horizontal plane. Hooper and Fozard continued their work and established that further improvements could be made by redesigning the engine nozzles so that the simple 'bent pipes' were replaced by a cascade of multiple vanes which turned the emerging air flow. There was also the question of gyroscopic effects which promised to be quite significant, but Fozard suggested that by counter-rotating the Olympus fan the gyroscopic

Continued on page 28

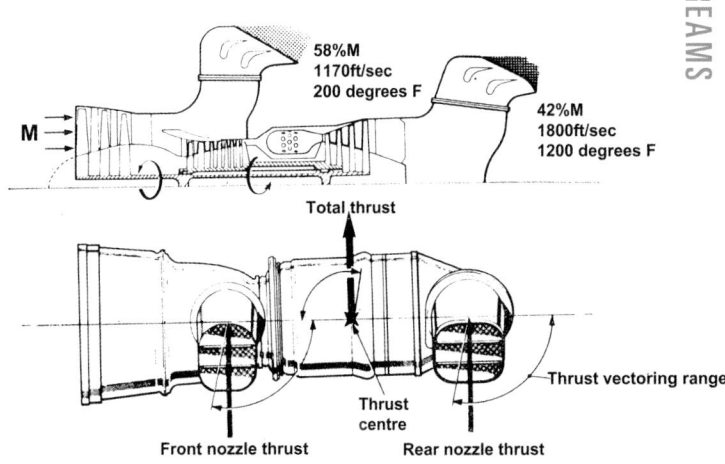

FRONT NOZZLES

REAR NOZZLES

H.P. COMPRESSOR

ANNULAR COMBUSTION CHAMBER

H.P. TURBINES

L.P. COMPRESSOR

L.P. TURBINES

	Front	Rear
Velocity	800 m.p.h. (350 m/sec.)	1200 m.p.h. (550 m/sec)
Temperature	150°C (200°F)	670°C (1240°F)

Jet Characteristics at Sea Level VTO rating

58%M
1170ft/sec
200 degrees F

42%M
1800ft/sec
1200 degrees F

M

Total thrust

Thrust vectoring range

Front nozzle thrust

Thrust centre

Rear nozzle thrust

Above: The interior of the Harrier's Pegasus engine, illustrating the forward 'cold' section (with compressed air feeding the forward nozzles and main engine core) and the rear 'hot' section with combusted air feeding the rear nozzles. (courtesy Rolls Royce)

Below: Illustration of some of the key Pegasus engine derivatives. (courtesy Rolls Royce)

Above right: The thrust output of the Pegasus engine is divided between the forward and rear nozzles, with 58 per cent of the total thrust being delivered through the front 'cold' pair, and the remaining 42 per cent emerging through the rear 'hot' exhausts. Both sets of nozzles can be shifted from just head of the vertical position through to horizontal. (courtesy Rolls Royce)

PEGASUS 3

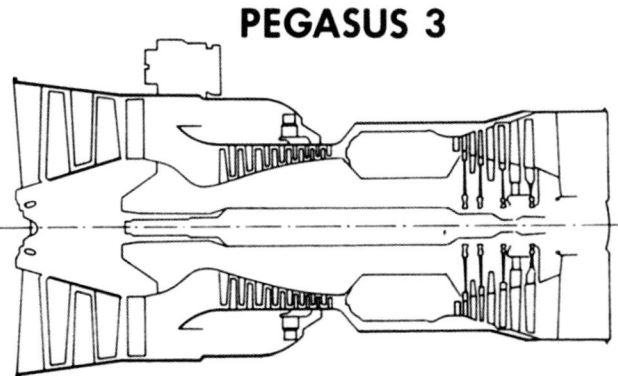

Introduced additional stage to HP compressor and second stage added to HP turbine. 14,000 lb take-off thrust; 4·94 lb/lb installed thrust.

PEGASUS 5

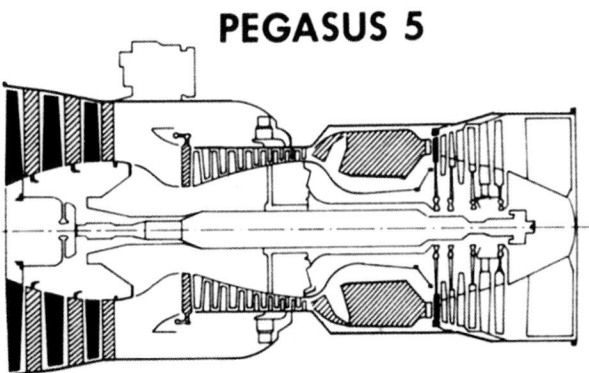

Three-stage LP compressor with inlet guide vanes deleted; variable HP inlet guide vanes; annular combustion chamber; cooling to first stage of HP turbine. 15,500 lb take-off thrust; 4·58 lb/lb installed thrust.

PEGASUS 6

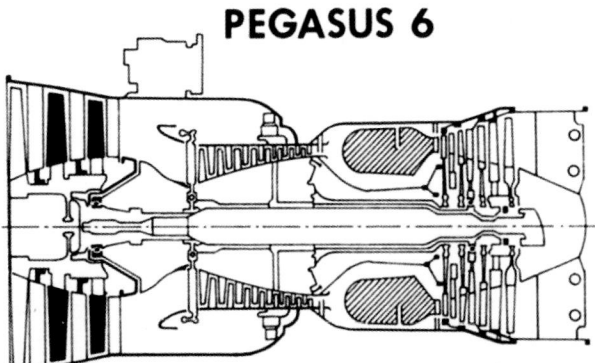

Short-Rating introduced with water injection; all-titanium fan; cooling to both stages of HP turbine; two-vane exhaust nozzles; additional fuel system controls; life recorder; 19,000 lb take-off thrust; 5·30 lb/lb installed thrust.

PEGASUS 11

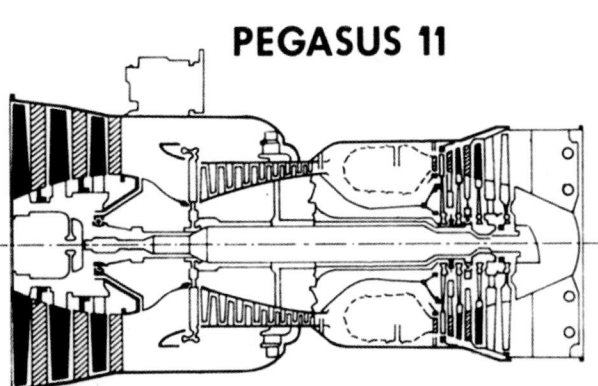

Rebladed LP compressor to increase mass flow; improved combustion chamber and water injection; increased cooling to HP turbine; naval version has improved anti-corrosion features. 21,500 lb take-off thrust; 5·79 lb/lb installed thrust.

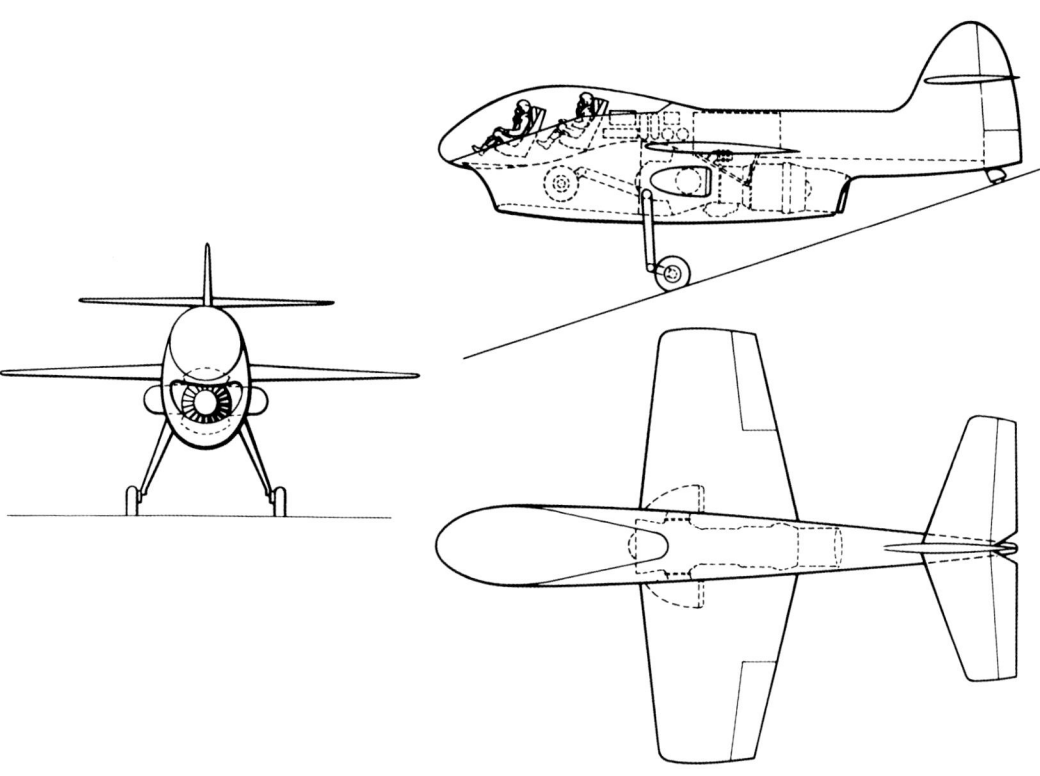

Above, below: The P.1127 first emerged as a very small and simple battlefield liaison aircraft. As can be seen from the early drawings, the design bore some resemblance to Hawker's Sea Hawk and was expected to possess only STOL (ie- not vertical) capabilities. (courtesy BAE Systems)

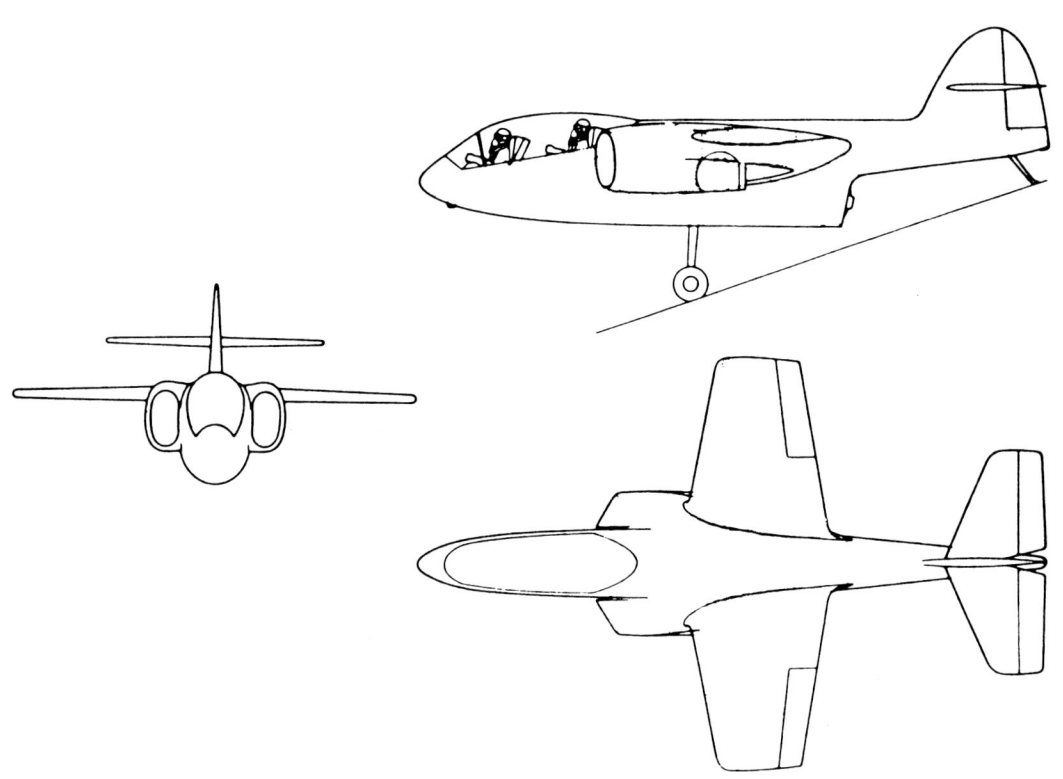

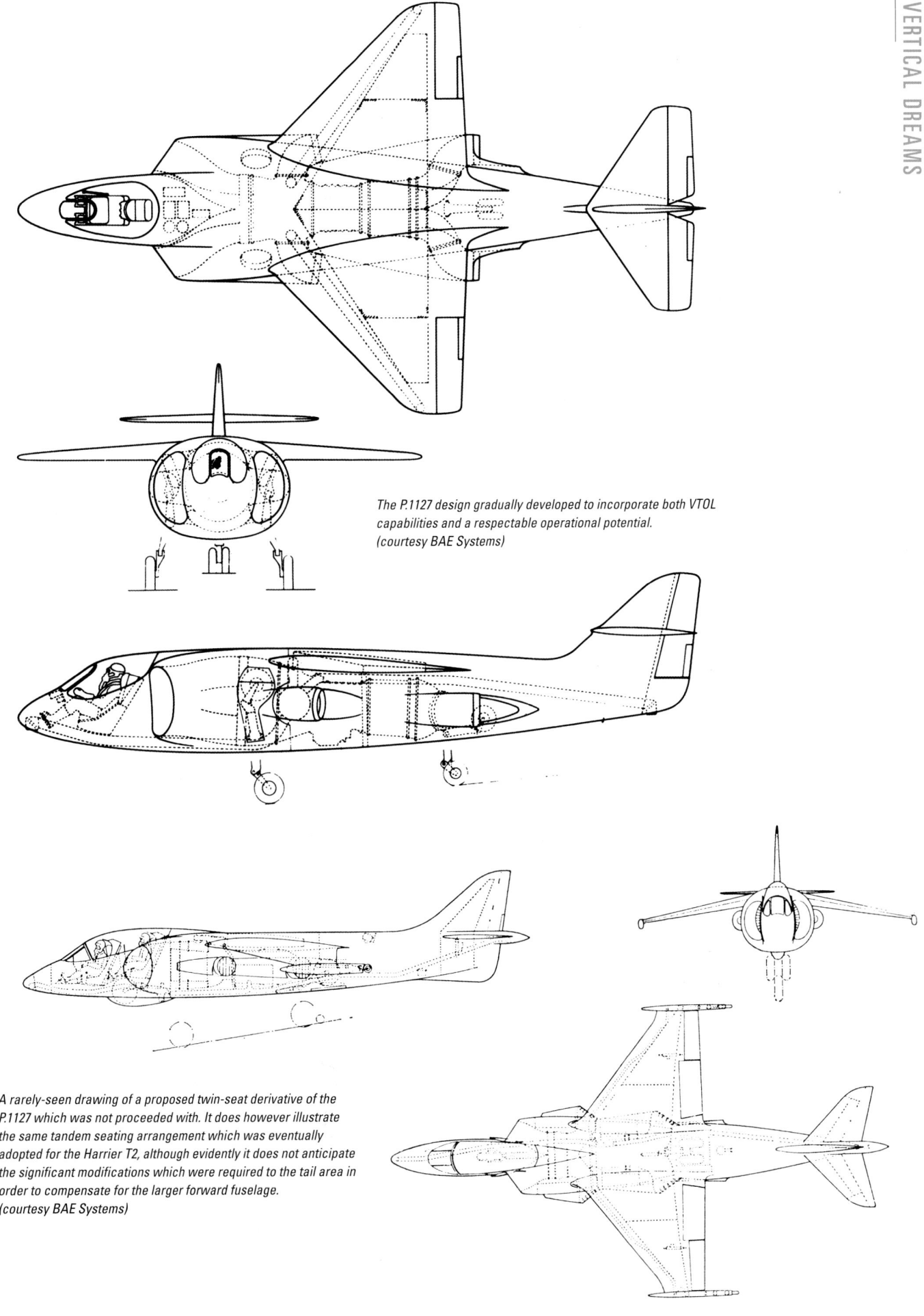

The P.1127 design gradually developed to incorporate both VTOL capabilities and a respectable operational potential.
(courtesy BAE Systems)

A rarely-seen drawing of a proposed twin-seat derivative of the P.1127 which was not proceeded with. It does however illustrate the same tandem seating arrangement which was eventually adopted for the Harrier T2, although evidently it does not anticipate the significant modifications which were required to the tail area in order to compensate for the larger forward fuselage.
(courtesy BAE Systems)

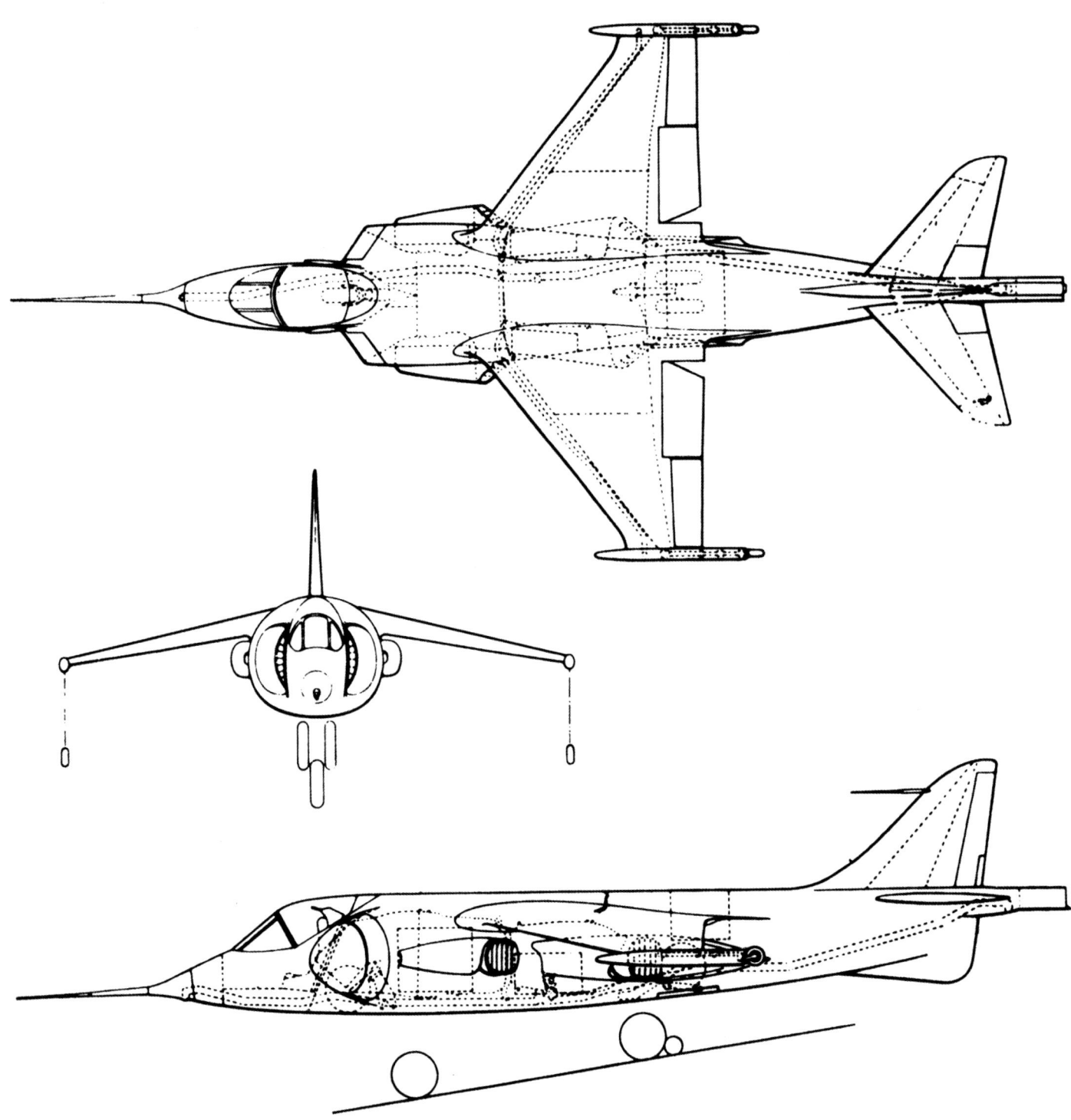

*Hawker's P.1127 in its original form with wing trailing edge notches,
early leading edge wing configuration, and horizontal tailplanes.
Minor alterations to the P.1127's overall shape continued until the
Harrier reached production standard. (courtesy BAE Systems)*

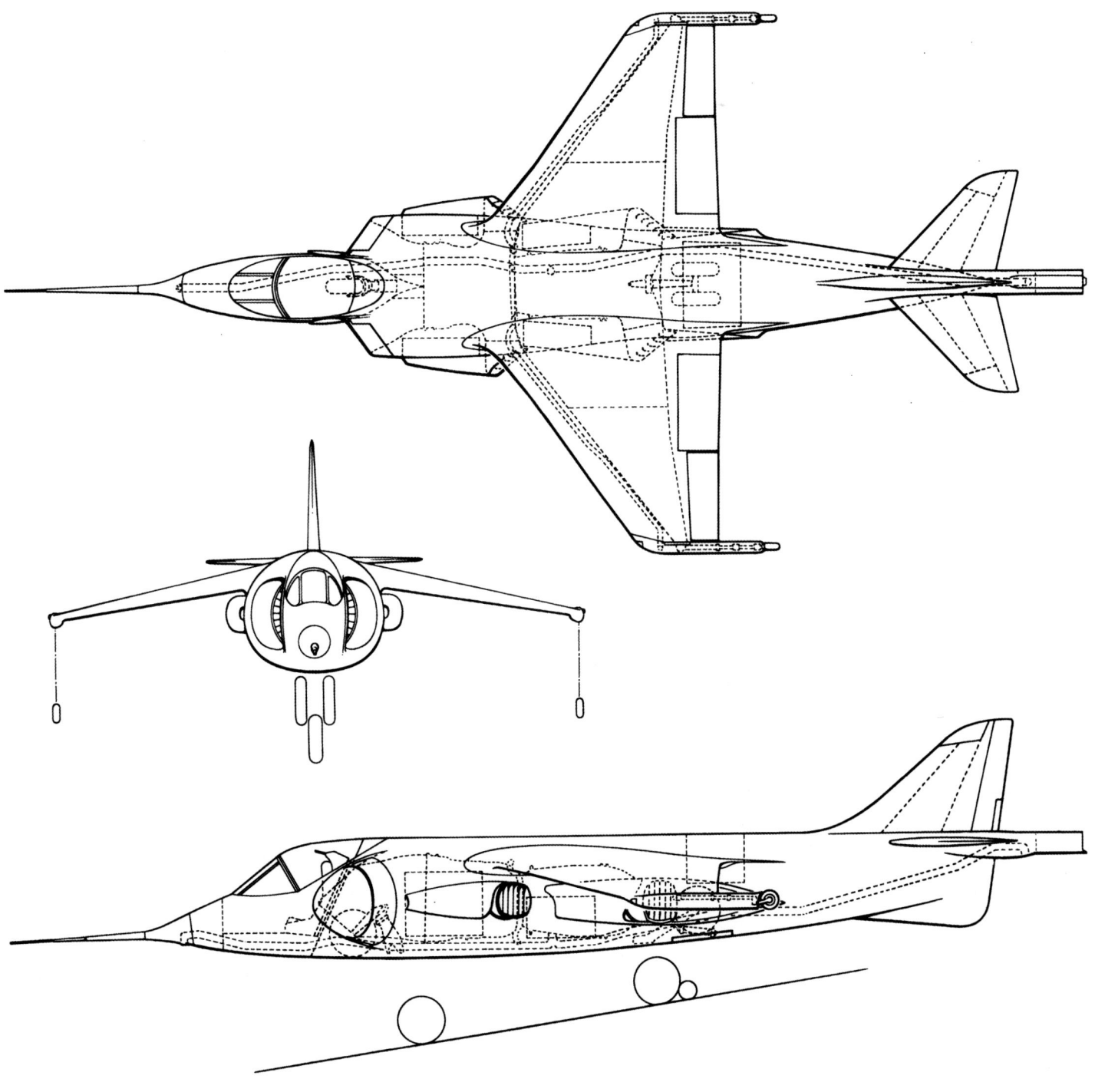

The P.1127 later in the design process, with re-designed wing leading edge, revised wing trailing edge and new outrigger fairings.(courtesy BAE Systems)

effect would be eliminated, thereby reducing any need for complicated stabilisation systems. Bristol was vaguely horrified by this proposal, having adopted the Olympus turbine as a simple and cheap component. The company claimed that the engine bearings would probably not be able to handle the loads, and that the cost of re-blading the Olympus component would be prohibitive. But eventually it was agreed that the advantages of this arrangement outweighed the cost of its development and the combined improvements created the basis for what eventually became one of the most successful and revolutionary jet engines ever created – the Pegasus. These fundamental changes to the engine prompted Sydney Camm to state that the project should now have a 'proper military capability' which meant that instead of being an unambitious liaison aircraft, the P.1127 would now be regarded as the foundation of a true warplane.

It was at this stage that Hawker's attention shifted elsewhere when the possibility of competing for the RAF's requirement for a Canberra replacement gradually emerged. Almost all of Kingston's design staff were pooled with those employed by Avro (both companies being part of the Hawker Siddeley Group) in order to concentrate on their pursuit of the RAF's strike aircraft requirements, and only a couple of people in Hawker's project office remained allocated to P.1127 during 1957. Ultimately, Hawker Siddeley's projected strike aircraft submission was judged to be capable of meeting the RAF's needs, but the Government eventually chose the equally impressive TSR2 design, largely as a political exercise designed to force the merger of English Electric and Vickers-Armstrongs into one company (BAC). At the same time that this news was delivered, the Ministry of Supply informed Hawker that there would be no financial support for the P.1127 project either, its interest in VTOL at that time being directed exclusively towards the Shorts SC.1. The prospect of privately funding both the new engine and the aircraft that it would power, was hardly the most encouraging news. However, in 1958 both Camm and Hooper again visited the offices of the MWDP and quickly learned that American money would be available to fund the P.1127 project. Bill Chapman was encouraged by the Hawker design but he felt that NATO would require something which provided almost double the projected radius of action proposed for P.1127. This led to more engine design work and the introduction of a water injection system which would boost the engine's take-off thrust and thereby almost double the amount of fuel which could be carried (although the changes and improvements to the engine design gradually increased deliverable thrust and the need for water injection subsequently diminished). In response to this encouraging news, a revised design was issued (the P.1127B), taking into account the drastically revised engine configuration which had been

changed still further by the introduction of a new two-stage transonic compressor fan which acted as a 'supercharger' on the original high-pressure compressor, creating what was, in effect, a 'high bypass' fan engine in which the bypass airflow emerged through the front 'cold' nozzles. The new P.1127 design was very different to the original proposal, and its proportions changed still further when the considerable bulk of the redesigned engine was taken into account. This necessitated a completely different undercarriage layout, Hooper and Fozard creating an unusual tandem wheel arrangement with small 'outrigger' wheels at the aircraft's wing tips. In order to minimise the length of these outriggers, the wing design incorporated significant anhedral, whilst still enabling the wing to remain intact as a one-piece structure running continuously across the aircraft's upper fuselage and engine (the entire wing section would be lifted out in order to access the engine). Further changes emerged when the issue of Reaction Control Valves (RCVs) was addressed. In forward flight the aircraft would be controlled by conventional ailerons, elevators and a rudder, but in a hover or vertical flight the aircraft's control surfaces (with no airflow over them) would be useless. Control would be achieved by applying small applications of jet exhaust at the aircraft's extremities through small control valves, providing sufficient thrust to stabilise the aircraft in all three axes. Bristol's Ralph Hooper had envisaged bleeding air from the system from the engine's forward fan through aluminium piping, but in order to achieve sufficient thrust to maintain control, it was discovered that the air would have to be delivered from the engine's high pressure (and higher temperature) section, and this would require stainless steel piping. Eventually a satisfactory RCV system was devised, incorporating a continuous bleed system feeding RCVs which vented downwards at the wing tips, nose and tail, with the fuselage RCVs also capable of rotation laterally in order to provide yaw control. Colonel Chapman and the MWDP liked Hawker's completed proposal and also agreed to Bristol's request that three-quarters of the engine's development cost should be funded by MWDP, leaving Bristol to finance the remaining quarter. In stark contrast, British official support was still virtually non-existent, the Ministry of Supply almost grudgingly agreeing to the possible provision of some wind tunnel facilities but still refusing to sanction a research contract, chiefly because there was no perceived civil potential for the project. Clearly, without the interest of America, the project would have been stillborn.

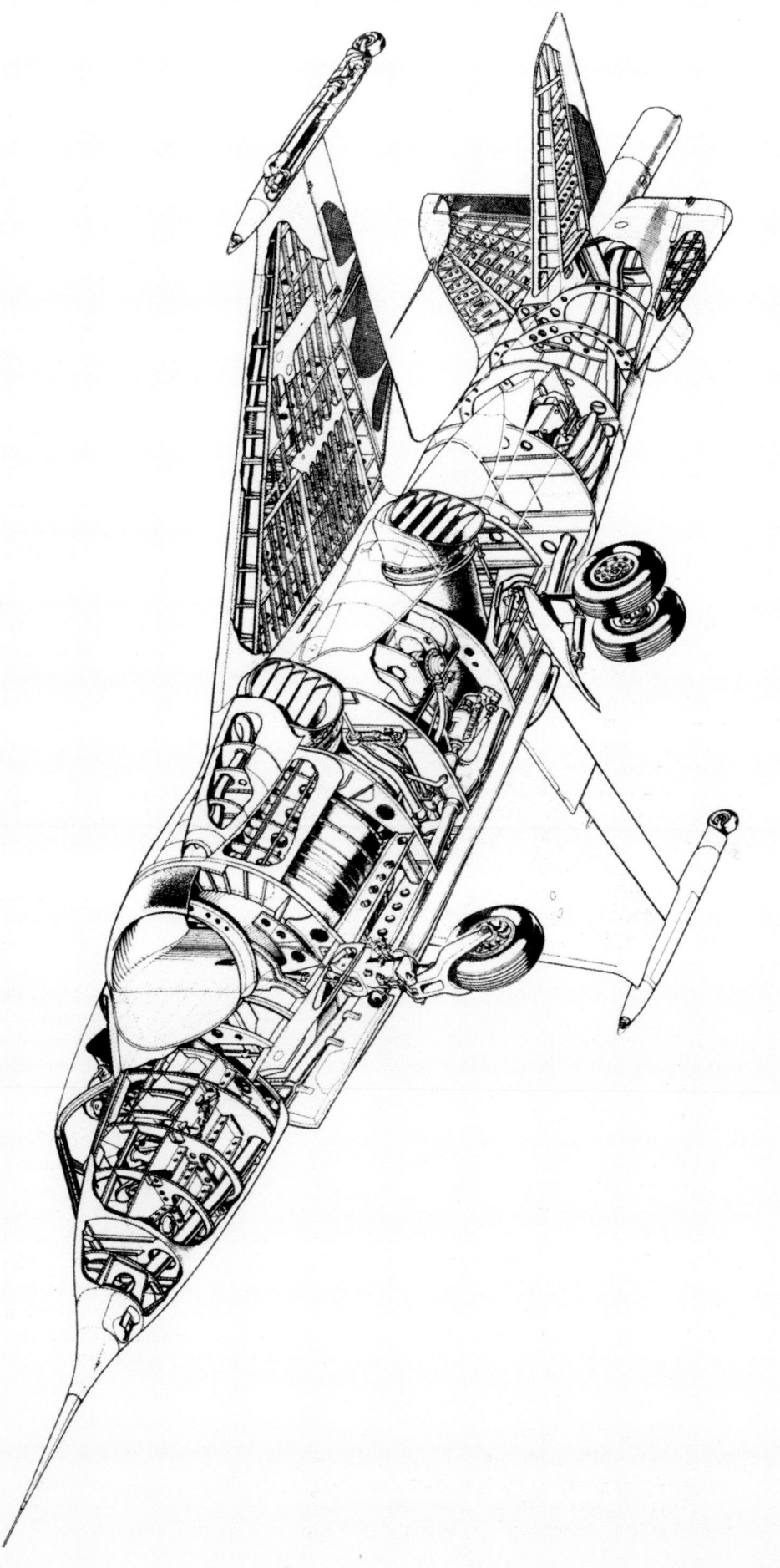

P.1127 cutaway diagram.
(courtesy BAE systems)

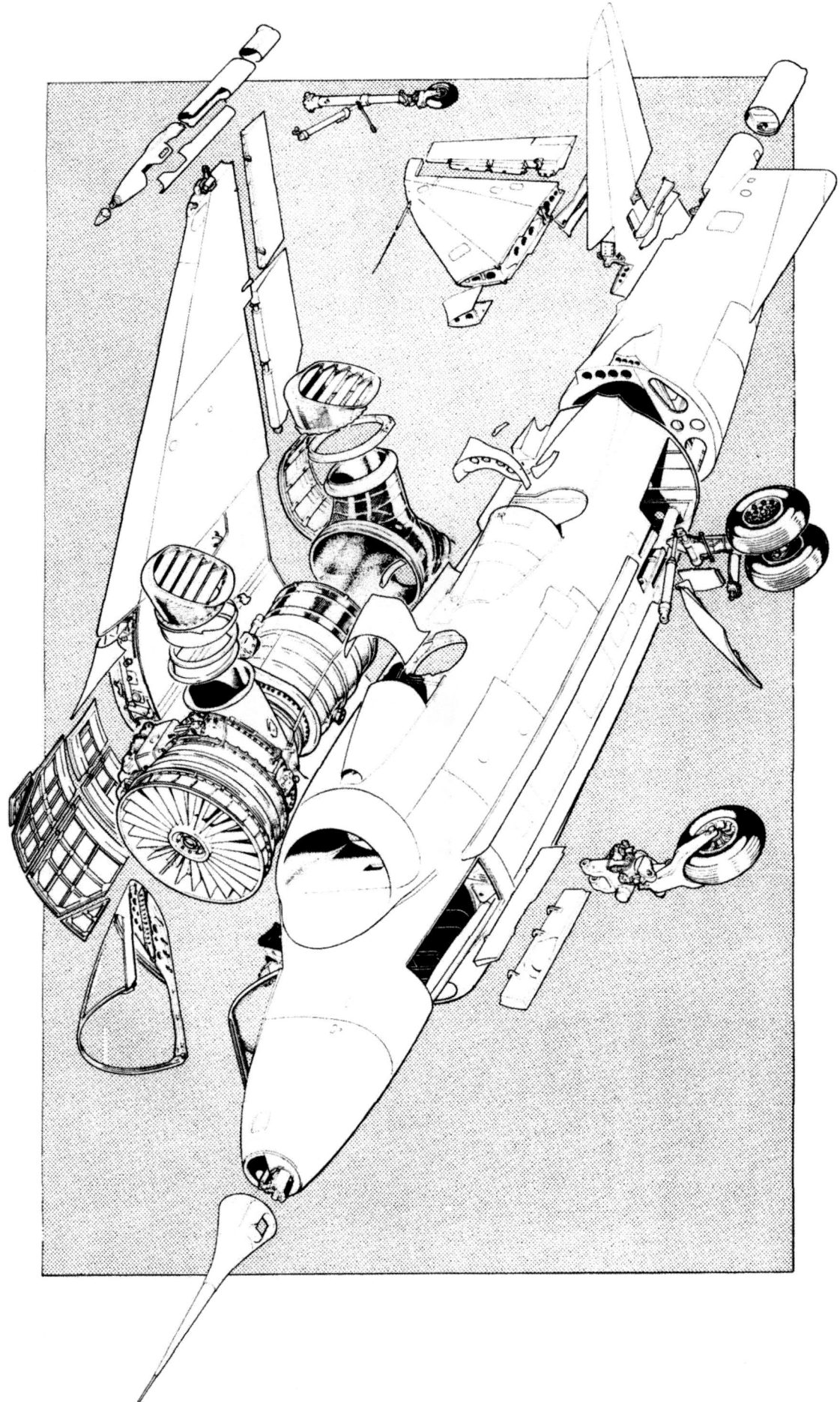

P.1127 major components diagram, illustrating the simple construction and the engine's location, enabling it to be 'dropped-in' to the upper fuselage when the wings are removed. (courtesy BAE Systems)

31

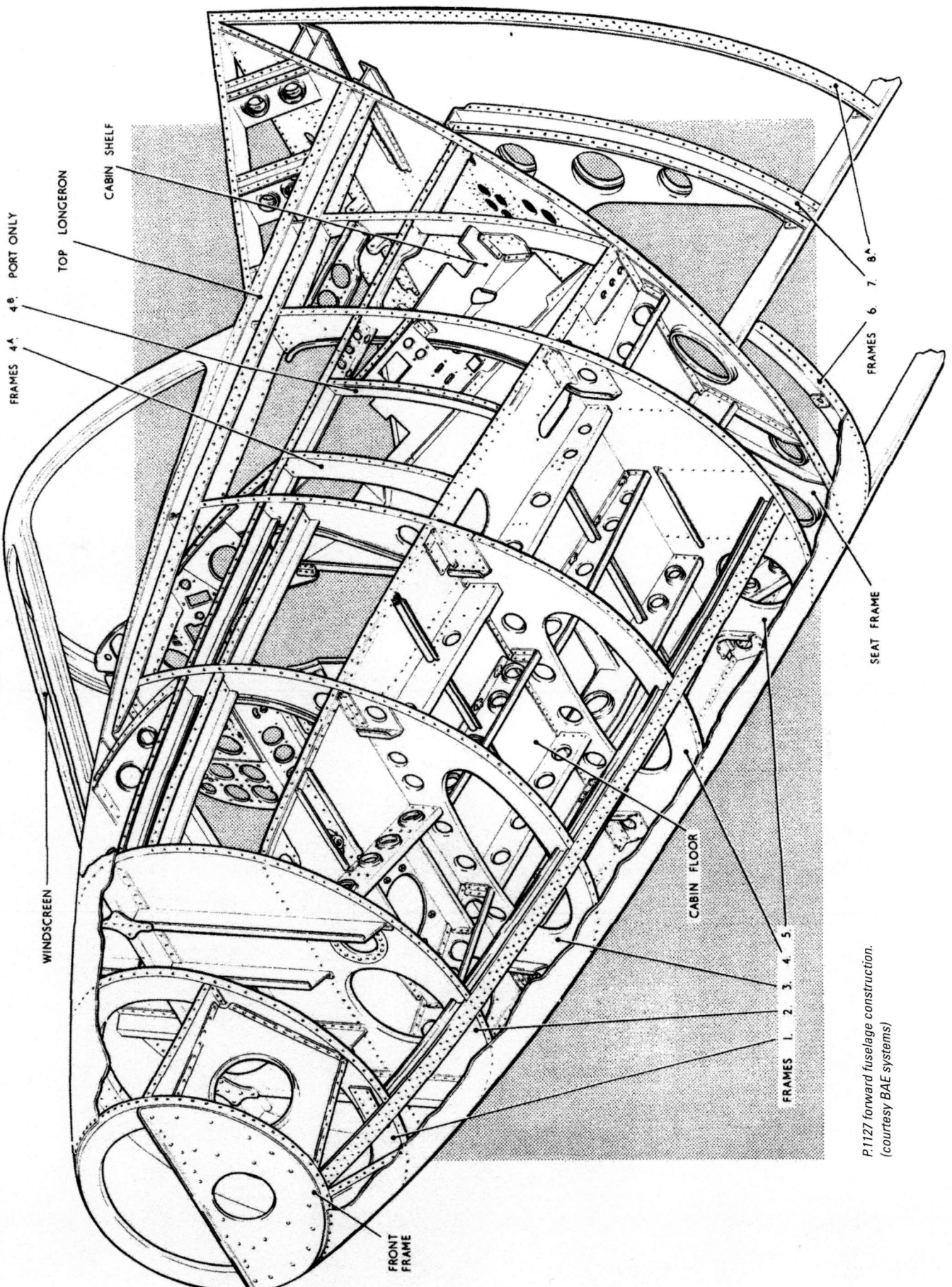

WINDSCREEN

FRONT FRAME

CABIN FLOOR

FRAMES 1. 2. 3. 4. 5

FRAMES 4ᴬ. 4ᴮ. PORT ONLY

TOP LONGERON

CABIN SHELF

FRAMES 6. 7. 8ᴬ.

SEAT FRAME

P.1127 forward fuselage construction.
(courtesy BAE systems)

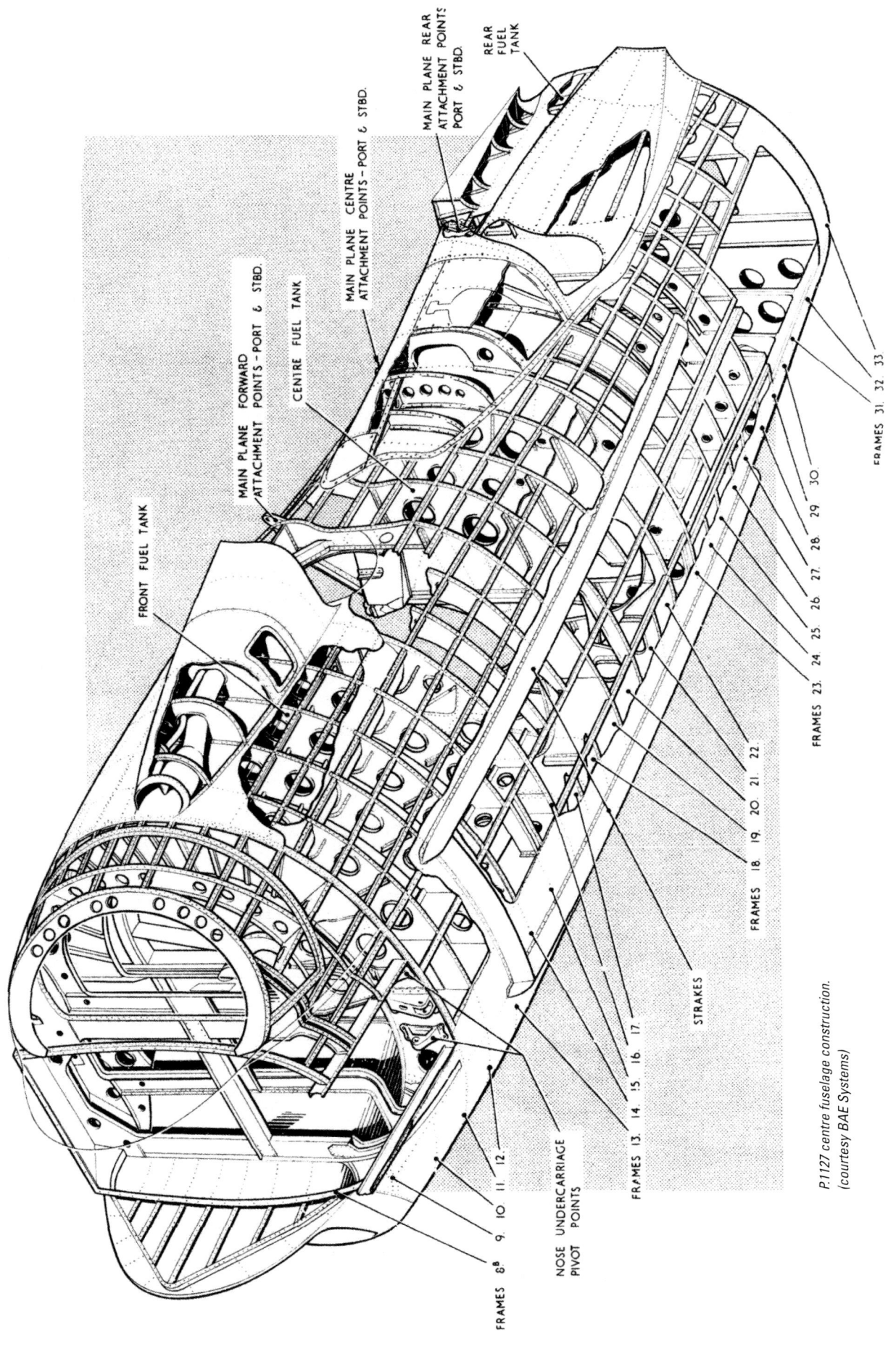

*P.1127 centre fuselage construction.
(courtesy BAE Systems)*

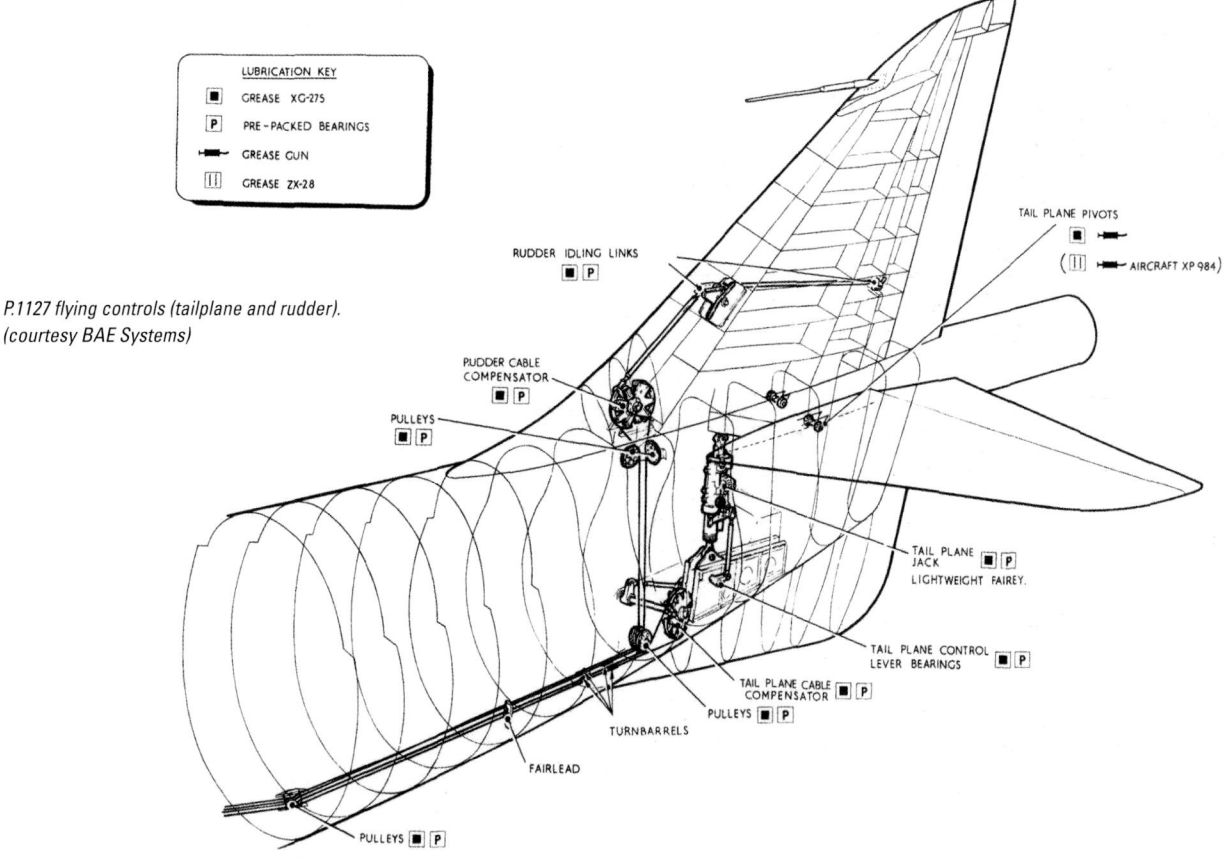

P.1127 rear fuselage construction.
(courtesy BAE systems)

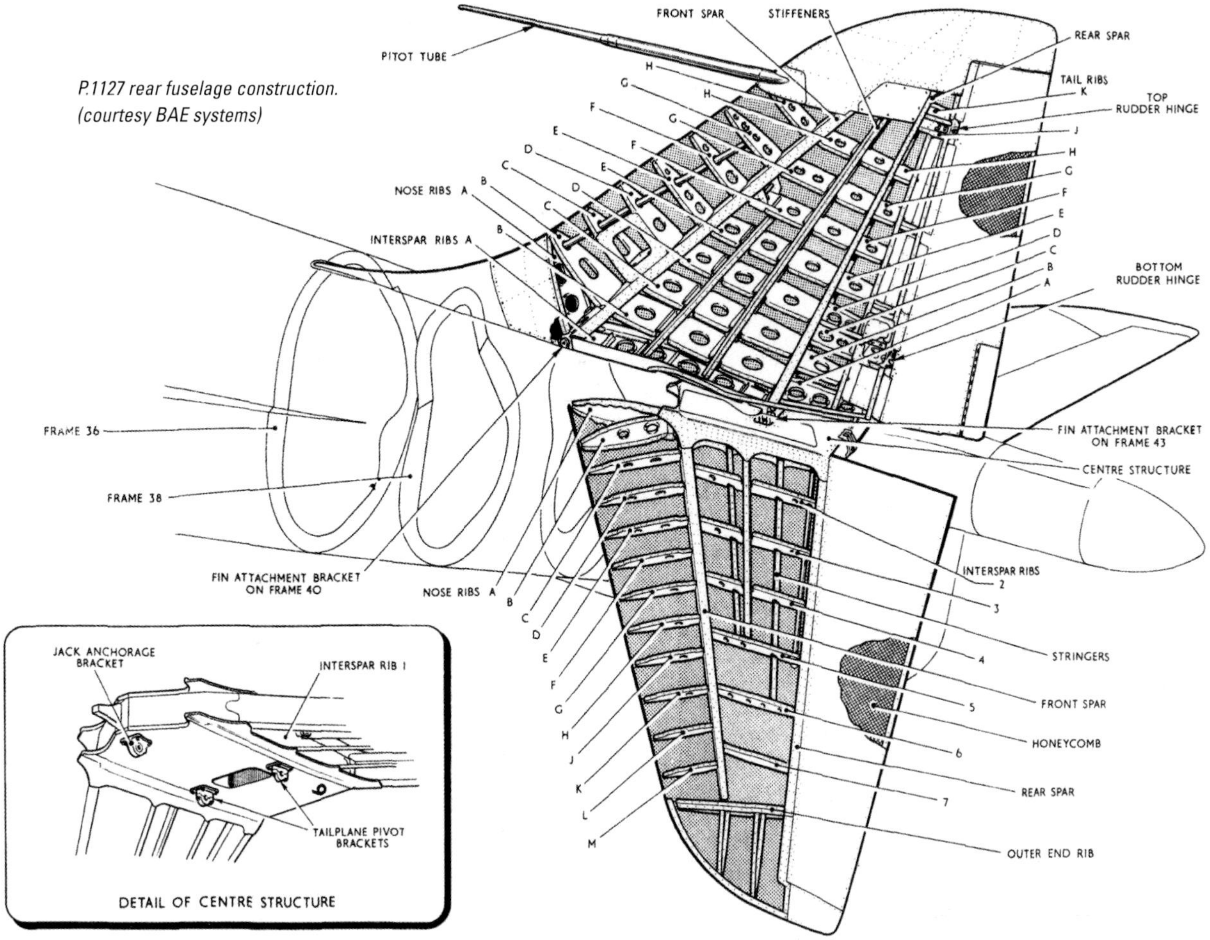

PITOT TUBE

FRONT SPAR   STIFFENERS

REAR SPAR

TAIL RIBS
K

TOP
RUDDER HINGE

H
G   H
F   G
E   F
D   E
C   D
B   C
B

NOSE RIBS A

INTERSPAR RIBS A

H
G
F
E
D
C
B
A

BOTTOM
RUDDER HINGE

FRAME 36

FRAME 38

FIN ATTACHMENT BRACKET
ON FRAME 40

NOSE RIBS A

FIN ATTACHMENT BRACKET
ON FRAME 43

CENTRE STRUCTURE

INTERSPAR RIBS
2
3

B
C
D
E
F
G
H
J
K
L
M

4

5

6

7

STRINGERS

FRONT SPAR

HONEYCOMB

REAR SPAR

OUTER END RIB

JACK ANCHORAGE
BRACKET

INTERSPAR RIB I

TAILPLANE PIVOT
BRACKETS

DETAIL OF CENTRE STRUCTURE

FIG.1 Tail unit (Full anhedral tail plane)

LUBRICATION KEY

■   GREASE XG-275

P   PRE-PACKED BEARINGS

⊷   GREASE GUN

⊞   GREASE ZX-28

P.1127 flying controls (tailplane and rudder).
(courtesy BAE Systems)

RUDDER IDLING LINKS
■ P

TAIL PLANE PIVOTS
■ ⊷
(⊞ ⊷ AIRCRAFT XP 984)

RUDDER CABLE
COMPENSATOR
■ P

PULLEYS
■ P

TAIL PLANE
JACK
LIGHTWEIGHT FAIREY.
■ P

TAIL PLANE CONTROL
LEVER BEARINGS
■ P

TAIL PLANE CABLE
COMPENSATOR
■ P

PULLEYS ■ P

TURNBARRELS

FAIRLEAD

PULLEYS ■ P

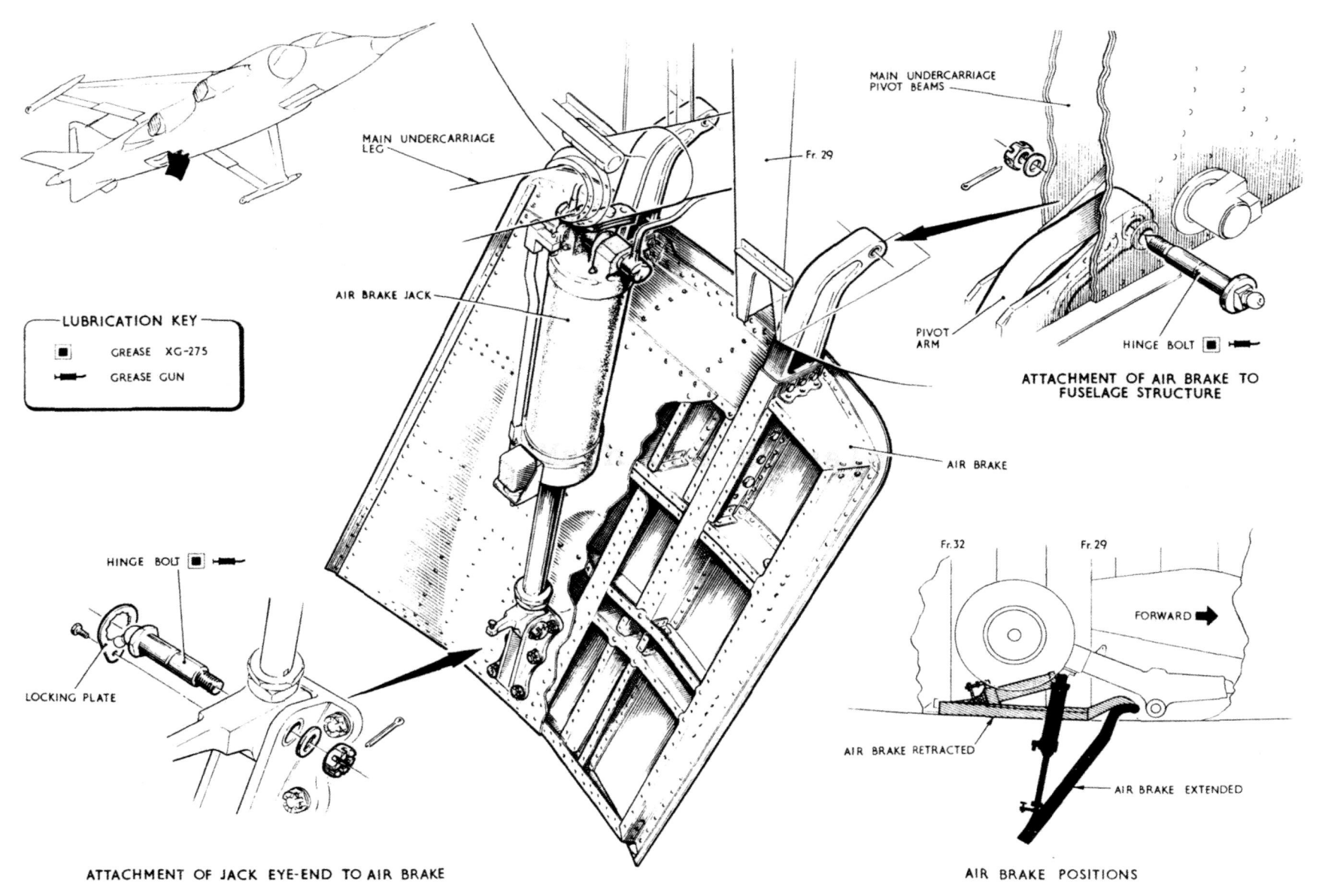

LUBRICATION KEY

■ GREASE XG-275

⊷ GREASE GUN

MAIN UNDERCARRIAGE LEG

AIR BRAKE JACK

MAIN UNDERCARRIAGE PIVOT BEAMS

Fr. 29

PIVOT ARM

HINGE BOLT ■ ⊷

ATTACHMENT OF AIR BRAKE TO FUSELAGE STRUCTURE

AIR BRAKE

HINGE BOLT ■ ⊷

LOCKING PLATE

ATTACHMENT OF JACK EYE-END TO AIR BRAKE

Fr. 32   Fr. 29

FORWARD ➤

AIR BRAKE RETRACTED

AIR BRAKE EXTENDED

AIR BRAKE POSITIONS

Air brake installation

P.1127 air brake installation. The air brake and main wheel bay door were combined into one unit. (courtesy BAE Systems)

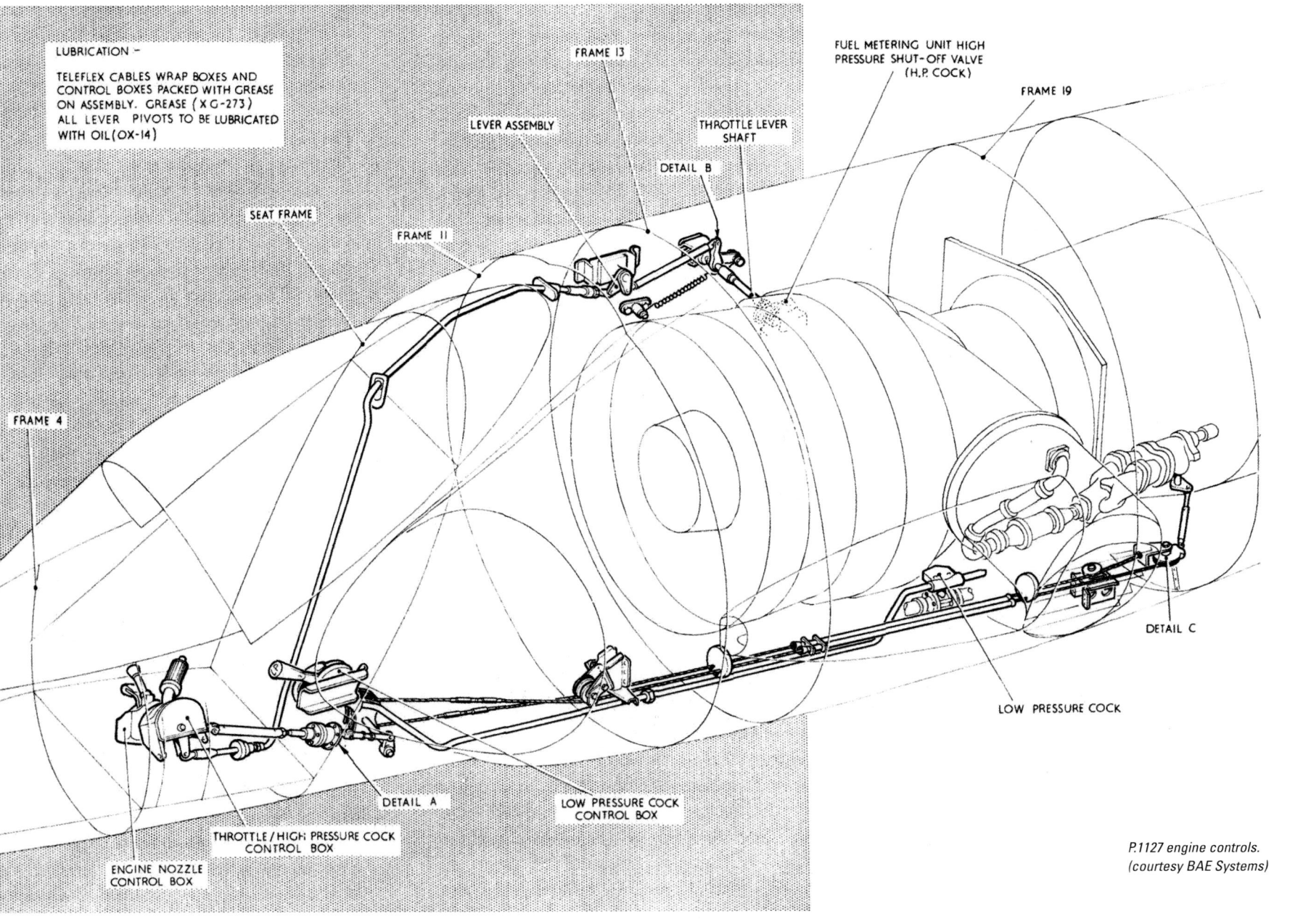

FRAME 13

LEVER ASSEMBLY

SEAT FRAME

THROTTLE LEVER
SHAFT

FRAME II

DETAIL B

FUEL METERING UNIT HIGH
PRESSURE SHUT-OFF VALVE
(H.P. COCK)

FRAME 19

FRAME 4

DETAIL C

LOW PRESSURE COCK

DETAIL A

LOW PRESSURE COCK
CONTROL BOX

THROTTLE / HIGH PRESSURE COCK
CONTROL BOX

ENGINE NOZZLE
CONTROL BOX

P.1127 engine controls.
(courtesy BAE Systems)

36

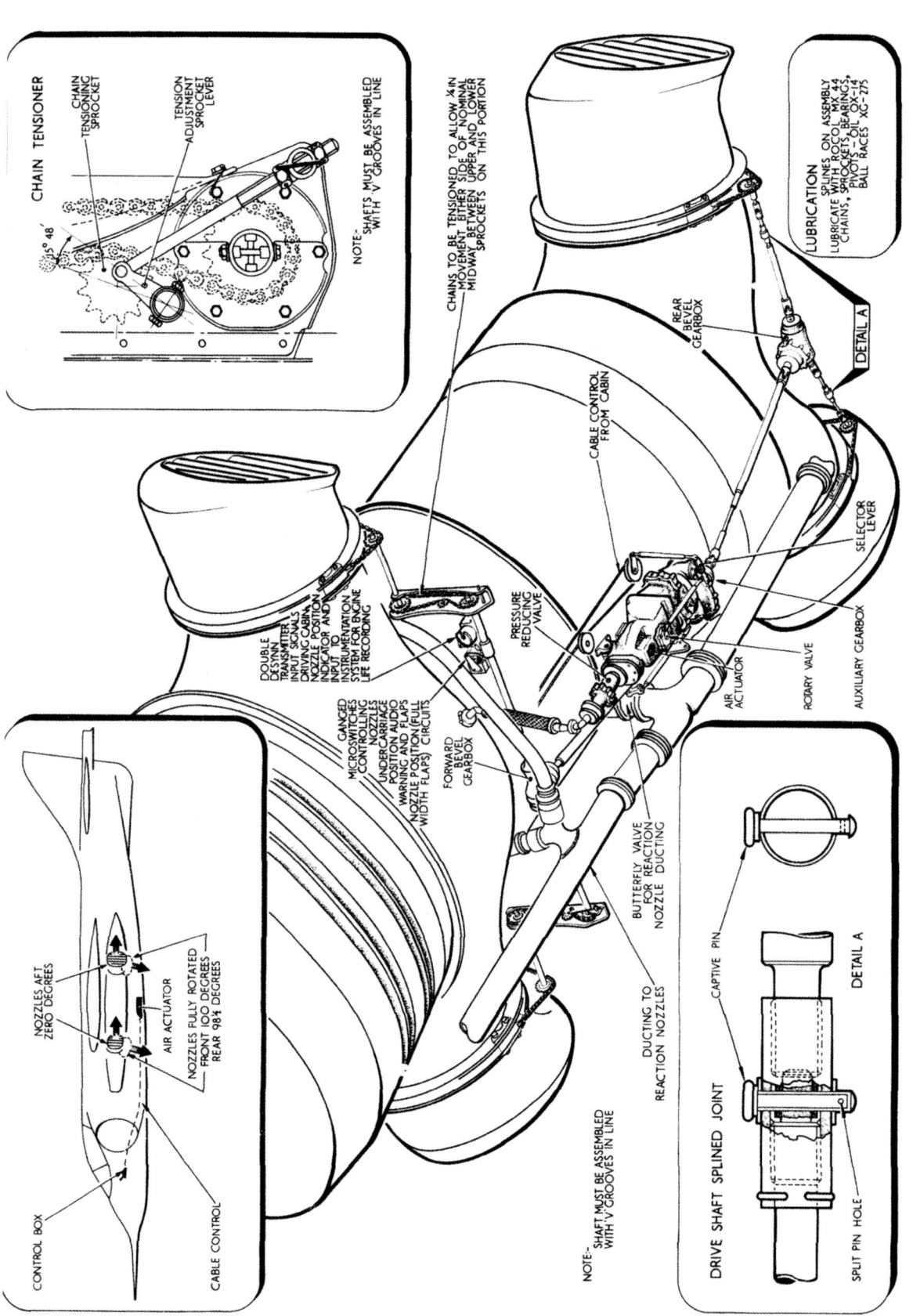

CHAIN TENSIONER

CHAIN TENSIONING SPROCKET

TENSION ADJUSTMENT SPROCKET LEVER

5° 48'

NOTE:- SHAFTS MUST BE ASSEMBLED WITH V GROOVES IN LINE

CHAINS TO BE TENSIONED TO ALLOW ¼ IN MOVEMENT EITHER SIDE OF NOMINAL MIDWAY BETWEEN UPPER AND LOWER SPROCKETS ON THIS PORTION

LUBRICATION
SPLINES ON ASSEMBLY LUBRICATE WITH ROCOL MX 44 CHAINS, SPROCKETS, BEARINGS, PIVOTS – OIL OX–14 BALL RACES XG–275

DETAIL A

REAR BEVEL GEARBOX

CABLE CONTROL FROM CABIN

SELECTOR LEVER

DOUBLE DESYNN TRANSMITTER INPUT SIGNALS DRIVING CABIN NOZZLE POSITION INDICATOR AND INPUT TO INSTRUMENTATION SYSTEM FOR ENGINE LIFE RECORDING

GANGED MICROSWITCHES CONTROLLING NOZZLES UNDERCARRIAGE POSITION AUDIO WARNING AND FLAPS NOZZLE POSITION (FULL WIDTH FLAPS) CIRCUITS

PRESSURE REDUCING VALVE

FORWARD BEVEL GEARBOX

AIR ACTUATOR

ROTARY VALVE

AUXILIARY GEARBOX

BUTTERFLY VALVE FOR REACTION NOZZLE DUCTING

DUCTING TO REACTION NOZZLES

NOTE:- SHAFT MUST BE ASSEMBLED WITH 'V' GROOVES IN LINE

NOZZLES AFT ZERO DEGREES

AIR ACTUATOR

NOZZLES FULLY ROTATED FRONT 100 DEGREES REAR 98½ DEGREES

CONTROL BOX

CABLE CONTROL

DRIVE SHAFT SPLINED JOINT

CAPTIVE PIN

DETAIL A

SPLIT PIN HOLE

Nozzle Control Mechanism – Schematic

P.1127 engine control mechanism.
(courtesy BAE Systems)

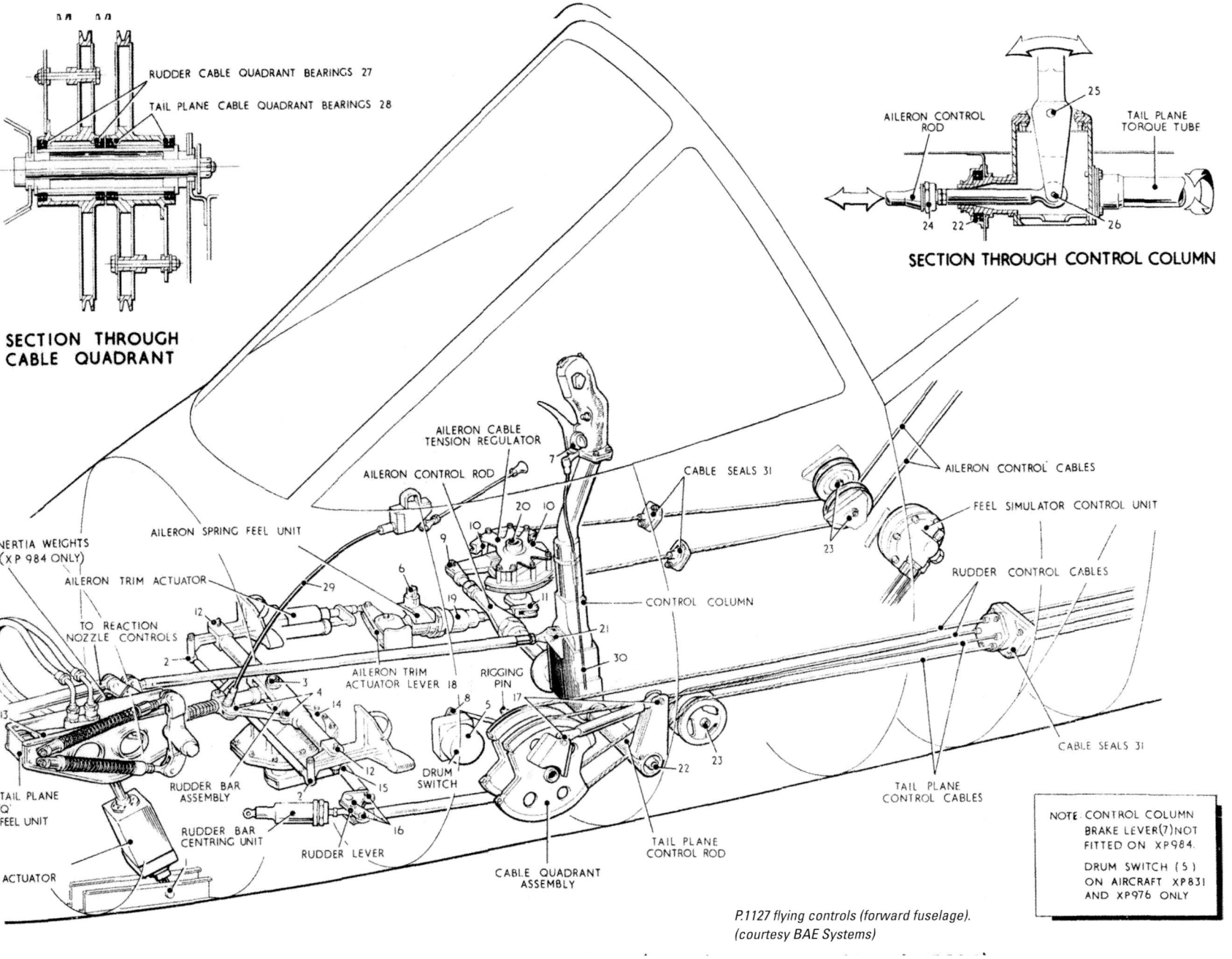

SECTION THROUGH
CABLE QUADRANT

RUDDER CABLE QUADRANT BEARINGS 27

TAIL PLANE CABLE QUADRANT BEARINGS 28

SECTION THROUGH CONTROL COLUMN

AILERON CONTROL
ROD

TAIL PLANE
TORQUE TUBE

25

24 22 26

INERTIA WEIGHTS
(XP 984 ONLY)

AILERON TRIM ACTUATOR

TO REACTION
NOZZLE CONTROLS

AILERON SPRING FEEL UNIT

AILERON CABLE
TENSION REGULATOR

AILERON CONTROL ROD

CABLE SEALS 31

AILERON CONTROL CABLES

FEEL SIMULATOR CONTROL UNIT

RUDDER CONTROL CABLES

CONTROL COLUMN

AILERON TRIM
ACTUATOR LEVER 18

RIGGING
PIN

DRUM
SWITCH

TAIL PLANE
'Q'
FEEL UNIT

RUDDER BAR
ASSEMBLY

RUDDER BAR
CENTRING UNIT

RUDDER LEVER

ACTUATOR

CABLE QUADRANT
ASSEMBLY

TAIL PLANE
CONTROL ROD

TAIL PLANE
CONTROL CABLES

CABLE SEALS 31

NOTE CONTROL COLUMN
BRAKE LEVER(7)NOT
FITTED ON XP984.

DRUM SWITCH (5)
ON AIRCRAFT XP831
AND XP976 ONLY

P.1127 flying controls (forward fuselage).
(courtesy BAE Systems)

38

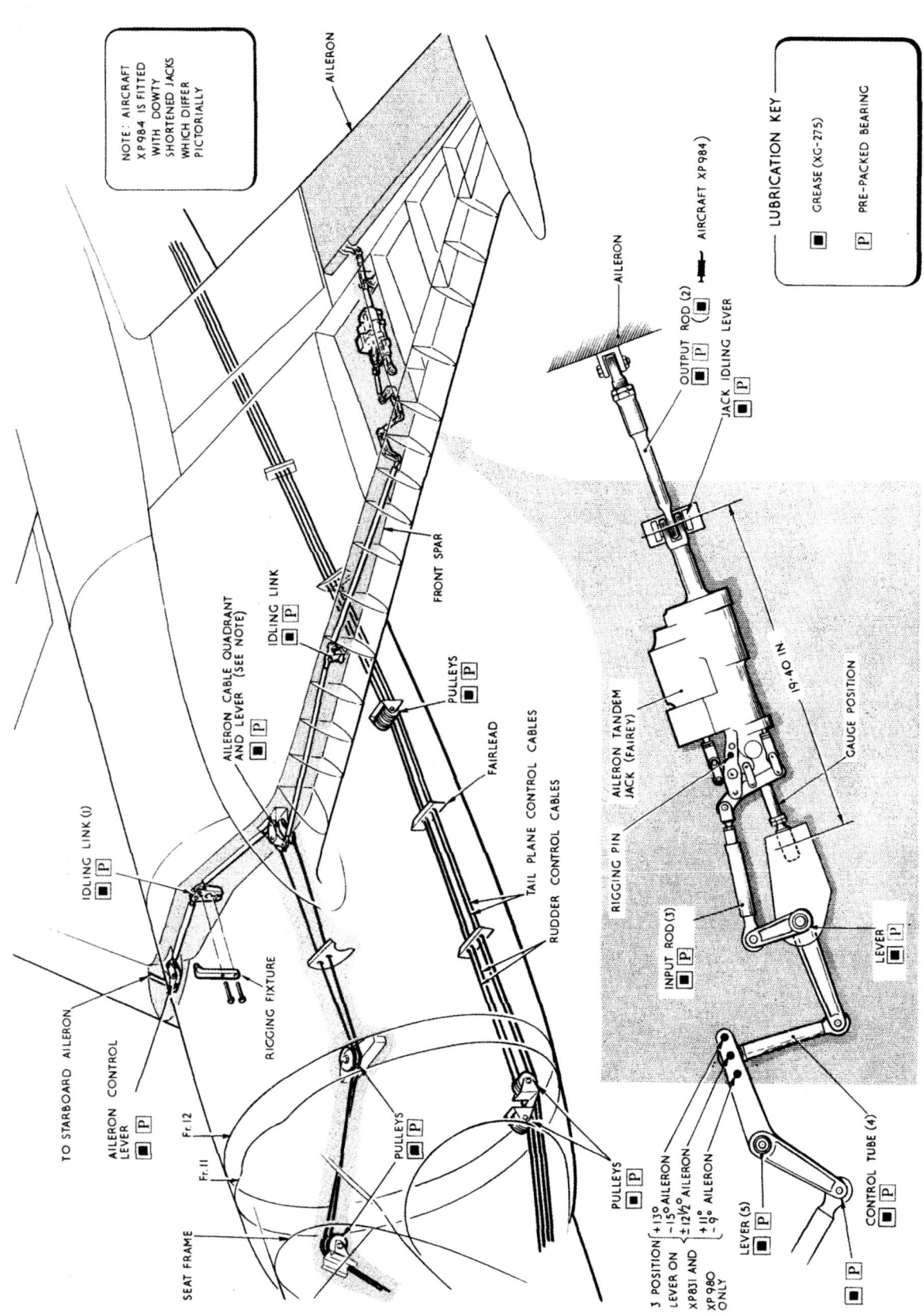

AILERON

NOTE: AIRCRAFT
XP984 IS FITTED
WITH DOWTY
SHORTENED JACKS
WHICH DIFFER
PICTORIALLY

AILERON

OUTPUT ROD (2) 🔲 P

JACK IDLING LEVER 🔲 P

LUBRICATION KEY

🔲 GREASE (XG-275)

P PRE-PACKED BEARING

AIRCRAFT XP 984

FRONT SPAR

IDLING LINK
🔲 P

AILERON CABLE QUADRANT
AND LEVER (SEE NOTE)
🔲 P

PULLEYS 🔲 P

FAIRLEAD

TAIL PLANE CONTROL CABLES

RUDDER CONTROL CABLES

AILERON TANDEM
JACK (FAIREY)

RIGGING PIN

19·40 IN.

GAUGE POSITION

IDLING LINK (I)
🔲 P

INPUT ROD (3)
🔲 P

LEVER
🔲 P

TO STARBOARD AILERON

AILERON CONTROL
LEVER
🔲 P

RIGGING FIXTURE

Fr.12

Fr.11

PULLEYS
🔲 P

PULLEYS
🔲 P

CONTROL TUBE (4)
🔲 P

SEAT FRAME

3 POSITION { +13°
LEVER ON { -15° AILERON
XP831 AND { ±12½° AILERON
XP980 { +11°
ONLY { -9° AILERON

LEVER (5)
🔲 P

P

*P.1127 flying controls (centre fuselage and wing).
(courtesy BAE Systems)*

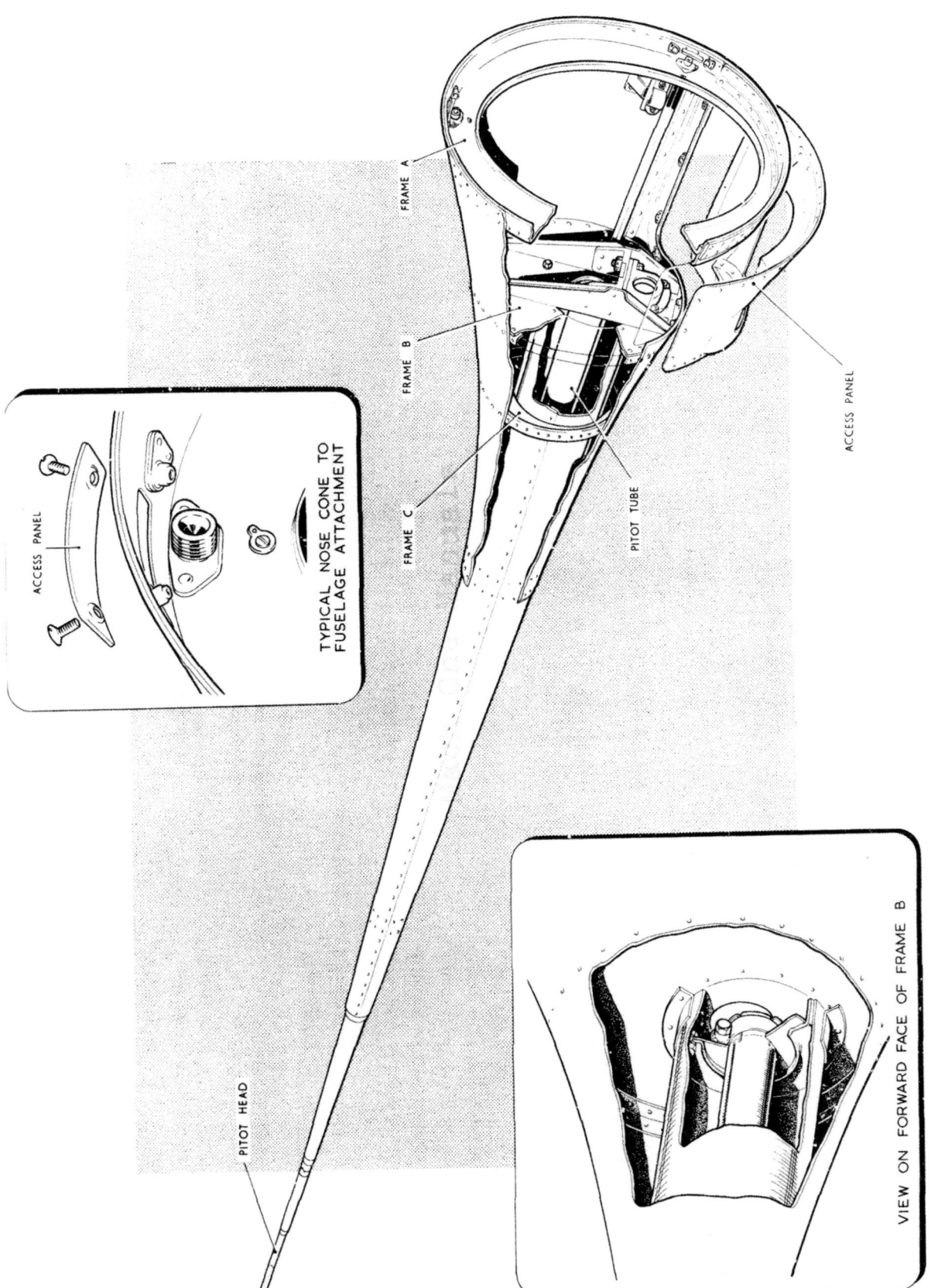

ACCESS PANEL

TYPICAL NOSE CONE TO
FUSELAGE ATTACHMENT

FRAME A

FRAME B

FRAME C

PITOT TUBE

ACCESS PANEL

PITOT HEAD

VIEW ON FORWARD FACE OF FRAME B

*P.1127 nose boom and pitot head.
(courtesy BAE Systems)*

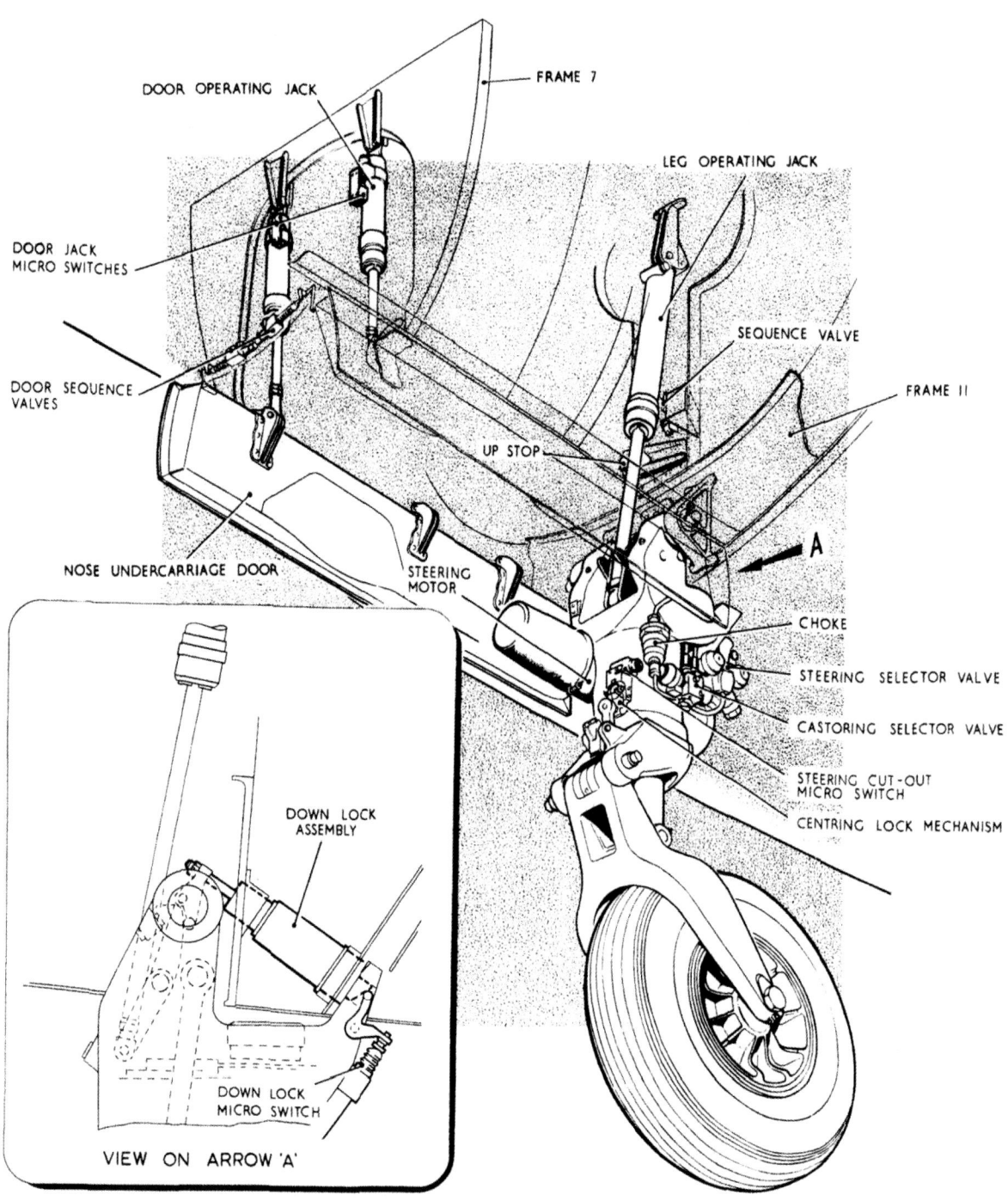

DOOR OPERATING JACK

FRAME 7

LEG OPERATING JACK

DOOR JACK
MICRO SWITCHES

SEQUENCE VALVE

DOOR SEQUENCE
VALVES

FRAME II

UP STOP

A

NOSE UNDERCARRIAGE DOOR

STEERING
MOTOR

CHOKE

STEERING SELECTOR VALVE

CASTORING SELECTOR VALVE

STEERING CUT-OUT
MICRO SWITCH

CENTRING LOCK MECHANISM

DOWN LOCK
ASSEMBLY

DOWN LOCK
MICRO SWITCH

VIEW ON ARROW 'A'

P.1127 nose landing gear assembly.
(courtesy BAE Systems)

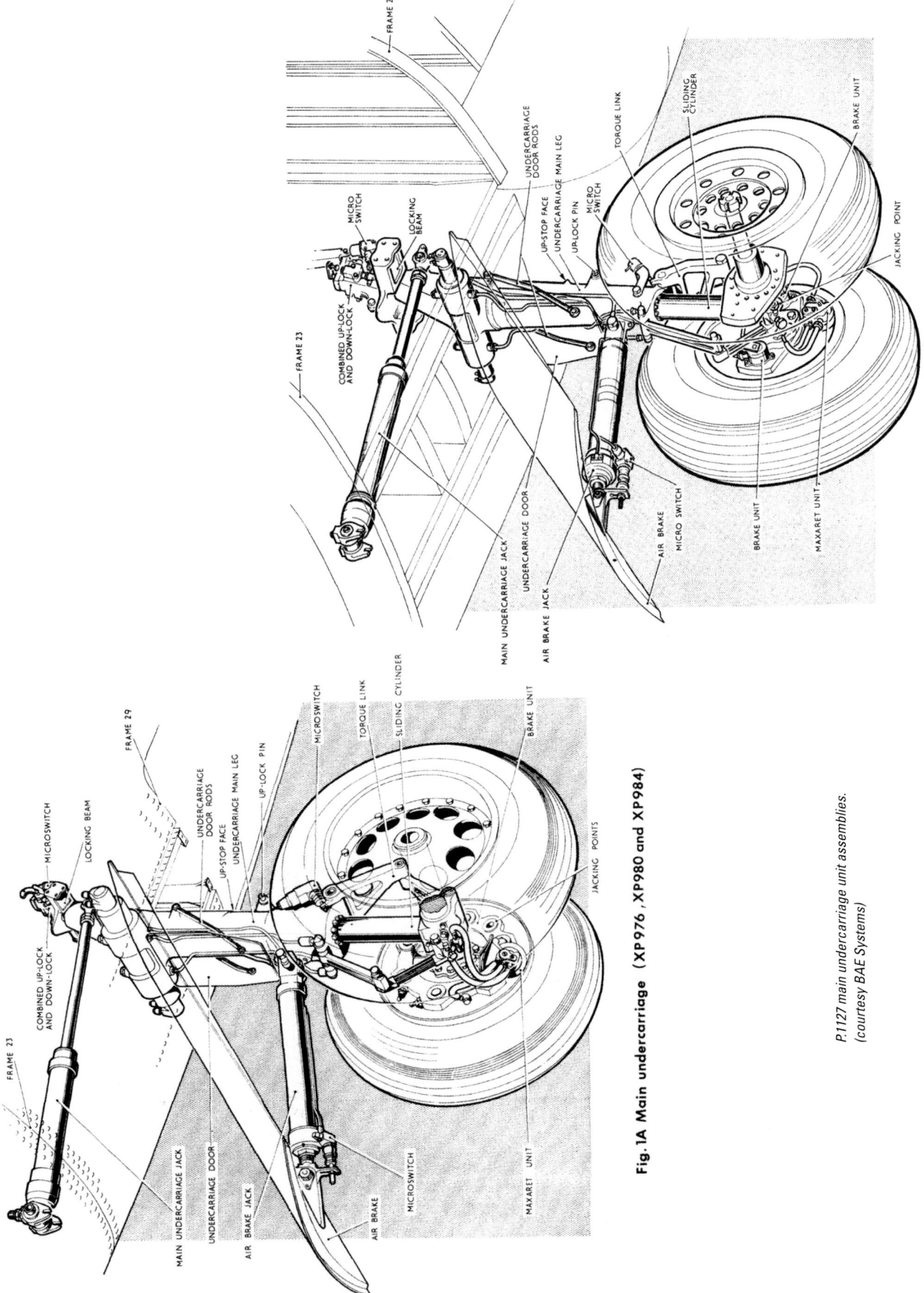

FRAME 29

FRAME 23

COMBINED UP-LOCK AND DOWN-LOCK

MICRO SWITCH

LOCKING BEAM

UNDERCARRIAGE DOOR RODS

UP-STOP FACE

UNDERCARRIAGE MAIN LEG

UP-LOCK PIN

MICRO SWITCH

TORQUE LINK

SLIDING CYLINDER

BRAKE UNIT

JACKING POINT

MAIN UNDERCARRIAGE JACK

UNDERCARRIAGE DOOR

AIR BRAKE JACK

AIR BRAKE

MICRO SWITCH

BRAKE UNIT

MAXARET UNIT

FRAME 29

FRAME 23

COMBINED UP-LOCK AND DOWN-LOCK

MICROSWITCH

LOCKING BEAM

UNDERCARRIAGE DOOR RODS

UP-STOP FACE

UNDERCARRIAGE MAIN LEG

UP-LOCK PIN

MICROSWITCH

TORQUE LINK

SLIDING CYLINDER

BRAKE UNIT

JACKING POINTS

MAIN UNDERCARRIAGE JACK

UNDERCARRIAGE DOOR

AIR BRAKE JACK

AIR BRAKE

MICROSWITCH

MAXARET UNIT

Fig.1A Main undercarriage (XP976 , XP980 and XP984)

P.1127 main undercarriage unit assemblies.
(courtesy BAE Systems)

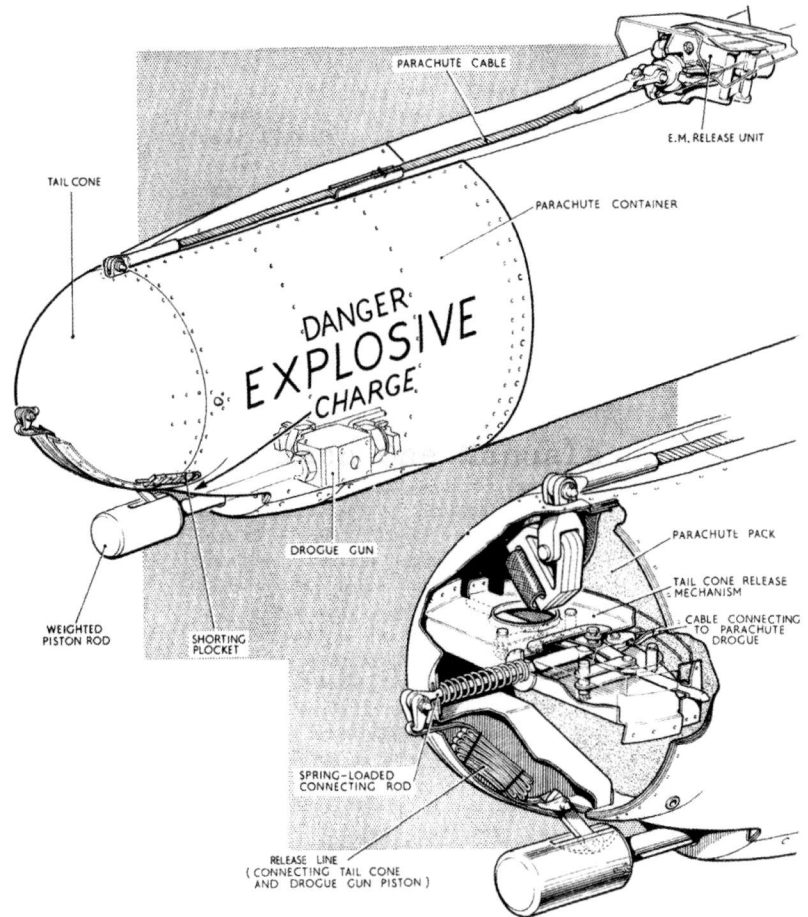

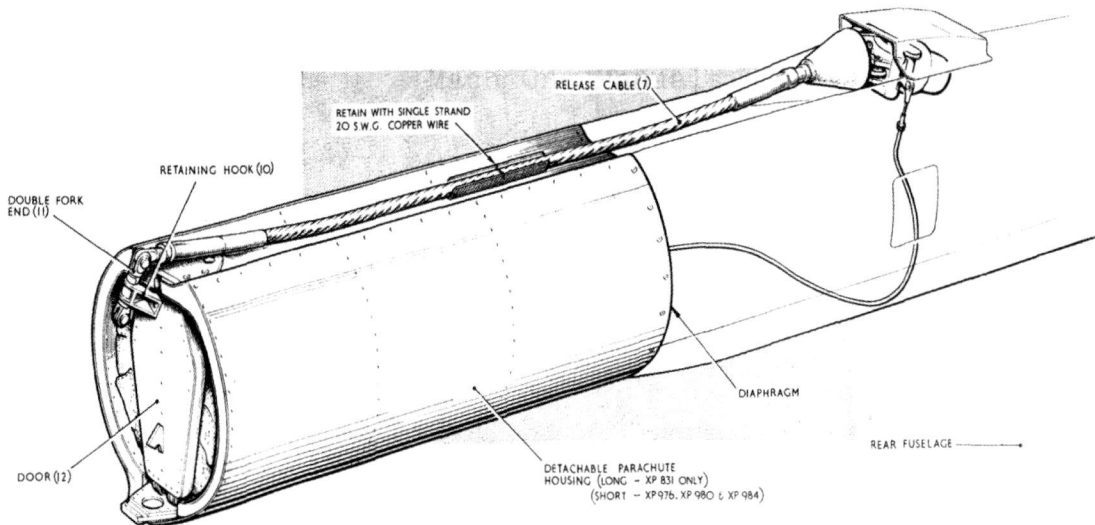

P.1127 spin parachute and brake parachute assemblies and fairings.
(courtesy BAE Systems)

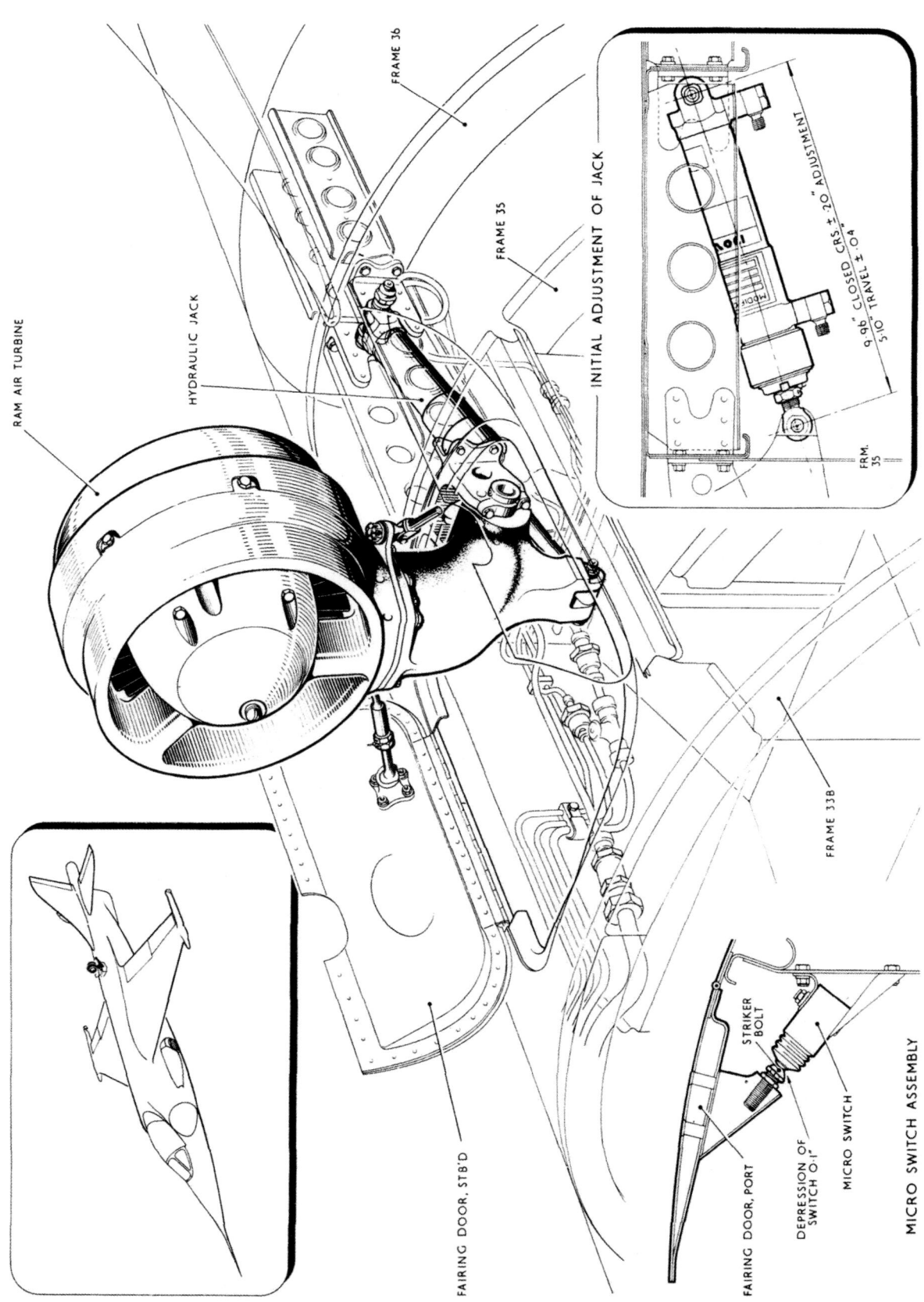

RAM AIR TURBINE

HYDRAULIC JACK

FRAME 36

FRAME 35

INITIAL ADJUSTMENT OF JACK

9.96" CLOSED CRS ± 20" ADJUSTMENT

5.10" TRAVEL ± 04

FRM. 35

FRAME 33B

FAIRING DOOR, STB'D

FAIRING DOOR, PORT

DEPRESSION OF SWITCH 0.1"

STRIKER BOLT

MICRO SWITCH

MICRO SWITCH ASSEMBLY

P.1127 Ram Air Turbine installation.
(courtesy BAE Systems)

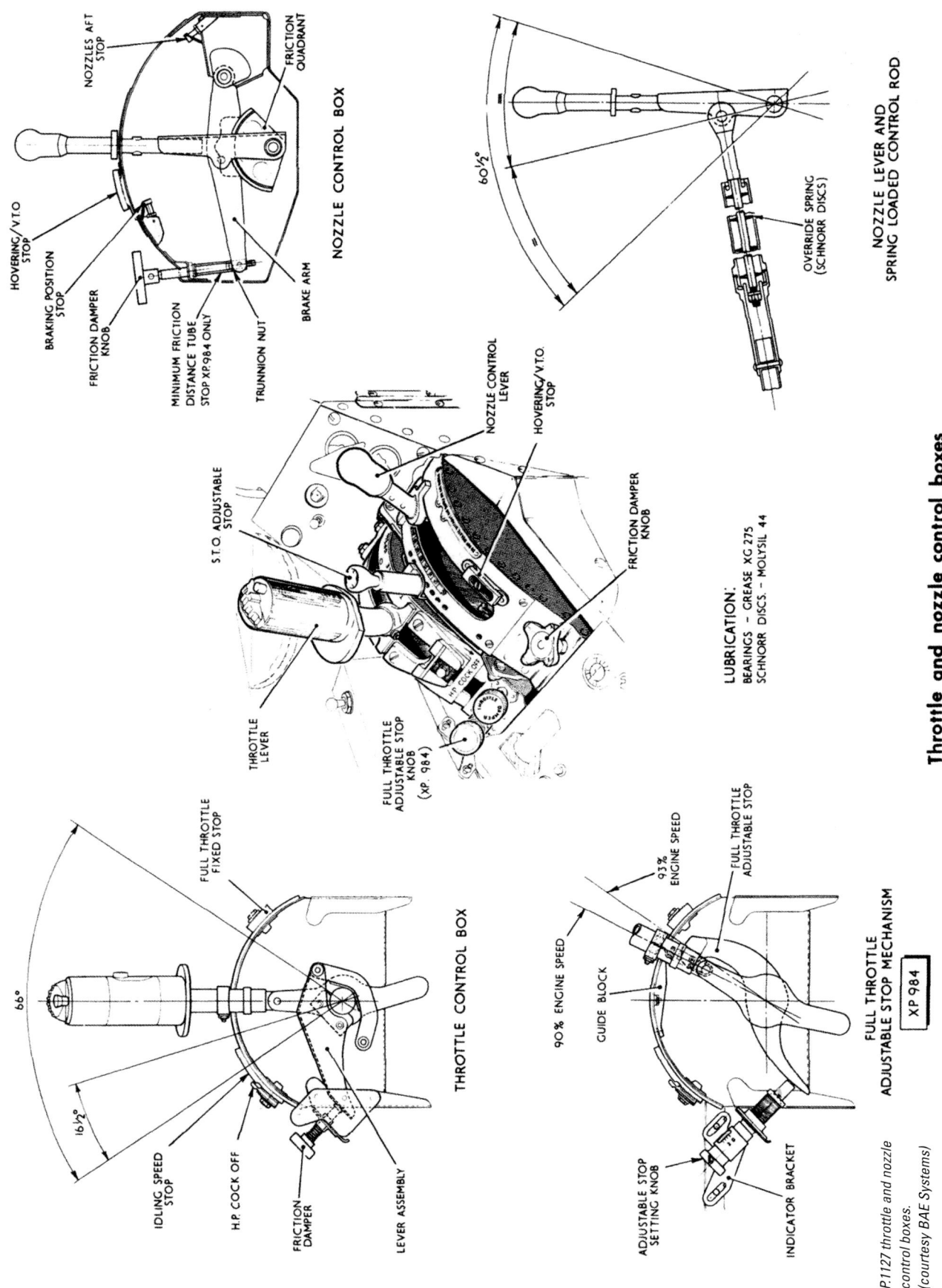

Throttle and nozzle control boxes

P.1127 throttle and nozzle control boxes.
(courtesy BAE Systems)

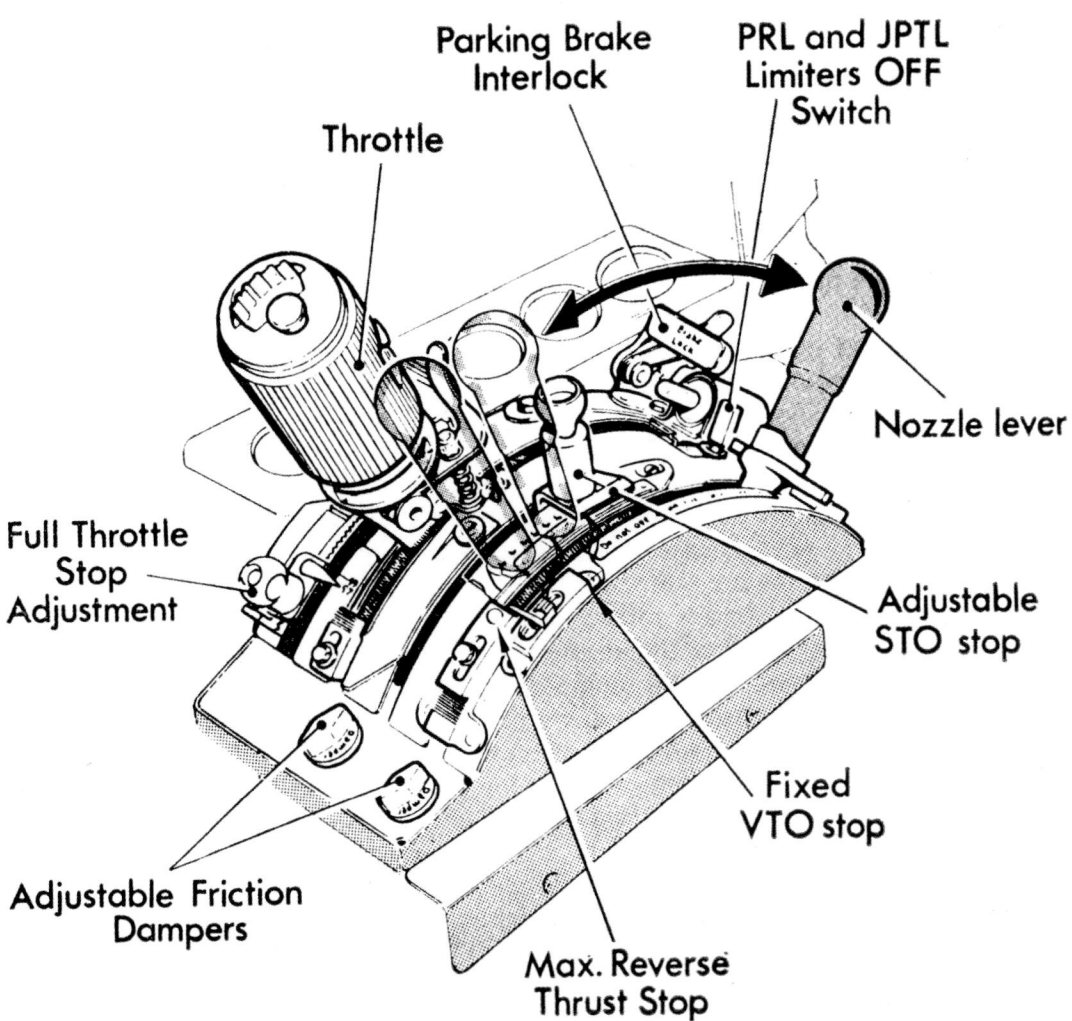

Parking Brake
Interlock

PRL and JPTL
Limiters OFF
Switch

Throttle

Nozzle lever

Full Throttle
Stop
Adjustment

Adjustable
STO stop

Adjustable Friction
Dampers

Fixed
VTO stop

Max. Reverse
Thrust Stop

*P.1127 throttle control box
illustrating the additional
nozzle angle lever,
peculiar to the
P.1129/Harrier.
(courtesy BAE Systems)*

SECTION THROUGH ENGINE/JET PIPE JOINT

Engine installation

P.1127 Engine Installation.
(courtesy BAE Systems)

HAWKER AIRCRAFT LIMITED
CANBURY PARK ROAD
KINGSTON·UPON·THAMES
SURREY

Design Dept.SC/PM

17th May, 1957.

Dr. S.G. Hooker,
The Bristol Aeroplane Co. Ltd.,
Filton House,
Filton,
Bristol.

Dear Dr. Hooker,

I saw recently a film on the Ryan V.T.O. aircraft and it started me wondering whether we ought to give more attention to this possible development I have also heard that you have given some consideration to it and I should like very much to have your views. My own view is that before we can go very far we would have to have in mind the practical application of the aircraft in other words it could not be merely a research aircraft.

There are many aspects, of course, of this development. Up to the present I have thought that the arrangement in which engines are carried merely for take-off and landing would be bad for the over all efficiency but Rolls, on the other hand, have suggested that this is probably the best arrangement.

I am sorry I omitted to discuss this with you when I was down at Bristol. Perhaps you could drop me a line about it.

Best wishes,

Yours sincerely,

The 1957 letter from
Sydney Camm to Stanley
Hooker, marking the very
beginnings of what
became the Harrier
programme.
(courtesy BAE Systems)

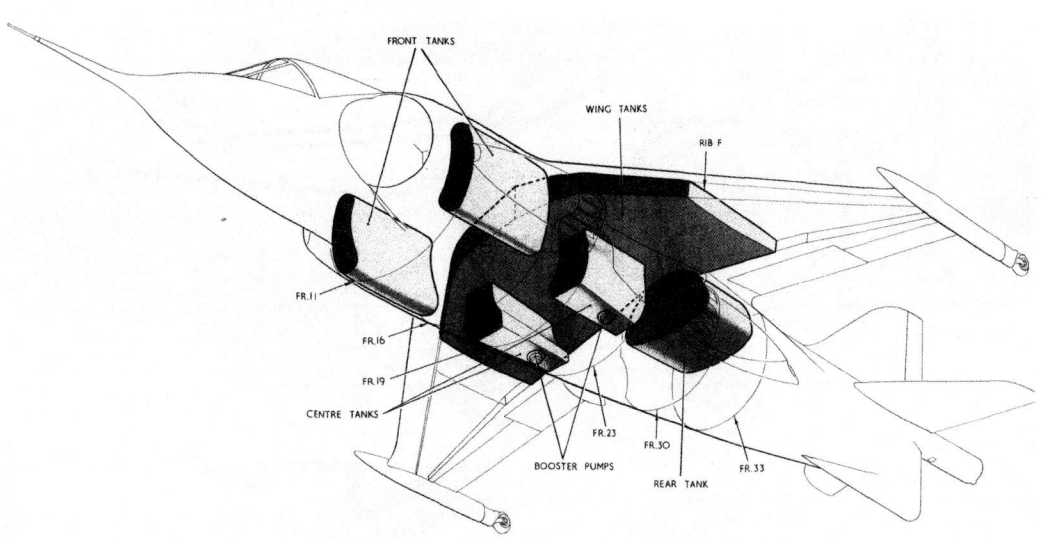

P.1127 fuel tank positions
diagram.
(courtesy BAE Systems)

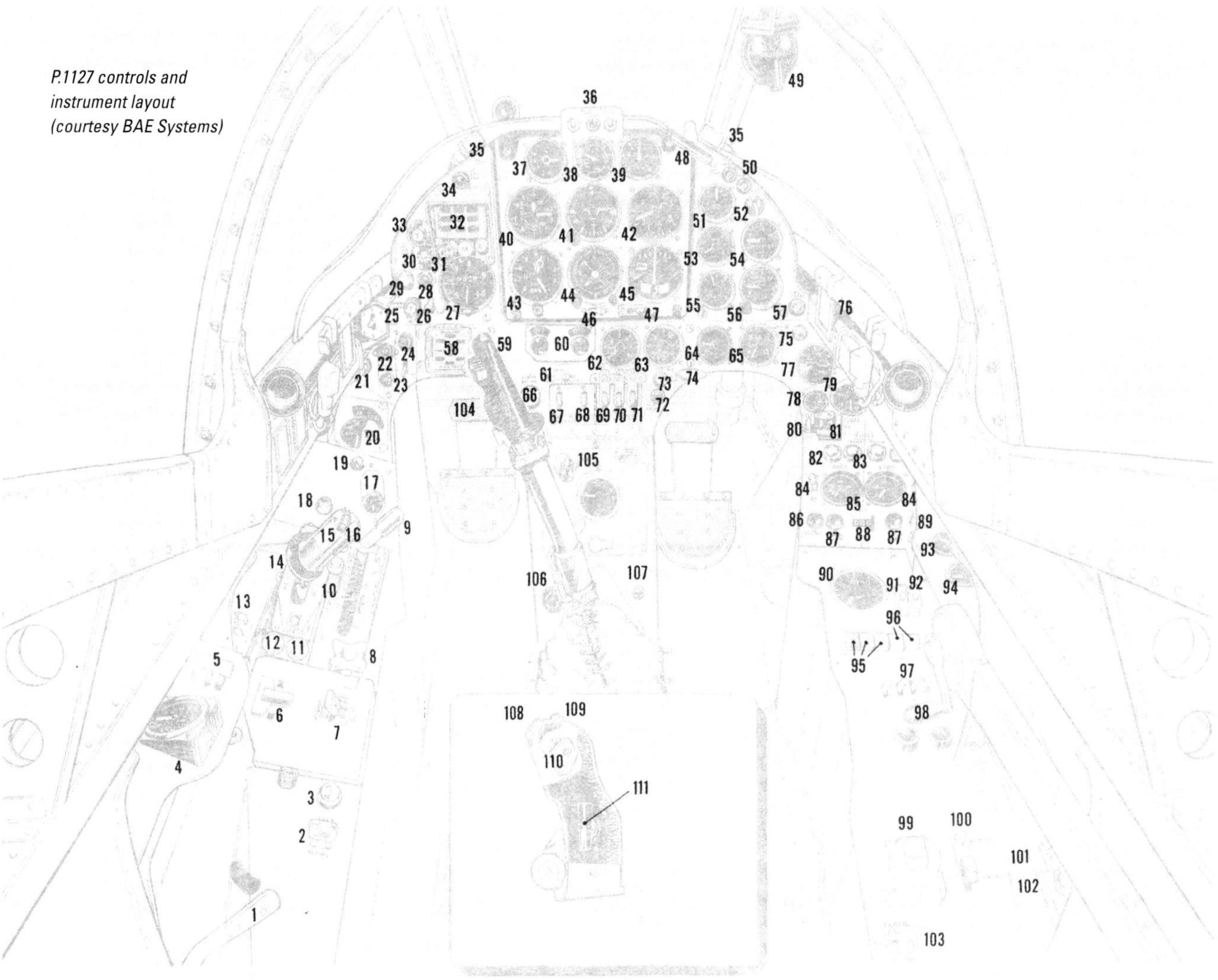

P.1127 controls and instrument layout (courtesy BAE Systems)

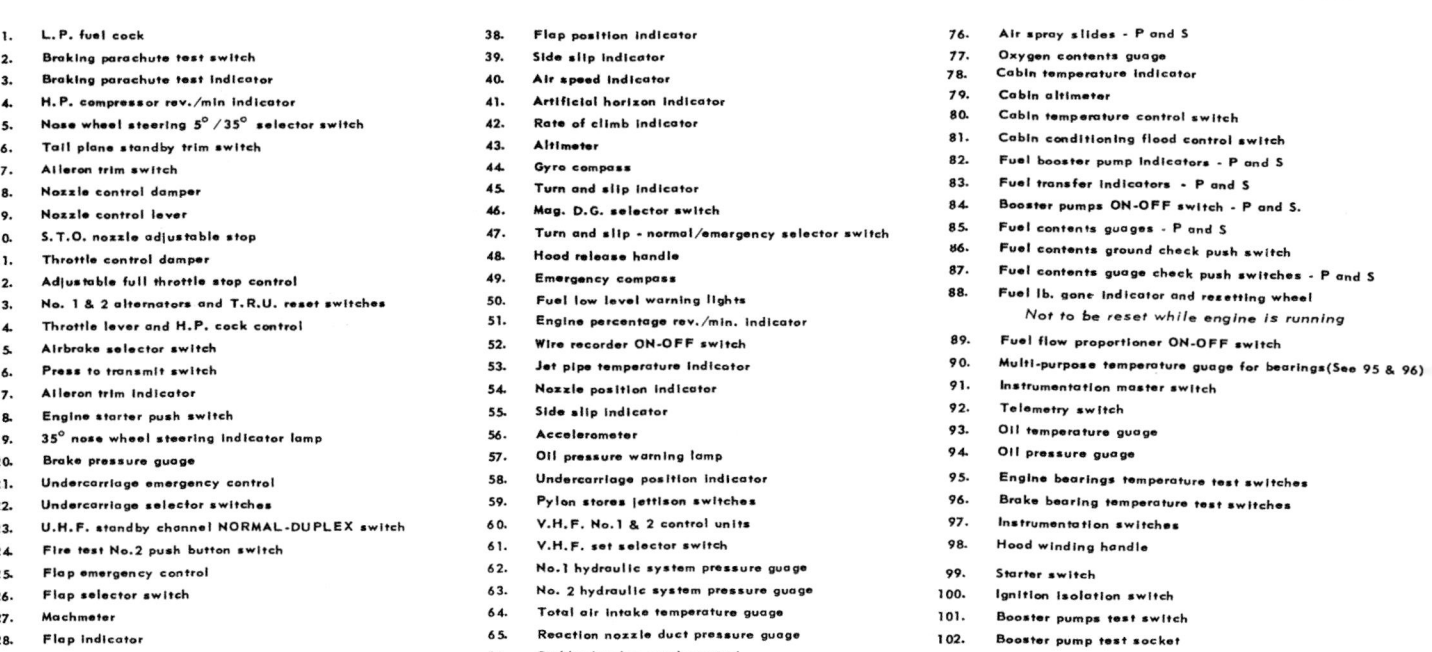

No.	Description	No.	Description	No.	Description
1.	L.P. fuel cock	38.	Flap position indicator	76.	Air spray slides - P and S
2.	Braking parachute test switch	39.	Side slip indicator	77.	Oxygen contents guage
3.	Braking parachute test indicator	40.	Air speed indicator	78.	Cabin temperature indicator
4.	H.P. compressor rev./min indicator	41.	Artificial horizon indicator	79.	Cabin altimeter
5.	Nose wheel steering 5°/35° selector switch	42.	Rate of climb indicator	80.	Cabin temperature control switch
6.	Tail plane standby trim switch	43.	Altimeter	81.	Cabin conditioning flood control switch
7.	Aileron trim switch	44.	Gyro compass	82.	Fuel booster pump indicators - P and S
8.	Nozzle control damper	45.	Turn and slip indicator	83.	Fuel transfer indicators - P and S
9.	Nozzle control lever	46.	Mag. D.G. selector switch	84.	Booster pumps ON-OFF switch - P and S.
10.	S.T.O. nozzle adjustable stop	47.	Turn and slip - normal/emergency selector switch	85.	Fuel contents guages - P and S
11.	Throttle control damper	48.	Hood release handle	86.	Fuel contents ground check push switch
12.	Adjustable full throttle stop control	49.	Emergency compass	87.	Fuel contents guage check push switches - P and S
13.	No. 1 & 2 alternators and T.R.U. reset switches	50.	Fuel low level warning lights	88.	Fuel lb. gone indicator and resetting wheel
14.	Throttle lever and H.P. cock control	51.	Engine percentage rev./min. indicator		*Not to be reset while engine is running*
15.	Airbrake selector switch	52.	Wire recorder ON-OFF switch	89.	Fuel flow proportioner ON-OFF switch
16.	Press to transmit switch	53.	Jet pipe temperature indicator	90.	Multi-purpose temperature guage for bearings (See 95 & 96)
17.	Aileron trim indicator	54.	Nozzle position indicator	91.	Instrumentation master switch
18.	Engine starter push switch	55.	Side slip indicator	92.	Telemetry switch
19.	35° nose wheel steering indicator lamp	56.	Accelerometer	93.	Oil temperature guage
20.	Brake pressure guage	57.	Oil pressure warning lamp	94.	Oil pressure guage
21.	Undercarriage emergency control	58.	Undercarriage position indicator	95.	Engine bearings temperature test switches
22.	Undercarriage selector switches	59.	Pylon stores jettison switches	96.	Brake bearing temperature test switches
23.	U.H.F. standby channel NORMAL-DUPLEX switch	60.	V.H.F. No.1 & 2 control units	97.	Instrumentation switches
24.	Fire test No.2 push button switch	61.	V.H.F. set selector switch	98.	Hood winding handle
25.	Flap emergency control	62.	No.1 hydraulic system pressure guage	99.	Starter switch
26.	Flap selector switch	63.	No. 2 hydraulic system pressure guage	100.	Ignition isolation switch
27.	Machmeter	64.	Total air intake temperature guage	101.	Booster pumps test switch
28.	Flap indicator	65.	Reaction nozzle duct pressure guage	102.	Booster pump test socket
29.	Air brake indicator	66.	Rudder bar leg reach control	103.	Navigation lights switch
30.	Braking parachute selector switch	67.	Battery master switch	104.	Brake toe pedals
31.	Combined fire warning lamp and extinguisher push switch	68.	Pitot head heater switch	105.	Oxygen regulator
32.	Standard warning panel with mute and cancel switches	69.	No.1 hydraulic system failure test switch	106.	Anti-spin parachute fuse
33.	S.W.P. test push switch	70.	No. 2 hydraulic system failure test switch	107.	Emergency battery fuse
34.	No. 1 T.R.U. failure warning indicator	71.	Ram air turbine test switch	108.	Tail plane twin switches seperator lever - ground test use
35.	Flashing indicator lamps - draw attention to S.W.P.	72.	Ram air turbine reset push switch	109.	Instrumentation push switch
36.	Anti-spin parachute control panel	73.	Ram air turbine indicator	110.	Tail plane trim switch
37.	Tail plane position indicator	74.	Parking brake control handle	111.	Auto control switch
		75.	Oxygen flow indicator		

CHAPTER TWO

Progress and Pipe Dreams

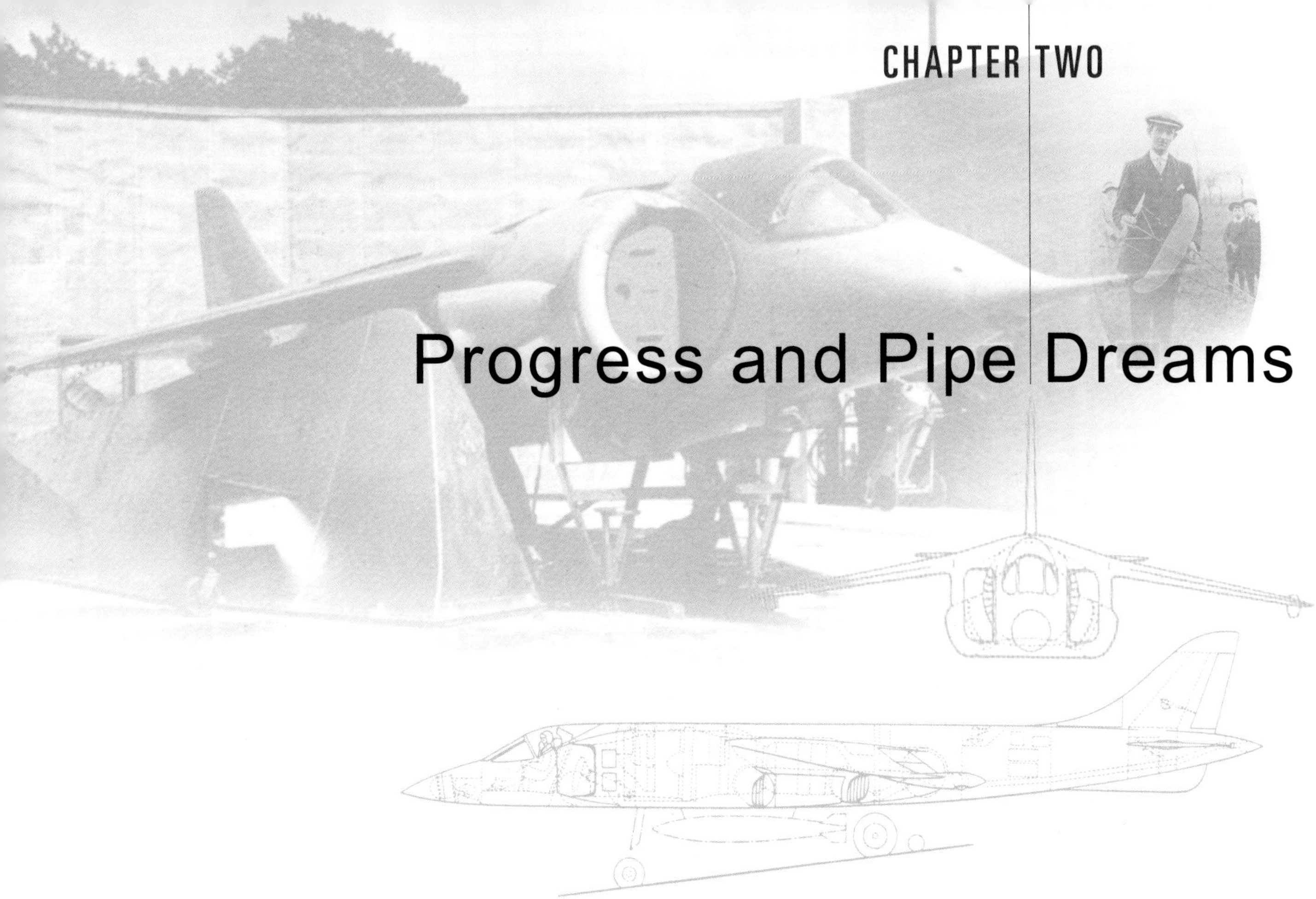

ITH the future of Bristol's engine now assured, it was the P.1127's future which still remained in some doubt. Hawker's officials continued to apply whatever pressure they could to persuade the Government to take a more active interest in the project, but progress was slow. During the 1958 Anglo-American Aeronautical Conference, Hawker had another chance to promote the project to the Ministry of Supply's Deputy Controller of Overseas Affairs (Mr. E.T. Jones), and emphasis was placed on the potential benefits which might be reaped from some Government investment in the design, now that there did appear to be some prospect of an operational aircraft being developed around Bristol's new engine. Slowly, official interest began to develop, the first hints of this being the Ministry of Supply's offer of wind tunnel facilities which gradually translated into direct liaison between Hawker and the RAE's Chief Scientific Officer (Structural Research) and the Head of the RAE's Transonic Wind Tunnel Department. The MWDP's interest in the project also continued and the USAF's Technical Adviser to NATO went so far as to suggest that NATO's ongoing plans to develop an advanced strike fighter (its NBMR-3 project) should be bypassed and replaced by a derivative of Hawker's P.1127. This combination of American interest and the slightly warmer enthusiasm being expressed by Britain's Ministry of Supply was sufficient to finally capture the attention of both the RAF and Royal Navy, from where a draft requirement for both a VTOL fighter and a VTOL

transport aircraft quickly emerged. In fact the requirement emerged rather too quickly and little practical thought was given to the precise nature of the fighter design in particular, which shifted in terms of performance, weapons load, equipment and even its basic role for almost two years. Thankfully this rather premature draft requirement never influenced development of the P.1127 otherwise it is doubtful whether any viable aircraft would ever have been completed. But at least it became clear that there was significant official British interest in the concept of VTOL even if it was not entirely clear whether it should be a fighter, bomber, reconnaissance aircraft or a combination of all three functions. In January 1959 official interest grew still further and the Hawker team was informed that the newly-created Ministry of Aviation was considering the procurement of two prototype aircraft, and by the end of that same month a representative from the MoA had discussed the idea directly with Hawker. On 23 January, Sydney Camm met with the Chief of the Air Staff (Operational Requirements) and learned – much to his surprise – that the RAF was effectively willing to ignore Defence Minister Sandys' ambitious claims that manned combat aircraft would no longer be necessary, and that, largely on the basis of its success in pursuing the purchase of TSR2, it now seemed reasonable to embark on other 'manned' projects, not least the design of an aircraft with which to replace the Hawker Hunter in the ground-attack support role. It was believed that a development of the new

Sir Sydney Camm, 'father' of the Harrier programme. (Brian Stanley collection)

P.1127 design would be an ideal candidate for this requirement. Just a week later, a draft RAF Specification had been drawn up and was already being circulated around Government departments.

Hawker Aircraft's team was understandably pleased that some tangible support was finally beginning to manifest itself within Britain's corridors of power, but consideration also had to be given to the MWDP from where so much support had first emerged (and through which the all-important engine was being financed). Indeed without the American MWDP money to finance the engine's development, the project would probably never have started. NATO was undoubtedly keen to encourage 'internationalisation' and the cooperation between countries on aircraft projects, and MWDP (influenced by NATO requirements and thinking) would be very unlikely to support continued development of the P.1127 if Hawker was seen to be 'going it alone' on what would be viewed as an all-British project. Hawker was therefore encouraged to seek some form of cooperation with a European partner, but although the concept of a joint project clearly had some merit (such as cost reductions and the likelihood of increased interest from potential NATO customers), Hawker did not want to run the risk of losing any commercial benefits from producing an exclusively British product. Mindful of the BE.53 engine which remained British, but largely funded by American money, Hawker was also only too aware of the relationship which was being forged between Rolls-Royce and Avions Marcel Dassault: Rolls-Royce's diminutive RB.108 lift engine was adopted for Dassault's VTOL adaptation of its trusty Mirage fighter (another project which ultimately came to nothing). The situation was complicated and confusing, not least because NATO's emerging requirement for a second-generation strike fighter was almost as nebulous as the RAF's shifting requirement had been. It was unclear what – if any – aircraft NATO would eventually require and it was equally unclear how such an aircraft would be funded, even if NATO did finally decide upon a specific design. Consequently, Hawker took the brave but very sensible decision to continue development of the P.1127 independently, having concluded that when both the RAF and NATO eventually established what kind of aircraft they really wanted, there was no guarantee that they might not require two conflicting designs, and the P.1127 would be unable to meet either. Hawker therefore proposed to continue developing the P.1127 as a research and proof-of-concept vehicle even though it already represented the most practical means of producing an operational VTOL warplane. Without any external financial support, Hawker issued manufacturing drawings to its Experimental Department during March 1959 and a month later the first metal was cut. It is to Hawker's great credit that so much faith was placed

in the project and that Hawker Siddeley's Board ultimately allowed the P.1127 to be funded at its own expense for two years. Having already lost more than £1 million on the abandoned P.1121 and while Bristol's engine was being financed to the tune of more than $10 million, Hawker's resolve must have been shaken at many stages. It is also fair to say that at least through the initial months of the project, Sydney Camm was still far from enthusiastic about it. It was only the gradual release of increasing numbers of engineers to work on the project that indicated a gradual shift of faith on the part of Camm and, as the project progressed, he became increasingly convinced that Hawker was backing a potentially revolutionary aeroplane.

Just a few weeks after the initial manufacturing process began, the RAF's draft GOR.345 requirement for a Hunter replacement was shown to the Hawker team. The general (and rather vague) requirements for a new ground-attack and fighter-reconnaissance aircraft suggested that RAF thinking on the Hunter's successor was still less than clear. It was also evident that, effectively, GOR.345 had been written around the P.1127 design, ensuring that the Operational Requirement did not place any unreasonable and unattainable demands on the new design. In fact the OR was surprisingly modest and in most respects it simply represented a new Hunter with VTOL capability – a Hunter 'flat riser' in effect. Simultaneously, the Ministry of Aviation requested that Hawker prepare costings and a manufacturing programme for two prototype aircraft, and a draft Research Specification (ER.204D) was shown to the company. Perhaps not surprisingly, this indication of growing British official support for the P.1127 prompted NATO to re-energise its interest in the new aircraft and Hawker officials were invited to Paris with Bristol and MoA representatives in order to discuss the possibility of meeting NATO's requirement for a new strike fighter aircraft. However, it soon became clear that NATO's requirements had shifted quite considerably towards a much more sophisticated all-weather aircraft and it was unlikely that the P.1127 could ever hope to meet this kind of demanding specification. Thus NATO's interest in the aircraft dwindled again, but Colonel Chapman's enthusiasm for the P.1127 remained as strong as ever and in the absence of any great NATO interest, he quickly fostered relations between Hawker and representatives of the US aircraft industry, with a variety of officials making visits to Kingston in order to learn more about the emerging project. This new relationship was not one-sided however, as both Ralph Hooper and Robert Marsh (Head of Projects at Hawker) visited NASA's facility at Langley Field and also explored the various VTOL designs which were being pursued by the Bell Aircraft Corporation. By this stage Bell (a company already associated with VTOL through its extensive experience with helicopters) was busy developing a tilt-rotor design,

An early picture of Sydney Camm with a rather basic flying machine which looks a long way from the mighty Harrier which he would create many years later.
(Brian Stanley collection)

a ducted-propeller aircraft and the X-14, a small and relatively simple aircraft powered by a pair of Rolls-Royce Viper turbojets. Its VTOL ability was achieved through the employment of thrust deflectors fitted behind the engines which directed the exhaust gases downwards in order to obtain jet lift. With a system of reaction control jets similar to those being created for the P.1127 and gyro-stabilisation problems, the Hawker and Bell teams had plenty to talk about. Hawker's reception at Langley Field had been even warmer and NASA's John Stack offered to conduct a series of free-flight model testing on the P.1127 design, while it was subsequently agreed that NASA would also undertake transonic wind tunnel testing. This test programme resulted in a one-sixth scale replica of the P.1127 which was equipped with working jet nozzles fed by internal fans. Eventually it was placed in NASA's huge 30 x 60 ft wind tunnel at Langley and a team of four controllers (each operating one variable) 'flew' a series of tests on the model, culminating in transitions from jet-powered hovers into conventional flight. Further tests were conducted in NASA's transonic tunnel with a smaller metal model, and rolling take-off and landing tests were performed outdoors, attached to a revolving arm device. Once again it had been American support for the project which enabled P.1127 to progress although on 21 October Hawker finally received a £75,000 contract from Britain's MoA for the continuing design work at Kingston.

The MoA's decision to finance two P.1127 prototypes resulted in a draft contract and proper funding on 1 June 1960 for these two machines – XP831 and XP836. Regarded as research machines, it was also deemed necessary to extend official endorsement of the aircraft's engine, clearing what became the Pegasus 2 for a maximum 15 hours of VTOL operation and some 20 hours of conventional flight. NATO's lingering, but often vague, interest in both the engine and the P.1127 had by this stage encouraged Bristol to develop a Stage 2 version of the Pegasus which could deliver a thrust of almost 20,000 lb. This would have been more suitable for NATO's ambitious requirements, although it also encouraged Rolls-Royce to increase its efforts to promote its fixed vertical lift jet engine concept, which it still believed offered greater flexibility in terms of both aircraft weight and overall performance (this belief was largely expressed through the ongoing French VSTOL projects). In February 1960 the MoA formally requested that Hawker should clarify the NATO situation once and for all and the company confirmed that, in its present form, both the P.1127 and its engine would be incapable of meeting NATO's demands as they stood. However it added that Bristol's Stage 2 engine might well be more suitable for its requirements if a suitable aircraft design emerged. Ironically, Bristol had just informed Hawker that the existing BE.53 Pegasus (which had been improved to BE.53/3 standard) would probably be capable of delivering just

10,000 lb – half of the Stage 2 engine's expected thrust. Frustratingly, Hawker had anticipated that the prototype P.1127 would probably weigh-in at 10,000 lb which prompted Stanley Hooker to carefully revise his design estimates. Recent bench running of the Pegasus had produced 11,500 lb thrust and this promised to offer a margin of power for the prototype's initial hovering trials. However, with additional power needed for the aircraft's reaction controls (fed by high pressure air bled from the engine), it was clear that the aircraft would be critically short of jet lift thrust. Further concern was raised when Hawker's Chief Experimental Test Pilot, Hugh Merewether, was involved in an accident whilst evaluating Bell's X-14 in April. After suffering gyroscopic coupling problems the aircraft ran out of available lift power and landed heavily and although Merewether was unhurt, the aircraft was severely damaged. It emphasised that the P.1127 would need a good reaction control system which had sufficient power to maintain hover stability in pitch, roll and yaw.

Sir Stanley Hooker, the ultimate creator of the Pegasus engine which enabled the Harrier family to be developed. (Brian Stanley collection)

Although at a stage when a final contract for the two prototypes had yet to be signed (this would finally be achieved on 22 June), on 12 April the MoA requested that Hawker should produce a tender for a further four prototypes. Meanwhile on 3 May the first Pegasus engine (No.905) was transported from Bristol to Kingston for installation in the first aircraft. Construction was well-advanced by this stage, and the transonic wind tunnel tests and free-flight model research being conducted by NASA were yielding useful results. Back in the UK, the aircraft's reaction control ducts and valves were tested at Gloster Aircraft's Brockworth factory while Martin Baker aircraft continued work on the ejection seat that would be fitted. The first run of an installed engine took place on 31 August (although this was not flight-cleared) and an 11,300 lb-thrust Pegasus 2 was installed on 13 October. Hawker accepted that these first engines would be life-limited and could only be used for short test-runs but this did not represent any setback to the development pro-gramme. It had already been agreed that the first 'flight' tests would actually be only jet-borne hovers, so that a full investigation of the aircraft's control characteristics could be explored in relative safety, just a

The P.1127 prototype's fuselage shell emerges from the Kingston factory. (Photo: BAE Systems)

XP831 at Dunsfold undergoing static engine runs prior to making its first 'hop'. (Photo: BAE Systems)

few feet above the ground. Obviously it made good sense to concentrate on the most challenging aspects of the aircraft's performance first, and to explore the aspects of the design of which, in many respects, still very much is unknown. In order to avoid problems with ground effects and the ingestion of exhaust gases, model tests of a projected grid pad were completed and a full-scale concrete pit was constructed at Hawker's test airfield at Dunsfold in Surrey. The pit was some 88 ft long and 40 ft wide, with a depth of 4 ft, with cascaded to deflect exhaust gas through a metal grid base and out through an upwards-sloping ramp at the end of the pit. A Pegasus engine was installed on the test grid on 22 September for a trial run, after which it was returned to Filton for examination and refurbishment. Meanwhile the first P.1127 (XP831) had been transported to Dunsfold for final assembly and system checks before being officially 'rolled out' on 31 August. After the aircraft had been weighed it was quickly assigned to ground engine runs in a specially-designed silencing pen, and although these runs went smoothly, XP831 did briefly catch fire during one of the tests when oil leaked from one of the engine's rear nozzles. Prompt action from the attendant fire personnel prevented what could have been the cause of a very serious delay. Further tests were then completed over the metal grid on 22 September and with no problems to address, the go-ahead was finally given for the first tethered 'flight' test. As mentioned previously, Merewether had already gained some VTOL experience with Bell's X-14 and the same opportunity was also given to Hawker's Chief Test Pilot, A.W. 'Bill' Bedford. Both pilots were also given 18-hour courses on helicopter-handling in

the expectation – or at least hope – that this would give them some basic grounding in VTOL handling, although of course the characteristics (and controls) of a helicopter bore very little similarity to the P.1127. Possibly more useful was a brief opportunity for each pilot to make a short and tethered hover in one of Short's SC.1 aircraft at its Belfast airfield, although some synthetic training had also been possible thanks to the creation of a Control Response Simulator. This was developed under the supervision of Hawker's Robin Balmer and comprised a computer system which could replicate the predicted control load characteristics of the Pegasus engine under different dynamic inputs. It was by no means as capable or ambitious as modern simulation programmes, but it was sufficient to give Hawker (and Bristol) a taste of things to come. In order to prepare for the P.1127's potential handling in conventional flight, some training was completed in Hunters, flown in 'dirty' configuration with flags and landing gear extended, as this was thought to be representative of the P.1127 in a fairly typical low-speed handling test flight. It also enabled the pilots to practise engine failures – something which would be as potentially serious in conventional flight as in the hover. Suitably prepared for the commencement of the P.1127's test-flight programme, Bill Bedford walked out to XP831 on Dunsfold's test grid pad on the morning of 21 October. At long last, Michel Wibault's bizarre proposal was finally going to be translated into what would be the very first full-scale test of his revolutionary concept.

Early trials of the Pegasus engine included in-flight testing performed through the use of a converted Valiant bomber fitted with a ventral fairing housing the engine test specimens.
(Photo: Rolls Royce)

XP831 out on the airfield at Dunsfold, still devoid of national insignia and serial numbers at the beginning of its test programme.
(Photo: BAE Systems)

Tethered hovering trials in progress at Dunsfold. XP831's initial instability was exacerbated by the unsatisfactory outrigger wheel and wing anhedral arrangement and the tethering system which compounded stability problems still further. (Photo: BAE Systems)

XP831, still minus its nose boom and wearing only calibration markings, inches skywards in a tethered hover at Dunsfold. (Photo: BAE Systems)

Pictured at a snowy Dunsfold later in her development career, XP831 resplendent in full national insignia, serials and titling. (Photo: BAE Systems)

Above right: XP980 fitted with inflatable rubber intake lips, pictured transitioning to forward flight from a hover. The intakes performed well but the lips could not withstand high speed flight and were eventually replaced by metal shrouds which were aerodynamically less efficient, but more reliable.
(Photo: BAE Systems)

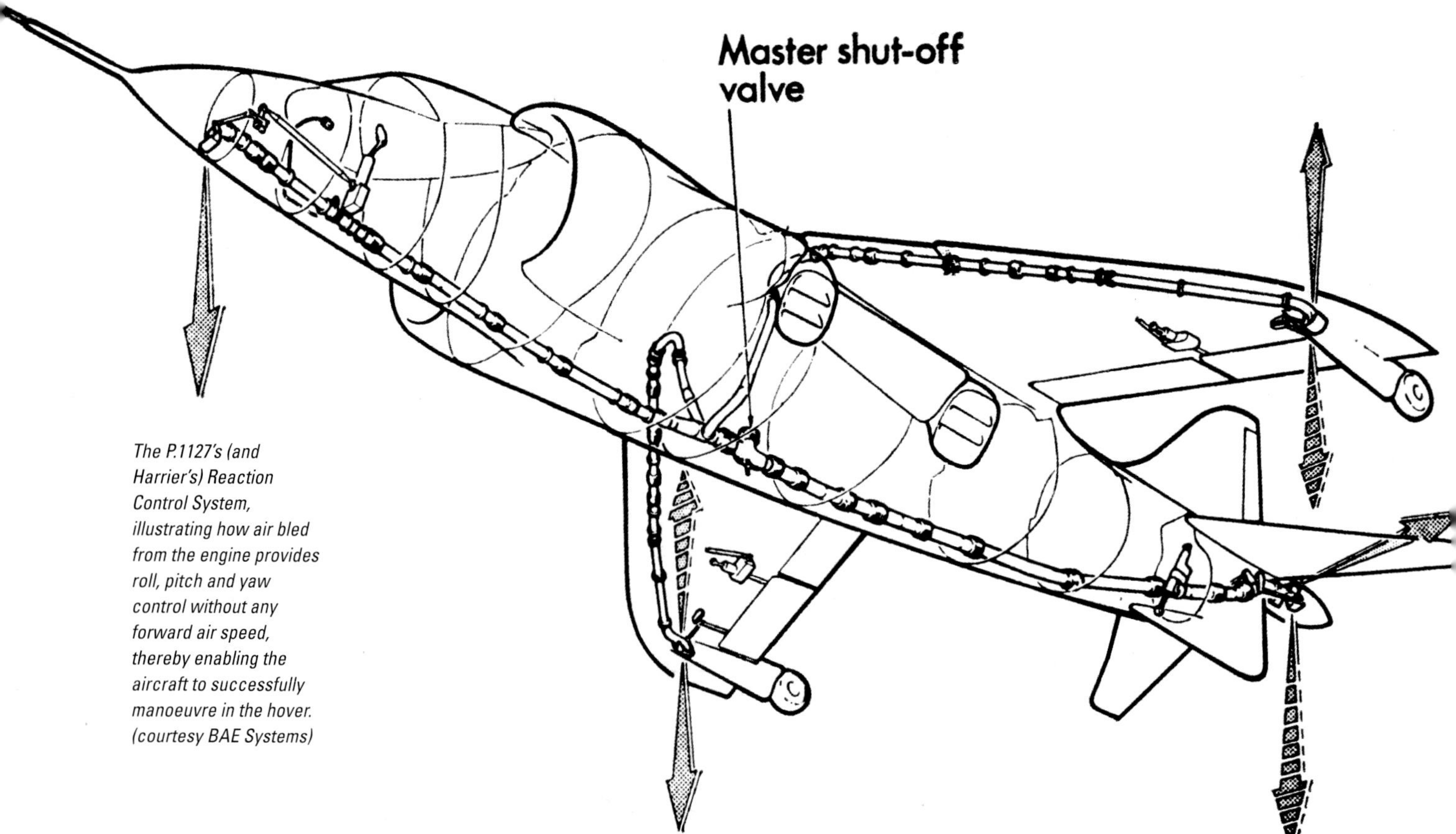

Master shut-off valve

The P.1127's (and Harrier's) Reaction Control System, illustrating how air bled from the engine provides roll, pitch and yaw control without any forward air speed, thereby enabling the aircraft to successfully manoeuvre in the hover.
(courtesy BAE Systems)

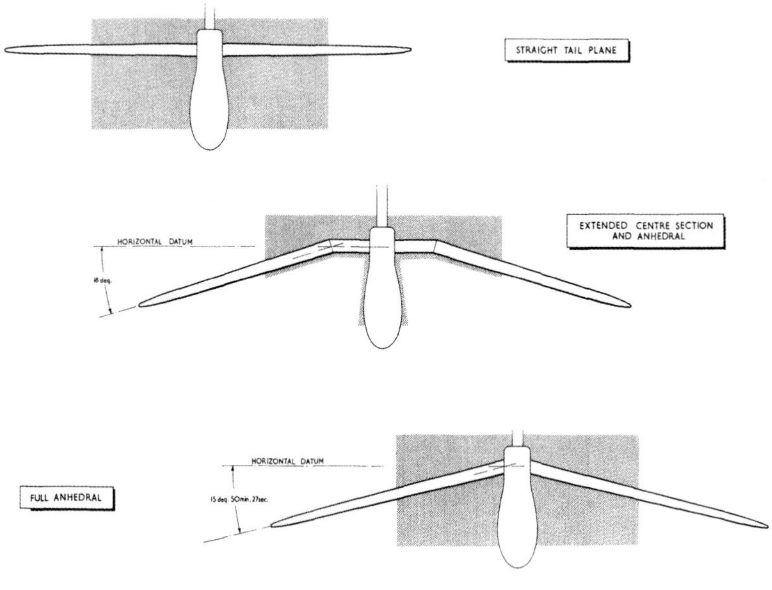

STRAIGHT TAIL PLANE

HORIZONTAL DATUM

EXTENDED CENTRE SECTION AND ANHEDRAL

Design of the P.1127's tail plane underwent various changes, including three distinct positions of anhedral as illustrated. Eventually a straight downward-angled configuration was adopted as standard.
(courtesy BAE Systems)

FULL ANHEDRAL

HORIZONTAL DATUM

XV276 was one of a small batch of Development Batch P.1127(RAF) aircraft. Although retaining the machine's familiar layout, this pre-production variant incorporated the later wing design ultimately fitted to the production-standard Harrier, and also incorporated a revised intake with inlet doors. (Photo: RAE Bedford)

XP831 at RAE Bedford, illustrating the long instrumentation pitot boom and straight wing leading edge. This aircraft spent most of its active life at Bedford assigned to research.
(Photo: RAE Bedford)

This unusual view of the P.1127 in forward flight emphasises the bulbous inflatable rubber intake lips which proved to be impractical for high-speed operations. They were subsequently replaced by fixed metal components. The air intakes were probably the most troublesome aspect of the design which required significant re-design and modification before a production standard was reached. (Photo: Brian Stanley collection)

A rare colour image of XP831 pictured after removal of the inflatable rubber intake lips. This view also emphases the fuselage fairings ahead of each nozzle which were re-designed prior to reaching a production standard. (Photo: BAE Systems)

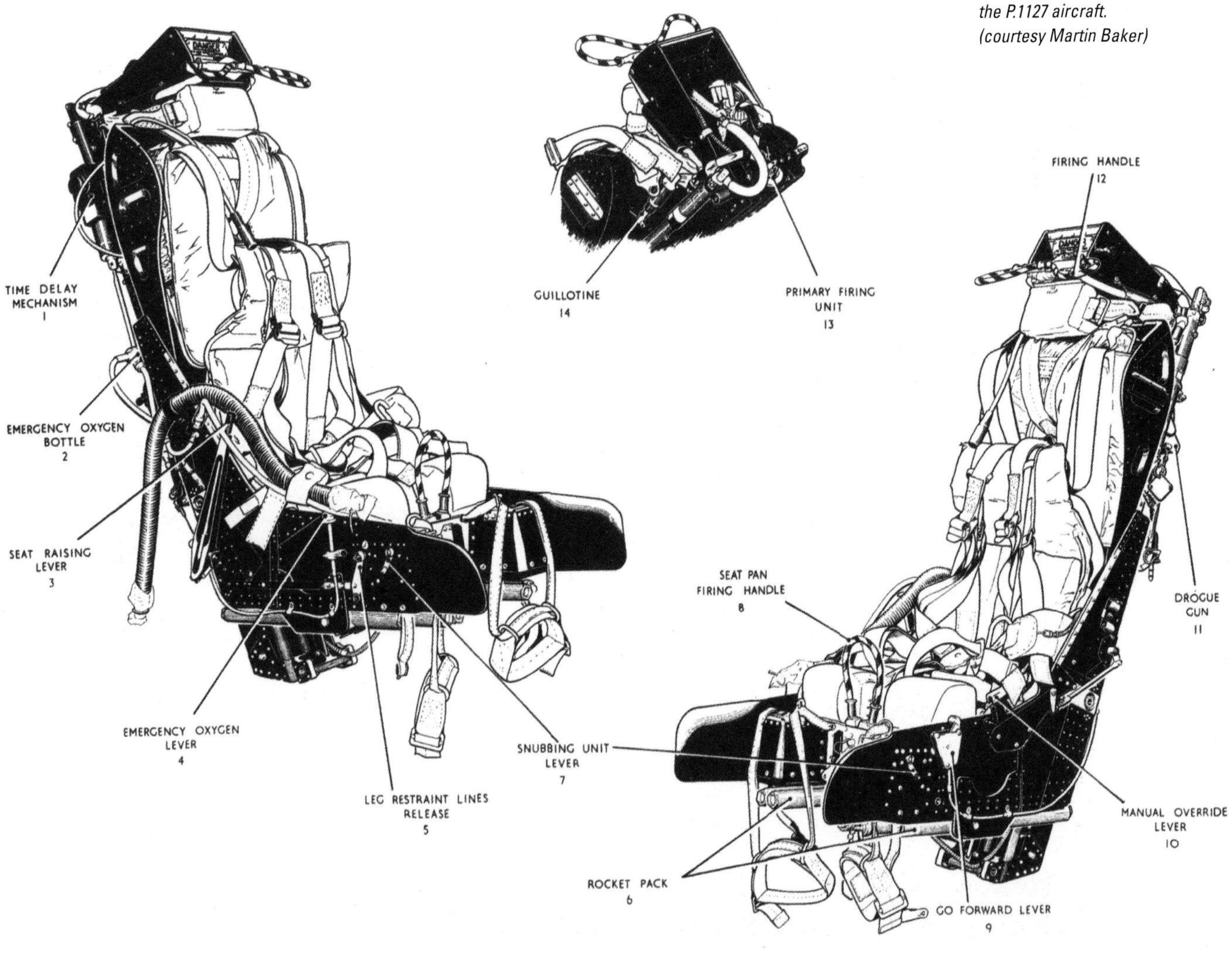

Martin Baker Type 6HA ejection seat as fitted to the P.1127 aircraft. (courtesy Martin Baker)

TIME DELAY
MECHANISM
I

EMERGENCY OXYGEN
BOTTLE
2

SEAT RAISING
LEVER
3

EMERGENCY OXYGEN
LEVER
4

LEG RESTRAINT LINES
RELEASE
5

GUILLOTINE
14

PRIMARY FIRING
UNIT
13

FIRING HANDLE
12

DROGUE
GUN
11

SEAT PAN
FIRING HANDLE
8

SNUBBING UNIT
LEVER
7

MANUAL OVERRIDE
LEVER
10

ROCKET PACK
6

GO FORWARD LEVER
9

60

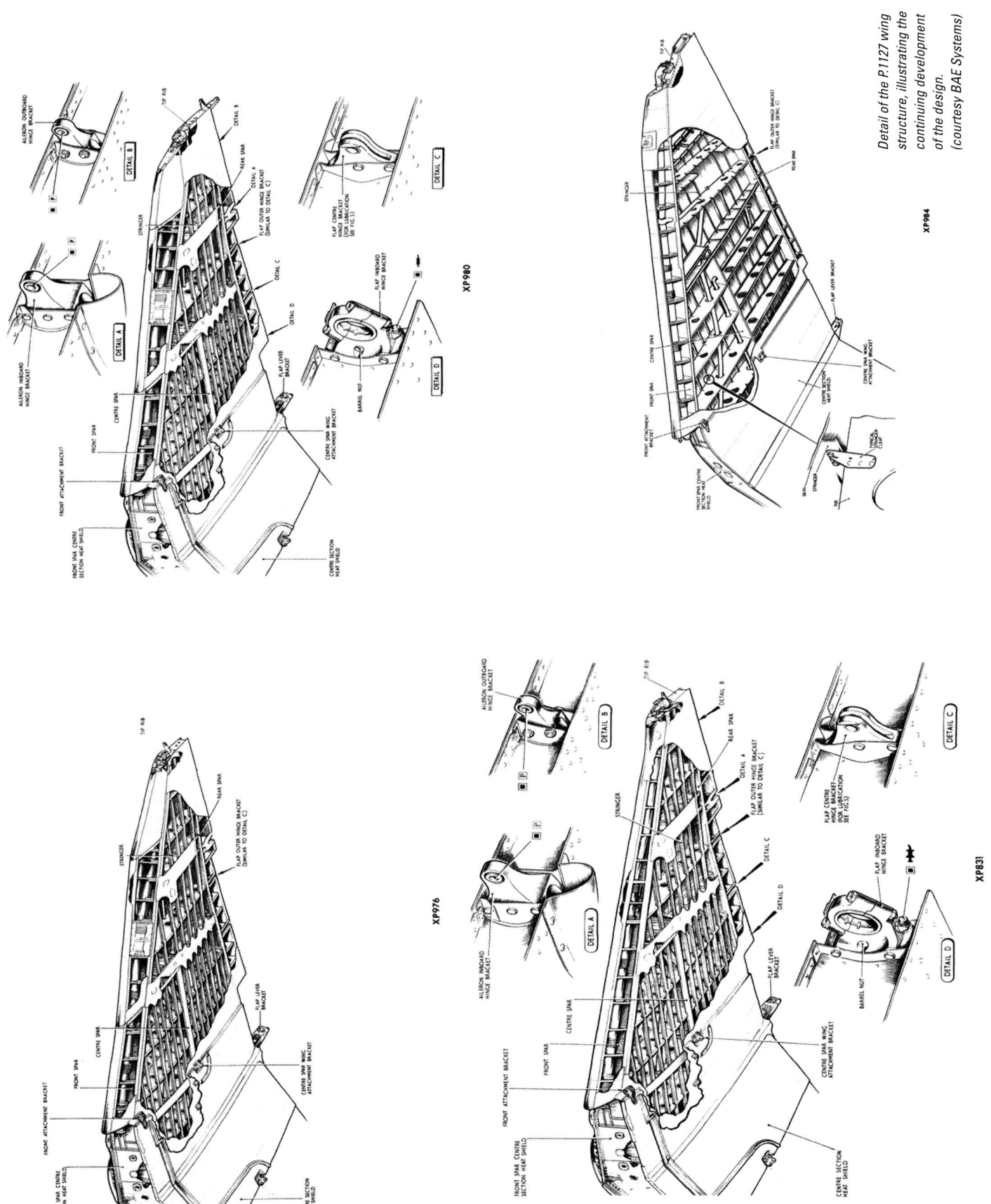

Detail of the P.1127 wing structure, illustrating the continuing development of the design. (courtesy BAE Systems)

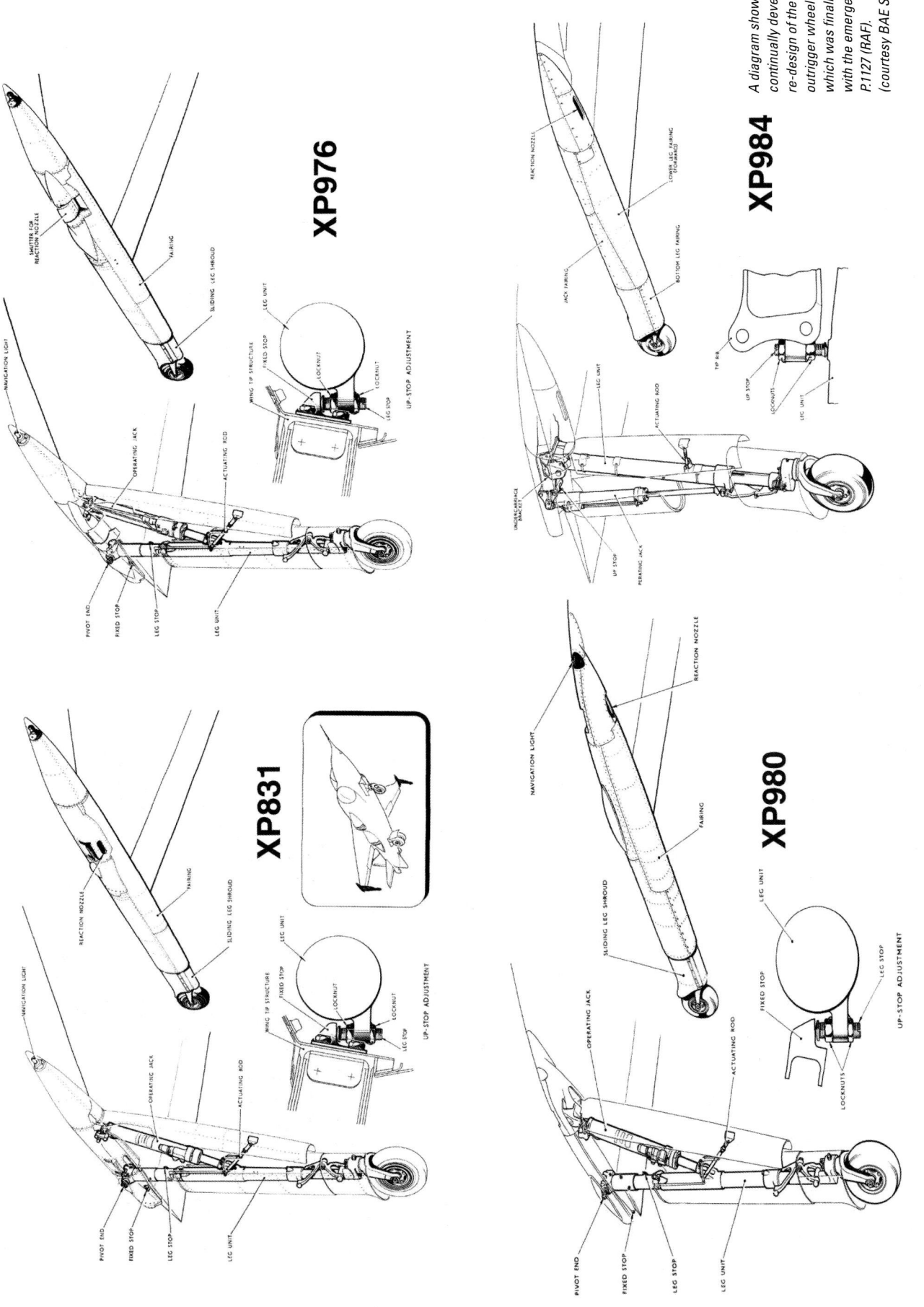

XP976

SHUTTER FOR REACTION NOZZLE

FAIRING

SLIDING LEG SHROUD

NAVIGATION LIGHT

OPERATING JACK

ACTUATING ROD

PIVOT END

FIXED STOP

LEG STOP

LEG UNIT

WING TIP STRUCTURE

FIXED STOP

LEG UNIT

LOCKNUT

LOCKNUT

LEG STOP

UP-STOP ADJUSTMENT

XP984

REACTION NOZZLE

LOWER LEG FAIRING (FORWARD)

JACK FAIRING

BOTTOM LEG FAIRING

TIP RIB

UP STOP

LOCKNUTS

LEG UNIT

LEG UNIT

ACTUATING ROD

UNDERCARRIAGE BRACKET

UP STOP

OPERATING JACK

A diagram showing the continually developing re-design of the P.1127's outrigger wheel fairings which was finally fixed with the emergence of the P.1127 (RAF).
(courtesy BAE Systems)

XP831

REACTION NOZZLE

FAIRING

SLIDING LEG SHROUD

NAVIGATION LIGHT

OPERATING JACK

ACTUATING ROD

PIVOT END

FIXED STOP

LEG STOP

LEG UNIT

WING TIP STRUCTURE

FIXED STOP

LEG UNIT

LOCKNUT

LOCKNUT

LEG STOP

UP-STOP ADJUSTMENT

XP980

REACTION NOZZLE

NAVIGATION LIGHT

FAIRING

SLIDING LEG SHROUD

OPERATING JACK

ACTUATING ROD

PIVOT END

FIXED STOP

LEG STOP

LEG UNIT

FIXED STOP

LEG UNIT

LEG STOP

LOCKNUTS

UP-STOP ADJUSTMENT

Bill Bedford brings XP831 aboard HMS Ark Royal in February 1963 to begin a short series of trials which confirmed the aircraft's suitability for ship-borne operations.
(Photo: Brian Stanley collection)

XP976, one of four Government-funded P.1127 development aircraft, pictured with the fuselage-mounted Ram Air Turbine extended. The extended tail boom houses an anti-spin parachute. (Photo: BAE Systems)

XS695 displaying to spectators at the Berlin air show in 1963, test boom removed.
(Photo: BAE Systems)

Rolls Royce's outstanding RB.108 lift engine which provided the basis for a variety of ambitious VSTOL designs, all of which were eventually abandoned when the versatility and potential of the Pegasus engine became evident. (Photo: Brian Stanley collection)

Left: P.1127(RAF) XV276 pictured in the hover at Dunsfold. (Photo: BAE Systems)

Left: XP984 hovering over RAE Bedford's runway. The later wing configuration can be seen, with vortex generators visible on the upper surface. (Photo: RAE Bedford)

XP831 pictured turning onto long final approach back to RAE Bedford shortly before retirement. Just visible are the wing tip lights which are incorporated into clear tips on the outrigger fairings. (Photo: RAE Bedford)

XP831, Aero Flight, RAE Bedford
XP831 as seen towards the end of her test career, assigned to the Aero Flight at RAE Bedford. Overall finish is dull silver (unpainted metal). (Chris Sandham-Bailey)

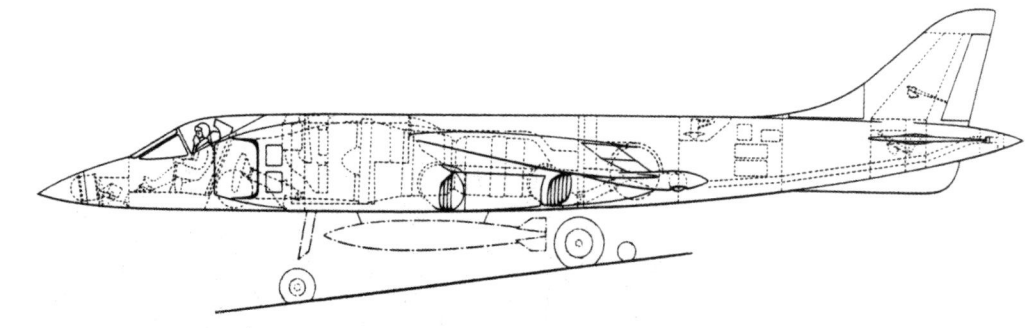

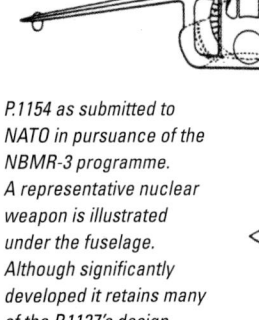

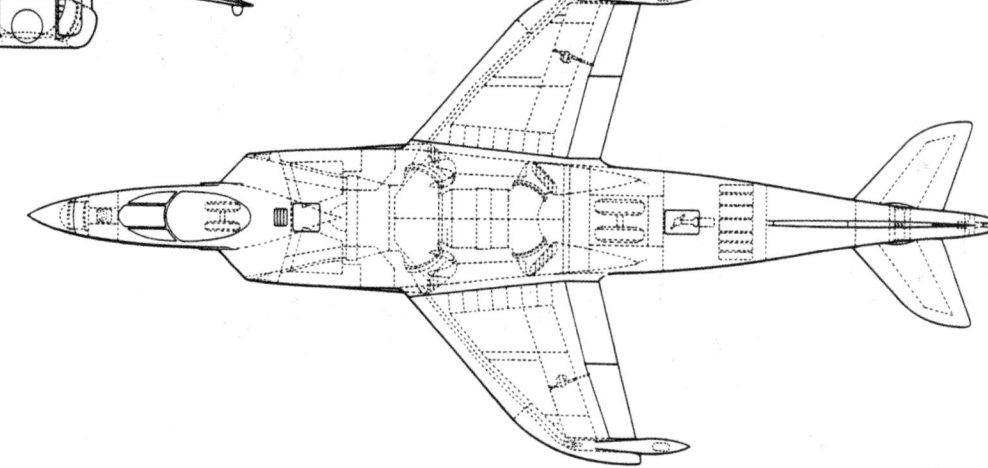

P.1154 as submitted to NATO in pursuance of the NBMR-3 programme. A representative nuclear weapon is illustrated under the fuselage. Although significantly developed it retains many of the P.1127's design features and the same wing as fitted to the Harrier.
(courtesy Brooklands Museum)

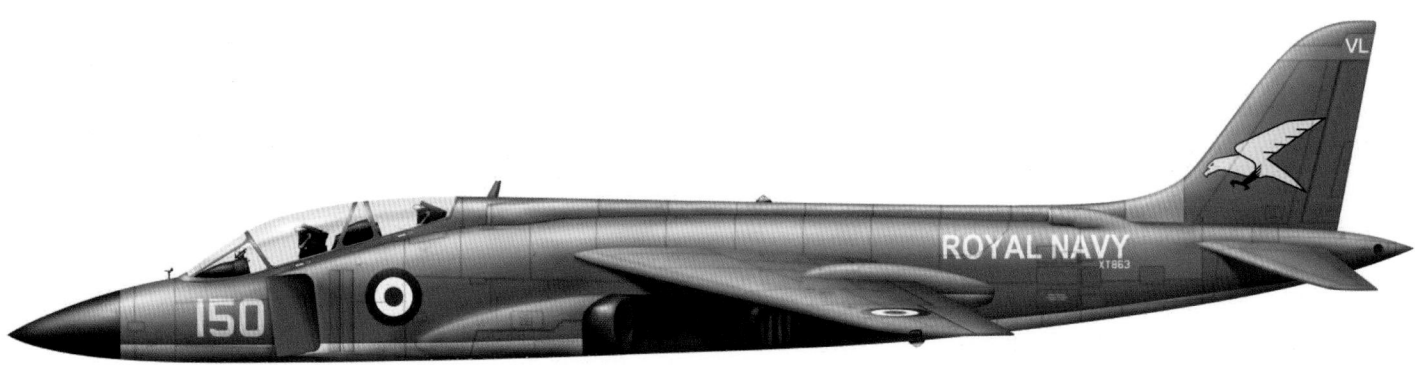

P.1154(RN) as the aircraft might have looked, had it reached service with the Fleet Air Arm.
(Chris Sandham-Bailey)

How the P.1154(RAF) might have looked had the aircraft entered RAF service. (Chris Sandham-Bailey)

Early model of the projected P.1154(RN) illustrating the unusual undercarriage layout (and associated wing fairings) necessitated by the carrier's catapult system. (courtesy Brooklands Museum)

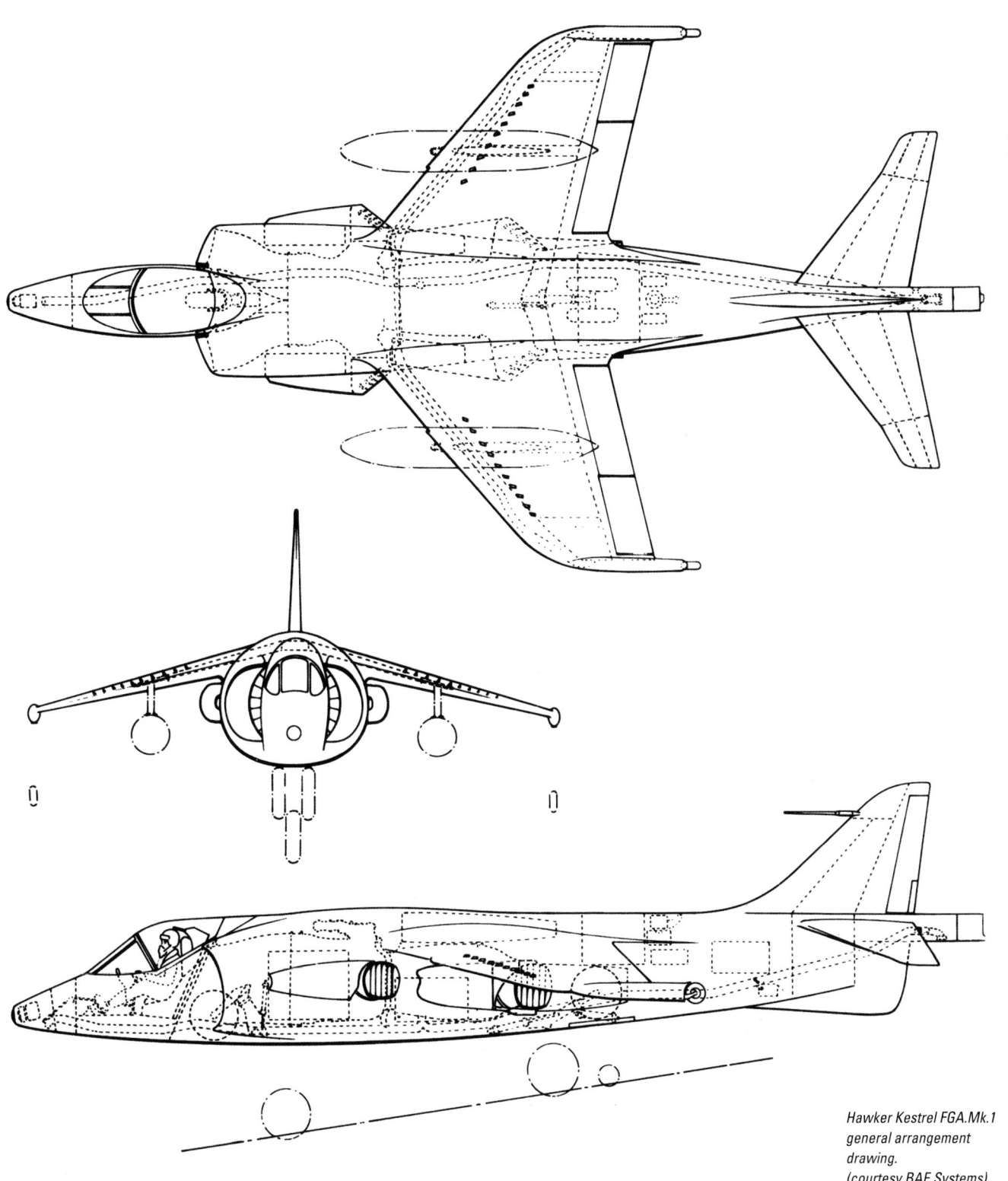

*Hawker Kestrel FGA.Mk.1
general arrangement
drawing.
(courtesy BAE Systems)*

*One of the first Kestrel aircraft pictured whilst still fitted with inflatable rubber
intake lips; these were replaced by metal intakes on the entire Kestrel Fleet.
Typical of a field deployment, the mown grass and scattered foliage blown up by
the thrust of the Pegasus engine is partially obscuring the aircraft.
(Photo: BAE Systems)*

*A Kestrel pictured on the Stanford Army range during a deployment from West Raynham, taxying through tree cover.
(Photo: BAE Systems)*

A quartet of Kestrels flying clean (with weapons pylons fitted) pictured on a sortie from West Raynham.
(Photo: BAE Systems)

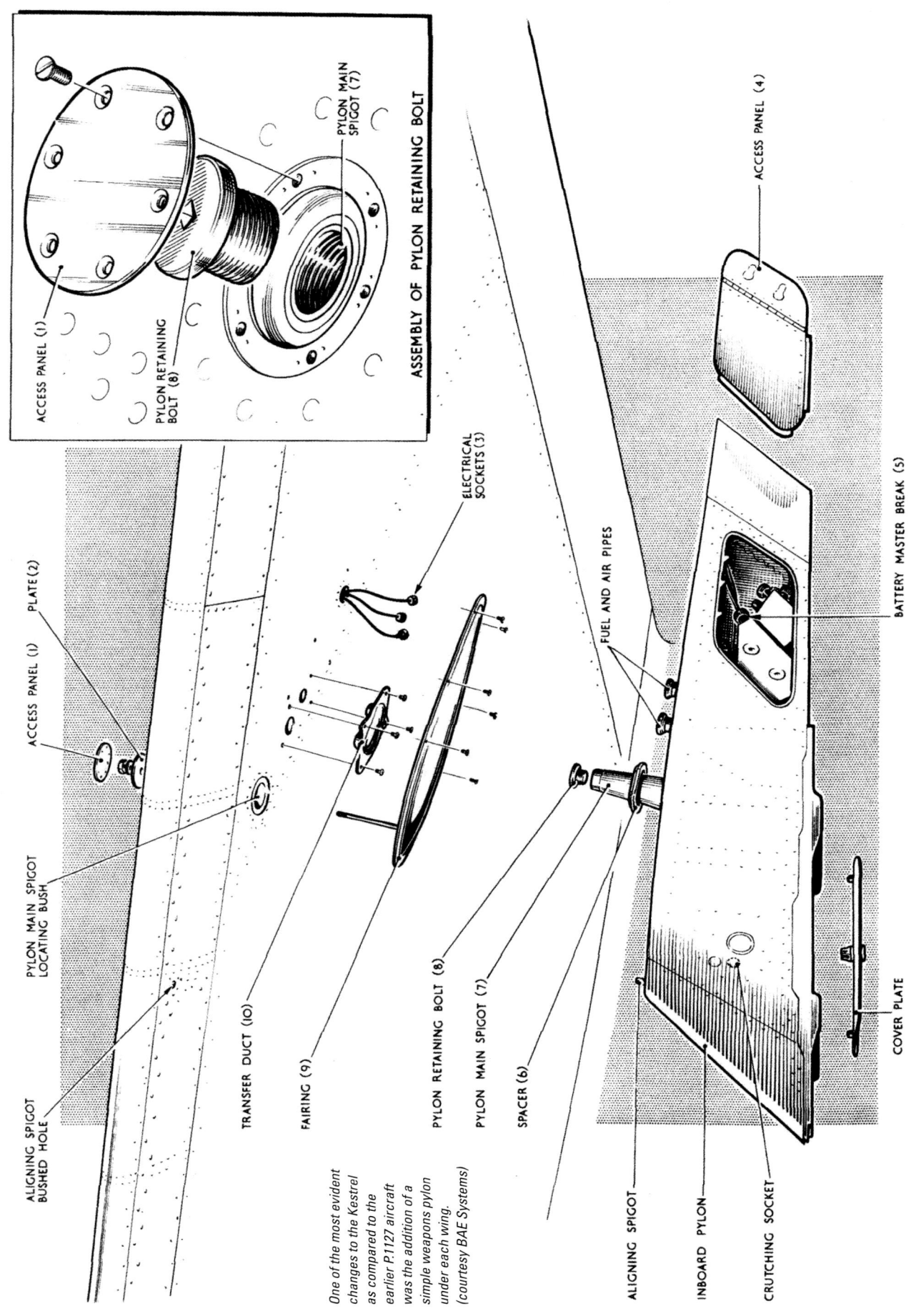

ACCESS PANEL (1)

PYLON RETAINING
BOLT (8)

PYLON MAIN
SPIGOT (7)

ASSEMBLY OF PYLON RETAINING BOLT

ELECTRICAL
SOCKETS (3)

ACCESS PANEL (4)

FUEL AND AIR PIPES

BATTERY MASTER BREAK (5)

PLATE (2)

ACCESS PANEL (1)

PYLON MAIN SPIGOT
LOCATING BUSH

ALIGNING SPIGOT
BUSHED HOLE

TRANSFER DUCT (10)

FAIRING (9)

PYLON RETAINING BOLT (8)

PYLON MAIN SPIGOT (7)

SPACER (6)

ALIGNING SPIGOT

INBOARD PYLON

CRUTCHING SOCKET

COVER PLATE

One of the most evident changes to the Kestrel as compared to the earlier P.1127 aircraft was the addition of a simple weapons pylon under each wing.
(courtesy BAE Systems)

A magnificent photograph of XS688. Unusually, this aircraft wore 'handed' tripartite wing insignia, Hawker titling on the nose, and retained inflatable rubber intake lips for some time.
(Photo: BAE Systems)

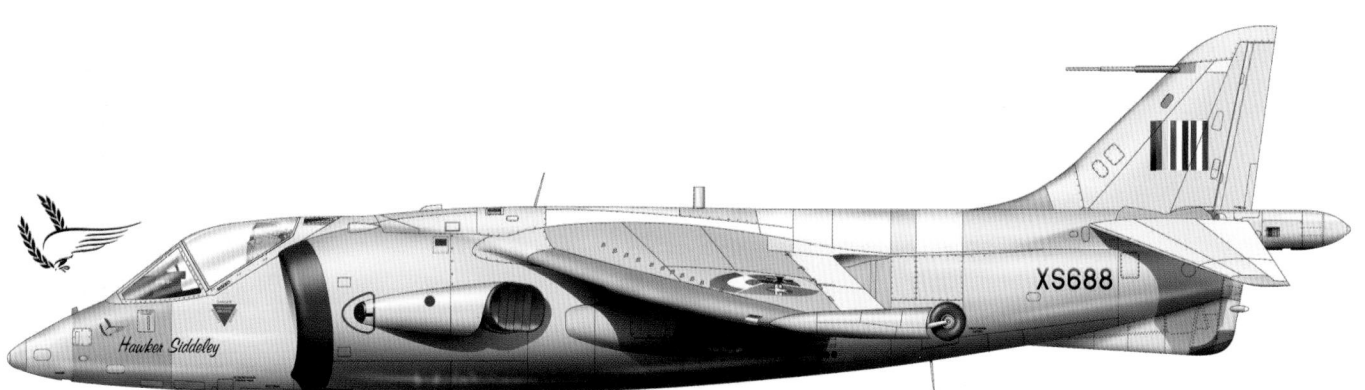

Hawker Siddeley Kestrel FG1 XS688, Tripartite Evaluation Squadron (TES), 1965.
Natural metal overall with black air intake lips; TES markings in four wing positions (exceptionally on this example, these were 'handed').
Black serial and logo on nose.

A damp morning on the TES flight line at West Raynham. Standard tripartite markings were applied to the Kestrel fleet together with individual fleet numbers. (Photo: BAE Systems)

XV-6A 'Nasa 520' pictured during her test career with Nasa's Langley Research Center. (Photo: Nasa)

After completion of test-flying at Langley, Nasa 520 was retained for permanent display on site. (Photo: Nasa)

One of two XV-6A Kestrels used by the Langley Research Center for several years and assigned to various test programmes. (Photo: Mick Roth collection)

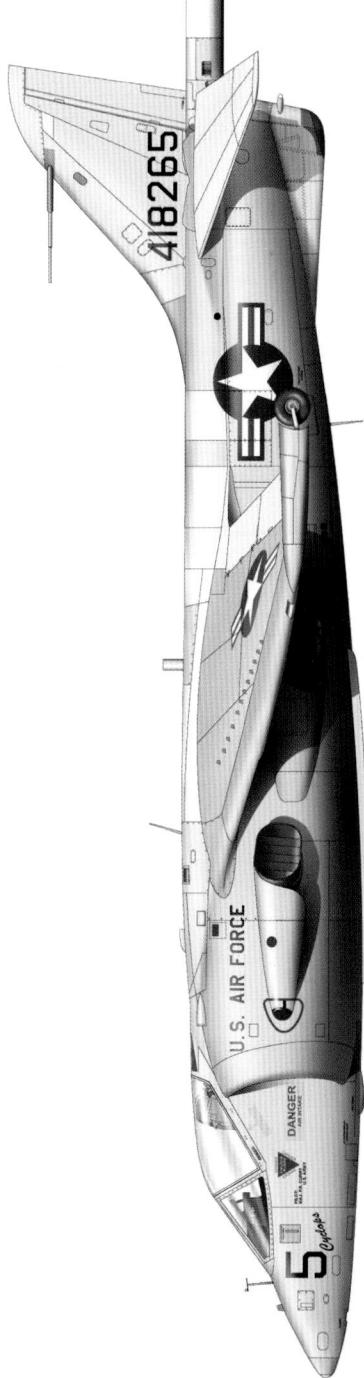

**Hawker Kestrel XV-6A, 418265/5, 'Cyclops',
Edwards Air Force Base,
Major P.R.Curry, US Army, 21 May 1967**
*Natural metal overall with standard USAF markings;
all lettering in and name on nose in black.*

XV-6A 418266 pictured
during evaluation at
Edwards AFB.
(Photo: USAF)

A former Kestrel which
was subsequently
shipped to the USA,
XV-6A 418262, is now
preserved as part of the
USAF Museum's
collection. (Photo: USAF)

CHAPTER THREE

Into Service

THE first production Harrier (XV738) took to the air for the first time on 28 December 1967, flown by Duncan Simpson. A contract for 60 aircraft, designated Harrier GR.Mk.1 (GR signifying the Ground-Attack and Reconnaissance roles) powered by the 19,000 lb Pegasus 6 (Mark 101) was drafted in February 1966, with a go-ahead for production given later that year before the contract was finalised early in 1967. A second contract followed which covered the two prototypes together with eight twin-seat dual-control variants designated Harrier T.Mk.2. The Harrier programme ran surprisingly smoothly, probably because so much preliminary work had already been completed on the P.1127 and even though the Harrier was in effect a completely different aircraft, it retained virtually all of the P.1127's basic design features, which enabled Hawker to 'leapfrog' many aspects of the Harrier programme. Indeed most of the flight development work was concerned with improvements in handling and the finalisation of the avionics and flight control systems. For example, the Ferranti INAS promised to be one of the more troublesome (or at least time-consuming) aspects of the programme, but in practice it was quickly perfected to deliver a navigational accuracy of little more than a 1nm error per hour of flight – which was far better than anything achieved by other aircraft at that time. By August 1967 all six Harrier development aircraft were flying and plans were already being made to improve the aircraft's performance even before it had settled into RAF

service. The Pegasus 10 was rated at 20,500 lb (thanks to better cooling of the engine's HP turbine blades and better water injection) and as the Mk.102 it was progressively retro-fitted to the new aircraft which were then redesignated as Harrier GR.Mk.1A. Meanwhile, five Harriers were deployed to Boscombe Down so that service evaluation of the aircraft could begin prior to achieving a CA Release, while two more machines conducted trials from Dunsfold with a variety of external fuel tanks, bombs, SNEB-Matra rocket pods and other equipment.

January 1969 marked the very beginnings of the Harrier's service with the RAF. At Dunsfold, under the leadership of Duncan Simpson, the Harrier Conversion Team was set up, comprising four experienced Hunter pilots (former Qualified Weapons Instructors) who had been selected, rather perversely, by weight as much as experience. As ever, the quest for an operational VSTOL aircraft was still being driven by a constant battle between power and weight. For some ten weeks the four-man team carefully studied all aspects of the Harrier's systems and learned as much as they could about the aircraft's aerodynamic properties from John Fozard. Their accumulated knowledge was then used as the basis for the HCT's Ground School syllabus through which the RAF's first Harrier pilots would be trained. The team's first hands-on flying took place at Chivenor, where the pilots completed a short refresher course on the Hunter before moving to Ternhill where they flew a six-hour course on Whirlwind helicopters,

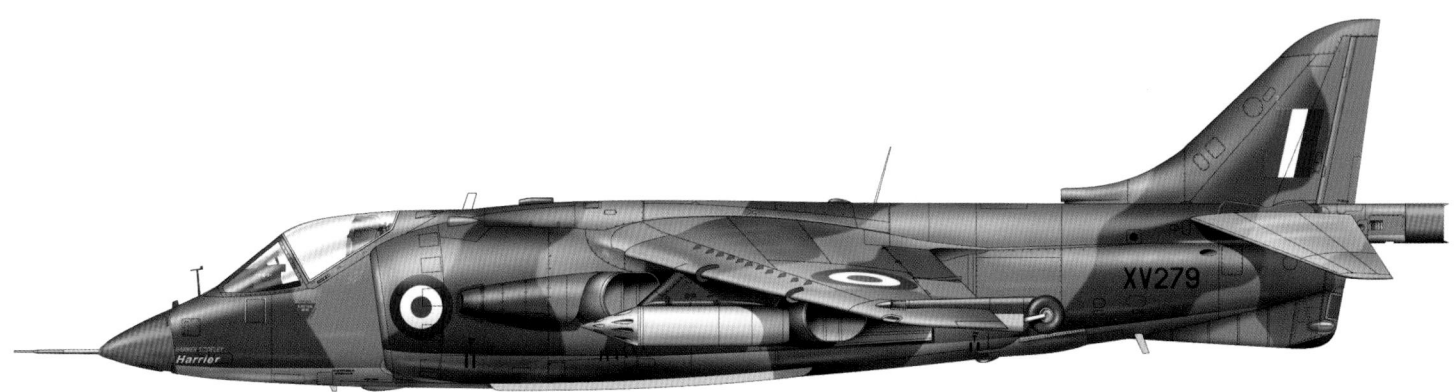

Harrier GR1 Mk.1, XV279, Dunsfold, June 1968
Dark Sea Grey/Dark Green/Light Aircraft Grey finish with national markings in bright colours; 36" diameter roundels above and below wings, 24" diameter roundels on air intakes. Black serial, repeated below wings. Dayglo nose cone and parachute tail housing

A rare colour image of an early Harrier Development Batch aircraft performing for the media at Dunsfold. The aircraft is unpainted and retains some panels painted in yellow primer. (Photo: Simon Watson)

studying all aspects of VTOL flying. There then followed eight hours of flying on the Harrier itself. At this stage there was still no dual-control variant of the aircraft available and each pilot had to become accustomed to the Harrier's handling qualities through a combination of study, trial and error, although some very unusual type conversion training techniques were employed. Most of the initial solo flights were accompanied by Simpson in a Hunter, starting with a conventional (i.e., an entirely wing-borne) flight that culminated in an equally conventional landing which (without jet lift) required the Harrier to touch down at some 160 knots – this was probably the most difficult and dangerous of all types of Harrier landing. Subsequent flights introduced the pilots to VSTOL operations and included some very unorthodox conversion flying in a Dove, piloted by Duncan

Simpson, with the four pilots carefully studying the recommended approach and departure procedures over Dunsfold (talked-through by Simpson) prior to practising transitions to and from jet-borne hovers in their Harriers. Finally, the pilots conducted a series of short take-offs and landings from both the runway and grass areas, and each made a vertical landing into a small 50 ft pad hidden in woodland near Boscombe Down. With only two dayglow markers on adjacent trees to act as visual cues, the pilots had to land into the clearing virtually blind, making visual contact with the pad at little more that 15 ft from touchdown. The HCT then moved to RAF Wittering on 16 May, taking their four aircraft to begin the task of converting RAF Hunter pilots onto the Harrier. Still equipped only with their batch of single-seat Harriers, a pair of twin-seat Hunter T7s (referred to at Wittering by air and ground crews as 'Fred' and 'Nuts') were also acquired from Chivenor to act as chase aircraft and procedures trainers. A significant proportion of the initial training was exported back to the Kestrel's former home at West Raynham, where the concrete pads built for the TES trials were already in place and ideal for Harrier VTOL training. Despite the absence of a dual-control Harrier, the HCT's activities proceeded rapidly and smoothly, and by August 1970 the HCT was busy training the first instructors for the new Harrier Operational Conversion Unit. Two months later the first Harrier T.Mk.2 was delivered and No.233 OCU was formed at Wittering, enabling the HCT to be wound down.

The first operational Harrier Squadron was one of the RAF's most famous – No.1 Squadron which had previously been operating Hunters at West Raynham. Its first Harrier aircraft (XV476) was delivered to Wittering on 18 April 1969 with another three aircraft delivered to the unit during the same month. Just two weeks later, the Harrier was revealed to the media and public in spectacular fashion when two of No.1 Squadron's aircraft (XV741 and XV744) were assigned to the 1969 Daily Mail Transatlantic Air Race – an exciting but ultimately pointless and expensive exercise designed to commemorate Alcock and Brown's historic Atlantic crossing, which the Fleet Air Arm had enthusiastically embraced as an opportunity to 'showcase' its new Phantoms. RAF support for the event was rather more muted and it was only by using the race to effectively 'trial' the Harrier's in-flight refuelling capabilities, that ultimately they were given approval to participate. On 9 April the two Harriers were flown to Boscombe Down so that the bolt-on refuelling probe and wing tip 'ferry' extensions could be test flown and cleared for use (this was in fact the first and only time that the Harrier's ferry wing tips were used, as they were found to be unnecessary for routine long-range flights). For the purposes of the race, the competitors were challenged to begin their journey at the Post Office Tower in London and complete it at the Empire State Building in New York. Not surprisingly, the supersonic Phantom achieved the fastest Atlantic crossing, but it was the RAF which was judged to be the overall winner point-to-point

XV20, illustrating the smaller (and more numerous) inlet doors fitted to the air intakes on P.1127(RAF) Development Batch aircraft. (Photo: Simon Watson)

An iconic image of the Harrier GR1: XV741 slows into a hover in front of captivated rail passengers at St.Pancras Station, 1969. (Photo: RAF Museum)

XV741 in the St.Pancras coal yard during the 1969 Trans-Atlantic Air Race. The bolt-on ferry wing tip tanks are clearly visible. (Tim McLelland collection)

The American side of the 1969 Trans-Atlantic Air Race: XV741 gets airborne in a cloud of dust in downtown Manhattan. (Tim McLelland collection)

(a time of 5 hours 57 mins westbound and 5 hours 31 mins eastbound), thanks to the Harrier's versatility which enabled the RAF pilots to reach their destinations much more rapidly. The faster Phantom had to operate from Wisley (the nearest suitable airfield to the starting point in London) and had to land at Floyd Bennet NAS, some considerable distance from New York's skyscrapers. By contrast, the Harrier was able to operate directly to the immediate vicinity of the two towers, with a suitable landing site in downtown Manhattan made available, and a coal yard adjacent to St.Pancras Station being used for the London leg. The jaw-dropping sight of an operational combat aircraft landing in full view of London's rail

travellers on the nearby platforms was an image which the world's media could not resist. Likewise, America's public was captivated by the bizarre spectacle of a foreign warplane touching down in the middle of New York City. It was attention-grabbing stuff by any standards. The Navy – having dismissed VTOL in favour of the mighty Phantom – must have wondered whether abandoning the P.1154 had been such a good idea after all.

By July 1970 No.1 Squadron had its full complement of 18 aircraft (although this process had been slowed not by technical problems, but by occasional bird strike and ingestion problems – factors that were to become a continual headache throughout the Harrier's service life) and

One of the Harrier Conversion Unit's Harrier GR1s pictured at Wittering, wearing early post-delivery full-colour national insignia. (Photo: Paul Tomlin)

re-equipment of the RAF's second unit, No.4 Squadron, then began. Its first aircraft (XV779) was joined by a further 14 aircraft by the end of the year and the unit established itself at Wildenrath, where RAF Germany's Harrier operations were to be concentrated. The second RAFG Harrier unit was No.20 Squadron which began conversion late in 1970 and was followed by No.3 Squadron early in 1972, the RAFG force being declared fully operational in January of that same year. Wildenrath, despite being a huge and well-equipped station, proved to be a less-than-ideal location for the RAFG Harrier force, being some considerable distance from the East German border. Consequently, supporting the Army's activities (which were always inevitably some distance away) required a considerable amount of expensive and complex logistical back-up which eventually encouraged the RAF to switch operations during 1977 to the more suitable airfield at Gütersloh, which was vacated by the resident Lightning squadrons (their air defence role being assumed by Phantoms at Wildenrath). Gütersloh, just 120 km from the border, and the RAF's most easterly 'allied' airfield, then became RAFG's permanent Harrier base, comprising two enlarged squadrons after No.20 Squadron gave up its aircraft in order to re-equip with the then new Jaguar, its relinquished Harriers being shared amongst the other two units. Thus, Nos. 3 and 4 Squadrons became RAFG's

'core' Harrier force, but under wartime conditions they also would have been supported by further aircraft from Wittering drawn from the OCU (flown by QFIs) which would, under such circumstances, have abandoned its training activities.

As described previously, initial Harrier conversion training was achieved without a dual-control variant of the aircraft. However the concept of creating a 'twin stick' Harrier had been anticipated ever since the GOR.345 specification had emerged. Creating a trainer derivative of a single-seat combat aircraft is inevitably a complicated business, but in most cases it is achieved without any significant design problems. Accommodating a second cockpit whilst maintaining the aircraft's performance is a task which can be achieved, but often results in a degraded range or speed capability – something that is not necessarily important for an aircraft which is primarily designed for training. However, in the case of the P.1127 there was much more to take into consideration. With so much of the aircraft's performance relying on jet thrust (and therefore necessitating minimal weight), adding a second cockpit would create new demands on the aircraft's available thrust and would also seriously affect the aircraft's all-important centre-of-gravity properties. From Hawker's experience with the Hunter and the successful side-by-side arrangement

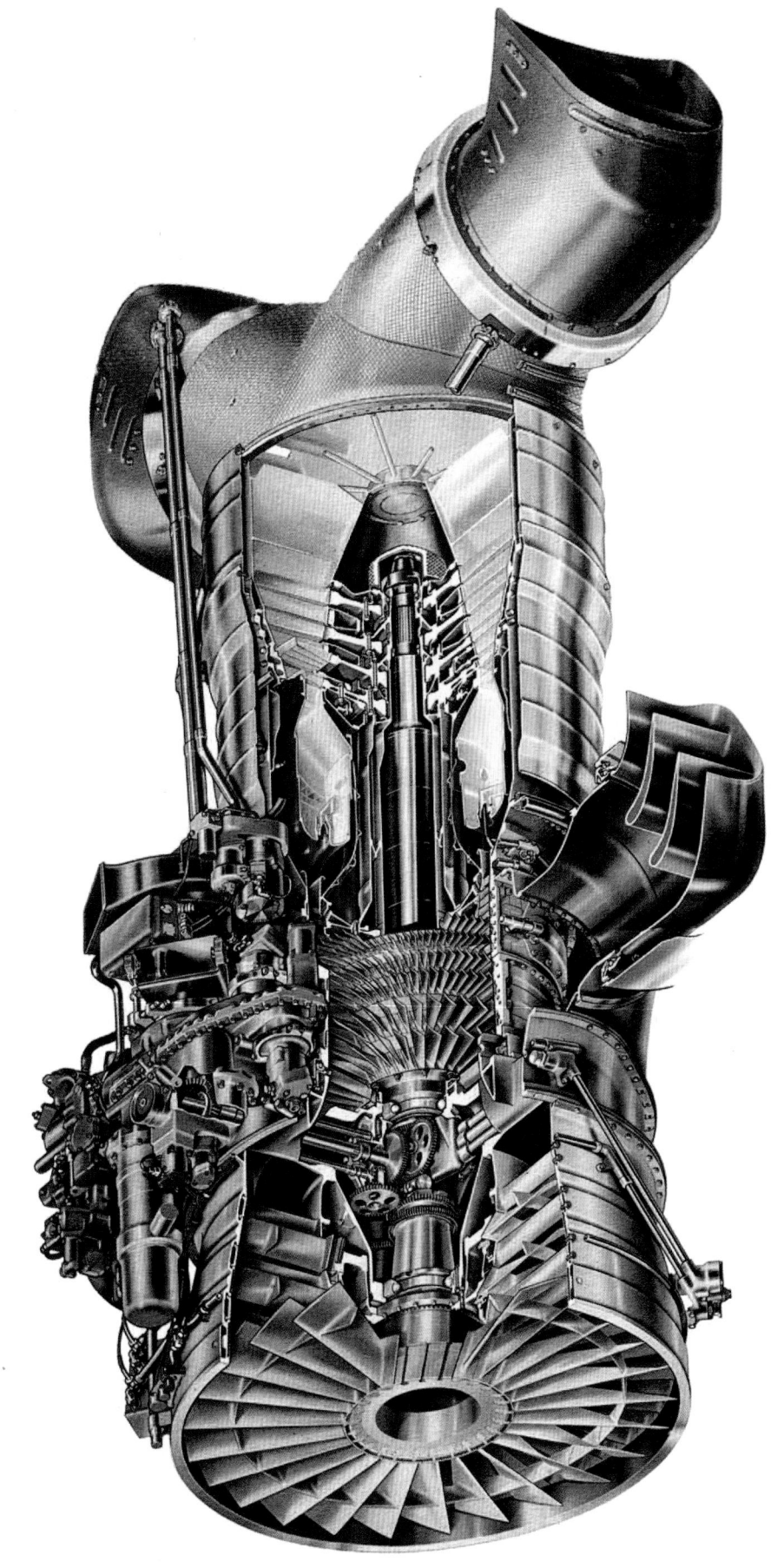

A cutaway diagram of the Pegasus engine, complete with rotatable nozzles.
(courtesy Rolls Royce)

Although the Harrier did not enter service with the FAA until 1979, the aircraft was by no means a stranger to the marine environment by this stage. During the late 1960s Harriers were deployed to Royal Navy vessels on sea trials, as illustrated by this image of HMS Hermes, and a trials aircraft wearing (rather prematurely) Royal Navy titling. (Photo: BAE Systems)

Harrier XV742 aboard
HMS Blake's tiny
helicopter deck during
trials in 1968.
(Photo: BAE Systems)

designed for that aircraft's trainer derivative, it seemed logical to adopt the same configuration for the P.1127. However, it was quickly realised that this would require a completely redesigned nose section and possibly a new forward and centre fuselage too, leading to all manner of delays and difficulties which would be created by the need to accommodate the airflow demands of the huge engine air intakes. In effect, it would be almost as problematical as creating a new design from scratch. Consequently, there was no other option than to adopt a tandem seating arrangement which required only a minimal redesign of the Harrier's fuselage and by March 1960 Hawker had

The first Harriers
deployed to Belize were
GR1s, as illustrated by this
aircraft from No.1
Squadron, proudly
wearing a locally-applied
shark's-mouth decoration.
(Photo: John Adams)

completed some preliminary drawings. It was not until February 1961 that the Air Ministry finally addressed the issue but with the growing importance of the P.1154 (and continuing development of P.1127 and eventually the Kestrel), attention drifted away from the trainer requirement until 1964 when it was agreed that a feasibility study would be undertaken by Hawker's team at Hamble. It was not until 1966 that a contract for a pair of twin-seaters was finally signed but once it had been agreed, development of the Harrier T.Mk.2 proceeded without further delay, much of the development being shared by the ongoing single-seat P.1127 programme (particularly the weapons system which would be common to both variants). The Air Staff specified that the trainer should retain as much commonality with the GR.Mk.1 as possible and that, if necessary, it would be capable of being flown from the front cockpit as a single-seater with the same weapons carriage ability, so that it could be included in the RAF's overall total of available Harriers for combat operations.

The redesign of the Harrier was achieved with minimal alterations, although the result was an aircraft which looked markedly different to its single-seat counterpart. The cockpit and nose structure was shifted forward to enable a 47-inch 'plug' to be inserted, providing space for a second

A gaggle of Harrier GR3s from No.4 Squadron making a refuelling rendezvous. Although bolt-on refuelling probes were often carried on the GR3, the bolt-on 'ferry' wing tips were never used. (Photo: Tim McLelland)

A Harrier GR3 of No.1 Squadron receiving attention under a camouflage 'hide' net during deployment to Belize.
(Photo: BAE Systems)

cockpit. The cabin conditioning system, placed immediately behind the GR1's ejection seat, was modified to handle the larger twin cockpit demands and moved to the rear of the second seat. The position of the nose wheel bay necessitated the new rear cockpit frame to be moved aft where it was now directly over the bay, requiring the rear seat to be raised some 18 ins above the front seat. This, coincidentally, improved the rear seat occupant's view which was of great benefit to QFIs (Qualified Flying Instructors) and QWIs (Qualified Weapons Instructors), affording them a clear view directly ahead over the head of the student occupying the front seat. With individual sideways-hinged canopies and a separate windscreen structure for the rear cockpit, the arrangement was described as a 'stepped tandem' – in effect two cockpits, the rear position slightly higher than the front. The centre-of-gravity considerations required the nose-mounted F95 camera and inertial platform to be moved to a new position under the rear cockpit and, to compensate for the extended nose profile, the rear fuselage (including the tail fin) was moved aft by some 33 ins and the fin structure was raised by 11 ins (and a revised ventral fin added) so that the aircraft's yaw stability could be maintained. By contrast, stability tests revealed that the tail plane position need not be changed and that

the repositioned nose RCV (now some 56 ins further forward, combined with the input of the balancing rear RCV) did not require any significantly higher volumes of bleed air in order to maintain control. The wing and centre fuselage structure remained identical to the single-seater, and the only other noticeable design modification was the addition of vibration dampers in the tail planes, necessary because of 'buzz' vibration caused during engine runs on the ground (the same harmonic problems were not created by the GR1). With almost indecently swift progress, XW174 was duly completed as the first Harrier T.Mk.2 – in effect a development aircraft rather than a prototype – and it took to the air in the hands of Duncan Simpson on 22 April 1969. Sadly, the aircraft was destroyed only six weeks later when a fuel system fault occurred during a test flight and Simpson was forced to eject from the aircraft near Boscombe

The Harrier GR3's Radar Warning receiver (RWR) arrangement with fore and aft-looking sensors attached to the tail fin and rear fuselage. (courtesy BAE systems)

A close-up view of the GR3's Laser Rangefinder and Marked Target Seeker (LRMTS) with the sensor head opened. (photo: BAE Systems)

A view of the Harrier Detachment dispersal at Belize which illustrates the somewhat primitive nature of the semi-permanent facilities provided for air and ground crew.
(Photo: BAE Systems)

Down, sustaining severe injuries in the process. Development of the T2 was not significantly delayed however, as the second aircraft (XW175) made its first flight on 14 July and flight-testing proceeded thereafter without any major difficulties. However, there was one significant problem which had not been foreseen. When the T2 was flown at high angles of attack within a very specific speed range, the test pilots found that they were experiencing a rolling tendency caused by sideslip. Because most of the T2 redesign had centred on the forward fuselage, it was believed that the cause of this directional instability was the redistributed airflow behind the cockpit breaking away, thereby reducing the fin's effectiveness. Further investigation revealed that this was not actually the case and that the problem laid within the fin structure itself. Various redesign fixes were investigated, starting with a simple and moderately successful 18-ins height extension to the fin tip. Flight-testing suggested that an even greater extension would improve results still further. Therefore the fin's disproportionately tall structure grew even further (this time by 23 ins) although Hawker's structural stress experts were reluctant to advocate the modification and eventually the test pilots were asked to re-evaluate the shorter fin design. This they did and it was agreed that the 18-inch extension was, in fact, sufficient to cure the 'weathercock' stability problem. During test-flying it had been discovered that when the aircraft was exhibiting its undesirable instability, extending the ventral air brake tended to improve handling and so the design team linked its operating circuit to that of the tail plane. Subsequently (and on all production aircraft), when the control column was pulled hard (beyond normal cruise flight movements) to attain high angles of attack, the air brake automatically extended to 26 degrees,

retracting when stick pressure was reduced. A batch of 12 Harrier T.Mk.2 aircraft was ordered in 1967 (later increased by an additional five airframes) and after completion of flight-testing and development (and attainment of a CA Release) the first trainer aircraft was delivered to the Harrier OCU at Wittering in July 1970. Further deliveries were made to Wittering and Wildenrath, and by 1972 all of the Harrier squadrons had their own dual-control aircraft which greatly eased the task of conversion training, instrument rating, weapons training and familiarisation/proficiency flying. As with the single-seater, the T.Mk.2 was also quickly retro-fitted with a more powerful 20,000 lb thrust Pegasus 102, and redesignated as the T.Mk.2A.

Experience with the Kestrel TES had a direct effect upon the ways in which the Harrier was utilised upon entering RAF service. The very clear reduction in wartime vulnerability was undoubtedly the aircraft's key asset, but it was also clear that the Harrier would give the RAF an ability to provide a swifter response to Close Air Support tasking. TES recommendations were studied and refined over a period of four years and provided the basis for two fundamental concepts proposed for the Harrier force. Firstly, the Wittering-based aircraft belonging to No.1 Squadron were assigned to direct support of the ACE Mobile Force (Air) on the NATO flanks, as part of SACEUR's Strategic Reserve (Air). Secondly, the larger RAF Germany force would be assigned to No.2 ATAF. When No.1 Squadron formed, the unit quickly explored the Harrier's operational potential and its aircraft were deployed to various dispersed sites around the UK as well as more distant locations in Norway and Cyprus. Operations from ships were also conducted (including a deployment to *Ark Royal*) and both Tromso in Norway and Vandel in Denmark were soon allocated as the squadron's primary operational forward bases, with another seven bases later being added as designated wartime sites. Typical wartime sorties were expected to be designed to counter Warsaw Pact armoured vehicles which would probably be moving west through Finland's and Norway's mountain passes. In order to counter these targets, BL.755 cluster bombs and SNEB 68 mm rockets, combined with the aircraft's semi-permanent ADEN cannon, were to be the Harrier pilot's weapons of choice. Typical sorties were expected to be of almost an hour in duration, extending to a radius of around 150nm, the aircraft carrying drop tanks for most missions. The Harrier's INAS and moving map display would provide the crews with essential navigational and attack information for every flight although target acquisition and a great deal of the en route navigation was to be performed visually, assisted by Forward Air Controllers (FAC) on the ground. Development of the Pegasus engine quickly resulted in a new Mk.103 version which delivered 21,500 lb thrust (permitting an increase in all-up VTOL weight) and the Harrier GR1A fleet was progressively refitted with this engine, being redesignated as Harrier GR.Mk.3 in the process. By 1975 the whole Harrier fleet, including the twin-seaters which were redesignated as the T.Mk.4, had been upgraded to this standard. As part of this process, the GR3 airframes were gradually equipped with a fin and tail-mounted passive Radar Warning Receiver (RWR) and a new Laser Rangefinder and Marked Target Seeker (LRMTS) system, housed in a new nose fairing, giving the aircraft an unusual 'dolphinesque' appearance (the twin-seaters were also progressively upgraded to the same standard). This device produced a laser pulse which provided the pilot with target range and location data whilst also providing a search capability, seeking infrared radiation scattered from a target being illuminated by a FAC on the ground. This enabled the FAC to designate a target by laser, so that the Harriers could deliver their weapons with extreme precision.

The enemy's defences were also taken into consideration and it was anticipated that mobile SA-6 and SA-7 missiles would be the primary threat, together with mobile anti-aircraft artillery in the form of the ZSU-23/4. This would demand some very skilled evasion tactics from the Harrier pilots and No.1 Squadron was soon well-versed in the art of low-level manoeuvring around the snow-covered fjords of Norway. The Harrier's new RWR system was an invaluable aid, providing the pilot with a cockpit display showing the direction and type of radar emission, in response to which the pilot would be obliged to take some very serious evasive action, aided by chaff and flare dispensers which were progressively fitted to the Harrier fleet. In addition to the risks of ground-based defences, the air threat was another important factor, and aircraft such as the MiG-21 'Fishbed' were expected

to be a very significant problem for the Harrier force. However the Harrier's small size, relatively light weight and excellent manoeuvrability (combined with the RWR, chaff and flares) suggested that in a combat environment, it would be more than capable of evading the attentions of marauding fighters. Maintaining a capacity to operate in this kind of hostile environment required No. 1 Squadron to support continual deployments away from its home base at Wittering. During summer months aircraft and crews would often deploy to Denmark (usually for a Tactical Evaluation exercise) and during winter months (usually in March) the squadron would deploy to Norway, where the unit's aircraft often appeared repainted in white 'Arctic' camouflage for the duration of each visit.

Meanwhile in Germany, RAFG Harrier operations centred around a WARLOC (Wartime Locations) concept, with a combined fleet of around 36 available aircraft (plus a reinforcement reserve of 12 aircraft from the OCU). The Harrier force was to be deployed forward from its main base at Wildenrath to locations within the Army's No.1(BR) Corps area of responsibility. There were six pre-surveyed flying sites, two assigned to each squadron with a capacity for up to eight aircraft at each location, together with a further six sites for 'step-up' operations, a Forward Wing Operations centre (FWOC) and a pair of logistics parks. This forward-based concept was both ambitious and difficult to maintain with huge support convoys and ground parties required to accompany the aircraft and crews to these remote locations across Germany. Wartime plans anticipated that initial sorties would be tasked to operate directly from Wildenrath, but with each aircraft landing at its wartime dispersed site only an hour later – no mean feat for either the air crews or supporting personnel on the ground. At the main base (Wildenrath), the Harrier pilots had the relative luxury of a long, concrete runway and parallel taxiways from which to operate, but in the field, recovery would be made vertically and departures achieved by short take-off. Many of these dispersed sites were selected strips of rural and urban roads which were built to 'Schnellweg' standard (the equivalent of the UK's B-class network). Larger main roads and autobahns would have been even more suitable but these were expected to be needed for emergency operation of less-versatile aircraft which required significant lengths of concrete from which to operate and it was accepted that many roads would have to be kept free to be used as arterial convoy routes. Consequently, the Harrier sites were generally little more than small areas of clear road or, in some cases, fields onto which pads and tracking could be laid, adjacent to forest camouflage cover – in essence the same sort of sites from which the TES Kestrel crews had operated many years previously.

Harrier T2 XW264 enjoyed only a brief career, being written off en-route to the A&AEE at Boscombe Down on 11 July 1970.
(Photo: BAE Systems)

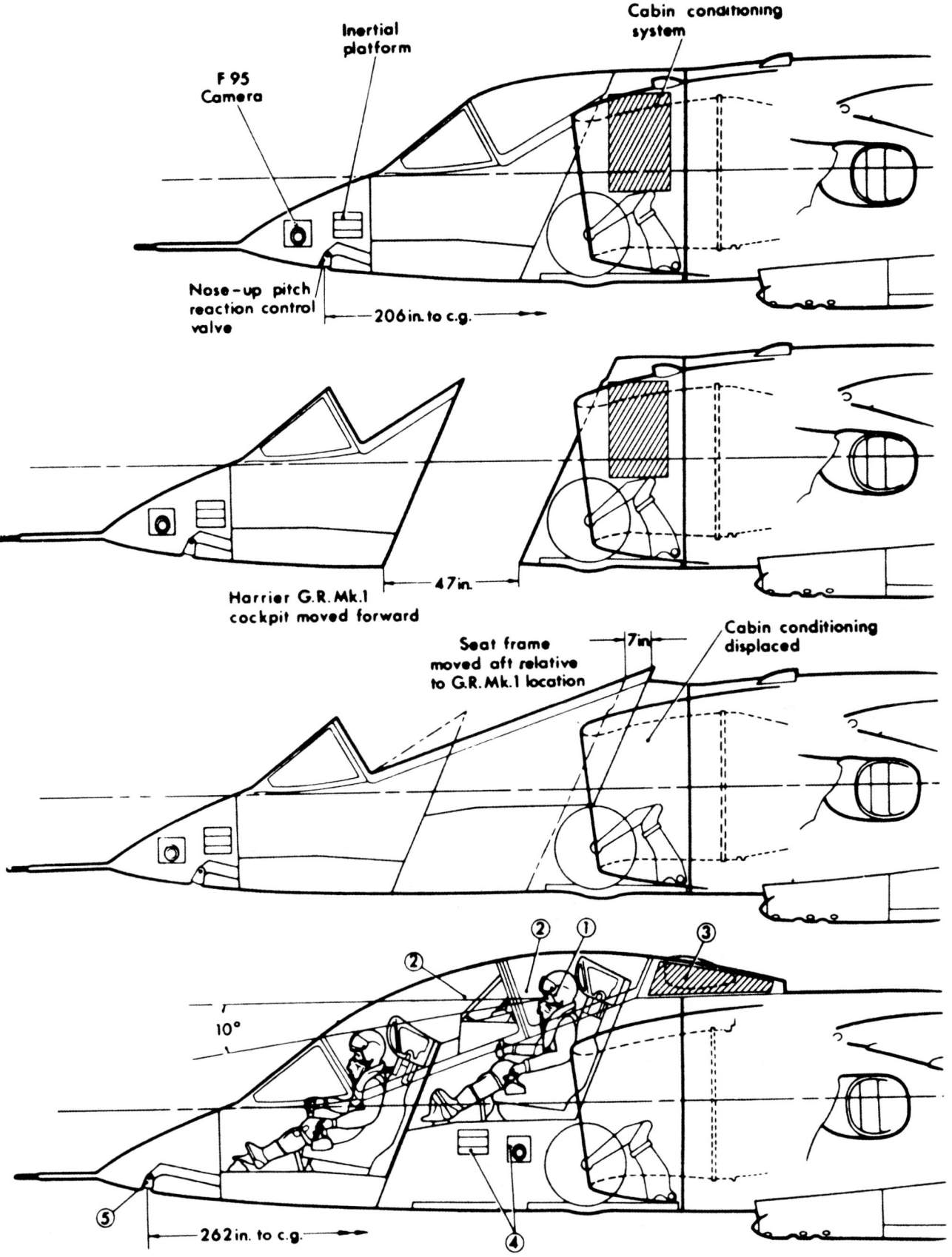

Cabin conditioning
system

Inertial
platform

F 95
Camera

Nose-up pitch
reaction control
valve

206 in. to c.g.

Harrier G.R.Mk.1
cockpit moved forward

47 in.

Seat frame
moved aft relative
to G.R.Mk.1 location

7 in.

Cabin conditioning
displaced

10°

262 in. to c.g.

Harrier T2 forward
fuselage modifications.
(courtesy BAE Systems)

A rare image of a Harrier carrying a WE.177 weapon. Although this trials aircraft is a GR3, the WE.177 was only carried operationally by the Sea Harrier and was not adopted for use by the RAF. (Photo: Tim McLelland collection)

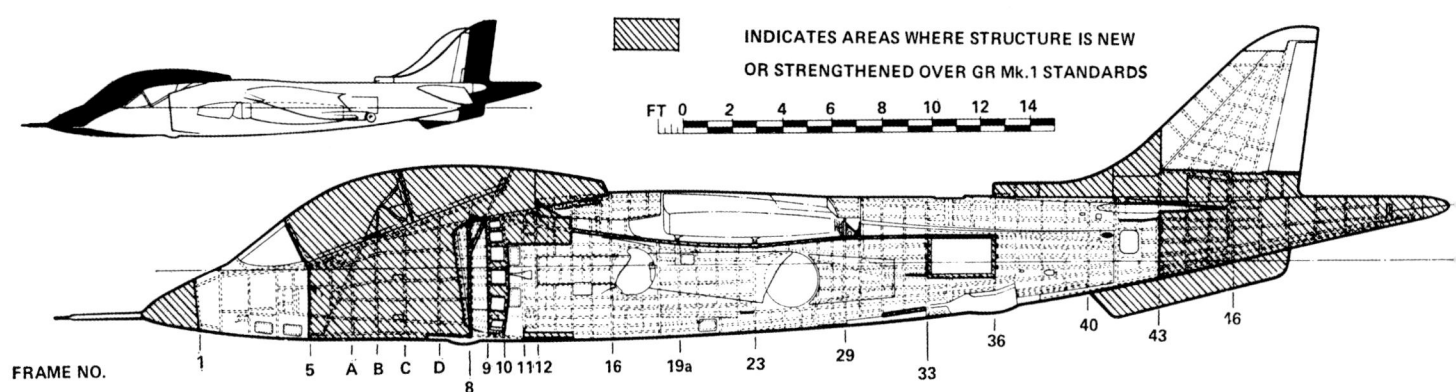

INDICATES AREAS WHERE STRUCTURE IS NEW
OR STRENGTHENED OVER GR Mk.1 STANDARDS

FT 0   2   4   6   8   10   12   14

FRAME NO.   1   5   A B C D   9 10 11 12   16   19a   23   29   33   36   40   43   16
                                    8

Below: Harrier T2 structural diagram (courtsey BAE Systems)

Pretty in pink: an exchange visit to France resulted in this No.1 Squadron aircraft receiving some particularly colourful decorations (applied overnight by French ground crews) which were swiftly removed when the aircraft was flown home to Wittering. (Photo: John Adams)

The twin-seat Harrier's early tail fin modification as applied to T2 aircraft. (courtesy BAE Systems)

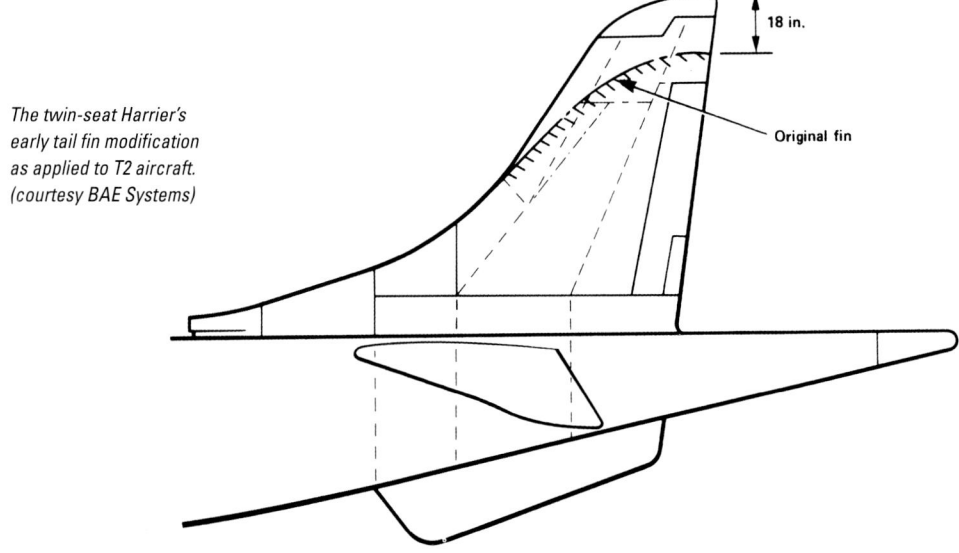

18 in.

Original fin

Harrier T2 XW175 pictured getting airborne from RAE Bedford's adjustable-angle 'ski jump' ramp during initial trials.
(Photo: RAE Bedford)

Harrier GR1/3 and Harrier T4/4 wing structure. (courtesy BAE Systems)

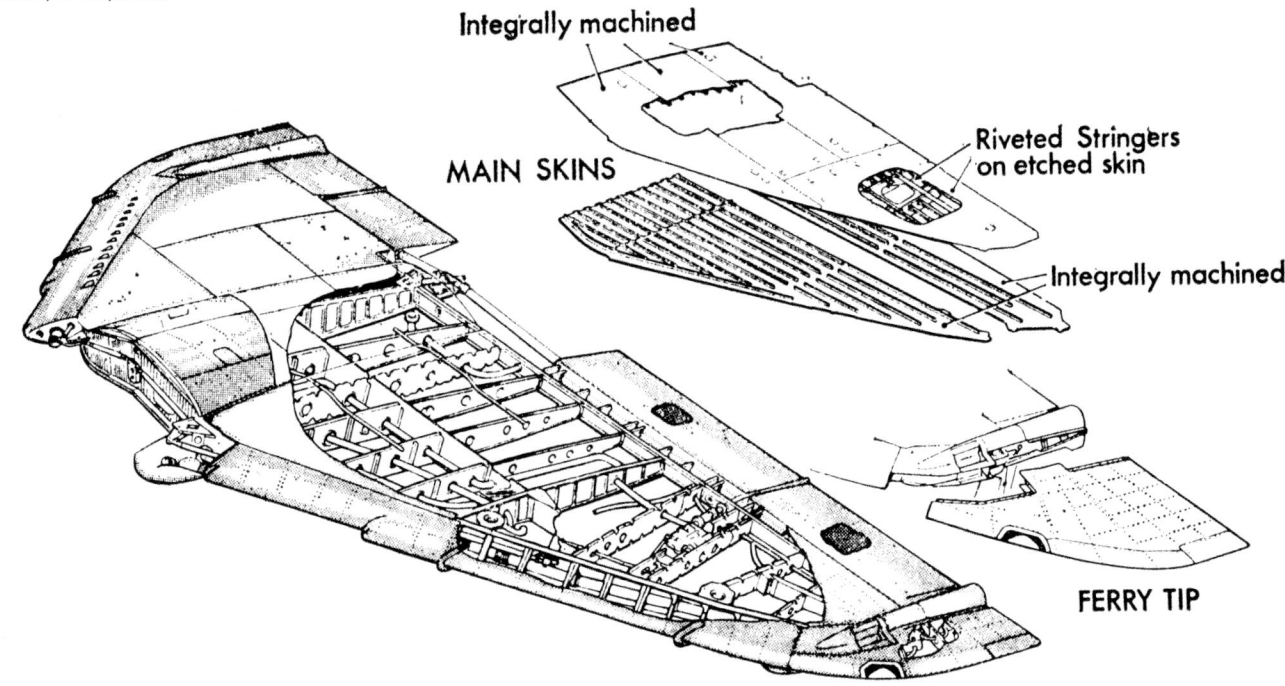

Integrally machined

MAIN SKINS

Riveted Stringers on etched skin

Integrally machined

FERRY TIP

The Harrier T.Mk.4, illustrating the proportions of the twin-seater's longer fuselage, combined with the addition of the LRMTS nose modification, introduced on the GR3. (Photo: Tim McLelland collection)

Harrier GR3 XZ989 which made a heavy landing at the San Carlos Forward Operating Base in the Falklands, following an unexpected loss of engine thrust in the hover. (via John Simons)

HMS Hermes, with RAF
Harriers ready to embark
on missions over the
Falklands, carrying
Paveway laser-guided
weapons and cluster
bombs. The Sea Harrier
is armed with a pair of
Sidewinders.
(Photo: BAE Systems)

The flight deck on HMS Hermes as seen during the Falklands Conflict, with a mix of RAF Harrier GR3s and FAA Sea Harriers visible. (Photo: BAE Systems)

The San Carlos Forward Operating Base in the Falklands with a pair of Harriers returning from a mission, utilising the temporarily-laid metal track matting. (courtesy No.4 Squadron Association)

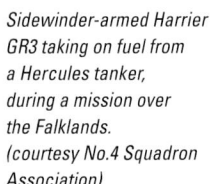

Sidewinder-armed Harrier GR3 taking on fuel from a Hercules tanker, during a mission over the Falklands. (courtesy No.4 Squadron Association)

CHAPTER FOUR

The Harrier Hands-On

PETE MEARS was one of the RAF's all-important ground crew, responsible for supporting Harrier operations in Germany. He recalls his time with the Harrier: 'I joined No. 4 Squadron as a twenty-year-old in 1971, the year after the squadron had reformed at RAF Wildenrath with its first four Harrier GR1s. By the time that I joined the squadron, its strength had increased to around twelve aircraft plus four aircraft which, although it carried 3 Squadron markings, were also being operated by our squadron. These aircraft were:

A	XV779
B	XV780
C	XV781
D	XV782
E	XV783
F	XV784
G	XV789
H	XV790
J	XV791
K	XV794
L	XV808
M	XW269 This was a T2 dual-control version
	XW763 in 3 Sqn markings
	XW764 in 3 Sqn markings
	XW917 in 3 Sqn markings
	XW918 in 3 Sqn markings

'Aircraft were eventually moved around between the squadrons (including the units based back in the UK at RAF Wittering), to replace losses, balance the Harrier fleet's flying hours and fatigue indexes, modifications, servicing requirements, and to introduce new airframes, and so on. In my trade as an Air Photo Operator or "photog", I was responsible – along with three other people at that time – for the day-to-day maintenance of the camera systems fitted to the aircraft. These were principally the port facing oblique (PFO) F95 70 mm reconnaissance camera fitted in the nose, the Telford 16 mm pilot's display recorder (PDR) mounted in front of the pilot's head and recording through the head-up display (HUD) screen and, when fitted, the five cameras (4 x F95 oblique and 1 x F135 vertical) inside the reconnaissance pod carried on the centre line station under the fuselage.

'I worked mainly on the Flight Line as a "Liney" along with other trades such as airframes "riggers", the armourers or "plumbers", engine specialists known as "sooties", electricians or "leckies", navigational instruments specialists or "insties" and communications/radio "comms" mechanics and technicians. Other trades were also present that did not work on the aircraft directly, but were nevertheless important to the operational efficiency of the squadron, like safety equipment specialists – the "squippers or rag packers", the administration people who we referred to as the "shinies", the stores and supply people known as the "blanket stackers" and so on, and when we deployed, trades such as catering, mechanical transport, medical, ground engineering, photographic processors/analysts and interpreters, RAF police, RAF regiment and our Army

Two Hunter T7s were assigned to the Harrier Conversion Unit, and utilised as chase aircraft and conversion trainers, pending delivery of dual-control Harriers. (Photo: Paul Tomlin)

colleagues such as Royal Engineers and signals all contributed to the overall effort. Line day-to-day tasks revolved around ensuring that the aircraft were towed out of the hangar, prepared for flight (by each trade carrying out a before-flight inspection) and if weapons were to be flown and dropped, the armourers would load the appropriate stores. Fuel for the sortie would be checked and adjusted. Engine and hydraulic fluid levels together with pneumatic pressures would be checked, replenished or adjusted, along with liquid oxygen (LOX) requirements. The recce pod and cameras would be loaded and function-tested, the ejection seat checked and the engine and airframe visually checked to ensure that there was no damage or defects.

'Once all the trades had carried out their respective work they would "sign up" in the aircraft maintenance and history log, the Form 700. All this activity was carried out under the watchful eye of the Line Corporal, an experienced and trusted trades person who would, when necessary, "kick backsides" to ensure the work was running to schedule. He, in turn, reported to the line sergeant or chief technician, who coordinated the process. Once all required aircraft were declared serviceable, squadron ops was informed, who then allocated aircrew to aircraft with a "crew walk" time given. The "crews walking" call was the signal for the "see-off" team to go out to their allocated jets, sometimes accompanying "their" pilot after he'd signed the F700, and sometimes heading out earlier to ensure all was ready for when he arrived at the

aircraft. The Harrier's start-up procedure sometimes consisted of a two-man crew, but usually it was carried out by one man – although when operating out of the closed confines of a camouflaged "hide" on deployment, at least two wingmen would be in place to ensure that the Harrier did not strike any obstructions on its way to the take-off position. A long-lead and head set, with throat microphone could be used to communicate with the pilot, but standard practice was to carry out the see-off without one, using recognised hand signals instead. The routine was as follows:

1. Remove all the aircraft blanks and locks (except the outrigger wheels locks), i.e., engine intake blanks, air direction detector (ADD) cover, rear bay coolant bung, main and nose wheel undercarriage locks.
2. Walk round aircraft with the pilot, and whilst doing so remove the five external stores ejector release unit (ERU) pins. If aircraft was armed have an armourer stand by.
3. Apply external power to aircraft from the Houchin generator set.
4. Assist pilot to strap-in to his ejection seat and as he leans forward, visually check and confirm that there are three red ties on the parachute flap.
5. Ask pilot for "four greens" (confirmation that the undercarriage is down and locked), and if positive remove the two outrigger locks.
6. When the armourer has connected the ADEN cannon firing leads and fastened the access doors, remove the red armament safety break

Harrier GR1 XV760 was one of the first Harriers to enter RAF service, joining the Harrier Conversion Unit at Wittering. The HCU's grasshopper motif is visible under the cockpit.
(Photo: Steve Bond)

The HCU's XV475 making one of the Harrier's first public appearances in Manchester's Heaton Park, August 1971. (Photo: Paul Tomlin)

Below: With the arrival of dual-control aircraft and more single-seaters, the HCU became No.233 Operational Conversion Unit. XV758 is pictured at Wittering proudly wearing the OCU's newly-applied markings. (Photo: Steve Bond)

(rear starboard side of aircraft behind the aft hot nozzle) and pass it up to pilot for stowage in cockpit (in case the aircraft diverts to another airfield or operating site).

7. On the pilot's instruction, trip the external power switch, remove the electrical power cable, fasten the panel and after checking the area, give the pilot the start engine signal. Stand by with the CO2 fire extinguishers and be vigilant to quickly respond to an engine or fuel spill fire.

8. Once the engine is running, confirm the operation of the Ram Air Turbine (RAT) extension and retraction. Show the pilot five fingers and visually check that he responds with five fingers to confirm that all of the ejection seat pins are removed and stowed correctly.

9. Check that the nose wheel doors closed fully on engine start and scan the aircraft for oil and fuel leaks or anything else out of the ordinary.

10. Remove the nose wheel chock and when clear, marshal the aircraft out.

'Once the Harriers had returned from their sortie and shut down, there would be frenzied activity to either refuel or rearm and prepare the aircraft for another sortie by virtue of a "turn-round" servicing; aircraft that were unserviceable or not required for further flying that day would be downloaded of any weapons and undergo an "after-

XV754 at Wittering pictured in No.1 Squadron's initial paint scheme (which laster little more than a few weeks) consisting of full colour national insignia combined with the unit's badge on the tail fin.
(Photo: Steve Bond)

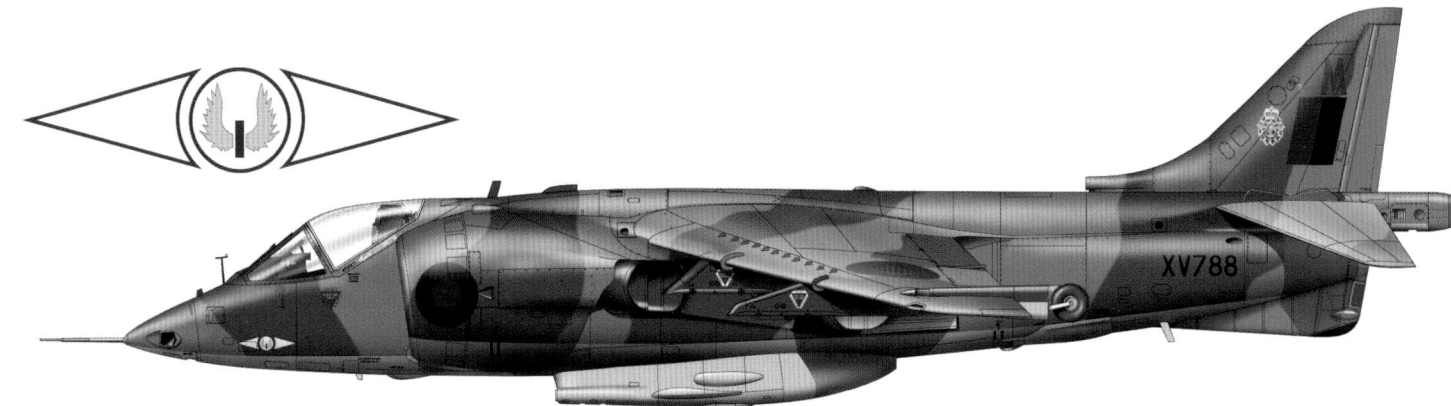

Harrier GR1 Mk.1, XV788/M, No. 1 Squadron RAF, Malta, August 1973
Dark Sea Grey/Dark Green/Light Aircraft Grey finish with Blue/Red national markings; serial in black, repeated below the wings.
Code 'M' in red on fin; unit badge, flanked by red/white arrowheads, on nose and Tri-Service badge on fin

Harrier GR3 Mk.3, XV781/O, No. 3 Squadron, 1978
Dark Sea Grey/Dark Green/Light Aircraft Grey finish with Blue/Red national markings; serial in black, repeated below the wings.
Code 'O' in yellow on fin; unit marking with yellow/green flash on nose

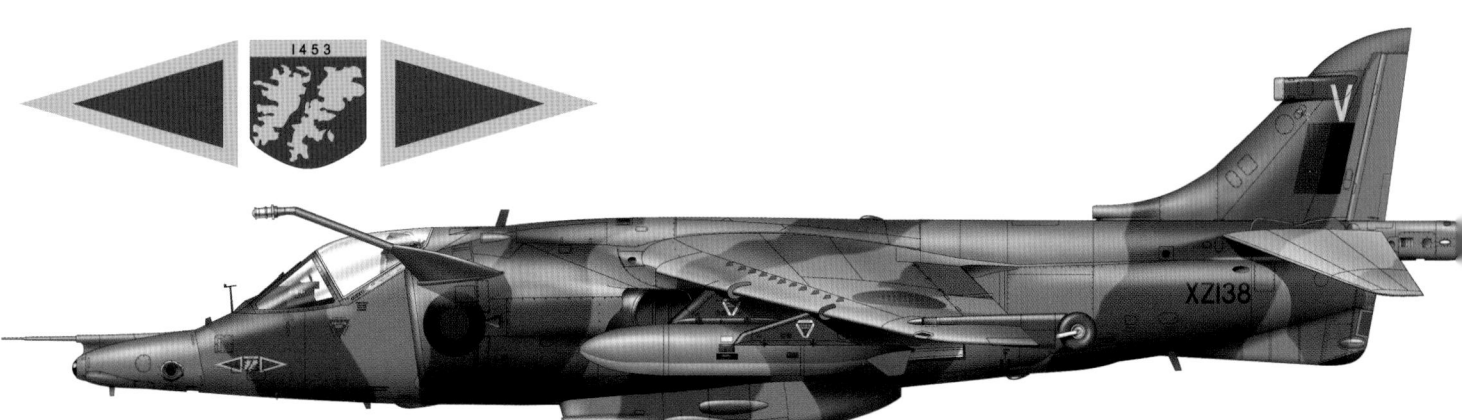

Harrier GR3 MK.3, XZ138/V, No. 1453 Flight RAF, Falkland Islands, late 1984
Dark Sea Grey/Dark Green wrap-around finish with Blue/Red national markings; serial in black, code in yellow. Blue/yellow unit badge
flanked by arrowheads; note air-to-air refuelling probe and Sidewinder missiles

No.1 Squadron's flight line at Wittering: evidently this Harrier GR1 has enjoyed the attention of a USAF crew, which appears to have applied its own additions to the more standard unit markings on the aircraft's nose.
(Photo: Steve Bond)

Pictured at Wittering shortly after the unit reformed on Harriers, one of No.20 Squadron's first GR.Mk.1s. (Photo: Steve Bond)

Harrier GR.Mk.1 from No. 3 Squadron, revealing what appears to be a much-used ADEN cannon, streaked with oil and soot. (Photo: Steve Bond)

Harrier GR1 wearing newly-applied 4 Squadron markings, pictured at Wittering in 1973. (Photo: Steve Bond)

flight" servicing. And so it would go on, throughout the day (or occasional night flying), until the final sorties had landed, when all of the remaining aircraft would be "after-flighted" and towed back into the hangar, ready to start the whole process again the following day. Of course, 4 Squadron ground operations did not just consist of the flight line. Another parallel shift of maintenance personnel worked in the hangar, whose role was to repair and maintain those aircraft that could not be dealt with at flight line-level. Often, to meet squadron operational requirements and to provide experience and improve competence, maintenance personnel would alternate between the line and the

XV752 at Wittering, pictured wearing temporary 'Arctic' camouflage for deployment to Norway. The white paint was applied over the aircraft's green camouflage. (Photo: Steve Bond)

Harrier GR1 from No.1 Squadron pictured during deployment to Norway in typical winter conditions. The temporary 'Arctic' camouflage appears to be working well in the harsh environment. (Photo via No.4 Squadron Association)

Harrier GR1 XV780 makes a short landing on one of Wildenrath's perimeter tracks shortly after delivery to No.4 Squadron. (Photo via No.4 Squadron Association)

XW921 pictured being marshalled onto a local road from a forward base at Ahden in 1973. (Photo: via Pete Mears)

hangar. Throughout the 1970s in RAF Germany, we were all acutely aware of the reason why we were there. The threat of a sudden attack on the West with massed Warsaw Pact armour, infantry and air power was taken extremely seriously and was, in fact, looked at as a matter of not "if", but "when"! Consequently everything we did was done with one eye on the fact that we might at any time be expected to do it for real. We had frequent station generation and survival exercises called "MinEvals" and RAF Germany command-level generations called "MaxEvals" which were all geared up to prepare us for the annual dreaded NATO-generated "TacEval". All these generations invariably began with the station alert "hooter" being sounded at some God-awful hour in the morning that resulted in the whole station turning in to "generate" the station's aircraft in their war-role fit. This was all carried out whilst wearing a nuclear, biological and chemical (NBC) suit, and when incoming air raids were detected, respirators and "tin hats" were donned and all personnel went to shelter. Once the raid had passed, essential personnel would leave the shelter to launch aircraft, deal with unexploded bombs or UXBs and so on, and continue working in a possible "contaminated"

chemical or biological environment in full NBC attire, sometimes for hours on end – not a comfortable experience when trying to carry out technical work on aircraft.

'Recognising the vulnerability of static airfields in the pre-hardened aircraft shelter days, the Harrier force's war role was to disperse and operate from non-airfield sites to aid survival. Operating forward in "field sites", Close Air Support (CAS) and Recce missions were flown mainly in support of 1(BR) Corps, conducting cockpit turn-rounds to increase sortie rates and reduce reaction times when responding to CAS/Recce requests. On 1 September 1972, Four Squadron adopted the dual role of attack and tactical reconnaissance. To support the recce role a Reconnaissance Intelligence Centre or "RIC" was attached to the squadron to facilitate recce exploitation. In June 1972 we deployed to Soest, a recently evacuated Canadian army camp that was ideal for our needs. The weather was superb and made a change from the gales, rain and freezing conditions we had to put up with during deployments in the winter months, and this time no biting insects were present during the hot German summer months when deployed! It was on this deployment that one of our Harriers had an unfortunate encounter with a Phantom FGR2 from 31 Squadron at RAF Bruggen, which could have resulted in the loss of both aircraft. On 8 June, Harrier XV784, coded "F", took off from the field strip at Soest on a routine sortie. Phantom XV431 had carried out a low-level interdiction exercise over northern Germany and on the return part of the journey, the pilot informed his navigator that he was in visual contact with a Harrier. The Phantom pilot turned to put the Harrier in his gunsight in order to make a simulated Sparrow missile launch. On completion of the simulated missile launch the Phantom broke right, applying full military power, and a heavy jolt was felt by the crew. The pilot realised he had hit the Harrier. Both pilots retained control of their aircraft and both diverted to Hopsten airfield, landing without further incident. I was given the Phantom's PDR cockpit camera and told that I must not let it out of my sight until the investigation team arrived. I kept it with me in my sleeping bag that night! The subsequent investigation revealed the Phantom pilot had exceeded his authorisation in engaging in air combat training, and it was probable the collision would not have occurred if he had completed his sortie as briefed. Thankfully everybody survived the incident unscathed. I eventually completed my tour on 4 Squadron in November 1973 after carrying out numerous squadron detachments to places like Sardinia, Denmark, Norway and Cyprus together with umpteen field deployments to places like Bad Lippspringe, Soest, Ahden, Geseke, Mandalay and others. However, looking back after almost forty years to my time on 4 Squadron which was the first operational Harrier squadron in the RAF Germany

Harrier Force, I still marvel at the aircraft's unique ability to operate out of rough sites and in conditions that no other aircraft could – and arguably still can't; but most of all I salute the camaraderie and professionalism of the air and ground crews alike, who made the squadron into the success that it undoubtedly was.'

Back in Britain, Steve Bond was part of Wittering's ground crew from 1973 to 1975, and he recalls his experiences of the Harrier's early years, shortly after the aircraft had settled into RAF service:

'The early Harrier was a pain for the engineers to work on. Engine life between overhauls was extremely short, with very limited time allowed for operations in the hover. Replacing the engine meant taking the wing completely off, so it took a very long time and some of the key connections were actually underneath the engine, so it was not easy – to say the least – to gain access to them. The main problem was that we were working on what was styled essentially a "product ionised" experimental aeroplane, which was never really designed to withstand the grind of daily operations – at least in our opinion. The term "maintainability" had certainly not been invented at that time! Although the aircraft were reasonably reliable except for the International Navigation System which seemed to fall-over with monotonous regularity, there were still some aspects that we "lineys" used to dislike. One was grass landing checks; the OCU students had to land away somewhere on an unpaved surface to get used to how they would operate in the field on a squadron. RAF Newton was used at one point for these landings, and on one memorable occasion a student carried out a perfect vertical landing there with his wheels still neatly tucked away! Even without such dramas, turn-round or after-flight checks following a grass landing required the removal, checking and cleaning of a number of air filters to make sure they were not choked with bits of mother nature.

'The back-end of the aircraft was perpetually filthy with all the soot from the hot nozzles, so we airmen also tended to look somewhat grubby on a semi-permanent basis. When on a land-away, the pilot's bag was hung up behind a panel in this same area, and returning from trips to RAF Germany meant the lineys had to remove the bags very carefully to avoid breaking any of the duty-free bottles stuffed inside! It was an unwritten law that at least one of the jockeys would donate a bottle to the airmen's tea-swindle as thanks, but there was one squadron leader who routinely failed to honour this until a couple of the lads "accidentally" dropped his bag when carrying it across the pan… *crash, tinkle, tinkle…*! Bottles also used to get hidden in other places, including inside the ground lock stowage and even under the ejection seat! There were incidents a-plenty too. One day an OCU instructor was due to take a T-bird on a solo trip, but sadly for him he failed to carry out his rear

cockpit switch checks correctly, with the result that as he started the engine and the hydraulic pressure came up, the undercarriage started to retract. The rear cockpit selector was in the "up" position and he had missed it. The outriggers were the first to whip up – the ground crew frantically gave the pilot the engine cut signal, but not before the rear main-wheel had started retracting. The aircraft finally settled very low down at the rear, and leaning to port at quite an alarming angle, fortunately with minimal damage, but the boss was not best pleased with his pilot.

'On another occasion, the OCU borrowed one of the rare, precious, and very expensive reconnaissance pods from neighbouring No.1 Squadron, which was known by the OCU people as "F Troop" after a popular TV series at the time about a US Army Cavalry outfit. Anyway, off went the student to do a recce sortie and when he came back, the pod – which was carried under the centre line – and both under-wing drop tanks were nowhere to be seen. He had inadvertently jettisoned them somewhere over Yorkshire, and the rumour doing the rounds was that a farmer was claiming salvage rights for the recce pod. One of the OCU instructors was "Dutch" Holland, well known in the Harrier world as a larger-than-life character who enjoyed his flying. One day he and his wingman found themselves in the vicinity of Upper Heyford, which was occupied by USAF F-111s at the time. Apparently the pair of them proceeded to beat-up the base to good effect. Not long afterwards, we were sitting in the crew room on the line, probably playing yet another game of uckers, when there was an almighty bang directly overhead, followed by the sound of jet aircraft rapidly disappearing into the distance. Playing cards, cups and everything else went flying, and we all rushed outside to see what the Hell had happened. Fading away in the distance was a pair of very low-flying F-111s, who had just taken revenge with a beat-up of our flight-line. Then there was the student who was not too sure of his left and right, so he really did have "left" and "right" written on the back of his flying gloves.

'The OCU pan had quite a marked downhill slope at one end; the end where we used to park the T-birds. One of these was towed out at the start of the day and let's just say the towing team were less than precise with their parking drills, because as the tractor drove away to go for the next aeroplane, the unmanned Harrier gently pushed the chock behind the nose wheel aside and started to roll backwards. Panic set in, and a few vain attempts to throw a chock behind a wheel ensued, before it was clear that the aircraft had to be left to its own fate. Across the pan it went, then across the taxiway, and onto the grass where the slope was much more marked, with a rather substantial building at the bottom of it. Luckily for all concerned, the weather had been awful, the ground was sodden, and the Harrier bogged down in the mud. Being still very

A typical situation for RAFG Harriers, with a GR1 manoeuvring onto a MEXE pad for take-off from a forward base. (Photo: via Pete Mears)

XW924 gets airborne from the grass at Ahden in 1974. (Photo: via Pete Mears)

early in the morning, a successful attempt was made to pull it out and clean off the mud and grass including on the taxiway. In theory, no-one was ever the wiser, although the wheel marks in the grass were a bit hard to explain! Access to the engine accessories was through the top panels over the centre fuselage, which meant clambering up the wing to reach them, which could be interesting on a wet or frosty day. Fine, except you had to be very careful when sliding back down again to make sure you didn't go off the leading edge, when the boundary-layer fences (or the wing tip puffer-ducts) could spoil your day! The 233 OCU hangar was built for Blue Steel missiles during the Victor era. The space available for up to about 16 Harriers was quite a challenge, and in this day and age would not be accepted, as there was absolutely no escape route to evacuate aircraft in the event of a fire. I also

remember a trip we did to Gaydon – the last flying display before the airfield was taken over by cars. We positioned two Harriers there, one flying plus a spare, and I was the only ground support. The big challenge was to find somewhere to park them, as the airfield had been out of use for donkey's years, and the available V-force dispersals were very tatty and largely overgrown. I recruited some ATC cadets to carry out a FOD plod for me, which sort of worked OK, as Harriers are very effective Hoovers of anything on the ground. We shared the dispersal with the Swords Jet Provost aerobatic team from Linton-on-Ouse. OK, except that there was only one fuel bowser, brought in especially from the nearest active RAF station, Little Rissington, which did not have enough on board to refuel four JPs and two Harriers. *Haha!* I got in first… never did hear how the JPs coped.'

As mentioned previously, although operations from the Harrier's first base at Wittering were consolidated and expanded, over in Germany RAF Wildenrath was not an ideal location for RAFG's Harrier operations. For most training exercises it took supporting convoys (which could total some 400 vehicles) around six hours to reach the forward sites and without the availability of helicopter support (the RAFG helicopters were assigned to NATO's COMTWOATAF), this was a logistical nightmare. Worse still, it degraded the Harrier force's wartime capability. Intelligence suggested that if a conflict looked likely, NATO's forces would move from a Reinforced to General Alert posture, giving RAFG time to begin the redistribution of assets. However, second-guessing Soviet intentions was never a precise science, and even though Intelligence experts insisted that a 'counter surprise' attack would never happen, it was a possibility which worried commanders. Consequently, the withdrawal of the RAFG Lightning force in 1976 provided an opportunity for the Harriers to move to the former Second World War *Luftwaffe* base at Gütersloh, near No.1(BR) Corps' headquarters at Bielefeld. From here the Harriers were far closer to their projected operational areas and much better placed to counter a Warsaw Pact armoured advance from the inner German border, north of the Harz Mountains. The reorganised force comprised two squadrons for two reasons: firstly, No.20 Squadron re-equipped with Jaguars, but Gütersloh accommodation was only geared towards the support of two units, and so Nos. 3 and 4 Squadrons were expanded so that each unit had a complement of 18 aircraft. Gütersloh was far smaller than Wildenrath but various areas of the airfield were gradually redesigned to accommodate Harrier training. In addition to the main runway and taxiways, two MEXE pads were laid down and a representative road strip was constructed, together with other less-permanent landing areas. However a great deal of training was conducted off base, not least during the main two-week deployments which were made three times every year. These were usually set up at field sites within the British Army's Sennelager training area to the east of Gutersloh, and generally comprised a grass area cleared for VSTOL flying, and an area covered by temporary metal planking which was deemed necessary in case weather conditions were poor (usually a MEXE pad with a metal access strip). Areas of adjacent woodland were normally used to house the aircraft for servicing, arming and refuelling. Some deployments were less routine and were made to more urban sites. Using public roads for Harrier operations required authorisation from the German highways department, and in practice these sites were generally sections of road that were scheduled for maintenance, so that the temporary closure could be combined with routine works. Once set up, the urban sites were undoubtedly easier to operate from (being little different from normal runways – just rather smaller), but Harrier operations from field sites were also undertaken without any major practical difficulties, with plenty of support being available from the force's own personnel, and also from the Royal Engineers who became adept at rescuing Harriers from inhospitable areas of soggy German fields.

As the RAFG Harriers settled into service, semi-permanent training sites on sections of road within the Sennelager area were established, perhaps the most well known being a tank road at Eberhardt which was first surveyed in 1974 and after becoming operational in 1975 it remained in use for another 20 years. Further areas followed and were used for routine training although occasional intensive exercises were conducted during which live weapons were brought in to enable ground crews to train with full weapons loads. Probably the least popular of the field exercises was the annual winter deployment which provided the force with experience of operations in sub-zero conditions. Of course, many other sites would be required for a 'real' wartime situation, and it was the responsibility of the Harrier Plans Office (part of Operations Wing) to oversee the reconnaissance and selection of these sites which were kept strictly secret and known only to Site Commanders and a few other key personnel within the supporting RAF and Army units. These sites were selected meticulously and discreetly, the Site Commander with a few Signals and Sappers personnel arriving in civilian clothing, armed only with maps and reconnaissance photographs. After parking some distance from the proposed site, a closer inspection was made to establish whether the site would meet the standard criteria for a straight, unobstructed stretch of road no shorter than 500 metres, and at least 10 metres wide. It also required access to operational areas, the FWOC and other temporary support structures (and a good link to the Bruin secure telephone network). Generally, this meant an industrial estate, a large supermarket or service station area which could provide not only the landing area, but also suitable locations for the support infrastructure. It is not known whether the German locals ever realised what the small groups of casually dressed people were up to, as they paced out seemingly uninteresting stretches of road and carefully scrutinised the most mundane of buildings which normally never attracted even the slightest attention. RAFG's Harrier operations changed very little in their nature from their inception, right through to the very end, by which stage a completely different version of the Harrier was in use, and the Warsaw Pact's threat had dwindled significantly.

Of course, during many years of operational service the RAF's Harrier operations ventured beyond the East-West German borders and the Norwegian arctic wastes. It was during 1975 that the first political situation arose which called for the Harrier force to deploy far from its usual areas of operation. Guatemala was embroiled in a bitter and bloody civil war which began to show every sign of developing into a wider conflict which could involve neighbouring Belize, a British dependency. A resident British Army garrison was already in place to defend Belize but it was agreed that a more substantial show of force was required to prevent the war spreading. No.1 Squadron (placed on seven days' notice after having just returned from an Armament Practice Camp at Decimomannu in Sardinia) was tasked with deploying six Harrier GR1s to Ladyville Airport during October 1975 for a temporary detachment which would enable the RAF to indulge in some 'high visibility' flying around the area, in order to demonstrate to Guatemala that Britain was prepared to defend Belize if necessary. Initially, the Harriers were to have been fitted with 'ferry' wing tips but in order to avoid the time-consuming complexity of removing them upon arrival, the idea was dropped and the Harriers were on Combat Air Patrol (CAP) only twenty minutes after their arrival. The 'flag-waving' exercise was judged to be a success and following Guatemala's renunciation of its territorial claim to Belize, the Harriers returned to Wittering in April of the following year. However, with no end to the situation in sight and a renewed threat of invasion, a second detachment was planned and in June 1977 the RAF established HarDet Belize, with six aircraft (this time Harrier GR3s) which were assigned to six purpose-built hides situated around the Airport. Operated on a rolling detachment basis with crews rotating from the UK and Germany, the HarDet became No.1417 (Tactical Ground-Attack) Flight on 18 April 1980. The distinctly temporary hides were progressively improved to a more permanent standard and support facilities were gradually developed until the Flight was able to operate freely in relatively comfortable (considering the remote location) and practical conditions. The detachment was immensely popular with Harrier crews, the ground personnel enjoying the rudimentary (but distinctly tropical) conditions, far away from the formal life back at Wittering, while the pilots were able to enjoy an almost unrestricted programme of flying, combining training and proficiency requirements (and routine Combat Air Patrols) with the more general aims of 'flag-waving' (or 'sabre-rattling'). In many respects the freedom to fly in Belize was a Harrier pilot's 'dream ticket'. The Flight's presence at Belize continued without any major incidents (and no real risk of any confrontation with Guatemala), and it was only more 'routine' losses (including a very serious bird strike) which marred what was otherwise a trouble-free episode in the Harrier force's history. No.1417's stay at Belize ended on 6 July 1993 and the resident Harriers returned to Wittering.

The Belize experience also had a direct effect upon the Harrier's future with the RAF as by 1975 serious consideration was being given to the question of what aircraft would eventually replace the Harrier in RAF service. The initial step in this process had taken place just as the Harrier GR1 was entering service. In keeping with standard procurement timescales, a long-term requirement for a Harrier and Jaguar replacement was issued in 1969 as AST396. Air Staff thinking at this time was still influenced by the turbulent 1960s during which time so much of the RAF's future procurement policy had been severely affected by political thinking, inter-service manoeuvring and cost-cutting. The Air Staff undoubtedly regarded the Harrier as little more than a 'stop gap' design on the way towards something more ambitious (and to some extent the Labour Government had encouraged this notion), and it was sanctioned by the Government almost as a 'pay-off' for the loss of P.1154 and TSR2 (and F-111, AFVG, etc).

The Jaguar was regarded with equal cynicism and, without any operational experience on which to make a more sound judgement, an aircraft capable of replacing both types was thought to be vital. The Air Staff responsible for creating AST.396 had no experience of the Harrier's abilities and concluded that STOVL was a concept which did not need to be incorporated into the new aircraft, not least because it would preclude an 'off the shelf' purchase of the new F-16 or F-18, or indeed a successful European collaborative project. Dwelling largely on knowledge of the Kestrel's evaluation and early experience with the fledgling Harrier force, the prospect of sacrificing performance for STOVL simply did not make sense, especially when the Air Staff were now fostering a much greater interest in air combat performance. Likewise, the difficulties (and cost) of logistical support for off-base operations also served to colour opinion and in many respects the Air Staff had concluded (rather foolishly and prematurely) that STOVL was an imaginative but ultimately impractical concept. It was therefore assumed that the Harrier would be replaced from 1985 and that funding for the aircraft would be confined to only minimal operational upgrades and flight safety modifications. It was the 1975 deployment to Belize which prompted the Air Staff to reconsider. Clearly, the Harrier was the only combat aircraft capable of operating from the small runway at Ladyville Airport and realistically it was the only aircraft appropriate for the ground support (and limited air defence) role in that unusual and relatively unsophisticated environment. The benefits of operational flexibility were brought home with some clarity and this factor (together with the gradual appearance of Staff Officers with direct Harrier experience) was sufficient to shift the pervasive anti-Harrier atmosphere. The quest for a short-term Harrier replacement was dropped and an order for 24 new-build Harrier GR3s was placed.

This change in the Harrier's fortunes proved to be invaluable not only for the aircraft itself, but for the RAF and the United Kingdom. During March 1982 No.1 Squadron was busy operating in Norway as part of its ongoing commitment to NATO's Northern Region. As the crews and aircraft returned to Wittering, a warning order was issued on 8 April which suggested that the squadron would soon be deploying again, but this time 8,000 miles south. By April the Falklands crisis was unfolding and it looked increasingly likely that the RAF's Harriers would be involved, but nobody at Wittering was entirely sure how. Air-to-ground operations of some sort seemed inevitable but it was by no means impossible that air-to-air engagements might also be necessary. There was also no indication of whether the Harriers would be deployed to a land base on the Falkland Islands or whether they would operate from the Navy's carriers. To the RAF pilots it seemed most likely that the Harriers would be used as attrition replacements for the Navy's aircraft which were expected to be lost at a rate of perhaps one aircraft per day. All that was known was that the Harriers would be employed within the British-imposed Total Exclusion Zone around the islands. Regardless of the chosen role for the aircraft, it was clear that the Harriers would deploy south on a Navy carrier, and this would require the aircraft to be suitably modified for operations at sea. The Harrier had already operated from *Ark Royal* during trials in 1971 and therefore the basic concept of carrier operations was not an issue. However in order to equip the aircraft for the journey south, each Harrier was protected against salt water (panels sealed), and shackles were fitted so that the aircraft could be shackled to the carrier deck. Installation of an I-Band transponder was also necessary so that the aircraft could recover safely to the carrier in poor weather conditions. All of these modifications were subsequently proved to have been vital.

A more fundamental modification was the introduction of an air-to-air missile capability, something which had first been planned for the Belize deployments but subsequently overlooked. Given the likely air threat around the Falklands and the absence of any other British 'fighter' asset (other than the Navy's Sea Harriers), compatibility with the AIM-9l Sidewinder was tested and cleared in a space of just three weeks. The Harriers were also fitted with chaff and flare dispensers, and modified to launch laser-guided bombs and American-supplied anti-radiation missiles. Meanwhile, the crews concentrated on training, flying ACM missions with French Mirage and Super Etendard units, performing missile launches, new weapon delivery profiles, and learning to take off from the Navy's 'ski jump' ramp.

It was decided subsequently, following a survey carried out at Liverpool Docks, that with the carriers already full to capacity, the RAF's Harriers would be shipped south on a container ship and the *Atlantic Conveyor* was selected to undertake this task. Eventually a mixed fleet of eight Sea Harriers, six Harrier GR3s, plus six Wessex and four Chinook helicopters was loaded on board either directly from the UK or the at the 'halfway' staging post at Ascension Island. Landing onto the *Atlantic Conveyor* was far from easy, especially in the rough sea conditions off Ascension Island, but with all of the aircraft secured on deck (and sealed against the elements), the vessel set course for the Falklands. These vital air assets undoubtedly captured Argentina's attention and as a high-value target, *Atlantic Conveyor* was protected by its own air power courtesy of a Sea Harrier maintained on alert, ready to launch from the vessel if any sign of enemy attention was detected – a classic example of the Harrier's versatility. During the ten-day journey the Harrier crews prepared their planning for the

XV809 at Wildenrath pictured with 330-gallon ferry tanks in preparation for deployment to Armament Practice Camp at Cyprus during December 1972. (Photo: Pete Mears)

anticipated operations while the on-board engineers worked hard to modify the Harrier GR3's inertial platform so that it could align itself from a moving deck–in order that the INAS system could be used operationally, rather than relying only on traditional map, stopwatch and fixed weapon sighting techniques. Just a month after the initial order to deploy had been given, the RAF Harriers were in action over the South Atlantic. The first mission (performed after a day of acclimatisation flying) was an attack on a fuel dump at Fox Bay, and a further 125 sorties were to follow between 20 May and 13 June, during which four Harriers were lost. Operations were conducted directly from the carriers or from forward sites on the Falklands – most notably at Goose Green where a fairly standard Harrier forward site was set up. Although most of the RAF Harrier contribution to 'Operation Corporate' was judged to be invaluable, not every aspect was regarded as successful. For example, the aircraft were employed on missions to disable Port Stanley's runway, which firstly had been perfectly bisected by an historic long-range mission flown by a Vulcan crew. Keeping the runway disabled required further effort and the Harriers were tasked with delivering retarded 1,000 lb HE bombs from low level, but thanks to an error in bomb-fusing, the bombs skipped before exploding, reducing their effect. Further attacks on various targets involved loft delivery profiles made in conjunction with Navy Sea Harriers relying on their inertial attack computers, but the results were less than certain. Without laser-marking (normally provided by FACs), bombs were also delivered using the Harrier GR3's own LRMTS system, but it was then discovered that the free-fall laser-guided bombs were incompatible with the LRMTS. These 'snags' were annoying and wasteful, but none were directly attributable to the Harrier itself. In fact the Harrier was of course vital to Britain's recapture of the Islands. No other combat aircraft could have been deployed to the South Atlantic and, without

the Harrier, it seems certain that the whole operation would have been a non-starter. Laser Target Markers were later introduced with the land forces and on 12 June they were employed during pinpoint loft deliveries which proved to be highly successful. The use of this system was the first example of Precision Guided Munitions (PGMs) being used operationally by the RAF and paved the way for what became a fundamental part of RAF operations in subsequent years. The Harrier's versatility was to have been stretched still further, when American-supplied Shrike anti-radar missiles were delivered (dropped into the sea from a Hercules, alongside HMS *Hermes*) for possible use. The Harrier ground crews worked hard to achieve aircraft and missile compatibility (using instructions which had been dropped-in with the missiles) but

by the time the first operational Shrike round was declared ready for use, the Argentine forces had surrendered the day before. Throughout the conflict, the main threat to RAF Harriers had been the Argentine ground-to-air weapons, both in the form of small arms fire and SAM systems. In addition to Roland and Tigercat, Russian SA-7 and Blowpipe systems were used, but the employment of low-level evasive flying (part of a Harrier pilot's routine training) ensured that most of these ground threats were ineffective. However the first RAF Harrier to be shot down was probably hit by Blowpipe. Anti Aircraft Artillery (AAA) was present in the form of 20 mm to 35 mm guns, some of which were linked to Fire Control Radars. One aircraft succumbed to AAA during a raid on Goose Green and although the main concentrations of fire

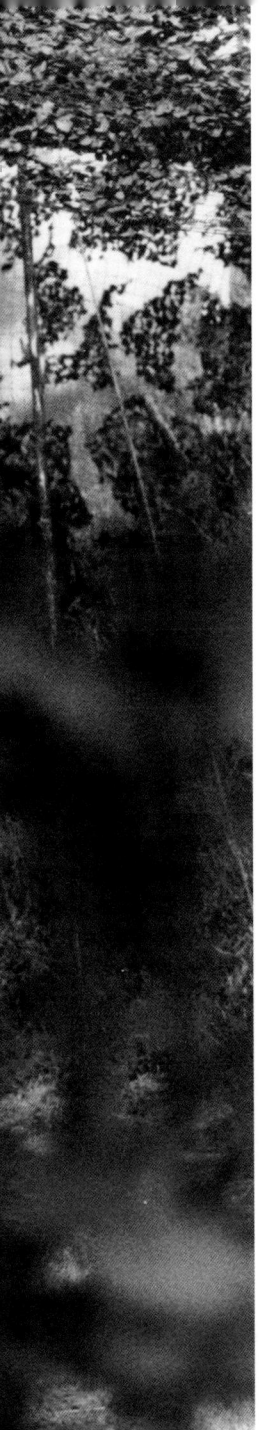

were in known locations, it remained a significant threat at all times. Likewise, small arms fire caused continual problems and when the attack missions took the Harriers towards Stanley, for every four aircraft launched at least one would inevitably return with holes. But apart from one aircraft which failed to survive long enough to return to the carrier, all other aircraft continued to operate and no aircraft spent more than 48 hours undergoing repairs.

By 8 June losses had totalled four (the fourth being a crash-landing at the forward base established at San Carlos), and replacement aircraft were delivered, this time directly by air from Ascension Island, supported by Victor tankers. This was no mean feat, and an unenviable task for the Harrier pilots who had to endure nearly nine hours of flying before making their first ever deck landing. After the Argentine surrender, the RAF Harrier force was established at Stanley Airport and the aircraft were assigned to the air defence role, armed with Sidewinder missiles. They remained on duty there until May 1985 (accompanied by RAF Phantoms in a limited capacity – Stanley's runway being far too short for routine Phantom operations), at which stage a new purpose-built airfield was completed at Mount Pleasant, enabling the RAF to provide air defence for the islands on a more permanent and conventional basis. The Harriers returned to the UK. As with the earlier detachments to Belize, 'Operation Corporate' had demonstrated that, under the right circumstances, the Harrier was not only a versatile combat aircraft, but it was also a vital asset without which the whole

operation would have been impossible. Those amongst the Air Staff who had initially poured scorn on the RAF's 'interim' STOVL jet must have been relieved that their views had not been accepted too literally.

Peter Collins, currently a civilian test pilot, was one of RAF Germany's elite Harrier GR3 pilots who enjoyed a long and enjoyable association with the aircraft. He recalls some of his time at Gütersloh and remembers one Harrier flight which he would rather forget:

'It was the summer of 1980, in those days, seemingly long ago, when we did actually have a summer in Northern Europe. I was based at RAF Gütersloh, in the Bielefeld area of West Germany (FRG as it then was) and close to the East German border. The Cold War was still at its height and we were part of RAF Germany (RAFG) and the 2nd Allied Tactical Air Force (2 ATAF). It was my first tour on the outstanding No.3 (Fighter) Squadron and I was flying the simply incredible and versatile Harrier GR3. No.3 (F) Squadron was declared to NATO as one hundred per cent ground-attack in role but with a secondary role of reconnaissance, if tasked. Our sister squadron of the Harrier Wing at Gütersloh, No.4 (Army Co-operation) Squadron, was declared to NATO as fifty per cent ground-attack and fifty per cent reconnaissance in role. The Reconnaissance Interpretation Centre (RIC) was therefore attached to No.4 (AC) in a supporting function and No.4 (AC) held most of the stock of Harrier recce pods (of which more in detail later). Each squadron had a certain number of "specialist" pilots who had undergone other post-graduation pilot qualification courses including Qualified Flying Instructor (QFI), Qualified Weapons Instructor (QWI), Electronic Warfare Officers (EWO) and Fighter Reconnaissance Instructor (FRI). The FRI qualification was a throwback to the days of the dedicated photo-recce (PR) Hunter squadrons (which had an array of fixed cameras in a "recce" nose) but this formal qualification had lapsed in the eyes of the official RAF with regard to the Harrier. In the bizarre world of RAF bureaucracy, I was unable to later quote my FRI qualification on my annual Assessment Report having gained the FRI qualification on a fully planned post-grad Operational Conversion Unit (OCU) course, whereas the QWI qualification, in comparison, conferred upon the owner an almost divine-like status in the eyes of the RAF...no friction there then! As to CFS and QFIs, perhaps the less said by me the better...

'However, the RAFG Harrier Squadrons recognised that the FRI specialisation was worth keeping, so, after foolishly volunteering, I was selected from No.3 (F), along with Tom Hammond from No.4 (AC), to return to the Harrier OCU at RAF Wittering, near Stamford, in mid-summer 1980 to attend the 10 week (No.7) FRI course and to gain the FRI rating as a squadron specialist. The Harrier GR3 was in many ways, at least in my

Above and below: Although the Harrier T2 and T4 fleet eventually standardised on the smaller (broader chord) tail, Harriers continued to fly for some considerable time with the early 'tall fin' configuration as illustrated by trainers from the OCU and No.1 Squadron on the flight line at Wittering, displaying both types of tail unit. Worthy of note are the Hunters of Nos.45 and 58 Squadron in the background. (Photos: Steve Bond)

opinion, a Short Take Off, Vertical Landing (STOVL) Hunter. Yes, it had a moving map linked to an Inertial Navigation and Attack System (INAS) platform (reputedly a piece of equipment carried over from the TSR2 programme), but the moving map often a had drift rate of 2-3nm per flight hour (even on a good day and much, much worse on a bad one...) so you always continued to map read in flight at low level using the 1:500,000 low level charts for route navigation and then switched to 1:50,000 maps for attack/recce IP-Target navigation. Most used the moving map as an "I'm somewhere around here" navigation aid/orientation "comfort blanket." The INAS also drove the Head-Up Display (HUD) symbology, but this was a very early generation, narrow field of view HUD even though it was the first in the RAF to be used entirely by the pilot as the primary instrument throughout the sortie for all flight, navigation and attack (ground weapons and air-to-air guns) events. All head-down flight instruments were treated as secondary instruments. Unbelievably (to me) today, 32 years after my initial Harrier GR3/T4 OCU course in 1978, the Hawk T1s at RAF Valley presently used for all RAF Fast Jet advanced flying and tactical weapons unit training (formerly the Hunter was used when I went through), still do not have a HUD. That's progress for you – RAF style!

'In 1980 the GR3 attack weapons consisted of primarily the BL755 cluster bomb and the 1,000 lb retarded bomb, delivered level over the top of the target at around 200 ft agl, and the SNEB 68 mm rocket pod (unguided with 18 or 19 rocket tubes per pod) plus the 30 mm cannon (two in individual belly pods) delivered from a 'pop up' to around 1,500 ft agl with a 10 degree dive to aim and fire. All peacetime squadron attack-type flying was conducted by day in Visual Met Conditions and the limits could become very "elastic" on TACEVAL exercise if the CO or the Station Commander needed that NATO tick. It was always at low level – to give us some feeling of protection against Soviet type SAMs and AAA threats – at 250 ft above ground level when within the designated Germany Low Fly Areas (LFAs) and 500 ft agl (or almost, as it seemed stratospheric when you were up there) outside the Low Flying Areas. All routine low-level flying was conducted at 420 kts cruise with an acceleration to 450 or 480kt for attack or recce runs simulating enemy defences. Mainly, when within ground Military Training Areas, you could drop it down to 100 ft agl and stoke it up to 510kts, but that is where the GR3, with combat wing tanks on, maxed out. Tanks off, the GR3 would do 540kt, but the shake and rattle through the cockpit then became seriously worrying! Clean wing, the GR3 fuel capacity was 5,000 lb and with 2 x combat tanks (inner wing wet pylon only) it was 6,400 lb. At 420kts, low-level cruise fuel flow was around 110-120 lb per min. If fuel was a little tight, setting a fuel flow of 100 lb per min gave a 400kt cruise. As a comparison, in the hover, fuel flow was around 200 lb/min.

'The recce pod was like the aircraft: simple, strong and sturdy with a fan of five cameras that covered from (just below) horizon to horizon with the wings level. The pod was mounted on the central pylon between the two gun pods and its position meant it was very close to the ground as the Harrier squatted on its undercarriage. The cameras used "wet film". The two outer fan cameras were F95 type with a 6-ins focal length lens (more telescopic as they looked at a longer range). The two inner fan cameras were F95 type with 3-ins focal length lens (more a wide angle as they looked at closer range). Directly vertical was a F135 type camera which had a control in the cockpit where the pilot could set the speed and height of the aircraft to adjust the F135 but most pilots left it at 200 ft/450kt. Controls for the cameras were on the right-hand side of the cockpit, essentially just to turn them on and, when running, the green 'on' lights would flash. However, all 'aiming' of the cameras was done manually; there was no cockpit 'screen' you could view and there was no indication of the 'film remaining' in any camera. Normally, a pilot would try and capture a target image using one of the outer F95 cameras as this gave the greatest clarity. I always drew two chinagraph pencil lines horizontally along the inner canopy – left and right sides – to give me an aiming reference for where I thought the F95 outer cameras, port and starboard, would 'capture' even if I was wing down and close into the target. The F95 was a very clever camera that utilised a moving film and a moving shutter to compensate for aircraft movement past the stationary ground target. The image was normally good for 100 ft/480kt but the image could blur beyond this if the target was close into the aircraft. The images were also overlapping so could be viewed and analysed stereoscopically after being developed and laid on the light tables in one of the RIC cabins.

'For the sortie in question, I had launched from RAF Wittering for a 3 x recce target, singleton aircraft sortie. This was in the initial phase of the FRI course with the intention of getting our (the student's) recce skills back up to scratch prior to the instructional 'give back' phase and the final 'operational' phase. The first target was a 'line search' of a minor road running along high ground on the western side of the Pennines in the area north-east of Manchester. The target type I was looking for was "possible" POL (petrol/oil/ lubricants). The line search was planned to be flown at 250ft agl and 450 kt. The planned "line" for this target was something like 15nm in length (not counting the IP-start line search point) so it would take something like 2 min to complete. Line searches of roads were, for most, the trickiest recce targets to fly since the aircraft had to be positioned "off the line" to give the best lateral view of the road (you didn't fly directly over the line to deliberately follow it because of likely defences and visual blanking under the nose); roads at low level are notoriously difficult to see with any aircraft lateral offset because they have no vertical extent; roads twist and fall behind terrain or tree lines so that a combination of these facts can throw you off the line without you realising it (450kt equates to 250 m/sec); terrain and man-made obstacles have to be avoided whilst still navigating at 7.5 nm/min. You end up part flying by eyeball, part flying by precise navigation whist holding a 1:50,000 scale map that gives you orientation, timing marks, planned turn checkpoints and planned 'line' headings to use from the HUD as guidance and all the time scanning the ground along and around the line. All in all, it was always a very high workload event and combined with very hard manoeuvring to stay 'on the line' in order to capture any potential target with one or more of the cameras.

'Completing the line search, I set course towards target no. 2 at 250 ft agl and throttled back to 420kt. As the jet stabilised in the cruise I went back over the 1:50,000 target map I had just used to study where I had been and what I had seen. I had noticed a lone petrol station during the line search and I had mentally noted the time from the stopwatch which timed the run from the IP (a wind-up stopwatch on the starboard cockpit combing that ran as minutes and seconds) as I went past it. With that time as reference plus the terrain features I had noted I was able to plot reasonably accurately where the petrol station position was and how my aircraft and its cameras were orientated when I filmed it. Additionally, I needed to note anything else I had seen, like stored POL barrels, pipelines, tanker trucks, defences, RWR returns from radar, communication masts, etc which would add to the "intelligence" value of the picture. Whilst doing the above post-target actions, and what I have described was being done very rapidly, a small bell went off in my head which said "...mate, you've been head-in too long, look up." When I looked up I saw an image that lives with me to this day. Everything within the canopy was green/brown and that green/brown extended significantly above the canopy arch and completely around my right-hand side. To my left-hand side there was some daylight, but not much. Whilst studying the map I had unknowingly descended into a "bowl" in the hills as I cruised along towards my second target. To this day I do not know which hand was on the control column; as I write right-handed, so I could have been flying with my left hand having set a fixed power to keep 420kt whilst scribbling with my right hand. Whichever hand was on the "stick" pulled it back instantly and violently to hit the back stop. The jet immediately reacted by starting to drop into deep wing rock which for a swept wing jet is a sign to the pilot that he is demanding too much angle of attack (AOA) and therefore not getting the optimum lift from the wing. Just as violently, I smashed the stick forward (I heard the metallic "clang") and brought it back to settle the wing at the "light burble" which is the indication to the pilot of optimum lift. All this occurred in an instant but for the next few seconds, time literally stood still as my life really did flash before my eyes. Like an old 16 mm film, I then watched a series of images that "clicked" to show the aircraft's nose starting to rise as the ridge I was flying towards hurtled towards me but in a freeze-frame motion. In each succeeding frame, the nose stepped up a little more and the ridge stepped closer. Unbelievably, I was fascinated by this and completely engrossed in the analysis of what would get there first – the ridge into the aircraft or the nose above the horizon. I remember 4 or 5 freeze-frame "clicks" and just as I steeled myself to meet the Grim Reaper, the nose cleared the ridge – but so low to the ground that I saw boulders and grass flash past the side of my canopy at above head height (when you fly very low and very close to the ground your peripheral vision gives you this impression). I had missed the ridge but I estimate by no more than 30 ft, maybe less.

'I levelled at around 2,000 ft to be hit by a massive injection of adrenaline as I realised just how close I had come. However, there was then an immediate decision to make: go back to low level immediately and finish the sortie or chuck it all in, fly back medium level to Wittering and give up Harrier and Fast Jet flying altogether. I couldn't see a middle way. Reluctantly and with gritted teeth, I pushed the stick forward and went back to low level, said a prayer of thank you to whatever God rocks your boat and completed the sortie and the further two recce targets. On return to Wittering, I signed over the jet, debriefed the targets and viewed the film in the RIC and then retired to the OCU aircrew crew room. I sat in a corner and lit a cigarette (I've given up now because of the health risk). I couldn't speak and must have had a "thousand-yard stare" on my face. One of the OCU instructors, the incomparable Iain Huzzard, asked me if I was OK and I think I was able to nod. He asked me if I had had a close call with the ground and I nodded again. He asked if I had learnt from it and I managed to utter a single syllable "Yes". So for all you pilots still flying around on low-level, high-speed, single-seat, single-engine operations (not too many of those around in the UK these days), my advice is this; if you have to go "head-in" inside the cockpit on any task when at high speed/low-level then make that time "head-in" very short; split the task up into several individual "head-in" events and spend lots and lots of time, in between events, looking out and clearing your flight path visually. In the eternal battle throughout history, between aircraft and the ground, the ground has never lost. It was close call for me on that occasion but I guess my final luck was that there were no sheep grazing on that ridge!'

A trio of Harrier GR3s from No.3 Squadron. The centre aircraft illustrates the 'wrap round' camouflage scheme which was eventually applied to all RAF Harriers, with the upper surface colours repeated over the undersides.

(Photo: BAE Systems)

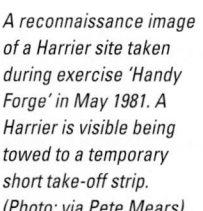

Typical of 'off-base' deployments to forward base sites, a Harrier GR3 hovers over a German parking lot adjacent to a country road. (Photo: RAF Germany)

A typical scene at a forward base with Harriers from No.3 Squadron operating from temporarily-constructed vertical and short take-off pads. (Photo: via Pete Mears)

A reconnaissance image of a Harrier site taken during exercise 'Handy Forge' in May 1981. A Harrier is visible being towed to a temporary short take-off strip. (Photo: via Pete Mears)

A Harrier GR3 getting airborne from a stretch of German Autobahn. (Photo: RAF Germany)

Right: A September 1984 reconnaissance image of a 'Hazel Flute' exercise with Harriers deployed to a large operating site comprising a camouflaged central area (under trees) adjacent to a scattering of seven VTOL pads and a short take-off strip, all linked by temporary tracking. Also visible are seven camouflaged 'hides' for individual aircraft. (Photo: RAF Germany)

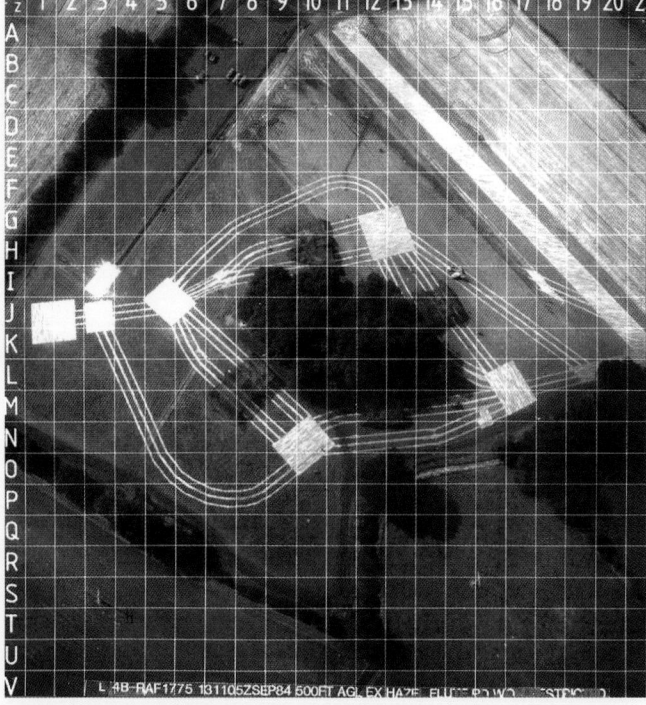

Pilot's-eye view of Harrier GR3s from No.4 Squadron at low level over Germany.
(Photo: BAE Systems)

XW268 pictured shortly after delivery to the Harrier Conversion Unit at Wittering. Mindful of the T2's longer tail boom (and the potential for ground collisions), the extremity has been painted Day-Glo orange - a practice which did not last for long. (Photo: Steve Bond)

A Harrier T4 with a GR3 in the distance. The yellow patches on the T4 appear to be replacement panels attached during maintenance, awaiting repainting.
(Photo: Tim McLelland)

XW175 leaps into the air from RAE Bedford's ramp during initial 'Ski Jump' trials. The same aircraft later went to Boscombe Down to re-emerge as the VAAC trials platform.
(Photo: RAE Bedford)

CHAPTER FIVE

Sea Jets

IT is quite possible that without America's support, the RAF would have never acquired a STOVL aircraft of any description. British official support for the concept of vertical take-off was lukewarm at best, and sometimes openly hostile. It was the persistent enthusiasm of Colonel Bill Chapman and the MWDT that translated the idea into practicality through the major funding which was eventually given to the development of the Pegasus engine. In total, almost three-quarters of the Pegasus development costs were paid for by America. It is all the more surprising, therefore, that America's armed forces (and particularly America's Government) were no more interested in an operational STOVL aircraft than the British for many years. Certainly the US supported the P.1127 and Kestrel programme, but in practical terms this was regarded as research for research's sake, with no serious intention of developing an aircraft from the results. Even the promise of an advanced warplane such as the P.1154 did not generate much serious interest across the Atlantic – apart from yet more vital funding for the development of Bristol's BS.100 engine with PCB burning. It is true that America's involvement in the Kestrel TES was based on the premise that a ground-support aircraft might possibly be produced by combining the TES findings with the work on P.1127 that was already advanced, but as the TES programme continued and then wound up, US interest became largely academic. The only practical interest in the programme had come from the US Army, and its concept of replacing the Grumman V-1 Mohawk

with a P.1127 derivative for operations in Germany. The idea progressed as far as a collaboration between Hawker and Northrop (which was to lead to development of the aircraft in the USA) but eventually it was politics which killed the project. Inter-service wrangling led to the establishment of specific roles and mission objectives which resulted in an overall weight limit being placed on aircraft operated by the US Army (a rather tawdry attempt to restrict the Army's equipment to helicopters and support aircraft). The P.1127 was way beyond these limits and so, effectively, the Army was forced to abandon any further interest in the aircraft.

The American-funded Kestrels (plus those that were no longer required by Germany) were used extensively for research duties after being shipped to the USA, and with the Army's interest having lapsed, it was the USAF, the US Navy and, for the first time, the US Marine Corps which explored the aircraft's properties. The Kestrels, now designated as the XV-6A, were re-evaluated as part of tri-service trials at Patuxent River and aircraft were deployed at sea on the *USS Independence* and *USS Raleigh* in May 1966 – some weeks before Britain performed similar trials on *HMS Bulwark*. USAF and US Navy interest in the trials was again largely academic, however, and neither service could (or would) project any operational use for a STOVL aircraft. Despite this, the USMC's interest was rather more serious. Tasked with the provision of air support for its ground forces, the USMC's aircraft are operated from US Navy vessels as necessary (the USMC does not possess its own

An early image of an AV-8A at sea, fitted with a bolt-on refuelling probe – an item of equipment which was used as required in much the same way as by RAF units across the Atlantic. (Photo: US Navy)

carriers or indeed any type of assault ship which could operate fixed-wing aircraft) and therefore the concept of a STOVL ground-support aircraft capable of operating more intimately with its forces was one which held considerable appeal. This interest eventually led to a rather unusual occurrence at the 1968 SBAC Show at Farnborough when, with almost no prior warning, Colonel Tom Miller (later to become Chief of Staff-Air for the USMC) and Lieutenant-Colonel Bud Baker, presented themselves to the Hawker Siddeley chalet and announced that they were in England to fly the Harrier, and would like to study the Pilot's Notes. Somewhat surprised, Hawker's team warmly welcomed the two pilots and just two weeks later they were at Dunsfold flying Harrier development aircraft. They were both greatly impressed with the Harrier's abilities and they returned to the US to give a favourable report to USMC and USN staff. By January, a US Navy team was in Britain conducting an evaluation of the aircraft and by June 1969 its findings led to funding approval for a batch of 12 Harriers as part of a wider plan to acquire 114 aircraft for the USMC. This was quite an achievement for Hawker as the United States rarely purchases aircraft that are not of American origin. Apart from the obvious fact that such a requirement seldom arises, there is inevitably strong political pressure for all defence equipment to be of indigenous design and manufacture, but in the case of the Harrier there was clearly no other aircraft which could even hope to replicate its unique abilities. Although the US

had been very supportive of the P.1127 programme, its interest (linked almost exclusively to research) had effectively delayed its own VTOL developments and most American-led research into the subject had ended – or was still being pursued without any operational purpose. Thus it was that, by accident or design, the only viable STOVL aircraft on the proverbial horizon was Harrier and the USMC purchase was approved, although it was stipulated that the purchase was to be an 'off the shelf' order for an aircraft that would require only minimal modifications in order to meet USMC

The AV-8A was equipped to carry Sidewinder missiles from the outset, resulting in a permanently-fixed weapons hard point being attached to the outer portion of the wing on this variant.
(Photo: US Navy)

A pair of AV-8As fitted with a full compliment of wing and fuselage weapons stations, although no weapons are being carried, with fuselage strakes attached in place of the absent ADEN cannon pods. (Photo: US Navy)

*Down below deck,
Marines at work
maintaining an AV-8A.
Although access to the
Pegasus engine was
relatively easy,
replacement of the engine
required the entire wing
section to be removed –
a time consuming, albeit
relatively simple, process.
(Photo: US Navy)*

requirements. It was also agreed that following completion of the first twelve, the subsequent aircraft would be largely manufactured in the USA (under a licence agreement from Hawker Siddeley). This led eventually to a 15-year agreement with McDonnell Douglas for the manufacture and sale of the Harrier in the USA, and also for the mutual exchange of design and development work conducted on the Harrier during the same period. A similar arrangement for manufacture of the Pegasus engine was also set up between Rolls-Royce Bristol and Pratt & Whitney. Eventually, the costs of setting up Harrier production in the US were judged to be uneconomic (with only a small batch of aircraft for the USMC being envisaged) and the subsequent aircraft were therefore manufactured in the UK – a rare and reverse situation to that which so often applies to aircraft procurement deals between the two countries.

As stipulated, changes to the USMC's Harriers were indeed minimal. Apart from the installation of an in-service naval radio fit instead of RAF-specific equipment, it was only the installation of a Sidewinder missile capability on the outer wing pylons which could have been regarded as a significant modification to the basic Harrier airframe. The Sidewinder capability was judged to be essential as the USMC had deliberately foregone the opportunity to purchase an additional batch of F-4J Phantoms in order to fund the Harriers, and

largely as a political consideration the service did not want to run any risk of the Harrier being perceived as an aircraft which could not defend itself. The 21,500 lb Pegasus Mk.103 was chosen to power the aircraft, but development of this engine derivative lagged behind the aircraft production process and so the first ten aircraft were fitted with Mk.102 engines and were re-engined at a later date. The only other change to the airframe was a weight-on-wheels switch to make safe all weapons once the aircraft was on the ground. Designated as the AV-8A, the aircraft were completed at Kingston, test-flown at Dunsfold and then partially dismantled for transportation to St.Louis by C-5 or C-141, after which they were reassembled and test-flown prior to being delivered to the USMC. The first aircraft went to Patuxent River in 1971 for a US Navy Board of Inspection and Survey trial, making further short deployments to the *USS Guadalcanal* and *USS Coronado*, before the AV-8A was officially approved for service use. From March 1971 the first batch of ten AV-8A aircraft was delivered to VMA-513 at Yuma in Arizona with further aircraft being delivered during the following year. Initial in-service experience was encouraging and only a few additional alterations to the aircraft were advised. The Ferranti 541 INAS was not popular with the Marines not only because of its relative complexity, but also the lengthy pre-take-off alignment time which compromised the USMC's rapid operational reaction ability. So from the sixtieth aircraft delivered, the INAS was omitted and a Smiths Weapons Aiming Computer was substituted – a system far less capable than the INAS but sufficient to provide necessary attack information, and free of alignment delays. The other major change was the removal of the Martin Baker Mk.9 ejection seat, as American policy was to develop an indigenous seat design which could be used in the AV-8A, the F-14 Tomcat and F-18 Hornet (and probably other aircraft too). The Stencel SEU-3/A model was chosen and after lengthy development and trials, it was progressively fitted from the ninetieth aircraft onwards. Although technically superior to the Martin Baker seat in some aspects (faster parachute deployment and an overall lighter construction), the seats were very similar and both achieved virtually identical success rates. Ultimately, the plan to make the Stencel seat a fleet-wide choice came to nothing and the decision to change from the Martin Baker model was – with hindsight – expensive and pointless.

The cost of these changes, plus others, such as the eventual removal of the ram air turbine, finally necessitated a reduction in the overall AV-8A order to 110 aircraft and, as there was a real risk that Congress would cut the order still further before the final aircraft had been delivered, the USMC deliberately delayed orders for a trainer derivative of the aircraft until FY (fiscal year) 1975. Eight trainer aircraft were eventually ordered, and these were similar to the RAF's T2 trainers, being direct dual-

control conversions of the AV-8A design with the same Stencel ejection seats, INAS replaced by the Smiths 'Baseline Attack System', and other alterations incorporated in line with the single seater's modifications. The first TAV-8A aircraft were delivered to VMA(T)-203 at Cherry Point during the summer of 1976. Meanwhile, the AV-8A settled into USMC service without any difficulties and quickly proved itself as a versatile and increasingly valued part of the Marine Corps inventory. Although USMC operations were in essence very similar to those being conducted by the RAF in Europe (albeit with a much greater global mobility), the USMC did gradually devise its own operating techniques, and some of this experience eventually became adopted by British Harrier pilots – most notably the concept of 'viffing'. This unique ability was first discovered during the initial AV-8A trials at Patuxent River when the Marine Corps Project Officer, Major Harry W. Blot, was conducting his own hands-on evaluation of the aircraft. He declared himself greatly impressed by the Harrier and its ground-support capabilities, but with fairly poor high-g manoeuvring (a symptom of the aircraft's small wing) and very poor rearwards visibility, he concluded that the aircraft was less than ideal as a fighter. Naturally, the Harrier was not designed for air-to-air combat, but the USMC did expect the aircraft to have at least some degree of self-defence ability – hence the decision to equip the AV-8A

An AV-8A baking under the Arizona sun. With poor air conditioning, the AV-8A was often an uncomfortable place to be when not airborne. This minor inconvenience was rectified in the second generation Harrier. (Photo: US Navy)

As part of the 'off the shelf' purchase of the Harrier, the USMC AV-8C retained the same camouflage paint scheme as that applied to RAF aircraft. The USMC markings were eventually 'toned down' and painted in black as illustrated. (Photo: Mick Roth collection)

AV-8A 158960 from VMA-513 at MCAS South Beaufort, July 1974. (Photo: Jim Tunney)

McDonnell Douglas AV-8A Harrier, 158703/703, USMC, USS Tarawa, 1981
This AV-8A Harrier is represented as it was seen during tests on USS Tarawa, 1981. Dark Sea Grey/Dark Green upper surfaces with Light Aircraft Grey undersides; International Orange fin and wingtips. Standard US national markings; lettering in black except '703' on nose which is white. 158703/703 was eventually lost in an accident during operations in the Pacific in 1981. (Photo at top: Mick Roth)

with Sidewinder. Blot had read reports about the possibility of shifting the Pegasus nozzles in conventional flight and the ways in which this vectored jet lift could, theoretically, be used to enhance the Harrier's manoeuvrability. He assumed that VIFF (vectoring in forward flight) had been explored by the RAF, but in fact it had not. Some pilots – particularly the more bold and flamboyant ones – had certainly played around with the capability but only on a distinctly unofficial basis. However, undeterred by the lack of technical advice on the matter, Blot got airborne in the first AV-8A and elected to try vectoring the aircraft's nozzles to their fullest extent – slamming them into fully-forward (reverse) thrust at 500 knots. In retrospect it was a crazy proposition but, without any firm advice to the contrary, Blot figured the easiest and swiftest way to investigate 'viffing' was to sample its maximum effects. With equal foolishness he had failed to properly secure his seat harness and anticipated timing the aircraft's deceleration from 500 to 300kt once the nozzles were shifted: 'With pencil in hand I slammed the nozzle lever into the braking stop (reverse thrust) position. The airplane started decelerating at an alarming rate, the magnitude of which I could not determine because

my nose was pressed up against the sight. A terrible way to be, even in an imagined conflict. My movements were even further constrained by the fact that the violence of the manoeuvre had dislodged me from the seat, and I was now straddling the stick with my right hand extended backwards between my legs, trying to hold on for dear life.'

Thankfully, Blot (and the aircraft) survived the incident and he concluded that 'viffing' could revolutionise the Harrier's fighting ability. NASA subsequently conducted a full VIFF test programme with an XV-6A Kestrel and a T-38 Talon during 1971, and air combat manoeuvring (ACM) trials were conducted by VMA-513 from Point Mugu. A second ACM trial (which included RAF personnel) was conducted at China Lake and this led to a combined USMC/RAF trial which was conducted at RAF Valley, over a period of ten days. A Harrier (with strengthened nozzle drive and instrumentation) was flown against a non-viffing Harrier, a Phantom and a Hunter and under all circumstances the 'viffing' Harrier emerged victorious. A second phase involved a Lightning F6 and also embraced a variety of ground-attack profiles. 'Viffing' was found to be of astounding

An AV-8A conducting a vertical landing ahead of aircraft preparing for (short) take offs.
(Photo: US Navy)

Like their RAF equivalents, the USMC's AV-8A aircraft occasionally, but far less frequently, received temporary camouflage schemes appropriate to specific exercises. (Photo: US Navy)

value and, in theory at least, virtually no aircraft would be capable of remaining behind a Harrier (to press home an attack) if 'viffing' was employed. Under most combat circumstances it was impossible for the attacking aircraft not to fly through and overshoot. With further nozzle and engine modifications (which enabled the nozzles to be vectored repeatedly for periods of up to 2.5

minutes), the Harrier pilot could use the technique for a wide variety of defensive manoeuvres, prompting Blot to comment that '...the Harrier had crossed the line from being good to being great… its ACM capability is absolutely eye-watering.'

The AV-8A was eventually subjected to a 'mid-life' modification programme and, from 1979, a total of 47 aircraft underwent conversion to

An AV-8A 159370 from VMA-231. The large VHF/FM blade aerial fixed to the upper fuselage was the only major external difference between the AV-8A and Harrier GR1. (Mick Roth collection)

AV-8C standard. ALR-45F/APR-43 radar warning receivers were fitted in the tail, wing tips and nose (this arrangement was preferred to the tail and fin-mounted system adopted by the RAF), and ALE-39 expendable munitions dispensers were fitted to the rear fuselage, together with an ALE-37 chaff dispenser, an on-board oxygen generation system and some lift improvement devices. The first of these aircraft entered service in 1983 and the AV-8C gradually supplemented the earlier variant with each USMC unit, although VMA-513 re-equipped exclusively with the C model. The AV-8A/C fleet remained in USMC service until the end of 1987, at which stage the USMC switched to the second-generation Harrier. However, this transition was not the end of the AV-8A's story. Spain had maintained an interest in the Harrier since 1972, as it had become increasingly apparent that the Harrier was an ideal aircraft for naval operations, being eminently capable of conducting combat missions from and to small carrier vessels. Unfortunately, Spain's Navy was not able to express its interest too vociferously through official channels as the country was not enjoying the best of relations with Britain at that time. Political issues – not least the endless debate over Gibraltar – strained relations. A Spanish order for British-built frigates had been cancelled and it was clear that the Harrier could not simply be purchased 'off the shelf' from Hawker Siddeley. Despite this, Hawker arranged for the Harrier to be demonstrated aboard Spain's *SNS Dedalo* (the former *USS Cabot*). In typical political fashion, Spain refused permission for the Harrier to over-fly Spanish territory and the Navy – still keen to see the Harrier at first-hand – arranged for the *Dedalo* to be sailed from the Mediterranean to

a point off the Portuguese coast. Test pilot John Farley flew a Harrier GR3 to the carrier non-stop and proceeded to demonstrate the aircraft's unique abilities. Thankfully the fears that the vessel's wooden deck would burst into flames were proved unfounded and apart from a few scorch marks, the visit was completed to everyone's satisfaction. In order to expedite a Spanish order (and to avoid the tedious political manoeuvrings), six AV-8A aircraft were simply added to the overall USMC order (Nos. 159557 to 159562) followed by a pair of dual-control TAV8-A airframes. These were then resold to Spain as the VA.1 Matador (designated as the AV-8S by the USMC and Harrier Mk.54 by Hawker, the twin-seat aircraft being the Mk.59 or TAV-8S). When relations between Britain and Spain improved, a further order for five aircraft (161174 to 161178) was placed in August 1977 and these were purchased directly from Hawker Siddeley, designated as the Mk.55. Outwardly identical to the AV-8A, the Spanish Harriers differed only in radio equipment and the eventual fitment of Sky Guardian RWR equipment. Conversion on to the Harrier took place in the US in 1976 (during which one aircraft was destroyed) and the aircraft were then ferried to Rota to be operated by the *Octava Escuadrilla* (8 Squadron), deploying to the *Dedalo* as required. When this vessel was retired, the new *Principe de Asturias* was introduced and Harrier operations were transferred to the new carrier, but by this stage (1989) the AV-8S was reaching the end of its operational career and it was progressively confined to shore-based training operations at Rota. The *Armada Espanola* had by this stage transitioned to the second-generation Harrier and the AV-8S was soon

AV-8C Harriers at sea. Some 47 A-model aircraft were upgraded to AV-8C standard and began entering USMC service in 1983 although they were all withdrawn, together with all remaining AV-8As, by the end of 1987. (Photo: US Navy)

redundant. However, interest in these aircraft was expressed by Thailand and a deal was signed for seven of the surviving AV-8S (and two TAV-8S) aircraft to be sold on to Thailand in September 1997. Refurbished by CASA prior to delivery and still retaining their Spanish paint schemes but with Thai insignia, the aircraft were assigned to the *HTMS Chakri Naruebet*, officially referred to as the OPHC-911 (Offshore Patrol Helicopter Carrier). During periods when the aircraft are not at sea, the Harriers (assigned to No.301 Squadron) operate from U-Tapao as part of No.3 Wing of the Thai Navy. Initial flying training was undertaken in the US, with conversion on to the Harrier taking place at Rota. As of 2011, Thailand's AV-8S are still in active service and, as such, they are the only surviving operational examples of the original Harrier Mk.1/AV-8A series.

Of course, the concept of operating the Harrier at sea had not been overlooked within Britain's armed forces. From the very first occasion in February 1963 when Bill Bedford operated the P.1127 from the deck of the *Ark Royal*, it had been clear that vertical jet lift would have a very obvious naval application if it could be developed into a viable combat aircraft. The subsequent trials with XV-6As aboard US vessels and the British trials on-board *HMS Blake's* small deck were sufficient to demonstrate that the Harrier was ideally suited to the maritime environment and in many respects was better suited than more conventional aircraft. For example, the Harrier enables its launch vessel to sail in any direction (wind over the deck being irrelevant other than in severe conditions), operating space is minimal with a spot clearance of less that 40 ft, and the costly and complicated launch catapult and arrester gear fitted to carriers is unnecessary. British Naval interest in the Harrier had centred on the abortive P.1154 – an aircraft which had the potential to become a formidable multi-role aircraft. But with a fixated interest in conventional aircraft (which fostered the notion that large aircraft carriers remained essential), the Royal Navy had embraced the Phantom, and the prospect of a new-build carrier to augment the four which were already in service. Any project which contradicted the notion of a strong fleet of carriers was probably doomed from the outset. It was only when Britain's costs and political considerations changed that the Harrier's maritime fortunes shifted. The Government, desperate to make cost savings, finally abandoned the planned new carrier and announced that the other existing carriers would also be withdrawn progressively, and with them all of the Navy's fixed-wing air power too. This was a massive blow to the Navy from which it took many years to recover and it was only through the adoption of the Harrier that the Royal Navy succeeded in its ambition to remain in the fixed-wing combat aircraft arena. In some respects it was surprising that the Navy had taken so little interest in the P.1127 when it first emerged, but in

fairness it must also be accepted that the P.1127 was first regarded as a 'proof of concept' design and then as a potential ground-support aircraft, and neither were of any direct relevance to the Navy's perceived future. The Navy required much more than a simple army support aircraft and would inevitably need a fleet defence fighter too, and so it was only when the P.1154 emerged that there seemed any realistic prospect of developing a multi-role aircraft which could meet all of the Navy's requirements. But as mentioned, the prospect of buying Phantoms proved to be irresistible. However, when the carriers were suddenly abandoned (together with the Phantoms and Buccaneers which would have operated from them), the Navy had to reappraise drastically its situation. It was assumed that the RAF would undertake future maritime missions and that its Harriers might also somehow go to sea. Precisely how, on what vessels, and for what exact purpose, was never properly established, nor did anyone question how the relatively small Harrier force could be expected to undertake its assigned roles in support of NATO and in Germany, and also take on a maritime commitment at the same time. But despite this, No.1 Squadron was cleared for ship deployment early in 1971, even though it did not take too long to realise that sustained operations at sea would not be possible. No.1 Squadron was assigned to wartime deployment in Norway and it could hardly be in two places at once. Likewise, the squadron had no capability to operate in the air defence role even if it had been able to handle two operational tasks at the same time. It was obvious that a dedicated maritime Harrier force was the only practical solution to Britain's needs.

It took until 1971 before the Navy finally embraced what was first referred to as the Maritime Support Harrier (this was subsequently abbreviated to Maritime Harrier and then Sea Harrier). Exploration of precisely what this aircraft would be took place over many months and included a variety of potentially exciting options, including the use of a new 25,000 lb Pegasus being developed by Rolls-Royce Bristol, and the employment of various weapons systems. However, it was also obvious to the Navy that there was very little money available, and whatever the Sea Harrier was to be, it would have to be something relatively modest if ever it was to be financed, not least because there was also the fundamental issue of from which ships the Harrier would operate – and the considerable cost that these would incur. In fact, the ships appear to have been openly considered before the Harriers and it was during 1969 that the concept of a 'through-deck cruiser' was first proposed by the RN Ship Department at Bath. This vessel was to be assigned to three main tasks, these being the deployment of anti-submarine helicopters; the command and control of naval and maritime air forces; and a 'contribution to air defence'. This latter category was vague, but it

AV-8A 159258 from VMA-542, complete with an AIM-9L Sidewinder training round under the port wing. (Photo: Jim Roth collection)

seems likely that this was the first indirect reference to the notion of reintroducing fixed-wing air power into the Navy, even if nobody had the will to overtly specify such a capability. There was clearly not the slightest chance of restoring the conventional carrier force but the prospect of creating a 'mini carrier' with a fleet of maritime Harriers evidently seemed far preferable to the prospect of having nothing at all. The Royal Navy believed that it stood a good chance of persuading the Government to finance such a proposal – especially if every opportunity was taken to portray the idea as being completely different (or at least far less ambitious) to the accepted concept of carrier power. The RAF, however, smelled a proverbial rat, and disputed the Navy's claims that any new aircraft carriers were needed or that an aircraft was needed for 'defence of the fleet'. Indeed, it asked – with tongue firmly in cheek – what fleet was to be protected, and precisely how much defence could be attained by maybe a dozen Harriers that would be facing maybe hundreds of supersonic, missile-armed Soviet bombers. More to the point, as far as the RAF was concerned, the introduction of Sea Harriers might convince politicians (who probably would not know any better) that the Navy was somehow capable of defending itself, and this might lead to the abandonment of orders for an air defence variant of the Tornado – a project which was regarded as

far more important. But the Sea Harrier concept persisted and it was agreed that the Royal Navy could pursue a Naval Staff Target for a minimum-change version of the existing Harrier, redesigned to achieve air defence ability over a range of up to 400nm at altitude, reconnaissance ability over an area of 20,000 square miles within one hour at low level, and a strike and ground-attack capability with a radius of action extending to 250nm. In effect, this specification outlined a truly multi-role aircraft albeit with a fairly modest capability, but one which could successfully be operated from a through-deck cruiser.

The changes to the Harrier airframe were divided between those which were necessary to meet these specified demands and those which were required for operation to and from a carrier. For the former category, the weapons system was revised to incorporate a Smiths HUD driven by digital computer, combining air-to-air and air-to-surface weapon-aiming capacity. Also included was a self-aligning attitude-reference platform, and of course a radar, in the shape of Ferranti's Blue Fox which was developed from the Seaspray system used in the Lynx helicopter. Appropriately modified for the air-to-air and air-to-surface requirements of the Harrier, it was also suitable for the hostile ECM environment in which the aircraft was expected to operate. Good though the new radar was, a plan to incorporate radar information into the HUD was

The diminutive AV-8A did not require any wing, nose or tail folding facility in order to be successfully accommodated by existing carrier lifts and hangar space. Likewise the aircraft could be parked in comparatively small deck areas, although the outrigger wheels prevented aircraft from being parked with their wings overhanging the deck – a common practice with other aircraft types. (Photo: US Navy)

Continued on page 143

Like their RAF counterparts, the USMC's AV-8As regularly carried ADEN cannon pods under the fuselage. The only obvious external differences between the Harrier GR1 and the AV-8A were the blade aerial atop the fuselage and the additional (fixed) wing pylons for Sidewinders. (Photo: Mick Roth collection)

Although USMC AV-8A aircraft were seen only rarely in non-standard paint schemes, this Harrier received an unusual application of brown paint which temporarily covered the existing green finish for a defence exercise in the 1980s. Unlike temporary finishes applied to RAF Harriers, the national insignia and serials appear to have been obscured. (Photo: Francesco Checuz)

AV-8C 159247 from VMA-542 was repainted with temporary brown and tan camouflage for an exercise at Nellis AFB during November 1984.
(Photo: Mick Roth collection)

Pictured at the beginning of a training mission, 158710 prepares to taxi to the runway, engine running and the intake auxiliary inlet doors all fully open. (Photo: Mick Roth collection)

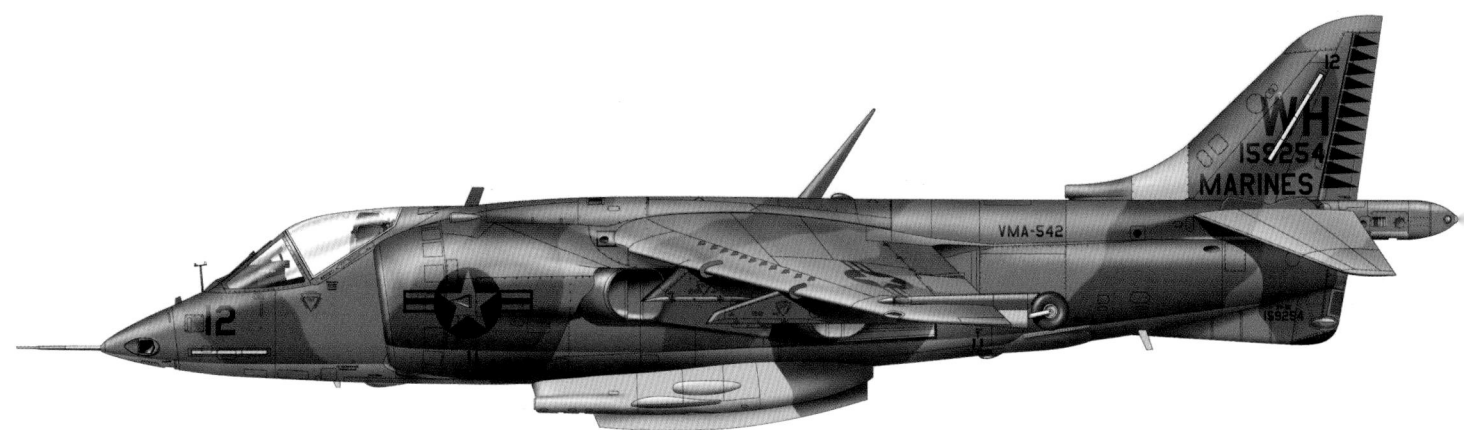

McDonnell Douglas AV-8C Harrier, 159254/12/WH, VMA-542, USMC, 1986
Dark Sea Grey/Dark Green upper surfaces with Light Aircraft Grey undersides; Low-Viz national markings in black. All lettering and rudder decoration in black

The USMC deliberately ordered its small fleet of twin-seat TAV-8A aircraft as a follow-on to the single-seaters. Although this was a sound planning decision, ensuring the security of the AV-8A order, it inevitably caused difficulties for early Harrier conversion training. (Photo: Mick Roth collection)

Right: An unusual image of a TAV-8A which appears to have been taken during initial USMC deck trials. The main and outrigger wheels have been painted white (with 'creep' markings) for photo calibration. (Photo: US Navy)

dropped thanks to cost considerations, and the radar's display became a head-down TV screen inside the cockpit. Most of the new equipment was designed to be self-checking and most fault diagnosis could be achieved without external equipment and easily fixed by replacement of the appropriate module. The five weapons pylons were similar to those fitted to the RAF's Harrier GR3 but with stronger release units. Compatibility with a wide range of weapons was incorporated from the start, including Sidewinder (outboard pylons), Martel and Harpoon. Perhaps most significantly, the Sea Harrier was afforded a Strike function and was cleared to carry the WE.177 nuclear store which gave the aircraft a destructive capability far beyond its more typical ground-attack capacity. For carrier operations, other changes were incorporated, such as the removal of many magnesium components which would suffer from salt corrosion and the incorporation of deck tie-downs (later fitted to RAF Harriers for operations in the Falklands). The other and most obvious change to the Harrier airframe was the redesign of the forward fuselage, necessitated by the new radar. The larger nose profile provided an opportunity to raise the cockpit and canopy so that it emerged beyond the height of the upper fuselage, thereby affording the pilot a greatly improved all-round vision which enhanced the Sea Harrier's potential as a fighter. This became a common feature to all subsequent Harrier developments.

In 1975 the Admiralty formally redesignated its new through-deck cruisers as 'Command Cruisers' in the shape of *HMS Ark Royal, Illustrious* and *Invincible*, each of which would ultimately accommodate six Sea Harriers. It was envisaged that two of these carriers might be deployed simultaneously, and, with this in mind, and a requirement for shore-based training, an order for 31 aircraft was issued (the total order eventually rose to 57 aircraft) together with three development aircraft, designated Sea Harrier FRS.Mk.1. It was not until May 1975 that this order was finally placed, such was the Government's indecisiveness. The initial contract for design study had been issued in 1972 but with national issues such as a fuel crisis, the 'three day week' and inflation, progress slowed until both customer and manufacturer began to accept that the order might never be placed at all. It was therefore something of a surprise to both Hawker Siddeley and the Navy when Defence Minister Roy Mason finally announced the Sea Harrier order – indeed John Fozard only learned of the order via the BBC News service as he flew into Dunsfold in a Dove. The first development aircraft to be completed was XZ439 and this aircraft took to the air still unpainted in yellow primer on 20 August 1978 in the hands of John Farley. Used primarily for handling trials, it was subsequently assigned to stores clearance work, which revolved around the release of unguided bombs and rocket pods,

although the Sea Eagle missile had also been envisaged as part of Sea Harrier's inventory for some time. Even before the Sea Harrier was manufactured (and before Sea Eagle became available), trials with a Harrier GR3 were flown using a Martel round (precursor to the Sea Eagle using the same missile body) with a balancing store on the other wing. It was demonstrated that the Harrier could hover and land vertically in this configuration – a fairly heavy store for the diminutive Harrier – and test pilot John Farley successfully fired a Martel round to demonstrate that the missile's exhaust plume did not affect the performance of the Pegasus engine. On 26 March 1979 *HMS Invincible* commenced sea trials and on 18 September, the first Sea Harrier unit – No.700A Naval Air Squadron – was commissioned at RNAS Yeovilton in Somerset, having taken delivery of Sea Harrier XZ451. This unit eventually operated the first five production Sea Harriers and, after completing its role as the Intensive Flying Trials Unit, it became No.899 NAS – the Navy's shore-based training unit. The three operational squadrons (800, 801 and 802) followed on as production of more Sea Harriers was completed. Oddly, no twin-seat derivative of the Sea Harrier was ordered, the Navy having concluded that specialist training for STOVL deck operations was not necessary. Conversion training on to the Harrier was undertaken by the RAF's OCU at Wittering and one of this unit's Harrier T4As (XZ455) was funded by the Navy as part of this arrangement. However, a handful of former RAF Harrier T4s was eventually transferred to 899 NAS at Yeovilton and redesignated as the Harrier T4N with three new-build aircraft subsequently delivered directly to the Navy, enabling 899 NAS eventually to assume all naval conversion training on the type.

Although not part of the Sea Harrier design process as such, another important development also accompanied the aircraft into operational service. Lieutenant-Commander Doug Taylor devised what became known as the 'Ski Jump' which greatly enhanced the Sea Harrier's capabilities and eventually influenced naval fixed-wing operations around the world. By creating an upward curve to the end of a carrier's take-off area, he proposed that the Harrier could take advantage of a 'free' input of vertical velocity, effectively 'throwing' the aircraft skywards. Not only would this enable the aircraft to take off with heavier fuel or weapons loads, but it would also enable deck sizes to be reduced and impart greater flight safety on every take-off (the aircraft would be physically directed upwards regardless of available thrust). For a normal short take-off (STO) the Harrier accelerates forwards at full power with the engine nozzles vectored aft. At the end of a carrier's deck the nozzles would be rotated to fifty degrees and the aircraft would become airborne on jet lift, combined with growing wing lift. With a suitable upwards-curved ramp, the aircraft could leave the

*Pictured shortly after delivery to the USMC, an AV-8A from VMA-513 equipped with rocket pods and ADEN cannon.
(Photo: Terry Panopalis collection)*

deck at a lower speed (perhaps 60kt instead of 90kt) and with an automatic upwards velocity it would reach 200 ft just a matter of seconds later, giving the pilot far more time to recognise any problems if there was an engine failure or other emergency. Likewise, normal STO departures from a flat surface must take into account the risk of a pitching deck which might be at the downwards part of its cycle at the critical point of take-off. With a ski jump, the aircraft will always have a positive vertical velocity regardless of the ship's attitude. The idea made great sense, and it was remarkably simple. By August 1977 a test rig had been constructed at RAE Bedford and the first Harrier take-off was performed successfully from the ramp on the 5th of that month. The six-degree ramp angle was then raised to 12 degrees by December and Harriers were able to demonstrate launches at speeds that were as low as 75kt, which was some 65kt less than a more typical STO. More than 1,000 ramp launches were performed and the ramp angle was tested at a variety of angles, eventually reaching 20 degrees – at which the Harrier's undercarriage oleos were reaching their maximum compression under a 4g load as they went up the ramp. The concept was brilliant and it was adopted immediately for the Navy's carriers. Unfortunately

both *Invincible* and *Illustrious* had already been completed with Sea Dart SAM positions on their bow structure and this restricted the incorporation of ramps to only 7 degrees. By comparison, *Ark Royal* was completed with a 12-degree ramp and *HMS Hermes* (which was still in service and adapted to handle Harriers) was fitted with a similar 12-degree facility.

Having barely settled into service, the Navy's Sea Harriers were soon in action. Initial Operational Capability had just been achieved by early 1982 but, as the crisis in the South Atlantic unfolded, the creation of a Task Force with which to recapture the Falkland Islands quickly emerged. It was obvious that the very core of this force would be carrier power and therefore the Sea Harrier, as this was the only combat aircraft which Britain could deploy in the South Atlantic. The RAF's Vulcan bombers could be (and were) operated as a 'strategic' asset, flying attack missions to and from Ascension Island, but this required a complicated, hugely expensive and risky journey over thousands of miles for each sortie. More to the point, the Vulcans could not operate 'in theatre' and could not directly support ground troops. Likewise they could not provide any air defence capability. The RAF's Phantoms, Tornados, Buccaneers and

Jaguars all required an airfield from which to operate and until the islands could be retaken, no such facility existed. Carrier aircraft were the only solution, and the Sea Harrier (supported by RAF Harriers) was the only option that Britain had. Of course the Sea Harrier was never intended to be operated in the South Atlantic. Designed to operate primarily as part of NATO, the Sea Harrier was expected to counter Soviet bombers or carrier-born Yak-38s. Nobody imagined that the Sea Harrier would ever be expected to fight Mirages. Even more alarming was the disturbing fact that the Navy did not even have any AEW (Airborne Early Warning) cover, their aged but adequate Gannets having been retired some years previously when the last conventional carrier, the *Ark Royal*, had been withdrawn. It was a perilous prospect, but with no other option available, the assembled Task Force set sail with every available Sea Harrier (24 aircraft) embarked on board *Hermes* and *Invincible*. History records that both the RAF's Harrier GR3s and the Navy's Sea Harriers achieved great success in the weeks that followed. It is true that the Argentine pilots were obliged to operate their aircraft at the very limits of their fuel endurance which prevented them from engaging in any significant air combat over the Falklands, but equally it is true that the skill and professionalism of the British pilots was a deciding factor in what seemed (at least to Britain) like an inevitable victory. In fact, it was a close-run affair and it was a combination of ingenuity, hard work, planning, skill and sheer good luck which enabled the British forces to prevail, but of course the Harrier was the key asset. Various last-minute upgrades were made to the aircraft. For example, the all-important AIM-9L Sidewinder was not even cleared for Sea Harrier use at the beginning of April 1982 and an emergency programme provided clearance in just a matter of days. Likewise, the aircraft's chaff and flare dispensers were not fitted at the start of the deployment south and they had to be dropped by parachute for fitment en route. But despite so many shortcomings and disadvantages, the Sea Harriers enabled crews to achieve the downing of 22 enemy aircraft plus a helicopter at the expense of only two losses, both of which were due to ground fire. Only four more aircraft were lost due to other accidents. The Falklands Crisis demonstrated clearly the value of carrier power and the versatility of the diminutive, unsophisticated but disproportionately potent Sea Harrier.

Naturally, the Falklands experience enabled the Navy to re-evaluate the Sea Harrier's effectiveness and plans for future improvements were revised accordingly. It had been envisaged that a radical re-winged Sea Harrier design would eventually be procured, but when a similar plan being pursued by the RAF was dropped in 1980, it seemed clear that the Sea Harrier's development would have to be more modest. Most importantly, the sinking of *HMS Sheffield* and the *Atlantic Conveyor* had demonstrated that a look-down radar capability was essential and that both aircraft- and sea-skimming missile detection would be a priority. It was also evident that the AIM-9L missile (and the 30 mm cannon) required Sea Harrier pilots to manoeuvre at close range if they were successfully to acquire a target, and the aircraft was not designed to be a dogfighter. Despite a great deal of ill-informed media hype, which often portrayed the Sea Harrier as a latter-day Spitfire, the combat pilots had a more realistic picture of the aircraft's capabilities with its relatively poor thrust compared to modern purpose-built fighters and a high wing loading which restricted the aircraft's turning ability. The Harrier's unique 'viffing' ability was certainly an asset but vectoring the aircraft's thrust inevitably resulted in a significant loss of energy and, although it gave pilots a formidable self-defence capability, it was of only limited use in terms of pressing home an attack. Thankfully for Britain, the Argentine pilots had been equipped with aircraft that were relatively old and did not have the advantage of a good BVR (Beyond Visual Range) radar and missile capacity, which they were obliged to operate at distances which used every drop of available fuel. Clearly, this balance of capabilities could not be relied upon for every conceivable conflict.

A Mid Life Update programme was therefore embarked upon and in the meantime a more immediate Phase One update was initiated, for completion in 1987. This gave the Sea Harrier some important improvements, most notably the incorporation of twin Sidewinder launch rails, thereby doubling the aircraft's missile capacity. A new 'nozzle inching' facility was introduced (enabling the pilot to trim the engine nozzle position by a further ten degrees to provide additional deceleration), and a new MADGE (Microwave Aircraft Digital Guidance Equipment) system was installed, roughly equivalent to the more common Instrument Landing System fitted to many combat aircraft, enabling the Sea Harrier to recover in poor weather without a talk-down facility. Development of the Sea Eagle missile continued and it entered service in 1987, providing Sea Harrier with an outstanding 'fire and forget' system which could be employed against surface targets at long range. More Sea Harrier FRS1 aircraft were ordered largely to replace those which had been lost (a total of 17 by this stage) and, at long last, an AEW system was re-acquired for the fleet, courtesy of the Sea King AEW2.

Of course after the cessation of hostilities, the British Government constructed a new purpose-built airfield on the Falklands which eventually enabled the RAF's Phantoms (subsequently replaced by Tornado F3s and finally by Typhoons) to operate directly from the Islands, and so the Navy's increased capabilities were arguably unnecessary – at least for deployment in the South Atlantic.

**Hawker Siddeley AV-8A Harrier, 159251/3/WF, VMA-513,
'The Flying Nightmares', Detachment 'A'**
Dark Sea Grey/Dark Green upper surfaces with Light Aircraft Grey
undersides; standard national markings. Serial and 'Marines' on fin
in black; all other lettering in mid-blue. Mid-blue rudder with white
stars

AV-8A 158975 proudly wearing the markings of VMA-513. This colour image reveals that the 'WF' tail code has been applied in dark blue (rather than black) paint. (Photo: Mick Roth collection)

Captured perfectly on camera, a TAV-8A (159379) from VMAT-203. Of note is the white line applied to the forward 'cold' engine nozzle, presumably intended to provide an easy visual guide to the nozzle's angle. (Photo: Francesco Checuz)

A rather 'battle-worn' TAV-8A illustrating how the repair of the paint finish has resulted in a distinctly patchy appearance. USMC Harrier trainers usually carried no external stores other than fuel tanks. (Photo: Mick Roth collection)

One former USMC AV-8A was assigned to NASA and was employed on VSTOL research duties at the Langley Research Center. Apart from the radical change of colour scheme it remained unchanged from USMC standard.
(Photo: Mick Roth collection)

Sea Harrier FRS1 XZ451 resplendent in the eye-catching colours of No.700A Naval Air Squadron. (Photo: Mick Roth collection)

Above left: Passing above Ark Royal, a Sea Harrier from No.800 NAS in pre-Falklands colours. (Photo: Royal Navy)

The illustrious Lt Cdr 'Sharky' Ward about to get airborne in a Sea Harrier FRS1.
(Photo: Royal Navy)

Sea Harrier FRS1 XZ454 pictured shortly after delivery, pristine in Dark Grey and White colours, with the insignia of No.800 NAS.
(Photo: Royal navy)

No.801 NAS became the second operational Sea Harrier unit when it reformed on 28th January 1981.
(Photo: Royal Navy)

A brace of Sea Harriers from No.800 NAS. The unit reformed with Harriers on 31 March 1980, initially for service on board HMS Invincible although the unit subsequently embarked upon HMS Hermes. (Photo: Terry Senior)

A poor but extremely rare clip of movie footage showing a Sea Harrier during A&AEE trials, dropping a WE.177 nuclear store. (Photo: QinetiQ)

Below: Clearance trials for the Sea Eagle missile continued after the Falklands Conflict, as illustrated by this operationally-camouflaged Sea Harrier FRS1, carrying a pair of Sea Eagle test rounds and Sidewinder 'acquisition rounds' on twin launcher rails attached to the outer wing pylons. (Photo: BAE Systems)

A pair of Sea Harrier FRS1s pictured shortly after delivery to the Royal Navy, wearing the markings of Nos. 899 NAS and 700A NAS, and tail codes denoting shore base at RNAS Yeovilton. No.700A NAS was eventually absorbed into No.899 NAS. (Photo: Royal Navy)

Fascinating image of HMS Hermes en-route to the Falklands with a gaggle of war-camouflaged jets visible below deck.
(Photo: Royal Navy)

Pictured during the Falklands conflict, a Sea Harrier FRS1 comes into the hover carrying Sidewinder missiles, external fuel tanks and ADEN gun pods.
(Photo: Royal Navy)

Sea Harriers from No.800 NAS in action over the North Sea, wearing post-Falklands low-visibility colours.
(Photo: BAE Systems)

Weapons clearance trials conducted at the RAE's West Freugh facility often ended with a spirited farewell from the participating pilots. Here a Sea Harrier FRS1 (carrying a camera recording pod) makes a low pass in front of the base hangars.
(Photo: BAE Systems)

CHAPTER SIX

Super Sea Jet

THE Sea Harrier's MLU Phase Two was intentionally more ambitious and in February 1985, British Aerospace (into which Hawker Siddeley was absorbed) and Marconi received a project definition contract for the upgrade of 30 aircraft as part of a Sea Harrier Improvement Programme (SHIP). At the core of this project was a new radar – the Ferranti Blue Vixen, and the Hughes (subsequently Raytheon) AIM-120 AMRAAM (Advanced Medium Range Air-to-Air Missile). The new pulse-Doppler radar was regarded as ideal for the much-needed look-down capability and work on a production system was advanced by the time an order was placed in December 1988 for the conversion of 29 FRS1 aircraft to the new FRS.Mk.2 standard (four more conversions were ordered in 1995 together with a batch of 18 new-build aircraft). With the new radar (designed with a high degree of automation) and the "fire and forget" AIM-20, the new Sea Harrier also incorporated a longer fuselage, courtesy of a 35 cm "plug" which provided extra space to house the radar's processor and other avionics equipment. The radar also required the aircraft's nose profile to be revised again, and this time a more bulbous nose cone was simply grafted on to the existing forward fuselage (some commentators suggested that it must have mysteriously evaded the attention of the aerodynamicists). Even with this modified fuselage, the Sea Harrier FRS2 was still no slouch and could theoretically maintain the top speed of Mach 1.2 attainable in the FRS1 although the later aircraft's stores were never cleared to such speeds. The design

of the aircraft's wing leading edge was changed in order to improve handling, with a new "kinked" shape, deletion of one of the vortex generators and an additional wing fence. Other improvements were also proposed (such as leading edge wing root extensions and additional missile capability) but, as ever, the projected costs prevented these from proceeding. The only other significant change made to the FRS2 was the incorporation of a slightly more powerful Pegasus Mk.106 engine with improved thrust at lower operating temperatures. The first completed FRS2 (ZA195) made its inaugural flight from Dunsfold on 19 September 1988 in the hands of test pilot Heinz Frick. The second prototype (XZ439) was shipped to the US on board a new *Atlantic Conveyor* in January 1993, after which it was used to carry out live firings of the AIM-20 missile against target drones, at Eglin AFB in Florida.

The Sea Harrier FRS2 completed evaluation at Boscombe Down and, after an official handing-over ceremony at Dunsfold on 2 April 1993, the first aircraft was delivered to 899 NAS at Yeovilton in the shape of ZA176 during September 1993. Taking the Sea Harrier FRS1 aircraft out of service for this MLU conversion created significant headaches for the FAA (the already-modest fleet was effectively cut still further while the aircraft were out of service) and it was the arrival of the new-build aircraft which finally eased the problems. With Kingston now gone, these aircraft were manufactured at BAE's Brough factory, before being dismantled and transported to Dunsfold for

final assembly and test-flying; quite why the aircraft could not have been flown out of Brough remains a mystery. Although new-build, the aircraft were fitted with what were actually rather older Pegasus engines, in the shape of "used" Pegasus Mk.103s which were taken from redundant RAF Harrier GR3s before being refurbished and modified to Mk.106 standard. In May 1994 the FRS2 designation was changed to Sea Harrier FA.Mk.2, reflecting the fact that the new aircraft no longer had a reconnaissance role, and also because the Strike capability had been abandoned. The WE.177 was withdrawn from naval service in June 1992, as indeed were all of Britain's air-launched nuclear weapons during the 1990s. In October 1994 No.801 NAS became the first operational unit to take delivery of the FA2 and the FRS1 was withdrawn from use over a period of months until the last example (ZD581) left No.800 NAS on 17 March 1995. Deliveries of FA2 aircraft were protracted and it was not until 24 December 1998 that the last (ZH813) was handed over to the FAA. This was in fact the very last of the "first-generation" Harriers to be completed and it therefore earned itself the distinction of becoming the very last all-British fighter to be manufactured – if the Sea Harrier could truly be described as a fighter in the traditional sense. Of course, the Falklands conflict was not the last time that the Navy's Harriers went into action. In subsequent years, the Gulf Wars, Balkans operations and Sierra Leone all called upon the Navy's participation and the Harrier (either in the form of the FA2 or the later GR7/9) continued to play a significant part in the Navy's order of battle until 2010. It was intended to retain the original Sea Harrier fleet in service until at least 2012 when the Navy was to acquire the all-new Lockheed Martin F-35 strike fighter, but as the projected delivery date for this complicated and expensive design slipped further and further away (and the likely cost grew ever

higher), the Government's thinking began to change. During 2002 – and without any serious hint of such a radical move – the Ministry of Defence announced that the Sea Harrier was to be withdrawn from 2006. The decision was ostensibly taken on grounds of capability, on the basis that there would be "difficulties" in upgrading the Sea Harrier still further (until F-35 was available) and that "other capabilities" were now available. This referred to the Type 45 anti-air warfare destroyer rather than any other aircraft type. It seems obvious, however, that despite protestations to the contrary, the decision to abandon the Sea Harrier was made purely on the basis of cost savings as it was accepted that early withdrawal of the aircraft would save £135 million and that a further £230 million could be saved by not implementing another engine upgrade for the fleet. The move was greeted with astonishment (particularly within the Fleet Air Arm) and an understandable amount of resentment, but the plan was indeed implemented and on 28 March 2008, No.801 NAS performed a five-aircraft flypast over Yeovilton to mark the rather premature retirement of the Sea Harrier from British service. The following day the remaining Sea Harriers were ferried to RAF Shawbury and placed in storage where – at the time of writing – most still remain.

Of course there is much, much more which could be said about the Sea Harrier, not least in terms of the many instances in which the aircraft has been used operationally. However, details of the Sea Harrier's active service are already well documented. What is rather less commonly explored is the viewpoint of a Sea Harrier pilot. Paul Tremeling is a former Sea Harrier pilot who served with Nos.800, 801 and 809 Naval Air Squadrons, and he also flew Harriers with the RAF's No.20 Squadron. Consequently, he probably knows the Harrier better than most and he recalls his association with the Sea Harrier, describing in the following paragraphs what flying the "Shar" was really like:

The Sea Harrier FA2's larger radar resulted in a re-designed nose cone which gave the aircraft a distinctly blunt-nosed appearance when compared to the more refined shape of the FRS1. The re-designed wing leading edge is also evident in this picture. (Photo: BAE Systems)

'The first thing that you would notice about the Sea Harrier FA2 if you walked up to one, would probably be its very obvious downward-sloping anhedral wing, which in turn would lead you to notice the unusual outriggers and their small tyres. You would also probably notice the bulbous nose of the aeroplane. Depending on your personal aesthetic tastes, this was either a step in the right direction from the pointy FRS1 or a massive step backwards. Whatever your personal preference, the radar that lurked behind this inflated subsonic nose cone was at the very heart of the machine and was simply excellent in every respect. The FA2 admittedly did a few things to only an average standard with its small wing and thrust pushed through four exhausts, giving it a turning performance that was not comparable to the currency fighters of the day, such as the F-16 and MiG-29. We had three things that could save us in the close-in fight, however. Our radius fight was actually fairly small, which was a good thing when engaging more capable fighters, and we could also fly slower than most platforms so our tactics invariably led to what we call scissors manoeuvres, either flat or rolling. To these, with a bit of practice, could be added VIFF, or vectoring in forward flight, used to pitch the nose beyond purely aerodynamic control. Great if you got it right, absolutely disastrous if you didn't! All FA2 pilots will have completely departed – lost control of – the aircraft at some stage, attempting to get a small advantage by using the nozzles. But what it lacked in the visual arena the FA2 made up for in the Beyond Visual Range world. This was due to three things. The jet was equipped with AMRAAM, the

Advanced Medium Range Air-to-Air Missile which was the best all-round air-to-air missile of the day, with less range than the Phoenix, but it could be carried by everyone. Likewise, not as manoeuvrable as AA-11 Archer but with far greater legs. If you could get the AMRAAM up high prior to launch then it performed brilliantly. The FA2 loved high altitude and we would regularly Combat Air Patrol in the low 'thirties (around 30,000 ft), or Block 3 as it became known. We would climb when we committed to enemy aircraft as well. This extra height, even though we would

A mock-up of the cockpit layout for the Sea Harrier FA2. In contrast to the cockpit of the FRS1, the FA2 featured more modern components including two large Multi-Function Display Units. (Photo: BAE Systems)

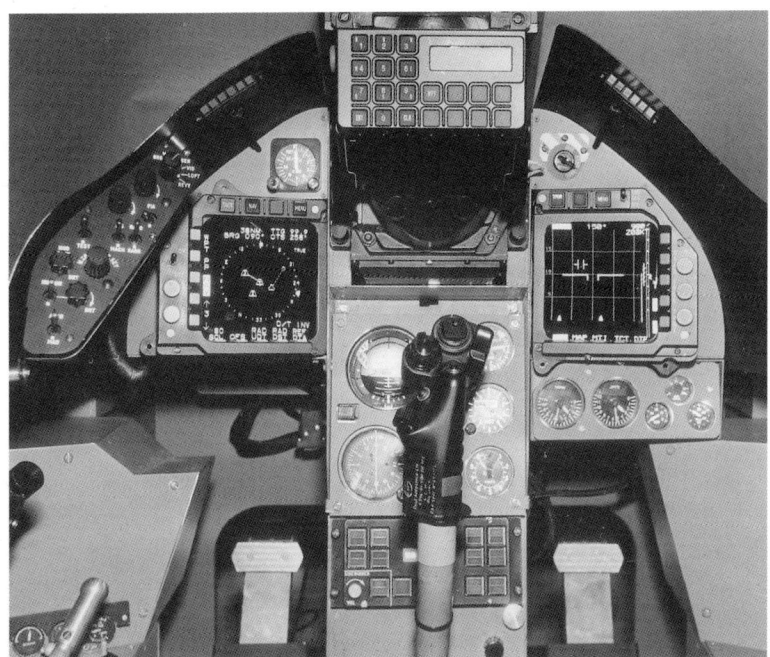

Carriage trials for the Sea Eagle missile included twin installations (as illustrated) and single rounds, with a counterweight (an external fuel tank) carried on the opposing wing. Live launches were also conducted over the West Freugh range. (Photo: BAE Systems)

Sea Harrier FA2 lashed to the deck between sorties. The launch pylons for the AIM-120 are visible under the fuselage. The pylons incorporate rams to push the missile away from the aircraft on launch. (Photo: Mark Rourke)

XZ439 was the second Sea Harrier FRS2 development aircraft and the first to receive radar, although it was not fitted until more than a year after its first flight in FRS2 configuration. (Photo: Terry Senior)

launch from subsonic speed, gave the AMRAAM longer legs than those fired from supersonic platforms which had a lower launch altitude, and that was a point lost on everyone from the general public to the Air Warfare Centre. The last strength of the Sea Harrier was Blue Vixen, an excellent radar. It worked in all three Pulse Repetition Frequencies – low, medium and high – with their attendant strengths and weaknesses. Low for long pick-ups, high for velocity tracks and medium for optimum support to the AMRAAM. This gave a very high fidelity track. The radar didn't have much power compared to other systems, so detection range was less than one would expect from Foxhunter radar, for example, but once a track had built, the radar wouldn't lose it. That's not to say that a wily bandit wouldn't drop a lock by using height or the Doppler notch, but rather that the radar didn't usually "coast" tracks it wasn't sure about. Some radars, due to a phenomenon called eclipsing, allow tracks to "coast", simply assuming they're still going the same way as the last definite contact on them. This is low fidelity stuff and doesn't allow for accurate AMRAAM computations. Not so with Blue Vixen. As a result the launch information for AMRAAM was kept updated and the kit could accurately show you how your weapon solution on a bandit was doing. Other radars that weren't able to perform this MPRF update couldn't accurately give a weapons solution and crews had to fire at predetermined ranges. The data link that flowed from radar to weapon, every half second, was superb, meaning that the weapon was updated continually during its trajectory, again a facility that wasn't always available to other AMRAAM users. Watching the radar contacts manoeuvre and trying to gauge whether they had done enough to avoid the inbound weapon was a skill in itself.

'The average FA2 sortie would be a pair of aircraft or a four-ship playing against what we'd call a "Red air" asset. The brief would be fairly short by most standards as everything we did was done in a standard way, therefore it didn't need explaining. The joy of this was that aircrew from different squadrons would be able to join the sortie at any time, even in the middle of it, and know what their role would be. The brief would be followed by the walk to the aircraft and the walk-round, and with all being well we would mount up. The norm was to sit with reliance placed on the auxiliary power unit or APU, allowing all the avionics to align and warm up prior to engine start and thereby saving petrol – one of the shortcomings of the jet was the fuel load. Navigation way points had to be punched in by hand which was onerous, but with only 10 to use, one of which was an offset and one of which was "Mum" (home base) it didn't take too long. Engine start and after-start tests were as per any aeroplane really, the big point being to get the radar up and running. Most snags could be cured by one of two Built-In Tests, although it would be disingenuous to suggest that no-one ever blasted off into the blue with a "lead nose" aircraft, that is, without the radar working. Sometimes an airborne re-boot was required to kick her into life. On the taxi out, however, things began to change from what normal fighter pilots get up to. First we had fuel galleries in the engine which needed filling by slamming the throttle fully open and then closing it again. Taxying FA2s would always be accompanied by the strange sound of engines winding up and then cutting as a direct result, whereas most jets will simply use a constant power. We had to measure the "low end acceleration" – how fast the engine spooled from low rpm to 55 per cent, and we had to check that with the nozzles down, high pressure air was actually going to them.

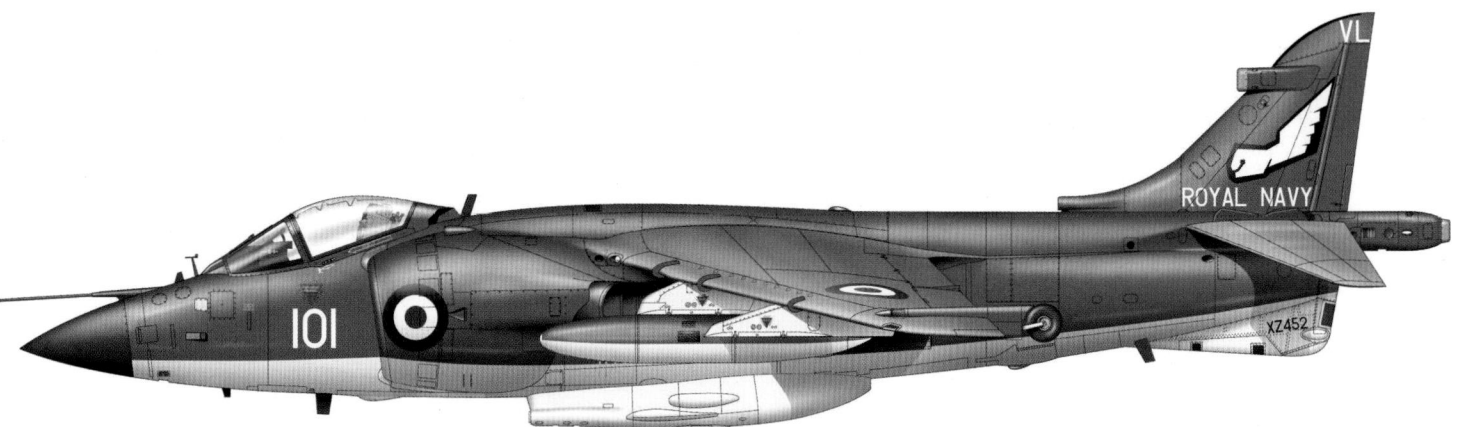

BAe Sea Harrier FRS.1, XZ451/VL-102, No. 899 Naval Air Squadron, 1981
Extra Dark Sea Grey/White finish with code in white and serial in black; unit badge in black and white on fin. Blue/White/Red roundels in six positions

A varied line-up of Harrier derivatives at Cottesmore. In the foreground is the Navy's T8, ahead of an FA2, with the RAF's T12 and GR7 in the background. JHF operations often resulted in a mix of types being present, from both RAF and FAA units. (Photo: Mark Rourke)

Hunter T8M pictured at Dunsfold. This particular aircraft was not assigned to Harrier training for some time and remained in use by British Aerospace on trials, used as an avionics integration aircraft for the Sea Harrier FRS1 programme. (Photo: Andy Lawson)

The take-off with a full load ashore was the 99 per cent Short Take-Off. Even doubters of FA2 performance would have to agree that out of the blocks it goes like a scalded cat; the numbers go up very quickly, it's just that they stop going up before they should – as my cousin, a Tornado pilot, told me when I took him for a ride. As with all aircraft the leader does his best to provide a stable platform, and the wingman simply hangs on. But there was a catch. The Sea Harrier was lifted from the ground cushion by selecting 50 degree nozzle at the leader's head nod, and this was followed by accelerating flight and raising the gear and flap on further nods. The rub was that if you dropped back you could nozzle out quicker to catch up, essentially using the

nozzle as a throttle, but physics always caught up somehow and you would need more power. Hence the "Harrier juggle", left hand jumping from nozzle lever to throttle and back again to keep the jet in formation. Worse case, if you used purely throttle to keep up and forward stick to keep the nose down, you could have two fighters side by side with vastly differing nozzle settings. "Getting caught on the wrong side of the nozzle", as we called it, was an odd place to be.

'Out of Yeovilton or "away from Mum" our first job was to get all the admin tasks done. We would roll through the ATC frequencies until we got to talk to the control agency. We would do this whilst carrying out our system checks. We'd confirm that our chaff and flares worked, that the radar would lock on, that AMRAAM worked in all its modes, that the close-in combat searches worked and the Sidewinders would lock; all done in your wingman's six o'clock position. When you were done he broke hard right and you flew straight; by breaking back to the left he would roll into your six position for his checks. This allowed you to check out your radar

AIM-120 missile attached to XZ439 whilst deployed to Eglin AFB for release trials. (Photo: via Dennis Jenkins)

warning gear. A good long "spike" told you that he was complete. At this signal you would break to the right, and when he "snipped" his lock you reversed the turn and were in perfect battle formation, line abreast. The flight itself was a wonderful place to be in the Sea Harrier. Loving the high block would mean that the FA2 was more often than not clear of the clouds, up in the bright, blue, piercing sky. We would establish a CAP through timing, lead and subordinate element flying the same six-minute race track, three minutes apart. The CAP was established at a point in space, the datum, and orientated to look "up threat". In places like Scotland where the ground relief has a set pattern it could be set up so that the "hot fighters" were looking directly up the valleys. It was common for us to see the enemy before the surface fleet did, sometimes we even outdid the AEW Sea King. We would fly the CAP in battle formation, or combat spread as the USAF would call it. At high altitude you had to be careful about keeping your speed up around 0.8M or the aircraft would descend, particularly in the turn, so we would nibble our way around the corners, usually making pretty patterns in the burning blue with our contrails, and this is where the work would start. Not to be underestimated, was the work required simply to stay in formation. Light grey, small fighters are very hard to see in the deep blue of the high troposphere.

'Most human beings possess the motor skills to fly an aeroplane and, given time, anyone can learn the basics. Some will possess the mental aptitude to fly an aircraft at high speed, approaching or even exceeding 500 knots. Of these some will be able to adequately perform the high end manoeuvres of combat and a smaller amount will in turn be able to keep up with a multi-faceted air battle with multiple friendly and enemy aircraft, in varying dispositions, attempting to claw each other out of the skies. The single-seat fighter pilot needed all these skills plus the ability to bring his radar and weapon system to bear on the enemy. The fight

therefore fell into five separate pieces. The first was the CAP, listening to the Fighter Controller or "Bag" and gaining as much SA (situational awareness) as possible prior to the combat itself. In this phase the priority was good formation and sound radar handling. Each fighter had an assigned area to search. The trick was to listen hard and talk only by exception. The second phase was the commit – the enemy having crossed the line where action became inevitable. We would commit in pairs, or maybe as a wall of four fighters, at full power climbing at 0.81M, radars searching ahead, left thumb slewing the radar, left fore and index finger moving the scanner up and down, left thumb changing range scale, left thumb keying the main radio into life. The second radio was activated using a switch on the port cockpit wall. Soft keys by the display allowed you to change the size of the beam, right hand worked access to AMRAAM or Sidewinder via the thumb, different buttons on the stick allowed you to accept a mode, designate a track and change AMRAAM modes. A good example of FA2 HOTAS or Hands-On Throttle And Stick, was the autopilot switch on the stick, sometimes called the 'paddle'. On the ground it activated nose wheel steering, in the air it turned the autopilot on and off – unless of course if you had the recce camera primed in which case it ran the film for the duration of the button press.

'Post commit would come the meat of the fight. Lead would tell you who to target, which of his fighters was going to kill which enemy. Within a pair you would wait until a given range comparing pictures using the radio, continually changing your heading and altitude to carry out a successful intercept. You had to keep the enemy from boxing round you, so horizontal disposition was crucial. You had to give the AMRAAM legs which required height, you had to be in a position to merge at the end of it all, which required the correct height differential between you and your foe. The radar couldn't accept too much look down, so a descending enemy needed to be

Whilst at Eglin AFB, XZ439 received an unusual shark mouth marking during AIM-120 launch trials. After completion of a series of test-firings the aircraft was returned to the UK by Hercules transport. (Photo: via Dennis Jenkins)

they would "strip" completely on their own. Keeping SA on complex fights was very hard indeed and it was always a relieving moment when the enemy showed up on the radar screen, your eyes having been glued to the right hand LCD for the entire intercept. It was important to avoid this tendency, as "scope boggling" led to aircraft in unusual positions and very disorientated pilots.

'When the enemy approached your briefed "shot criteria" it was time to let the AMRAAMs go. The third section. The call of "Fox 3" would be followed by a crank, a manoeuvre whereby you turned away from the enemy by 60 degrees, stopping you from getting too close. The BV had 70 degree gimbals, probably the best in the world at the time, so you would still be able to keep data link going to the missile in the crank. The crank also allowed you to get off the bandit's nose, so allowing you to flow-in aggressively if need be. Supporting the shot was critical and represented your fourth job. There were various cues in the head up display and on the radar screen to tell you how the missile was doing. Due to the frenetic nature of the air battle the crank would probably happen right on the boundary of the enemy weapon system's engagement zone, so was a maximum performance turn, using height to keep speed on the jet. In the crank you were waiting for the magical moment, peculiar to active weapon users, when the aircraft could let the weapon go on its own. Once the weapon went terminal you could

matched in the vertical. This had to be done in cloud or at night, sometimes both. The air battle was for those who could take all these contradictory requirements and continue to fight. If you were sure you had all "Red Air" accounted for you would meld and sort. Get both radars looking in the same place and decide who to shoot, so everyone got a weapon. This was standard, so could be done communications-out if necessary. In the event that the enemy wasn't helping, as was its wont, fighters would "float" or separate from lead but stay visual. If they needed more tactical freedom

Fleet Air Arm pilots enjoy a reputation for spirited flying, as exemplified by this specially-performed 'Top Gun' style formation by crews from No.801 NAS. (Photo: UK MoD Crown Copyright 2010)

ZH797 was one of a batch
of new-build Sea Harrier
FA2s delivered in
December 1995.
After retirement it was
assigned to the School
of Flight Deck Operations
at Culdrose.
(Photo: Andre Jans)

leave it. This is where you did one of three things, so essentially the fifth and final part of the intercept was this decision and your subsequent actions. If you had shot early enough you could turn in for another shot. If you had left it late you needed a max g abort, carving round in a sweeping turn, probably losing 10,000 ft doing it and running away bravely, waiting for SA that your weapon had worked. If command required a high risk mission then you would flow aggressively to the merge, into the within visual range game, firing as you went. It was technically possible to have four AMRAAMs in the air at once – the kit was capable of supporting them – but to keep four jets in the radar scan and action geometry on four intercepts at once took considerable brain power. The "Fox 3 quad" only really happened against mud movers such as Tornado GR1/4 crews who were unaware of us due to the low power of Beyond Visual; still they were sweet moments when they did happen. Four kills in one or two seconds.

'Following your intercept you might have to go and "de-louse" another fighter whose day hadn't gone quite so well and was now defensive, or flow into a fur ball of multiple fighters engaged in "one v one" visual combat. High workload moments with their own fair share of raised voices and pulses. Following a successful job then the trick of getting the formation back on CAP and in good order was a skill in itself. We would call out our positions in order to gain SA on each other. We would then attempt to join up en route to the CAP, where anyone unfortunate enough to have died in the fight would be waiting. There we would stay until relieved by the next section and then it was home James, now probably in very soggy goon bags having worked hard and sweated in suitable measure. The amusing thing, of course, was the oft trotted out truism that this is where the work really started. Most jets behave once the fight is over; the Sea Harrier didn't. The Harrier Two was very benign in the circuit and VSTOL regime, but not the earlier first-generation aircraft. One couldn't afford to be complacent in VSTOL, equally one couldn't get either rusty or scared of a particular manoeuvre. The jet was nimble even with the nozzles down. We would, in good weather, break into the circuit and then begin individual exercises, checking downwind what our fluid weight was, and therefore what the jet could and couldn't manage. Nozzle selection was fast and aircraft response brutal. The hard and fast rule was to stay out of the triangle of death, 30-120 knots, high alpha, sideslip. Do those three and the jet would roll over, probably too quickly to eject from. The circuit work demanded low fuel states to give an adequate thrust margin and we used to routinely fly without a diversion. Harrier ops are not for those that like looking at full fuel gauges. In the visual circuit the juggle commenced again with left hand controlling nozzle and throttle. At 100 knots you checked your engine to see if you had enough thrust, you then committed to the landing. Arriving in the hover you scanned the radar altimeter and markers laid out on the ground. Nose into wind and then power off to descend. Power back on to catch the rate of descent, then chop the throttle immediately on landing; failure to do so resulted in a "power bounce', very exciting. Obviously, if the petrol and thrust allowed it you could throw in a bow or pedal turn for practice. We also needed practice at the high speed landings, either with nozzles fully aft, using alpha to get the speed below the limit for the tyres – my least favourite event – or keeping the engine at a fixed power to simulate an emergency, using the nozzles as a throttle to bring back a "lame duck." After you were complete you would taxi back, canopy open and look forward to a brutally frank debrief that could last for hours, with everyone's HUD and radar tapes dissected in public. Life on the FA2 was happy. Single-seat air defence in the south west of England, or roving out into the North Sea with tanker support. Travelling the world as a very small unit of eight pilots, a true band of brothers. Flying a nimble aeroplane with great radar and big stick. Happy days indeed.

'The attractions of operating any aeroplane from the deck are obvious. The challenges faced by a carrier pilot are alien to any other aviator. The ship moves. It moves when you are taking off or landing, it moves when you're not there. The motor skills required to get back on board far outstrip those required to land at a static aerodrome. The art of finding the damned thing and the team work and fuel management involved can be very hard indeed. The vagaries of oceanic weather and the CVS' uncanny knack of finding the bad stuff all added a fairly exclusive feel to the club of being a naval aviator. Embarkation invariably started for us with a short trip through the Lulworth-Bournemouth gap and a joining up with "Mum" – in this case the carrier – somewhere near the Isle Of Wight. If we were lucky we would pass over the rotary types as they made their way up from Cornwall; there was always a romantic air to the Tailored Air Group re-forming and going back to sea. By this stage we would have worked hard, become au fait with the ramp at Yeovilton, done lots of hovering, even operated as per the deck with embarked procedures and timings. But this wasn't the same as actually finding Mum and landing on.

'It all started simply enough with Mum giving you an offset from a known location to find her. This wasn't fail safe as you had to be talking about the same location – and occasionally mistakes were made. You punched this data into your kit and then got Blue Vixen to look at the sea. This could be done simply by looking at a range and bearing, or by using the radar update software which centred the radar on your chosen lat/long. You improved your chances by bringing the scanner down a touch with the rocker switch on the throttle to ensure

your radar cover was hitting the sea in front of the carrier; the radar had an air-to-ground mode with sea and map modes. I don't remember ever using the map mode. Your "Charlie" time – the time you landed on – would be fixed, and woe betide anyone who missed it by too great a margin. Working back from there you would know at any given time how much fuel you needed to make Charlie with the correct load. Too much and you couldn't hover; too little and, well, the engine stopped. On every flight you would carry a lamb ladder, the calculation of the petrol required at all times through the sortie. If you reached this amount of fuel you simply set a fuel flow of 70 lb per minute and would have the correct amount alongside the boat. Sounds simple, but you try climbing or doing anything useful at 70 lb per minute. For some sorties, with a high but predictable fuel burn, you would know roughly when you would hit lamb; for others it came as a nasty surprise mid-combat.

'So you would leave your task at the correct time to get back with the correct fuel. If you had fuel to spare and performance required it, then you were compelled to jettison it into the sea. Overland we were limited to a minimum of 5,000 ft to dump petrol; over the sea you could pretty much do what you wanted. The FA2 could only dump to 2,200 lb, which was probably above hover weight, so you might be in the situation whereby you would have to dump to make hover fuel by Charlie time well before you saw the ship. A bit nerve-wracking, but something you got used to. Recovery would largely be one of two methods. Technically there were three, but case one and three made sense; case two was an unsatisfactory halfway house which I never trusted. Case one was a visual recovery to Mum at 1,000 or 1,500 ft; case three was an instrument recovery starting at 15 miles and ending 0.6nm behind the ship at 200 ft. Case two, the daft approach, was a 600 ft approach controlled by the ship. In my opinion, you were either big and bad enough to get in unaided (case one) or you weren't (case three); going for case two could end in tears – still in cloud over the ship, wishing you'd gone for case three but with no petrol left. So case one, screaming into the overhead, fuel flowing from the jettisons, getting into the "waits" at 1,000 ft for the low wait, 1500 ft for the high wait. Once there you would set 70 lb per minute and fly two and a half minute race tracks overhead Mum, orientated on the DFC. The ship didn't have to be on the DFC until two and a half minutes to go until Charlie, so sometimes the visuals were confusing until the wait and ship aligned. If you had too much petrol you could use airbrake or nozzle to increase your fuel flow. With someone on your wing you couldn't simply speed up to burn fuel off – he'd probably got it right in the first place and really didn't need you messing it up for him!

'The real trick to boat ops was looking good, being in an eye-pleasing formation on time. The waits were two and a half minutes long. You

An unusual underside view of a Sea Harrier FA2 as the aircraft climbs into a loop. In addition to ADEN cannon and external fuel tanks, two AIM-120 missiles are carried on the outer wing pylons. The engine is working hard with all of the auxiliary intake doors open. (Photo: UK MoD Crown Copyright 2010)

To mark the end of Sea Harrier operations No.800 NAS applied striking unit markings to one of its aircraft, shortly before it was withdrawn from service at Yeovilton.
(Photo: UK MoD Crown Copyright 2010)

took seconds off or added them to ensure you got it exactly right at the "slot", your pre-allotted time to break over Mum to make Charlie. With two and a half minutes to go you would slot, 360kts at 600 ft on the starboard side of the boat. Everyone should be able to get a slot within 10 seconds of the required time; there were always raised eyebrows from the skipper if you didn't. Lead would break ten seconds after passing the ship; dash two would break fifteen seconds later. The second pair would have offset on the other side of the wait, so would be following about 75 seconds behind. Here was where the fun began. Break to downwind using airbrake and nozzle to get the speed off, immediately followed by downwind checks, including a check to see if the water worked and that your reaction controls were working with nozzles down. Look out the left hand side of the jet, assess and correct your spacing on "Mum", begin your final turn depending on the wind –

slack wind you turned abeam the back of the ship; for stiff wind you needed to go abeam the back of the superstructure. Before you turned you needed 40 degrees nozzle. You then flew a level turn, head out to assess the turn and head in to get the alpha right. We flew alpha, that is the angle of attack, not air speed in the FA2. Halfway around the turn 60 nozzle started the speed coming back and the aircraft could descend a bit. By now you should be picking up the meatball on the superstructure as you rolled out of the turn pointing at Mum, with any luck intercepting the 200 ft, 0.6nm point that all landings featured. Looking to "fly the meatball" down to the deck. The ball is a white light between two bars of lights, the datums. If the ball is high on

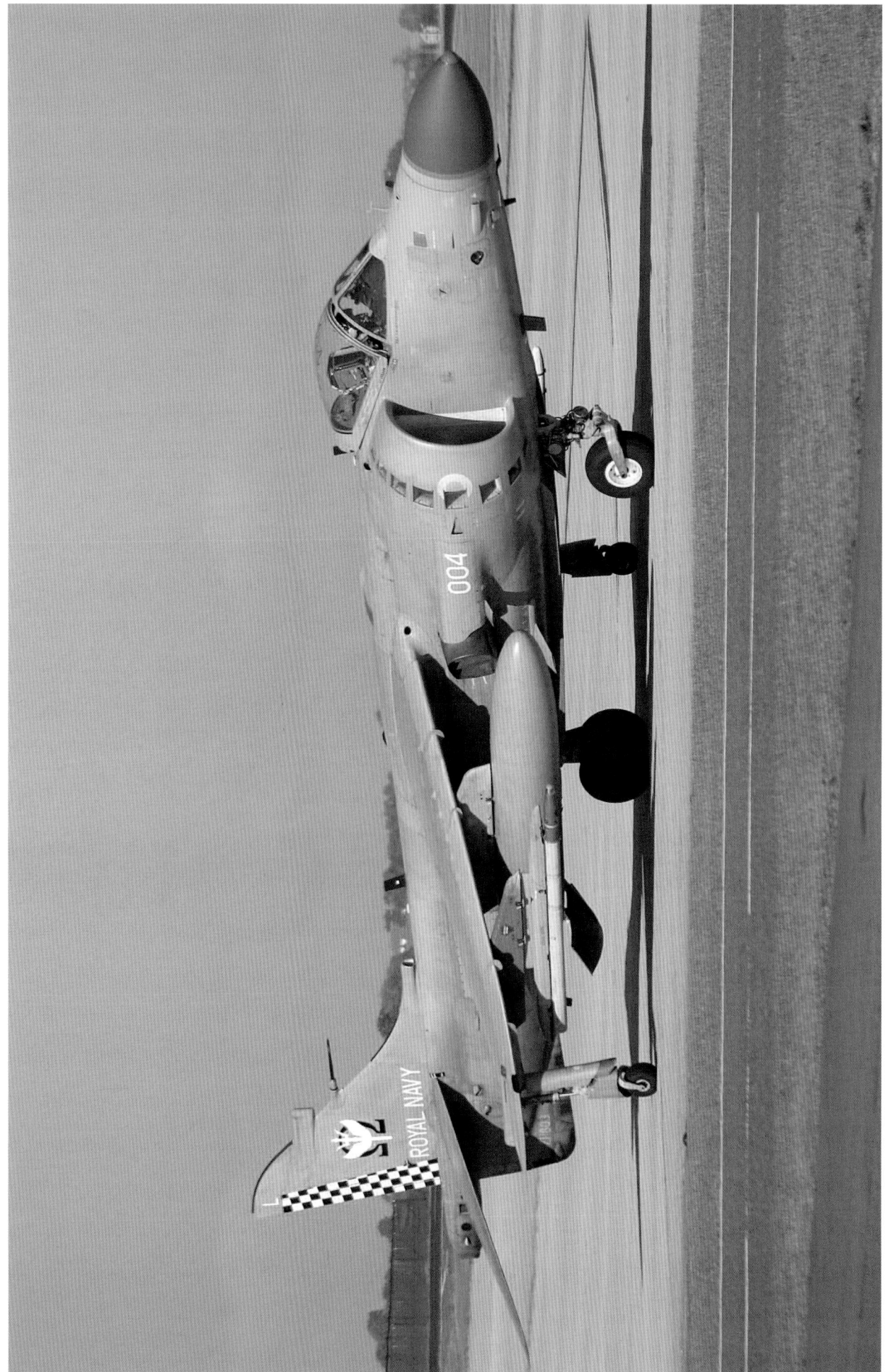

Pictured shortly before retirement, ZH803 wears the final version of No.801 Naval Air Squadron's markings. Visible is a Sidewinder 'acquisition' training round attached to the outer wing pylon.

(Photo: Rich Pittman)

the datums then you are high, if it is low then you are low. Flying the aircraft towards the boat you then took hover stop, 81 nozzle, to begin your final deceleration, still descending toward the bit of sea immediately to port of the boat. Now it was a game of juggling. Less power brought you down, more brought you up. If you needed more stopping power the nozzles needed to go to half or even full braking stop. Physically throwing exhaust forward to haul you to a stop. Full power in the braking stop got rid of speed as well as sending you up! By the round down everything would be under control, a nice stable pace as you came to the hover alongside the spot marked by a waving yellow coat, final few knots killed by half braking stop. Then you entered a simple scan, radar altimeter, height alongside the ship and forward and aft position. On a calm day you should hover at the same height as Flyco, so the horizon should go through Cdr (Air)'s head. On a bouncy day this was obviously impossible. The scan was simple, the motor skills very tricky. From the stable hover a steady transition over the deck to another stable hover. Pause… two…three… and down, a nice firm landing. Quickly through the after landing stuff and off the hot spot. All very simple when the ship is still, very hard to do when she's dancing away and your hands and feet try to follow her, no matter that your grey matter is telling you not to.

'Case three was the same in the final stages but was an instrument recovery from the "cake stand", our holding pattern offset 175 degrees from the ship's head at 15nm, everyone getting their own 1,000 ft level to marshal at. We flew in four minute circles until it was our time to push. We could let the ship arrange this or we could sort it out ourselves. We had the radar to keep up with the ship, or a microwave "ILS" called MADGE, or could simply put an inertial waypoint with a course and speed into the kit. Leav-

ing the cake stand we would descend to 1,000 ft and then either accept a talk-down or let the kit talk us down, a small letter in the HUD telling us whether it was R, the radar or M, the Madge, that was in charge. The HUD gave you steering to Mum and a height to be at. At 200 ft you would level out and peer ahead for the ship. The ship should be marked in the HUD by a cross, so finding it, even in poor weather, was hard but possible. All these techniques worked at night, which was strictly case three only. The difficulty came from the amount of information your brain gets from your peripheral vision. Going up, coming down, rate of descent, rate of closure are all things you calculate subconsciously. None of this is available at night. The techniques, therefore, are rigid scans aimed at offsetting this massive loss of SA. Night-flying a relatively unstable, single-seat fighter, below diversion fuel, with no EO aids was challenging; very challenging. This is why we approached night flying with all the respect we could muster, and also why we felt justifiably proud when we qualified to fly from the deck at night. You landed from most night deck landings absolutely wrung out. A hard tactical sortie followed by a night deck landing was definitely worth a CSB or two. Getting off the deck was simply a joy. The jets are so closely parked that you are right next to the guys in your formation. Everything is tightly controlled so times for starting and checking the engines are followed to the second. Jets are taxied within inches of each other and are shaken by each other's jet blast. When the jet in front slams to full power you are shaken and buffeted, sometimes the whole deck disappearing in the spray. The launch is simple. You are marshalled to the centre line. You are lined up above your minimum deck run, the distance your jet needs to get to flying speed, and below the maximum – the deck run that would see a heavy aircraft hit the ramp and fatally compress the nose wheel oleo. When every-

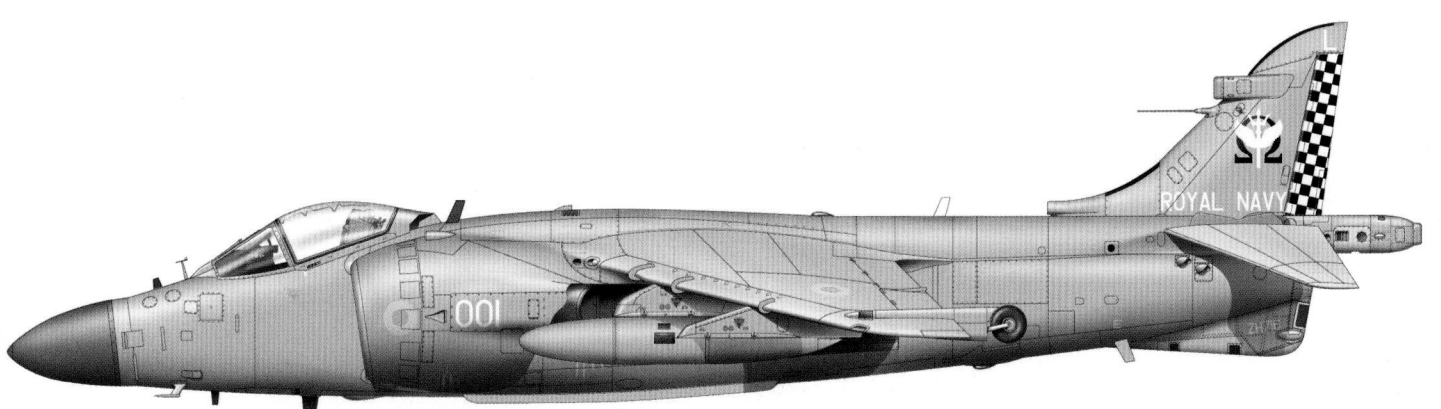

Sea Harrier FA.2, ZH761/001/L, No. 801 Naval Air Squadron, HMS Illustrious, Malta, November 2005
Medium Sea Grey overall with Dark Sea Grey radome; Pink/Pale Blue roundels on air intake fairings, above port and below starboard wings. All lettering in white; black/white check on rudder. Unit marking in black and white on fin; no pilot's name on either side of cockpit

A magnificent in-flight image of 899 Naval Air Squadron's ZH800 turning onto final approach at Yeovilton at the end of a training sortie. The bolt-on refuelling probe became a semi-permanent fit towards the end of the Sea Harrier's career. (Photo: Rich Pittman)

ZE690 leaps into the air from Yeovilton's ski jump. As a training unit, No.899 Naval Air Squadron's aircraft were normally land based at Yeovilton although occasional deployments to carriers were made, hence the tail code denoting HMS Illustrious. (Photo: Rich Pittman)

thing is ready in the cockpit you tell the world by switching on your nose wheel light. The Flyco team gives a "Green Deck Fixed Wing" on the traffic lights above you; the steady ones are for us, the flashing ones for the rotary types. Red means stop, amber means clear to taxi, green means "Wings" has said you can earn some flying pay. The Flight Deck Officer raises his green flag when he is content that all is ready. You sit at 55% and watch the bow. Up and down. As the bow goes down through the horizon you stand on the brakes and slam to full power. Engine RPM spools up incredibly quickly, matched by the engine guide vanes moving, and as you struggle to keep an eye on the gauges the jet begins to skid.

The brakes will never hold back the Pegasus, but you've given yourself the nanosecond you need to check the engine. Off brakes, aim at the ramp. Off the ramp, take nozzle. Guard the stick – don't fly the aircraft, the preset nozzle and trim will do that. Human input will simply mess things up. As the jet begins to fly you nozzle out steadily; too quick and your alpha will climb towards (or over) the limit. Once nozzled out you get the gear and flap up, roll silently to Homer, the ATC chap in the Ops room, wish him good morning and away you go. A simple, elegant, efficient and exciting way of getting a BVR fighter airborne.'

Looking particularly menacing with a pair of AIM-120 AMRAAMs under her wings, a Sea Harrier FA2 from No.801 NAS touches down vertically in a haze of exhaust heat at Yeovilton. (Photo: Rich Pittman)

Pilot's-eye view of flying Sea Harriers with No.800 NAS. (Photo: UK MoD Crown Copyright 2010)

Sea Harriers on the deck of HMS Illustrious armed with AIM-120B AMRAAMs. Up to four of these missiles could be carried by each aircraft, the weapon possessing a range in excess of 30 miles. (Photo: Mark Rourke)

Sea Harrier FA2 ZD579 lining-up for a short landing at Yeovilton, intake doors open and nozzles fully aft. (Photo: Rich Pittman)

Following their last-ever launches from the deck of HMS Illustrious late in 2005, the Sea Harriers of No.801 NAS performed a final low-level flypast prior to departure for Yeovilton. (Photo: UK MoD Crown Copyright 2010)

Celebrating 800 Naval Air Squadron's long association with the Sea Harrier, ZD613 seen resplendent in celebratory markings which even extend to the temporary under-fuselage strakes, fitted when the ADEN cannon pods were not carried. Not the 'R' tail code denoting HMS Ark Royal. (Photo: Rich Pittman)

No.899 Naval Air Squadron's gaggle of single-seat Harriers on the flight line at Yeovilton, basking in winter sunshine. (Photo: Rich Pittman)

A wintry scene at Yeovilton as a Sea Harrier FA2 carrying Sidewinder training rounds taxies for take-off amidst a snow shower. (Photo: Rich Pittman)

899 NAS celebrated the impending retirement of the Sea Harrier (and 5 years of operations on the type) by painting FA2 ZH809 in what was evidently meant to be a vague recreation of the Sea Harrier FRS1's delivery scheme. As can be seen, the result was striking, if not bizarre! (Photo: Tom Cheney)

ZH809 displaying typically flamboyant Naval sentiments shortly before the aircraft was withdrawn from service. (Photo: Tom Cheney)

Looking almost toy-like in her pre-retirement paint scheme, ZH809 heads for the runway in clean configuration, devoid of any external stores. (Photo: Rich Pittman)

Cdr Lawler trying his best to negotiate Yeovilton's taxiways in a heavy snow shower. This image illustrates the distinctly un-aerodynamic proportions of the Sea Harrier FA2's large and blunt nose cone, housing the Blue Vixen radar installation. (Photo: Rich Pittman)

The clear panel on the Sea Harrier FA2's nose denotes the position of the internal Vinten F.95 camera (with a 4in lens) which provided the aircraft with a medium-altitude oblique reconnaissance capability.
(Photo: Rich Pittman)

Taxying in front of Yeovilton's familiar control tower, the Sea Harrier's standard training fit of AIM-9L Sidewinder training rounds and 190 imp gal external tanks can be seen. ADEN gun pods were also carried as required.
(Photo: Rich Pittman)

Above and below: ZB603, a Harrier T.Mk.8 from No.899 NAS. The T8 remained similar to the first-generation Harrier T2 but featured a revised cockpit layout more representative of the FA2 with a new HUD and MFD screen and the FA2's Inertial Navigation System. The all-black paint scheme appears to have been adopted from what was a common standard for RAF trainer aircraft although – oddly – the national insignia was applied in low-visibility colours. (Photo top: Tom Cheney, Photo left: Rich Pittman)

A magnificent image of a Sea Harrier from No.801 NAS making a soggy short landing in miserable weather conditions at Yeovilton. (Photo: Rich Pittman)

CHAPTER SEVEN

Second Generation

REAR FUEL
TANK

AS is usually the case with any military aircraft procurement programme, while the Harrier's development programme was being completed, the search for a follow-on design was already underway. With Harriers starting their service lives on both sides of the Atlantic and both American and British manufacturers now committed to Harrier, it was inevitable that the future of the aircraft would be a multi-national one. The production and development agreement made between Hawker Siddeley and McDonnell Douglas (as part of the AV-8A programme described previously) and a similar arrangement between Rolls-Royce and Pratt & Whitney, included the potential for continued development of the design and in 1972 a joint US and UK Advanced Harrier programme was initiated. This was based largely around continued development of the original Pegasus engine which had been transformed into the 24,500 lb Pegasus 15. With a larger fan blade diameter and differing intake requirements, the engine could not be incorporated into existing Harrier derivatives and it was therefore only applicable to a significantly redesigned aircraft which would become a 'second-generation' Harrier design. On 12 April 1973, a project definition phase was approved, leading to a document which was issued in December detailing the proposed design requirements. For the United States, this would form the basis of an aircraft with which ultimately to replace the existing fleet of AV-8As when they reached the end of their useful lives, and also to replace the A-4 Skyhawk (the US

Navy's High Performance Attack Aircraft System). For Britain, the new aircraft would replace the RAF's Harrier GR1/3 derivatives and possibly provide the Royal Navy with an aircraft suitable for operation on its new through-deck cruisers (this project having first emerged before Sea Harrier). The result was the AV-16 although – rather confusingly – it was first designated as the AV-8C, and the AV-8B was to have been the dual-control variant. But the AV-8C designation was eventually re-applied to modified first-generation A models. At Kingston, some very basic studies were already being made for an aircraft which could take advantage of the Pegasus 15 and these were mostly created under one project designation – the HS.1184. However, at this time the Air Staff were not particularly interested in these developments, as the more conventional, but potentially even more versatile, Jaguar was now about to enter service and there did not seem to be any obvious need for a more advanced Harrier, which would in effect be a very similar aircraft to the Jaguar but with a STOVL capability. The Air Staff evidently believed that for the close air support mission the existing Harrier fleet was perfectly adequate. The American designation (AV-16) clearly demonstrated McDonnell Douglas' intention to double Harrier's effectiveness in terms of range and payload capability and the proposed aircraft was undoubtedly a significant improvement over the first-generation aircraft. With a new fuselage, supercritical wing, PCB-burning engine, new avionics and more weapons stations, the new design

The proposed AV-16 which was subsequently abandoned. This drawing illustrates the supersonic AV-16-S6 which was to have featured a much-modified Pegasus engine with Plenum Chamber Burning. Without British support McDonnell Douglas was unwilling to pursue the programme alone.
(courtesy BAE systems)

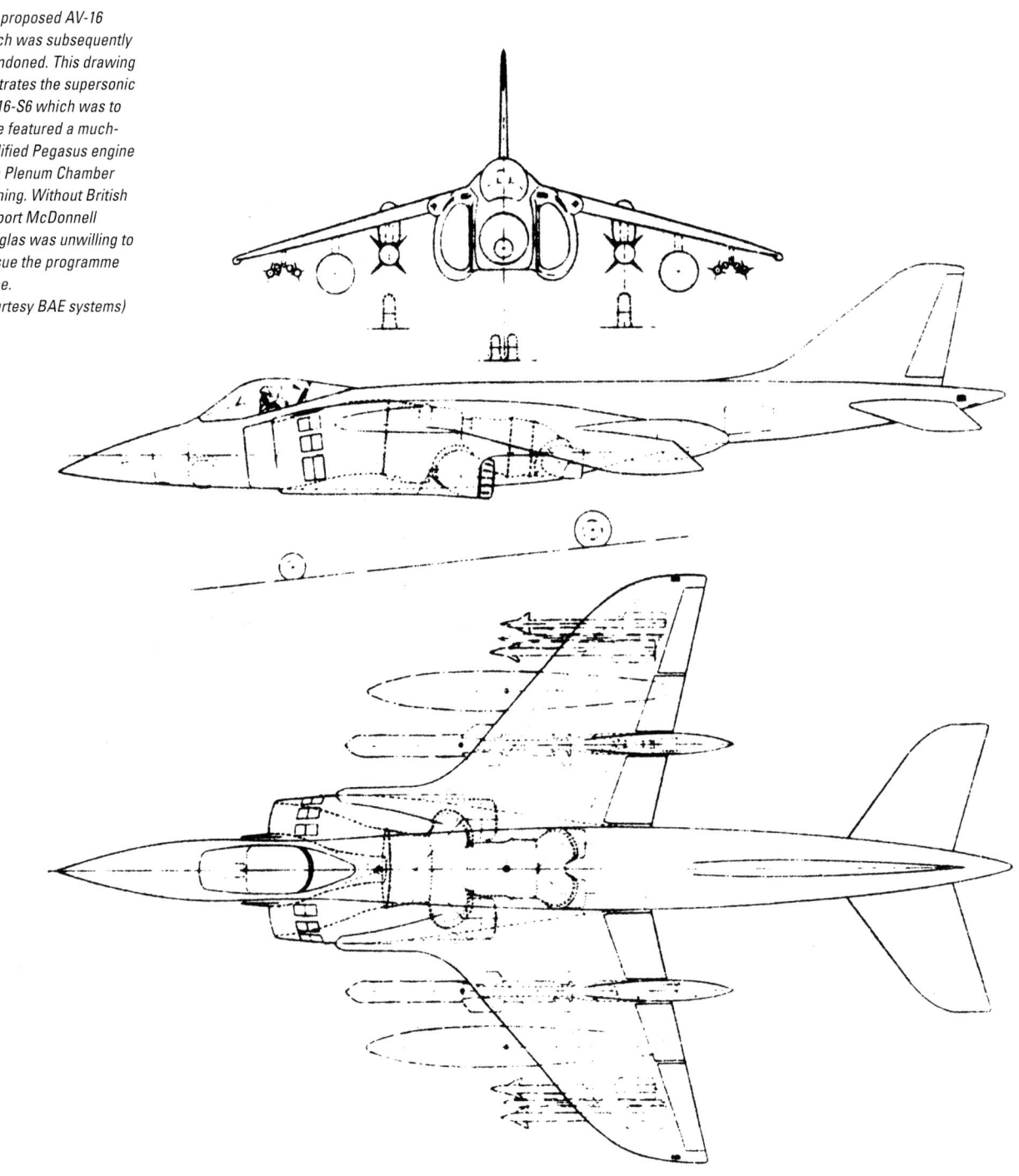

began to look remarkably like the abandoned P.1154 from many years previously and in just the same way as that aircraft had been dumped, the British Government eventually decided to abandon its interest in the AV-16 by 1975. The reason for the pull-out was a combination of two factors, the first being that, as described, the Air Staff was not particularly keen to pursue it (its attention having been drawn towards the Jaguar and – eventually – the MRCA, which became Tornado); the other key factor, naturally, was the projected cost which was

deemed to be far too high since AV-16 was, in effect, a new aircraft rather than merely a sequential development of the original Harrier. Without Britain's participation, ultimately America was also forced to accept that with an estimated cost of more than $2 billion, it could not afford to 'go it alone' and it too reluctantly abandoned AV-16. In fact by this stage the ending of the project was not regarded as a major loss by either country. The USMC was not too saddened by the project's demise as it was also beginning to believe (rather

like the RAF) that the projected aircraft was going to be far more advanced, complex and expensive than the basic 'mud mover' that it required. For the time being at least, the Harrier's development appeared to have stagnated.

With the prospect of a 'new' Harrier looking unlikely, Hawker Siddeley continued examining rather less ambitious ways in which the existing Harrier could be improved. It was clear that one of the aircraft's main deficiencies was its relatively poor ability to defend itself, and that a larger (and redesigned) wing would provide more lift and thereby improve the aircraft's capabilities. A larger wing would also enable more weapons hard points to be installed and would create additional volume for fuel capacity. By 1977 Kingston had received a feasibility study contract for what was known as the Big Wing – which would be designed to be retrofitted to existing Harrier GR3 and T4 aircraft. With a new supercritical design, three weapons points per side, leading edge wing root extensions and new slotted flaps, the new wing would be

combined with a new forward fuselage which repositioned the cockpit higher on the fuselage (in Sea Harrier fashion). Additionally, improvements were made to the exhaust flow pressure recovery achievable under the fuselage, by fitting larger strakes (or gun pods) and a retractable cross dam device which served to create lift from the mutual cross flow of the four nozzle exhausts, reflected back from the ground. As the Harrier GR.Mk.5, this reworked aircraft would be able to carry 1,500 lb more fuel or stores than the GR3, or 3,000 lb from a 1,000 ft STO ground run. Manoeuvrability (particularly turning ability) was also improved. However, while Hawker Siddeley was investigating its Big Wing's potential, other developments were taking place in the USA where McDonnell Douglas was also pursuing the possibility of improving the performance of the existing Harrier, rather than creating an entirely new one from scratch. Mindful of Kingston's activities, the American design team accepted that a new wing design was the key to creating a far

AV-8C and AV-8B together, illustrating the second-generation Harrier's much larger wing area, as seen on the YAV-8B prototype in the foreground. (Photo: McDonnell Douglas)

YAV-8C 158384 was originally one of the Harrier Mk.50 fleet built by Hawker. After operating on trials work with McDonnell Douglas, the aircraft crashed on 5 September 1980 on take-off from the USS Tarawa. (Photo: McDonnell Douglas)

YAV-8B 158394 pictured at the moment of take-off during ramp trials at NAS Patuxent River. Unlike production AV-8B aircraft, the prototype retained the AV-8A/C fuselage, with a lower cockpit and canopy. (Photo: McDonnell Douglas)

more capable aircraft. Likewise, it concluded that an improved engine combined with a completely new intake design (with two rows of pressure recovery inlet doors) would enable the thrust of the Pegasus 103 to be increased by more than 500 lb. McDonnell Douglas also embraced Kingston's lift improvement devices for the lower fuselage and the result was the AV-8B, a direct development of the first-generation Harrier which greatly improved capability. Of course it was not drastically different from the Harrier GR5 being proposed by HAS at Kingston, and Britain was therefore left with a stark choice between continuing to develop the Big Wing GR5, buying the American-designed AV-8B, or effectively doing nothing at all and simply updating the existing Harrier fleet more modestly. The prospect of adopting the AV-8B was, initially, less than popular, not least because it looked as though Britain was re-importing its own technology, and of course the aircraft was already being developed for American requirements,

without any design changes which might make the aircraft more suitable for RAF operations. On the other hand, the GR5 project was undoubtedly less ambitious, but significantly more expensive, whereas America would pay most of the bill for creating the AV-8B (and purchasing aircraft from a large production run would obviously be relatively inexpensive). Eventually it was agreed that an all-British programme was unnecessarily expensive and that the GR5 would be dropped. A Memorandum of Understanding was signed in August 1981 to purchase the AV-8B, incorporating some small modifications such as additional pylons for Sidewinder missiles catered to RAF requirements. This, rather than the Kingston design, would then become the Harrier GR.Mk.5. The AV-8B agreement divided the manufacturing of the aircraft between the US and the UK with McDonnell Douglas responsible for 60 per cent of the airframe (in terms of man hours), while British Aerospace (the successors of Hawker Siddeley) would be

The second FSD (Full Scale Development) AV-8B airframe 161397. Visible is the LERX (Leading Edge Root Extension) which was introduced in response to the RAF's requirement for better manoeuvrability. (Photo: McDonnell Douglas)

The first FSD (Full Scale Development) AV-8B airframe, 161396, positioned in front of McDonnell Douglas' factory shortly after roll-out. Worthy of note is the early intake configuration with a double row of auxiliary intake doors, and the instrumentation boom attached to the nose. (Photo: McDonnell Douglas)

The AV-8B FSD airframe was subjected to rigorous spinning tests. As a safety measure, an anti-spin parachute was fitted temporarily in a deployable pack, fixed to the aircraft's tail boom. (Photo: Mick Roth collection)

responsible for the remaining 40 per cent, particularly the rear fuselage, tail planes and the rudder assembly. Each nation would then complete assembly of its own aircraft, combining the components from each company, and incorporating the avionics and other modifications peculiar to each variant. A similar arrangement was established between Rolls-Royce and Pratt & Whitney with Rolls-Royce responsible for 75 per cent of the engine manufacture and all of the final assembly.

The first six completed rear fuselage sections were duly supplied by BAe to the US and these were incorporated into the first four Full Scale Development (FSD) airframes (161396 to 161399), together with a pair of non-flying test specimens.

Although retaining most of the original Harrier's general configuration, the AV-8B was (despite the lessons of AV-16) very much a new design, built around a new 28 ft wing which was at that time the largest structure to have been manufactured from carbon fibre composite materials. Some 300 lb lighter than the equivalent metal structure, it was also a staggering 400 per cent stronger. Incorporated into the wing were new single-slot flaps which circulated some of the engine exhaust flow when lowered, adding 7,600 lb of lift during STO. Added to this were the additional lift created by the new under-fuselage modifications and more improvements to overall manoeuvrability created by wing Leading Edge Root Extensions (LERX), which were eventually incorporated largely in response to RAF demands for better manoeuvrability. The larger wing enabled six weapons pylons to be fitted and the greater span enabled the RCV nozzles to be positioned further outboard, thereby improving lateral control without compromising engine bleed thrust. The forward fuselage was redesigned along similar lines to the Sea Harrier with a new raised cockpit, combined with a larger, bubbled, canopy which greatly improved all-round vision. Oddly, the outrigger wheels were moved slightly inboard and although this might have been seen as a retrograde step in terms of ground stability, it would enable the aircraft to operate successfully from smaller single-track roads when necessary. In essence, McDonnell Douglas had created a brilliant compromise design which provided many of the improvements of the abortive AV-16 whilst still utilising the original Harrier configuration. Formal US approval for the aircraft was issued on 27 July 1976 and the 'Harrier II' was born. While a redundant AV-8A (158385) was rebuilt to AV-8B aerodynamic standards for wind tunnel tests at NASA's Ames Research Center, two complete prototypes were manufactured from AV-8As (158394 and 158395), although they were only partially rebuilt, retaining the AV-8A's original nose section and shorter fuselage. They were, however, fitted with the new YF402-RR-404 engines and new redesigned 'zero-scarf' nozzles which fully enclosed the engine exhaust and prevented any of the engine thrust from splaying outwards, thereby increasing the engine's lift properties. The first of the prototypes took to the air on 19 February 1979 but its initial flight-testing programme was cut short when an engine flame-out resulted in the aircraft being lost on 15 November (the pilot ejected to safety). The prototypes proved the validity of the AV-8B design although to some extent the design teams were disappointed by the aircraft's slightly inferior speed performance, created by greater drag. Despite various attempts to improve this deficiency the USMC expressed satisfaction with the aircraft's overall performance and, with much better range, manoeuvrability and payload capability, it was accepted that a slight reduction in top speed was an acceptable compromise (flat-out speed was never a priority for the USMC). The first of the FSD aircraft achieved its inaugural flight on 5 November 1981 (flown by Charles A. Plummer) and the second and third aircraft followed on 7 and 10 April of the following year, the fourth aircraft making its maiden flight on 4 June 1983. The first two aircraft were fitted with instrumentation nose booms while the second pair received wing LERX modifications, this being a '70 per cent LERX' as opposed to a '100 per cent' derivative which appeared later. The last of the four FSD machines was completed to a more definitive standard and assigned to weapons release testing, including the new 25 mm cannon which had been created for

the AV-8B. The earlier ADEN 30 mm cannon had already proved to be very effective and reliable but as a British design, supply of components and ammunition had always been a headache. The new cannon comprised a GAU-12/U weapon housed in the left-hand gun pod, while the right-hand pod was used to house the ammunition, a 'bridge' across the lower fuselage to feed the gun being part of the design. With a firing rate of 3,600 rounds per minute it was similar to cannon fitted to USMC armoured vehicles, and this enabled a degree of commonality to be introduced. The same Hughes ASB-19(V)-2 Angle Rate Bombing System (ARBS) used in the A-4 Skyhawk was incorporated into the new design, linked to a mission computer (AYK-14) and a Head-Up Display. This system was designed to use collimated TV and laser spot-trackers located in the aircraft's nose to give the pilot a magnified (up to 6x) view on the pilot's display inside the cockpit, where the instrument layout was a generational leap from the earlier Harrier. Instead of a jumble of analogue instrumentation (little different from the equipment fitted to the aged Hawker Hunter), the new aircraft had multi-function display screens and a HOTAS (Hands On Throttle and Stick) system very similar to that fitted to the Marine's Hornets.

A three-axis Sperry Stability Augmentation and Attitude Hold System (SAAHS) was also fitted, giving the pilot a much easier workload when operating the aircraft in the hover and whilst transitioning to and from wing-borne flight. This system could be used to conduct a completely 'hands-off' vertical landing if necessary. This was ably demonstrated in February 1983 when test pilot, Bill Lowe, performed such a manoeuvre. Although not applicable to routine flying, it did demonstrate just how much automation was available to the pilot and how the challenging task of handling the Harrier had been significantly improved. The first production AV-8B (161573) made its first flight on 29 August 1983. Although design had been continually refined up until the completion of the first production machine, the aircraft had, in fact, changed little since the beginning of the design process. The only obvious external alteration was the deletion of the new twin set of blow-in doors, following another redesign of the ever-challenging inlet area. With the internal ducting re-contoured again, the design reverted to the more traditional single row of doors, similar to those found on first-generation Harriers. Production of dual-control derivatives of the AV-8B seemed certain but initially the USMC was reluctant to order any aircraft, believing that conversion training on to the new Harrier could be completed on the original TAV-8A airframes, the basic handling of the aircraft being virtually identical in most respects. However, the all-new cockpit with digital instrumentation was completely different to that found in the existing twin-seaters and students were not able to make the

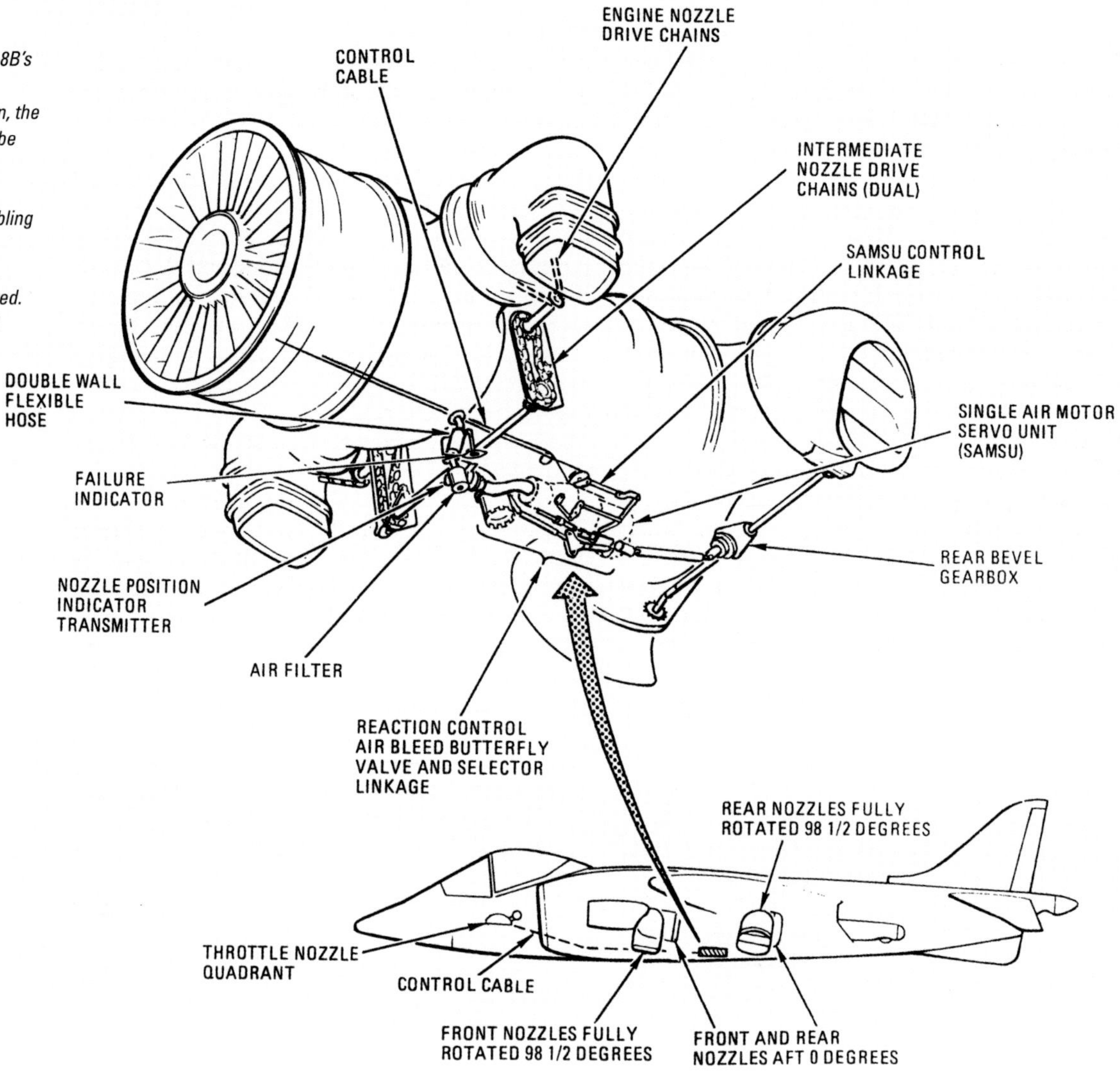

Illustration of the AV-8B's Pegasus engine installation. As shown, the exhaust nozzles can be rotated through 98.5 degrees, beyond the vertical, thereby enabling the aircraft to utilise engine thrust for deceleration if required. (courtesy McDonnell Douglas)

ENGINE NOZZLE DRIVE CHAINS

CONTROL CABLE

INTERMEDIATE NOZZLE DRIVE CHAINS (DUAL)

SAMSU CONTROL LINKAGE

SINGLE AIR MOTOR SERVO UNIT (SAMSU)

DOUBLE WALL FLEXIBLE HOSE

FAILURE INDICATOR

NOZZLE POSITION INDICATOR TRANSMITTER

AIR FILTER

REAR BEVEL GEARBOX

REACTION CONTROL AIR BLEED BUTTERFLY VALVE AND SELECTOR LINKAGE

REAR NOZZLES FULLY ROTATED 98 1/2 DEGREES

THROTTLE NOZZLE QUADRANT

CONTROL CABLE

FRONT NOZZLES FULLY ROTATED 98 1/2 DEGREES

FRONT AND REAR NOZZLES AFT 0 DEGREES

NOZZLES EXHAUST PATTERN

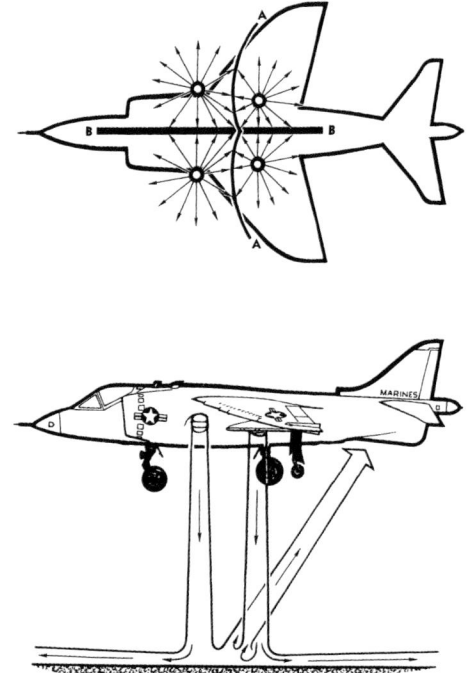

This simplified diagram from the AV-8A flight manual illustrates just one of many handling difficulties that Harrier pilots are presented with. As the aircraft hovers, the jet exhaust creates a varying about of lift as it reflects back to the aircraft from the ground. If the aircraft moves forward, the lift force moves aft, creating a nose-down pitch movement. (courtesy USMC)

transition on to the new aircraft without some difficulty. Therefore it was eventually decided that eight of the AV-8B aircraft on order would be cancelled, enabling funds to be shifted to the purchase of the TAV-8B. Some 28 aircraft were purchased, the first of these making its maiden flight on 21 October 1986. As with the creation of the Harrier T2, the TAV-8B is essentially a standard B-Model with a redesigned nose section, accommodating a second raised cockpit and a slightly larger fin area. The fuselage was also increased in length by some 3 ft 11 ins and this made an extended tail boom unnecessary. The only other significant alteration to the design was the deletion of stores points, and only two weapons pylons were fitted, these being used for training stores or external fuel tank (there was no intention to 'dual-role' the aircraft as an operationally-capable aircraft).

The first AV-8Bs entered USMC service in January 1985 when VMA-331 retired its A-4 Skyhawks. Meanwhile, across the Atlantic, Britain was also preparing to introduce its own version of this second-generation Harrier. It had been apparent during the 1970s that despite polite interest, the Air Staff was actually far more interested in adopting a completely new aircraft which could eventually replace both the Harrier and Jaguar, under its Air Staff Target 403 programme. When this AST was eventually abandoned in 1979 and a STOVL-specific replacement AST issued, it enabled BAe to pursue its 'Big Wing' Harrier GR5 design more vigorously, effectively revisiting much of the work which had been conducted on the abortive AV-16 design. It was proposed that 60 aircraft would be manufactured, while 40 existing Harriers would be modified to the same standard. The prospect of two remarkably similar aircraft being produced on each side of the Atlantic was one which seemed faintly ludicrous, but Britain had no enthusiasm for buying an American development of its own aircraft, while the US was seemingly content to 'go it alone' in order to meet the USMC's requirements. However, politics intervened yet again and in Washington there was a growing pressure for the AV-8B project

to be abandoned, unless its cost could be brought-down through the adoption of a foreign partner (in effect this meant Britain). When BAe looked at what was on offer, and realised that a part-share in the AV-8B would be more lucrative than pursuance of the entire indigenous GR5 programme, it was obvious that a joint UK and US programme made far more sense for both countries, and this led to the final abandonment of any British-designed second-generation Harrier. With an MoU signed between the aerospace companies and engine manufacturers in 1982, BAe had an agreement to provide 40 per cent of all AV-8B airframe manufacture and 50 per cent in the case of the RAF's Harrier GR5. The RAF ordered 60 aircraft, the first (ZD318) making its maiden flight at Dunsfold on 30 April 1985. Service deliveries began on 29 May 1987 when ZD325 arrived at RAF Wittering for engineering familiarisation. The OCU training courses shifted to the GR5 in July 1988 and No.1 Squadron became the first operational Harrier GR5 unit on 2 November 1989. Nos. 3 and 4 Squadrons then re-equipped

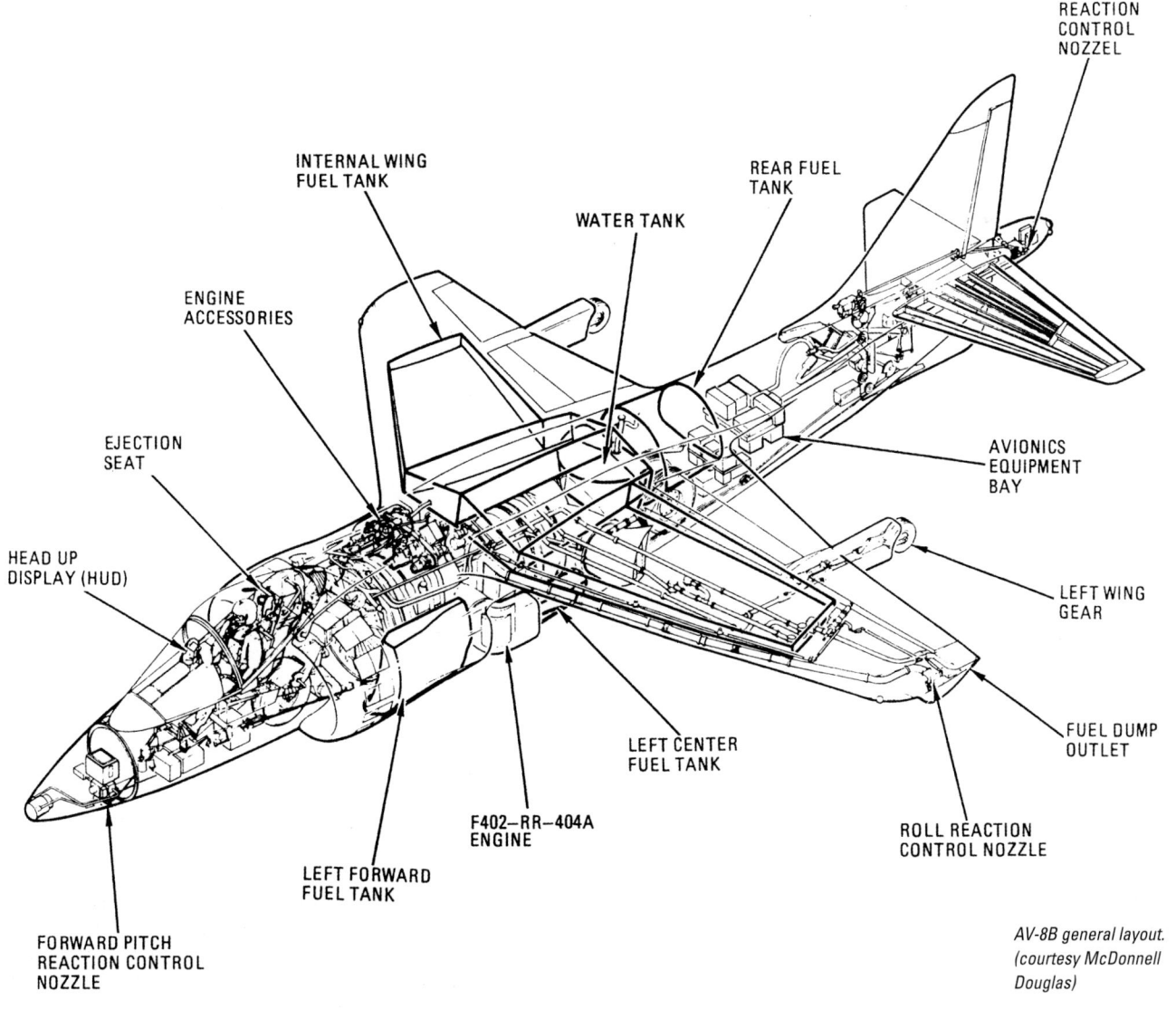

AV-8B general layout. (courtesy McDonnell Douglas)

Engine

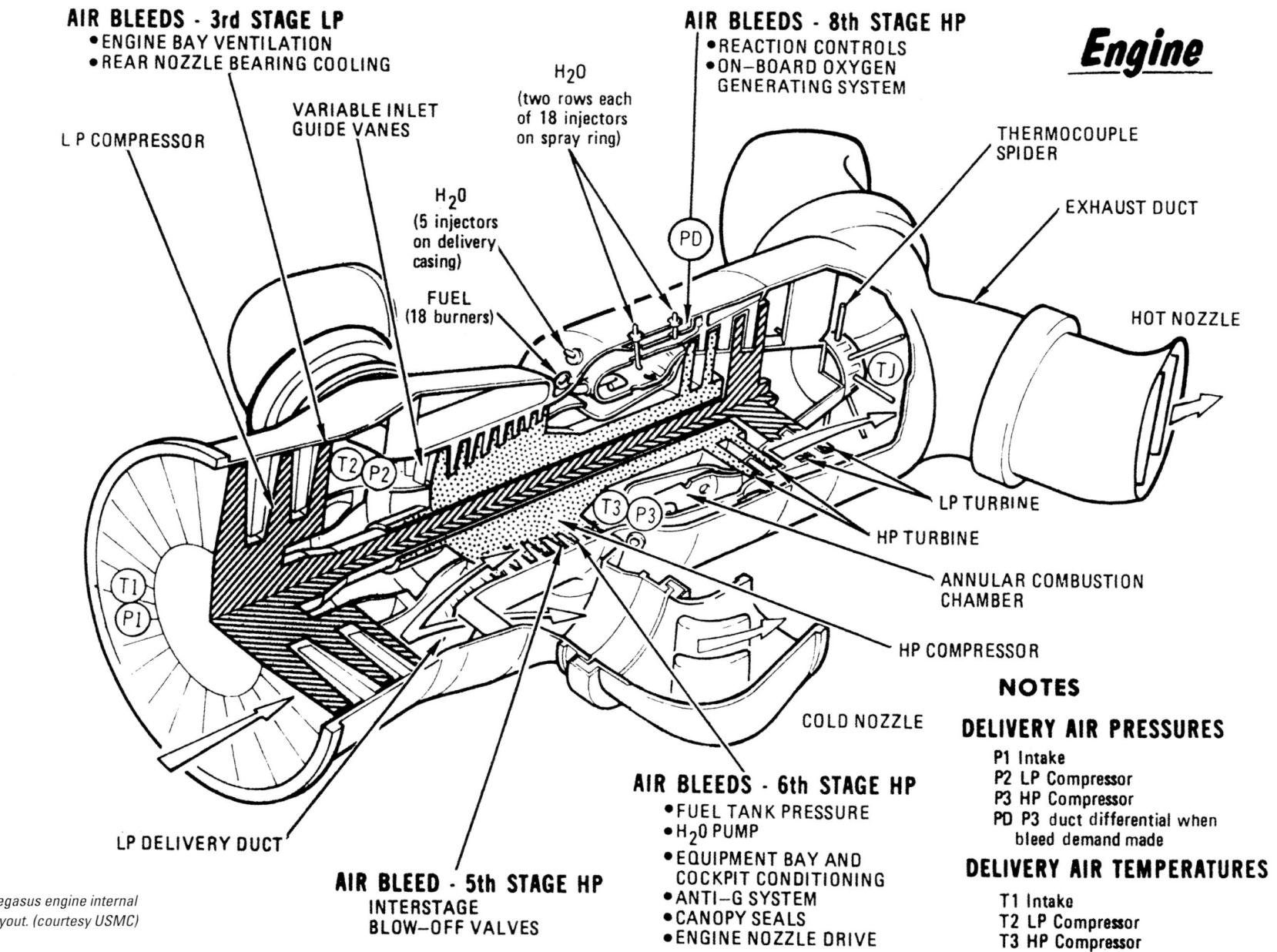

AIR BLEEDS - 3rd STAGE LP
- ENGINE BAY VENTILATION
- REAR NOZZLE BEARING COOLING

LP COMPRESSOR

VARIABLE INLET
GUIDE VANES

H_2O
(two rows each
of 18 injectors
on spray ring)

AIR BLEEDS - 8th STAGE HP
- REACTION CONTROLS
- ON—BOARD OXYGEN
  GENERATING SYSTEM

THERMOCOUPLE
SPIDER

EXHAUST DUCT

H_2O
(5 injectors
on delivery
casing)

FUEL
(18 burners)

HOT NOZZLE

PD

T2 P2

T1
P1

T3 P3

TJ

LP TURBINE

HP TURBINE

ANNULAR COMBUSTION
CHAMBER

HP COMPRESSOR

COLD NOZZLE

LP DELIVERY DUCT

AIR BLEED - 5th STAGE HP
INTERSTAGE
BLOW—OFF VALVES

AIR BLEEDS - 6th STAGE HP
- FUEL TANK PRESSURE
- H_2O PUMP
- EQUIPMENT BAY AND
  COCKPIT CONDITIONING
- ANTI—G SYSTEM
- CANOPY SEALS
- ENGINE NOZZLE DRIVE

NOTES

DELIVERY AIR PRESSURES

P1 Intake
P2 LP Compressor
P3 HP Compressor
PD P3 duct differential when
   bleed demand made

DELIVERY AIR TEMPERATURES

T1 Intake
T2 LP Compressor
T3 HP Compressor
TJ Exhaust duct

*Pegasus engine internal
layout. (courtesy USMC)*

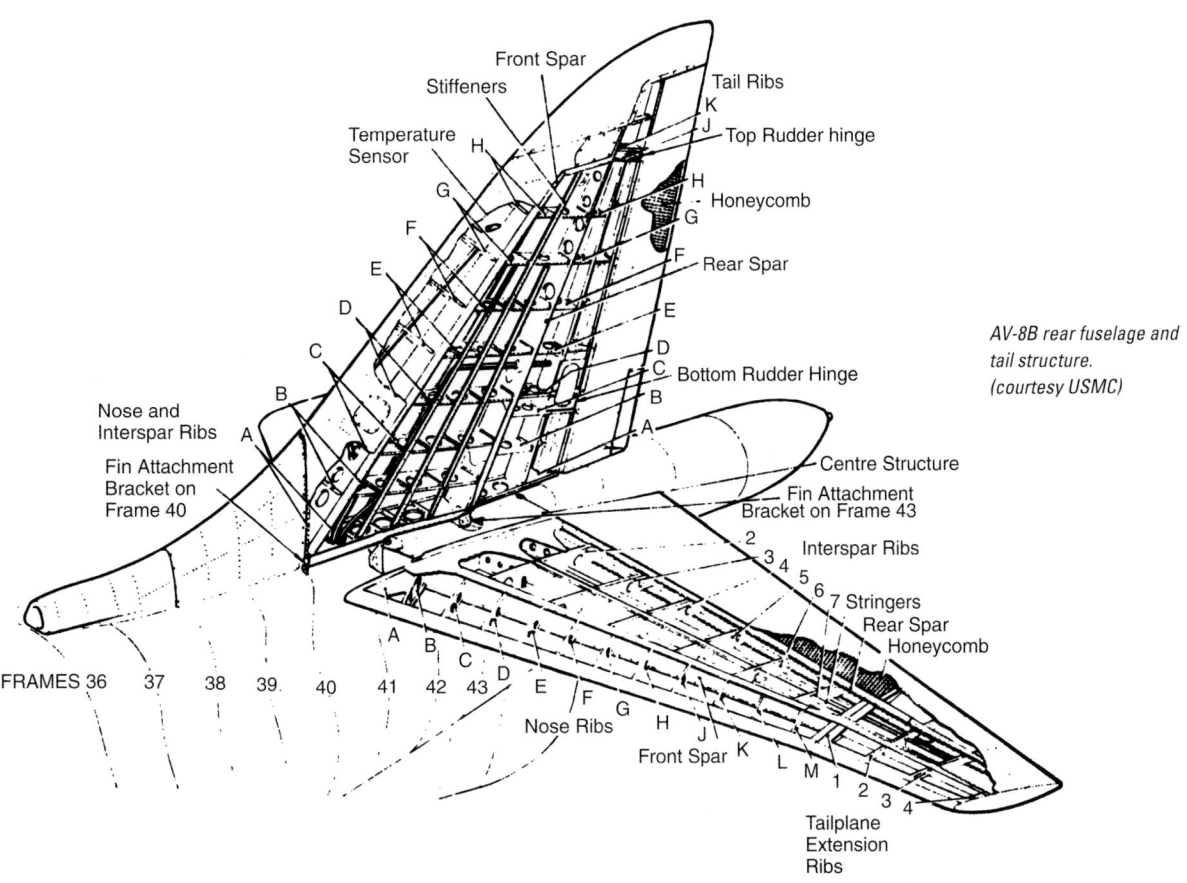

Front Spar
Stiffeners
Tail Ribs
Temperature Sensor
H
Top Rudder hinge
K
J
G
H
Honeycomb
F
G
E
F
Rear Spar
D
E
C
D
Bottom Rudder Hinge
B
C
A
B
A
Nose and Interspar Ribs
Centre Structure
Fin Attachment Bracket on Frame 40
Fin Attachment Bracket on Frame 43
2
3
Interspar Ribs
4
5
6
7 Stringers
Rear Spar
Honeycomb
FRAMES 36   37   38   39.   40   41   42   43
A
B
C
D
E
F
G
H
J
K
L
M
1
2
3
4
Nose Ribs
Front Spar
Tailplane Extension Ribs

AV-8B rear fuselage and tail structure. (courtesy USMC)

Ram Air Turbine (RAT) Housing

Ram Air Turbine (RAT) Mounting

Fin Fillet

Cooling Air Intake Duct

Fin Forward Attachment

Fin Rear Attachment

Tail Plane Pivot

Bullet Fairing

Air Brake Pivots

Frames 34 35 36 37 38

Accumulator and T.R.U. Mounting

Frames 39 40 41 42 43

Reaction Nozzle Apertures

Ventral Fin

Bumper Pad

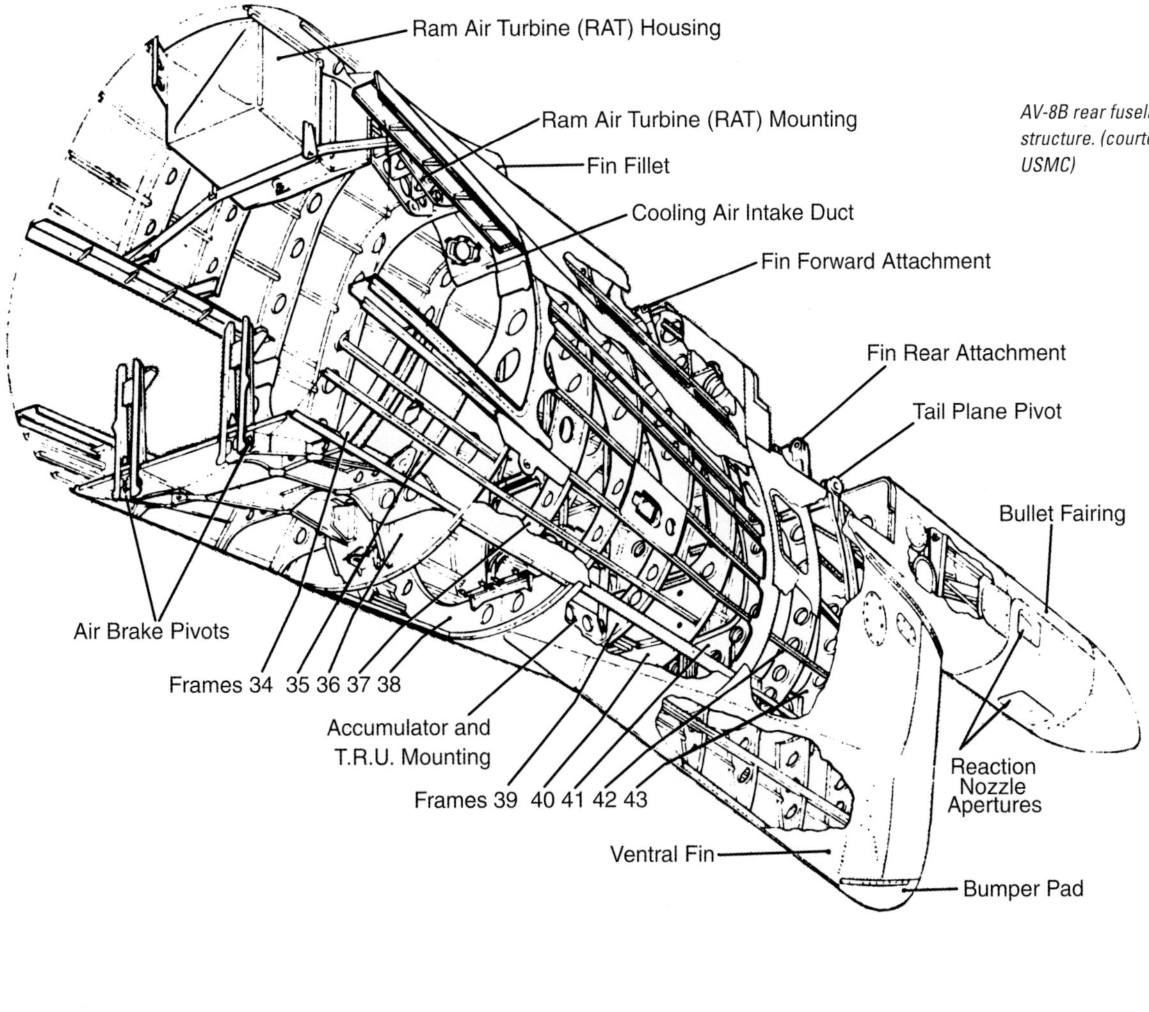

AV-8B rear fuselage structure. (courtesy USMC)

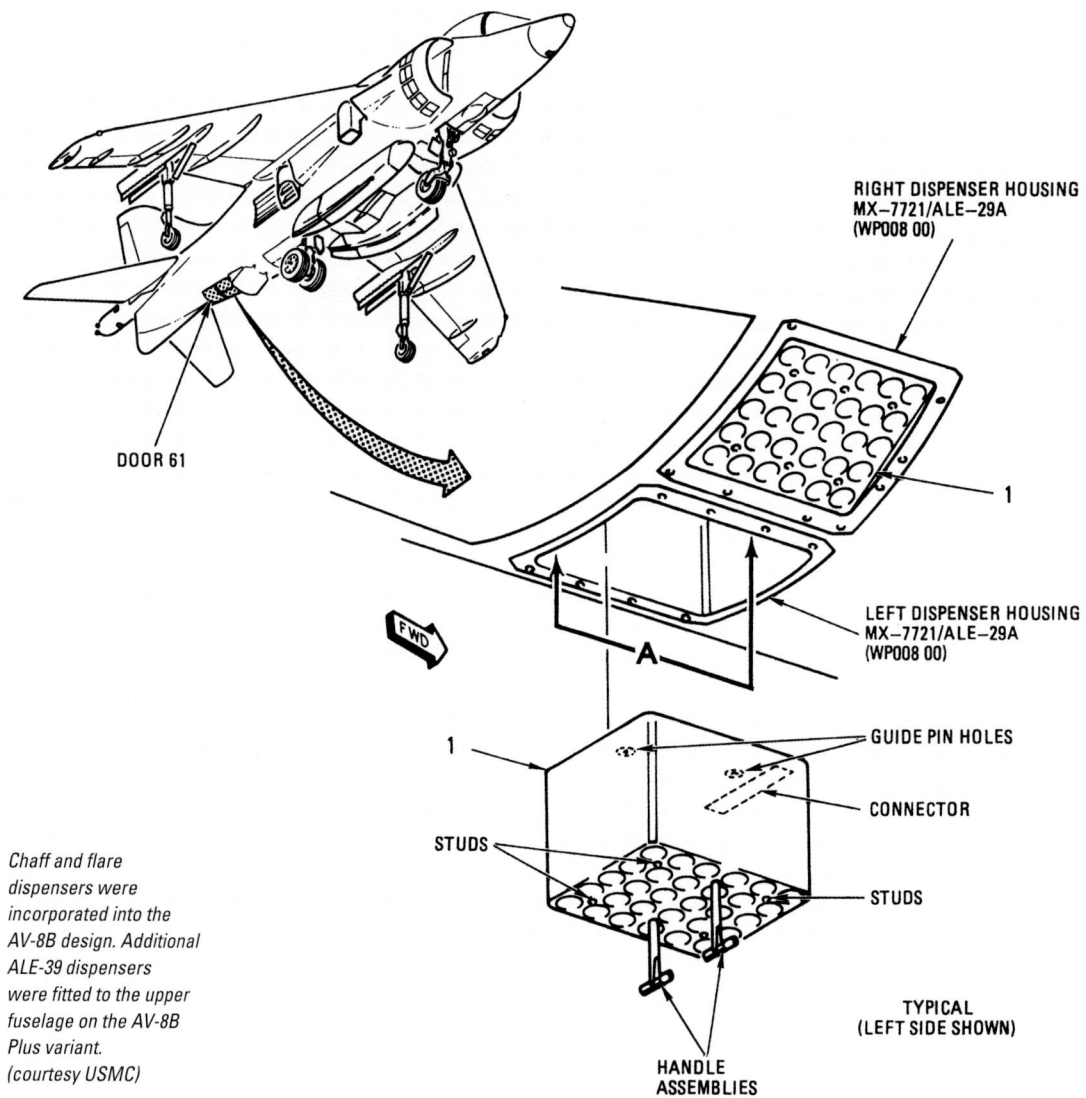

RIGHT DISPENSER HOUSING
MX–7721/ALE–29A
(WP008 00)

DOOR 61

LEFT DISPENSER HOUSING
MX–7721/ALE–29A
(WP008 00)

FWD

A

GUIDE PIN HOLES

CONNECTOR

STUDS

STUDS

TYPICAL
(LEFT SIDE SHOWN)

HANDLE
ASSEMBLIES

Chaff and flare dispensers were incorporated into the AV-8B design. Additional ALE-39 dispensers were fitted to the upper fuselage on the AV-8B Plus variant. (courtesy USMC)

with the type, leaving only the continuing Belize detachment operating the increasingly elderly Harrier GR3. Although manufacture of the AV-8B and Harrier GR5 was a truly shared experience (with components going across the Atlantic in both directions), the RAF's Harrier GR5 was substantially different to the AV-8B. While the USMC wanted a relatively simple and rugged CAS aircraft, the RAF wanted something more versatile and capable (now referred to as a Battlefield Air Interdiction aircraft, which could operate against second- and third- echelon forces) and as a result the GR5 is significantly heavier than its American counterpart. The GR5 cockpit included a Smiths SU-128/A HUD, a Hughes ASB-19 Angle Rate Bombing Set, and a Ferranti moving map display. Marconi Zeus RWR equipment was incorporated together with a Plessey Missile Approach Warning System (MAWS). ALE-40 expendable countermeasures (chaff and flares) were also included and the AV-8B's Litton ASN-130 INS was

adopted, in preference to the planned Ferranti FIN.1075, although this was eventually retrofitted. The Rolls-Royce Pegasus Mk.105 engine took advantage of a new Digital Engine Control System (DECS) which improved engine operation and provided smooth reliability throughout the engine's parameters (it was also incorporated into the Pegasus engines installed in AV-8Bs). The GR5's weapon pylons were also different to those fitted to the AV-8B. The RAF's use of the BL.755 cluster bomb (bigger and heavier than the USMC's 'standard' Mk.82 bomb) required redesigned pylons, and an additional outer pylon was also fitted for the carriage of Sidewinder missiles. Although this outer pylon was not capable of carrying anything else, it did of course free up the other pylons to carry heavier ordnance. The USMC's 25 mm cannon was not adopted, nor was the older ADEN 30 mm cannon. Instead, a new gas-operated ADEN 25 mm cannon was selected which provided a much better rate of fire and

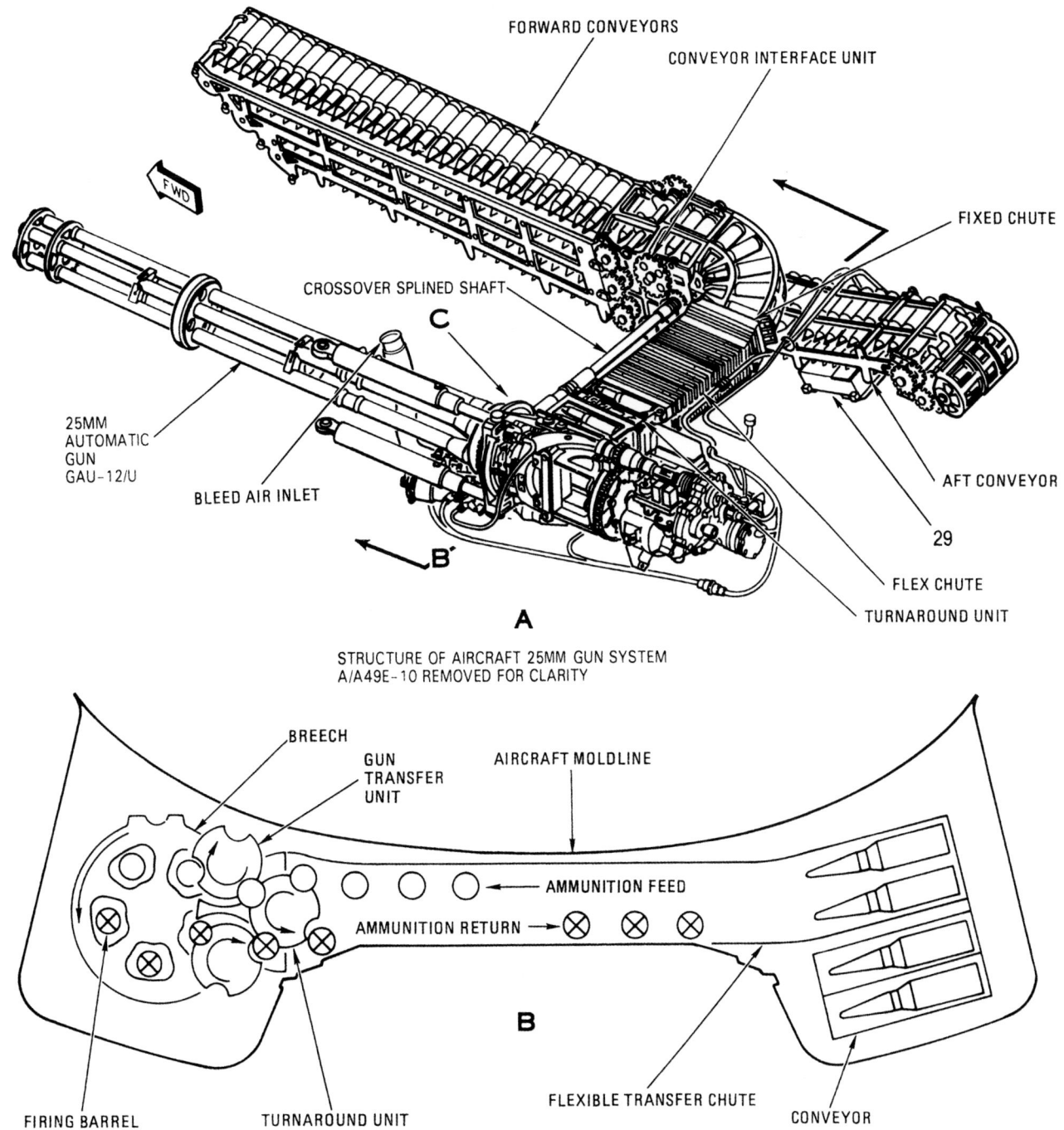

STRUCTURE OF AIRCRAFT 25MM GUN SYSTEM
A/A49E-10 REMOVED FOR CLARITY

FORWARD CONVEYORS

CONVEYOR INTERFACE UNIT

FIXED CHUTE

CROSSOVER SPLINED SHAFT

25MM
AUTOMATIC
GUN
GAU-12/U

BLEED AIR INLET

AFT CONVEYOR

29

FLEX CHUTE

TURNAROUND UNIT

A

BREECH

GUN
TRANSFER
UNIT

AIRCRAFT MOLDLINE

AMMUNITION FEED

AMMUNITION RETURN

B

FIRING BARREL

TURNAROUND UNIT

FLEXIBLE TRANSFER CHUTE

CONVEYOR

Figure 1. Aircraft 25mm Gun System A/A49E-10 Component Locator (Sheet 9)

higher muzzle velocity. However, development of the new cannon was troublesome and by 1999 these difficulties, compounded by increasing cost, led to the cannon being abandoned. Because the gun pods contributed to the Harrier's lift, they were still usually carried under the RAF's aircraft but only rarely did they actually carry cannon (some had already been delivered and were occasionally seen fitted, although it is doubtful whether they were ever fired). Also rather unusual was the distinctive 'chisel' fairing under the extreme nose

which was to have housed a Miniature Infrared Line Scan Equipment (MIRLS) system. Cost overruns eventually led to the equipment being cancelled, but by this time the Harrier GR5's nose was already being manufactured and so the redundant fairing survived, endowing the GR5 with a unique nose profile which ultimately served no practical purpose.

During the years since the AV-8B entered service, the greatly superior second-generation Harrier has been the subject of continual

In order to improve logistics, the AV-8A dispensed with the British ADEN cannon and utilised a system similar to that already used by USMC ground units. Although very different to existing equipment, the new cannon used the same 25 mm ammunition. (courtesy USMC)

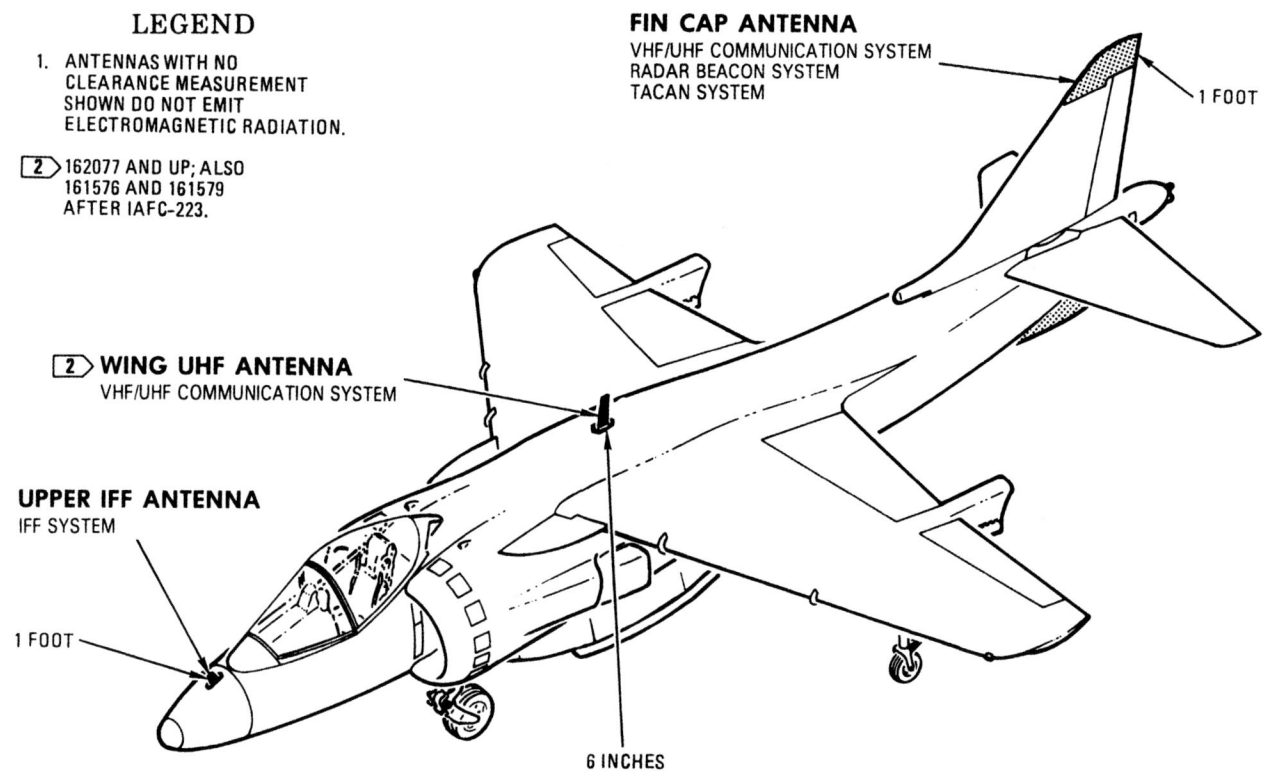

LEGEND

1. ANTENNAS WITH NO CLEARANCE MEASUREMENT SHOWN DO NOT EMIT ELECTROMAGNETIC RADIATION.

2 162077 AND UP; ALSO 161576 AND 161579 AFTER IAFC-223.

FIN CAP ANTENNA
VHF/UHF COMMUNICATION SYSTEM
RADAR BEACON SYSTEM
TACAN SYSTEM

1 FOOT

2 **WING UHF ANTENNA**
VHF/UHF COMMUNICATION SYSTEM

UPPER IFF ANTENNA
IFF SYSTEM

1 FOOT

6 INCHES

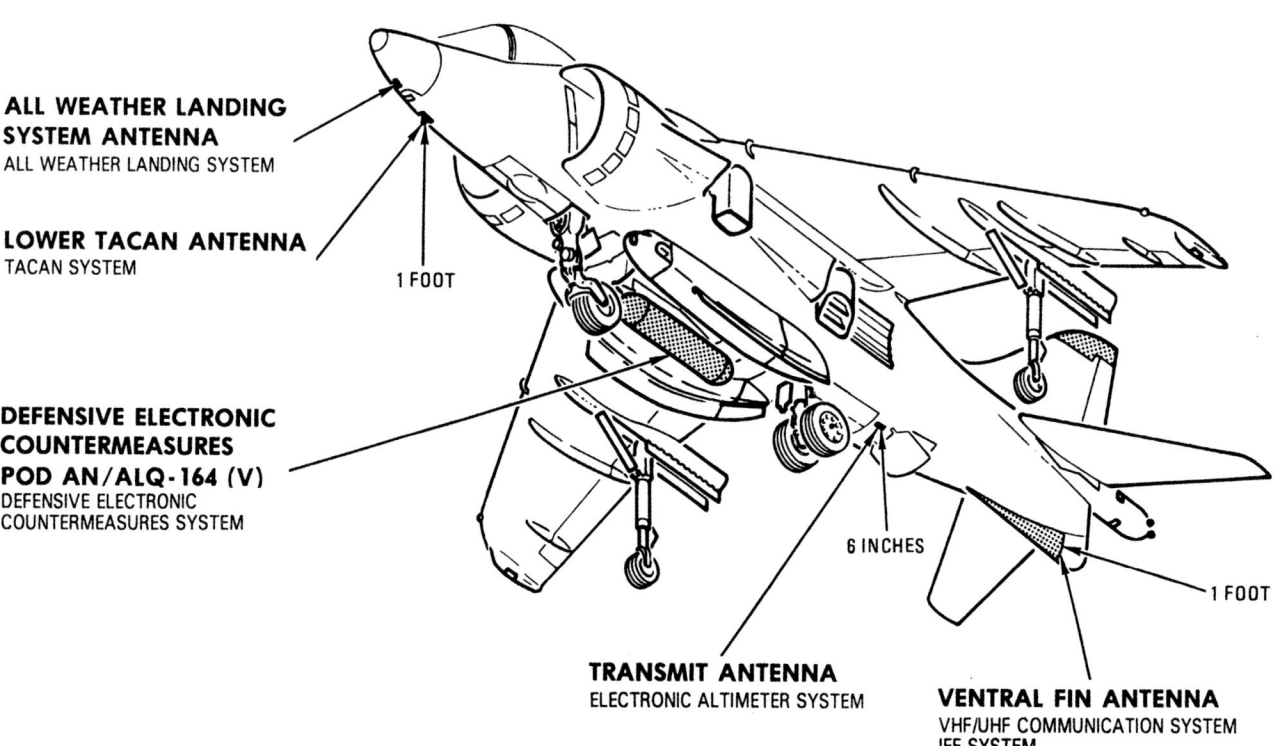

ALL WEATHER LANDING SYSTEM ANTENNA
ALL WEATHER LANDING SYSTEM

LOWER TACAN ANTENNA
TACAN SYSTEM

1 FOOT

DEFENSIVE ELECTRONIC COUNTERMEASURES POD AN/ALQ-164 (V)
DEFENSIVE ELECTRONIC COUNTERMEASURES SYSTEM

6 INCHES

TRANSMIT ANTENNA
ELECTRONIC ALTIMETER SYSTEM

VENTRAL FIN ANTENNA
VHF/UHF COMMUNICATION SYSTEM
IFF SYSTEM

1 FOOT

AV-8B antennae locations.
(courtesy USMC)

improvements and upgrades. The first major development was the creation of a night attack variant for the USMC, originally referred to as the AV-8D but later redesignated as the AV-8B(NA). Testing of a GEC-Marconi Forward Looking Infra Red (FLIR) system and GEC 'Cats Eyes' Night Vision Goggles (NVGs) was conducted at China Lake (using a TA-7C aircraft) and the trials were very successful, leading to the same equipment being incorporated into the modified aircraft, resulting in a distinctive fairing appearing above the nose cone. Also incorporated into the AV-8B(NA) was a new wide-field HUD, colour MFD screens, a digital map display and additional chaff/flare dispensers attached to the upper fuselage. The RAF's LERX was also fitted and the leading edge of the lower fin redesigned to incorporate a modified ram air intake. The prototype for this new configuration was AV-8B 162966 which flew as an AV-8B(NA) for the first time on 26 June 1987 and subsequent production aircraft were then completed to this standard, the first operational aircraft becoming available in September 1989. The second major development was the Harrier II Plus, which was derived from a design first created by McDonnell Douglas in 1987 (then referred to as the AV-8E). With a more powerful Pegasus engine, the E-model was designed to incorporate a new radar system with both air-to-air and air-to-ground modes. Interest in the project dwindled (largely due to budget restraints), but it re-emerged in 1988 when BAe and McDonnell Douglas announced a private-venture project to develop this design. Both Spain and Italy expressed interest in the proposal and eventually a four-nation deal was established with both Alenia and CASA taking a 15 per cent share of the programme. Of course this was not the first Harrier variant to carry a radar, as the hugely successful Sea Harrier FA2 was flying with the GEC-Marconi Blue Vixen system and it seemed logical that this equipment would be used for the AV-8B. Indeed it was suggested that the same radar should also be retrofitted to USMC Hornets as it was proving to be an excellent piece of kit, integrated with the equally successful AIM-20 missile. Sadly, cost considerations precluded the notion of re-equipping the Hornet Squadrons and the Hughes APG-73 was chosen for this aircraft instead. This effectively freed up the Hornet's older APG-65 radars and these were then used for the AV-8B. It was not an ideal solution, but certainly an affordable one. The resulting aircraft – the AV-8B Harrier II Plus – is, in effect, the AV-8B(NA) with a radar housed in a suitably redesigned forward nose section, embracing all of the modifications previously made to the night-attack variant. With existing AV-8B aircraft gradually being brought up to this standard, the AV-8B Plus is now the USMC's 'standard' Harrier variant, embracing all of the technological improvements developed over the preceding years plus more recent innovations such as GPS, a digital targeting data link, the Litening II

Targeting Pod system and new precision-guided munitions. As such, the Harrier Plus will remain at the forefront of the USMC's inventory until the all-new F-35 enters service. Only then will the Marine's long and hugely successful association with the Harrier finally come to an end.

The RAF also embraced some of the emerging AV-8B developments, most notably the same night-attack system, and this formed the basis of the Harrier GR.Mk.7. When the initial purchase of the Harrier GR5 was made in 1988, options on further aircraft were included and a batch of 34 Harrier GR7s was subsequently ordered, together with a plan to modify the earlier GR5s to the same standard. The complicated production process prompted BAe to complete some of these aircraft to GR5A standard, featuring most of the later variant's modifications, pending delivery and fitment of the avionics. When completed, these partially-modified aircraft were placed in storage pending final conversion and delivery as Mk.7s. Harrier ZD318 became the prototype GR7 and flew for the first time in this configuration on 20 November 1989. Distinguishable from the GR5 by virtue of a redesigned nose section, the GR7 featured a nose-top GEC-Marconi 1010 FLIR fairing (similar to that found on the AV-8B) and new under-nose fairings for the Marconi-Zeus ECM system. In other respects the aircraft was similar to the GR5 although, from the seventeenth new-build aircraft onwards, the LERX was switched to the later '100 per cent' design with deeper cross section and reshaped dimensions and this was progressively retrofitted to earlier aircraft (and most AV-8Bs) which featured the '75 per cent' LERX design. Unlike the USMC AV-8B(NA) the Harrier GR7 took advantage of an ingenious compressed air jettisoning system which ensures that the pilot's night vision goggles are safely separated from the wearer before ejection – the lack of a similar facility in USMC aircraft restricts night vision operations in some circumstances. It was envisaged that night-attack equipment could also be fitted to existing Harrier T4 trainers creating what would have been the Harrier Mk.6, but eventually the RAF received 13 Harrier Mk.10 aircraft which were essentially standard TAV-8B models with GR7 equipment, thereby retaining the dual training and combat capability preferred by the RAF. The Mk.6 would have presented the RAF with the logistical difficulties of supporting only a small fleet of first-generation Harriers which were to be used only for training. The first Harrier T.Mk.10 (ZH653) was assembled at Dunsfold and made its first flight there on 7 April 1994, although subsequent aircraft were assembled at Warton (Dunsfold was committed to Sea Harrier work at this time). The first Harrier T10 was delivered to the RAF on 30 January 1995. The final stage of the RAF's programme of modifications was the GR.Mk.9 which was a significantly updated development of the GR7, incorporating the ability

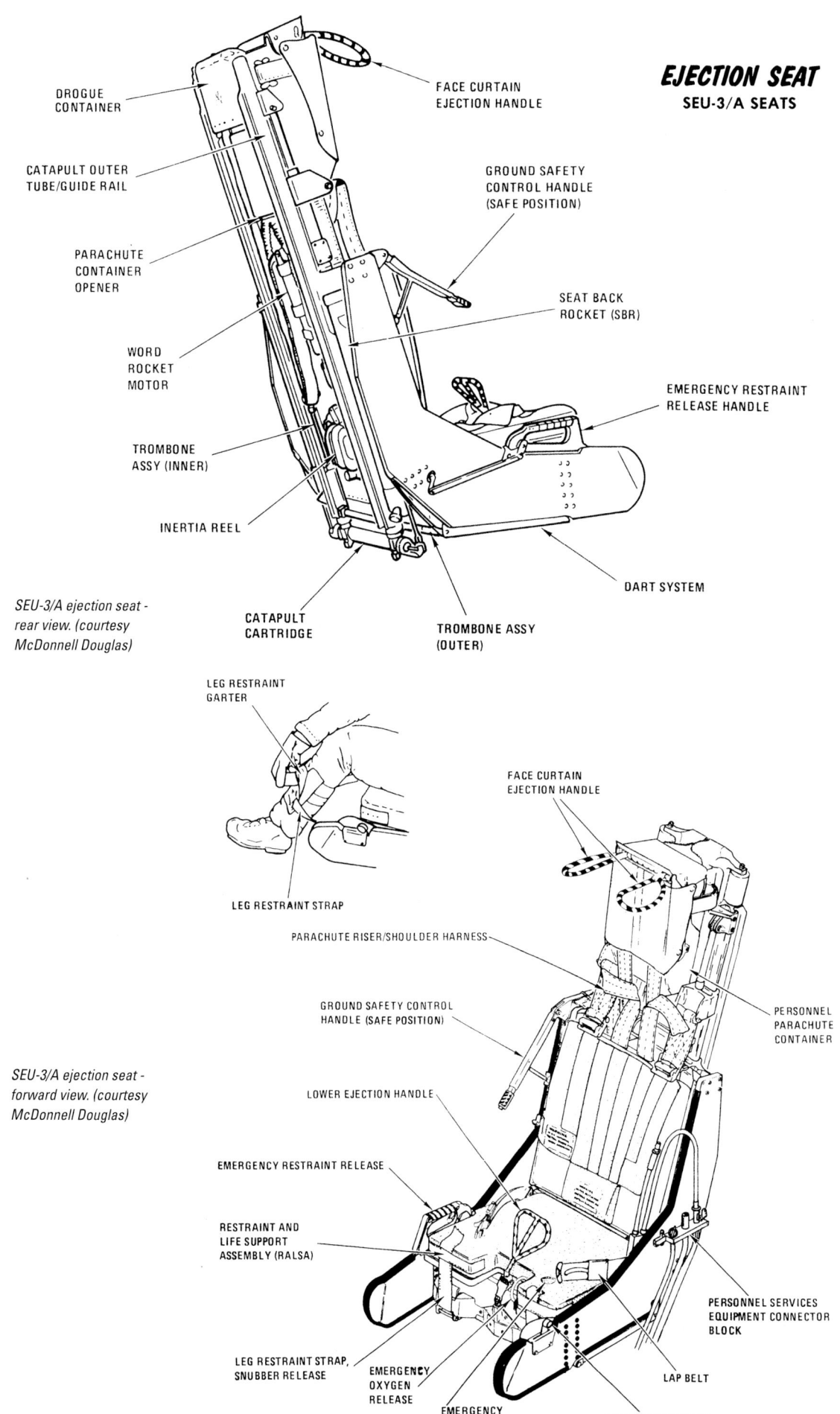

EJECTION SEAT
SEU-3/A SEATS

DROGUE
CONTAINER

FACE CURTAIN
EJECTION HANDLE

CATAPULT OUTER
TUBE/GUIDE RAIL

GROUND SAFETY
CONTROL HANDLE
(SAFE POSITION)

PARACHUTE
CONTAINER
OPENER

SEAT BACK
ROCKET (SBR)

WORD
ROCKET
MOTOR

EMERGENCY RESTRAINT
RELEASE HANDLE

TROMBONE
ASSY (INNER)

INERTIA REEL

DART SYSTEM

*SEU-3/A ejection seat -
rear view. (courtesy
McDonnell Douglas)*

CATAPULT
CARTRIDGE

TROMBONE ASSY
(OUTER)

LEG RESTRAINT
GARTER

FACE CURTAIN
EJECTION HANDLE

LEG RESTRAINT STRAP

PARACHUTE RISER/SHOULDER HARNESS

GROUND SAFETY CONTROL
HANDLE (SAFE POSITION)

PERSONNEL
PARACHUTE
CONTAINER

*SEU-3/A ejection seat -
forward view. (courtesy
McDonnell Douglas)*

LOWER EJECTION HANDLE

EMERGENCY RESTRAINT RELEASE

RESTRAINT AND
LIFE SUPPORT
ASSEMBLY (RALSA)

PERSONNEL SERVICES
EQUIPMENT CONNECTOR
BLOCK

LEG RESTRAINT STRAP,
SNUBBER RELEASE

EMERGENCY
OXYGEN
RELEASE

LAP BELT

EMERGENCY
OXYGEN
INDICATOR

SHOULDER HARNESS
LOCK LEVER

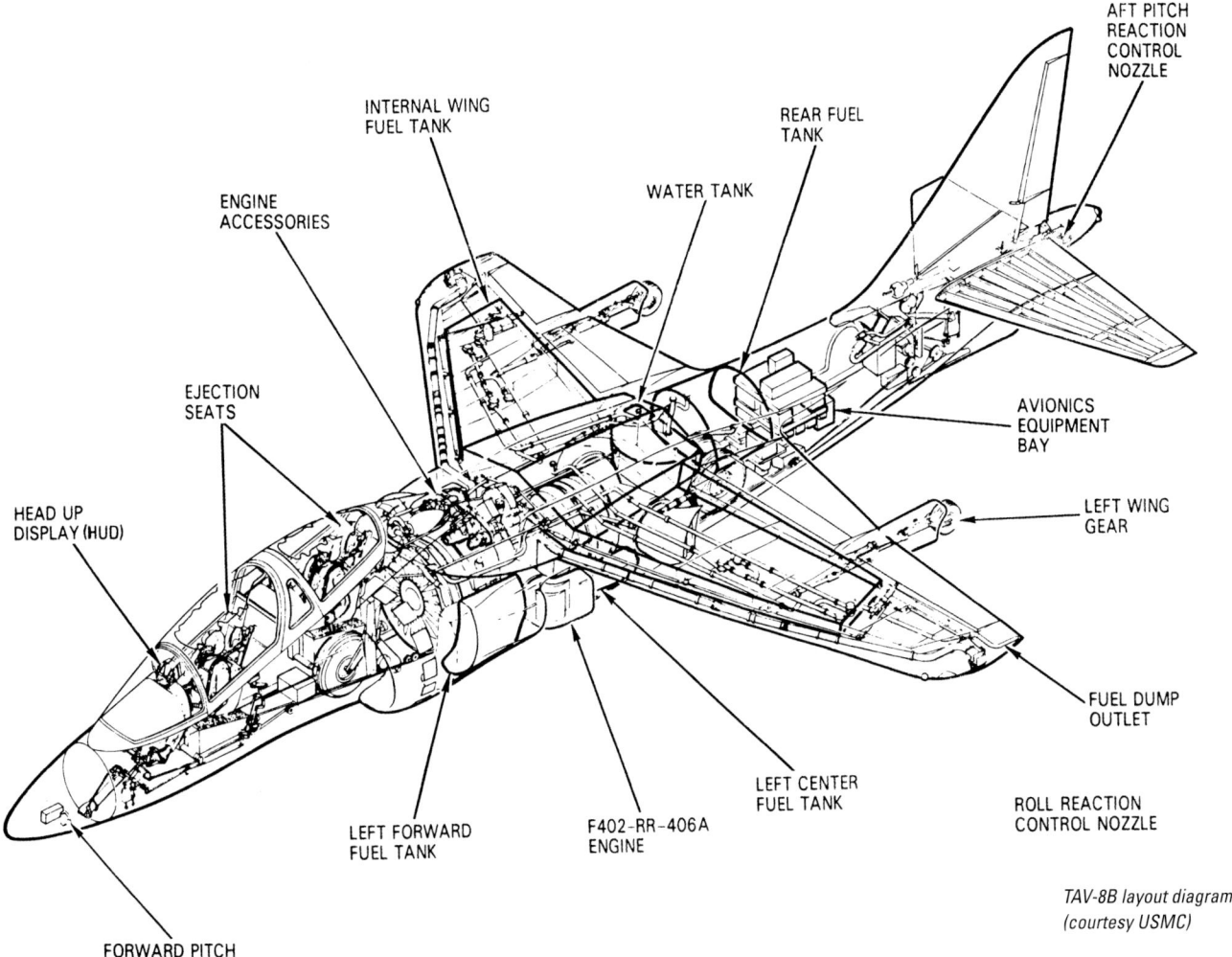

AFT PITCH
REACTION
CONTROL
NOZZLE

INTERNAL WING
FUEL TANK

REAR FUEL
TANK

ENGINE
ACCESSORIES

WATER TANK

AVIONICS
EQUIPMENT
BAY

EJECTION
SEATS

LEFT WING
GEAR

HEAD UP
DISPLAY (HUD)

FUEL DUMP
OUTLET

LEFT CENTER
FUEL TANK

ROLL REACTION
CONTROL NOZZLE

LEFT FORWARD
FUEL TANK

F402-RR-406A
ENGINE

TAV-8B layout diagram.
(courtesy USMC)

FORWARD PITCH
REACTION CONTROL
NOZZLE

to use a wide range of advanced precision weaponry, new communications, and systems and airframe upgrades. Integration and clearance of these weapons enabled the RAF to hit a wider range of targets harder, at longer range and with less risk to aircrew. The first of these improved aircraft equipped the new Joint Force Harrier Squadrons crewed by both Royal Air Force and Royal Navy personnel, following the withdrawal from service of the Royal Navy's Sea Harriers. The JFH concept effectively created a merged capability between the two services, comprising a force of four front line squadrons and one Operational Conversion Unit. The RAF supplied air and ground crew for two of the front line squadrons and the RN for the other two, while the OCU was subsequently jointly crewed. Operations were concentrated at the RAF's 'twin bases' at Cottesmore and Wittering, with training activities largely confined to the latter base, units deploying to sea on a regular basis. Alongside the GR9 upgrade programme, aircraft were fitted with more powerful engines to enable them to perform with increased efficiency in extremely hot climates, which degraded the performance of the existing Pegasus Mk.105

turbofan. Aircraft with the improved engines were designated GR9A. Under a £100 million contract awarded to BAe Systems in 2004, new digital weapons integrated into the GR9 included an advanced Global Positioning System and laser-guided Paveway IV bomb, and infrared and television variants of the Maverick missile to achieve high precision ground-attack capabilities. The aircraft was also cleared to carry up to six Paveway IV bombs, linked by a new on-board computer. The Successor Identification Friend or Foe system also enhanced the aircraft's versatility, making it less vulnerable on operational missions. The aircraft was later fitted to carry the advanced Brimstone 'fire and forget' anti-armour missile. Part of longer term plans for the aircraft included secure communications, a ground proximity warning system and, for training, the Rangeless Airborne Instrumentation and Debriefing System (RAIDS). The programme also extended to an equivalent upgrade for the two-seater T10 training aircraft to T.Mk.12 standard.

With this enhanced capability, Joint Force Harrier was expected to remain very much in business until around 2015 when deliveries of a

Lockheed Martin F-35 variant were expected, and this new aircraft was to have been a direct replacement for the entire surviving Harrier fleet. However, Britain's dire financial situation forced another round of severe defence cuts and high on the list of potential savings was JFH. Despite ongoing commitments in theatres such as Afghanistan, in October 2010, as part of a sweeping Strategic Defence Review, the British Ministry of Defence concluded that the purchase of two new full-sized aircraft carriers should go ahead and that they would still eventually be equipped with the new F-35 Joint Strike Fighter. However, the original plan to acquire the STOVL variant of the new aircraft (the F-35B) was dropped in favour of the conventional non-STOVL F-35C, which could operate from the new 'full-sized' carriers without any need for a short or vertical take-off/landing ability. The decision made perfect sense in that the development of the complex F-35B looked likely to be far more protracted and expensive than the equivalent F-35C programme, and the new carriers did not require the F-35B's capabilities in any case; but of course it also implied that in a much wider sense, both the RAF and Royal Navy no longer saw any practical need for a STOVL aircraft of any sort. This was a fundamental choice which the MoD seemed to have made with little

consideration and very little fuss but, almost at a stroke, Britain's interest in jet VTOL was effectively over for good. As if this was not enough to digest, the MoD also decided that rather than continue Harrier operations until the new carriers and F-35C aircraft were available, the entire Harrier fleet, and the mighty *Ark Royal* from which it would have operated, would be withdrawn with immediate effect in order to make substantial cost savings.

The decision was met with disbelief both within the RAF and throughout the British media and on the day that the news was released, RAF and FAA Harrier operations were immediately drawn down, some crews literally being stopped in their tracks as they prepared to fly training missions. Harriers would be withdrawn from service completely by April 2011, although in a matter of days from the SDR announcement it became clear that most operations would effectively come to an end in December 2010. Suddenly, and with little warning, the Harrier's illustrious career was over. Even though there was no prospect of the new carriers and F-35s coming into service for another five years at least, all fixed-wing carrier power would immediately be abandoned.

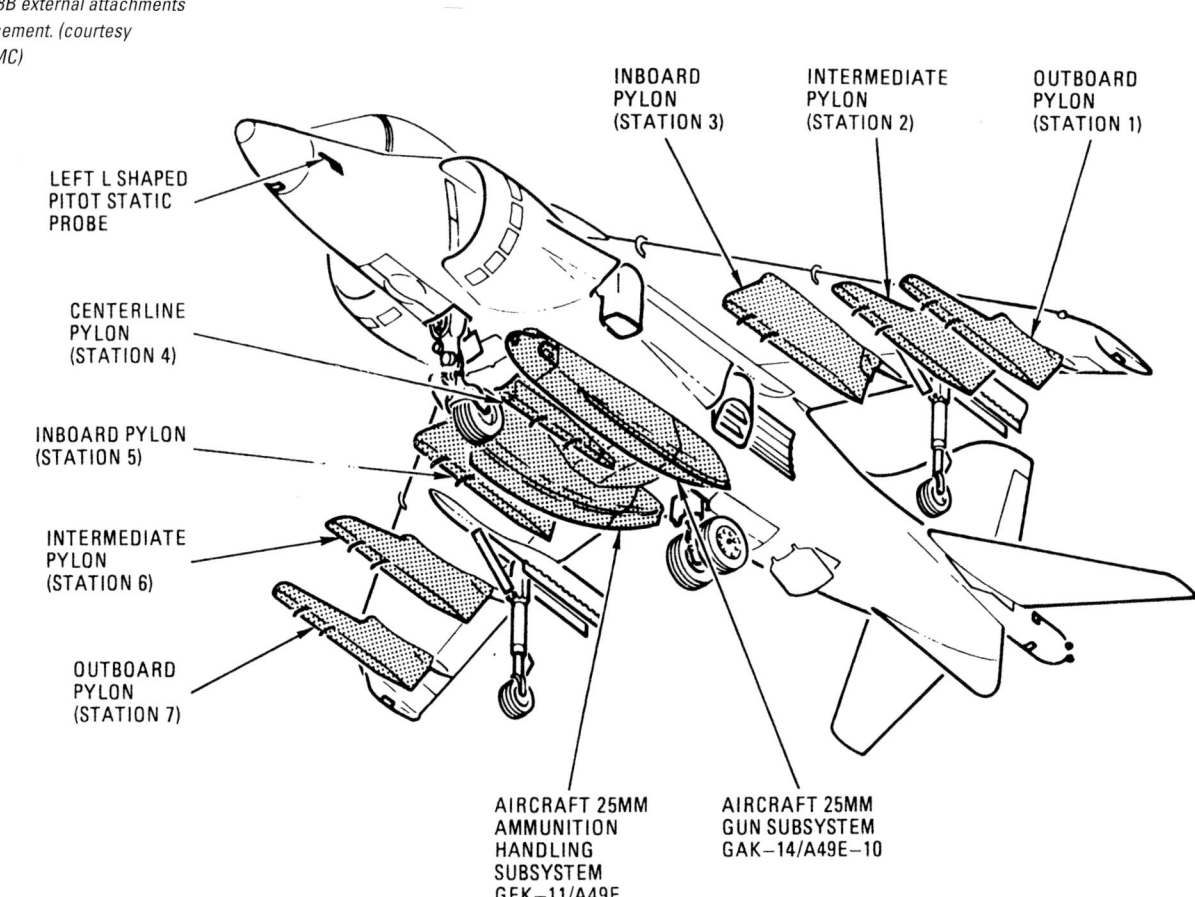

AV-8B external attachments placement. (courtesy USMC)

AV-8B 163687 from VMA-231 pictured at Cecil Field, Florida, in a relatively short-lived blue/grey camouflage scheme which was introduced for operations in the Gulf.
(Photo: Francesco Checuz)

McDonnell Douglas AV-8B Harrier II, 162732/CG-08, VMA-231, US Marine Corps
Wrap-around camouflage in FS.36320 and FS.36009 with all markings in dark grey, except for '08' on fin which is in white; unit badge on nose

To celebrate the completion of the 100th Av-8B, 163183 was suitably decorated for a publicity photo call. (Photo: McDonnell Douglas)

AV-8B from VMA-331 'Bumblebees' low over the Arizona desert, carrying 500 lb Snakeye retarded bombs. (Photo: McDonnell Douglas)

The YAV-8B prototype was eventually assigned to NASA's Ames Research Center where it was employed on various trials including microwave landing systems and control equipment research. (Photo: Nasa)

Rarely seen AV-8B assigned to the NAWC, wearing high-visibility red panels on the wings and tail. (Photo: via Dennis Jenkins)

British Aerospace's 'Advanced Harrier', better known as the 'Big Wing' or 'Tin Wing' Harrier GR5 which was eventually abandoned. (courtesy BAE Systems)

Harrier GR5 carrying what was originally envisaged as the type's standard weapons load of seven BL755 cluster bombs together with a pair of Sidewinder missiles. The bombs illustrated are inert loads used for clearance trials, painted in high-visibility markings for tracking purposes. (Photo: BAE Systems)

Harrier GR5 ZD319 pictured during pre-delivery trials. The grey colour scheme was abandoned before the Harrier GR5 entered RAF service in favour of a green paint scheme. (Photo: BAE Systems)

ZD319 at West Freugh during weapons release trials. Behind the GR5 are first generation Harrier GR3s from No.1 Squadron.
(Photo: BAE Systems)

Factory-fresh Harrier GR5s pictured shortly after delivery to No.233 Operational Conversion Unit at Wittering.
(Photo: Tim McLelland)

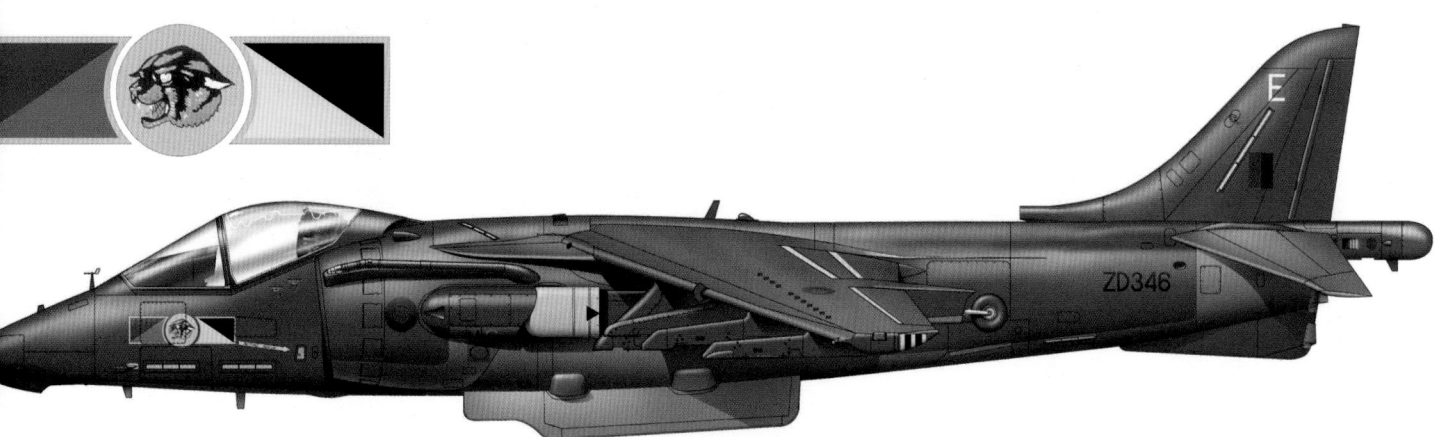

BAe Harrier GR Mk.5, ZD346/E, No. 233 Operational Conversion Unit, 1989
NATO Green BS 381C:285 upper surfaces with Lichen Green BS 4800:12-B-25 undersides; blue/red national markings. Black serial, white code; unit badge on nose flanked by grey/red/yellow/black flash, outlined in light blue

Harrier GR5 cockpit. As can be seen, the instrument panel is dominated by Multi-Function Display screens. The windscreen is visibly larger than that fitted to first generation Harriers, affording much better forward visibility. (Photo: BAE Systems)

Martin Baker Mk.12 'zero zero'
ejection seat as fitted to second
generation RAF Harrier variants.
(Photo: Martin Baker)

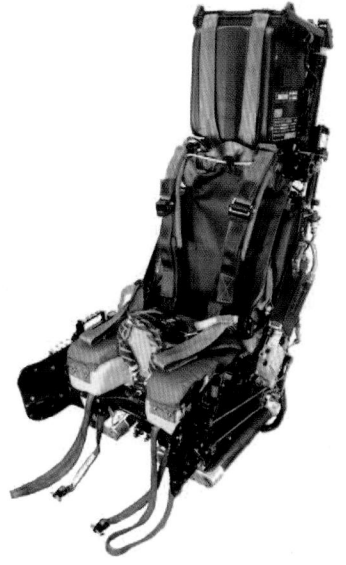

A Pegasus engine being
winched into the fuselage
of a Sea Harrier FA2 on
board HMS Illustrious.
(Photo: UK MoD Crown
Copyright 2010)

Prior to the Harrier's premature
withdrawal from RAF service,
changes to the RAF's structure had
already seen some significant
changes. No.3 Squadron at
Cottesmore exchanged its Harriers for
Typhoons on 31 March 2006, moving
to Coningsby as part of the process.
In this photograph Harriers from
Nos. 1 and 20(R) Squadrons overfly
Cottesmore in company with No.3
Squadron's first (unmarked) Typhoon.
(Photo: RAF Cottesmore)

RAF Harrier GR9s high over Nevada during a Red Flag exercise. Armed with an impressive mix of ordnance, this unusual image was captured from the ramp of a USMC KC-130 Hercules which was providing aerial refuelling support for the Harriers during the exercise. (Photo: BAE Systems)

Harrier GR9s pictured at Nellis AFB in Nevada during a Red Flag exercise. The RAF is a regular participant in the USAF's Flag exercises and Harriers were occasionally deployed to the United States for these exercises, operating with many USAF, US Navy, USMC and other NATO units. (Photo: BAE Systems)

CHAPTER EIGHT

Afghanistan Action

URING December 2010 *Ark Royal* bade farewell to the last deployment of Harriers and sailed to Portsmouth for retirement. Harrier operations continued for a short period until the remaining Harriers at Wittering made the short journey northwards to Cottesmore. On 15 December JFH flew a magnificent 16-ship formation of Harriers around Lincolnshire to mark the aircraft's retirement from RAF and Royal Navy service. The flypast was to have been repeated the following day for media and invited guests but typically gloomy British weather prevented this and the Harriers returned to Cottesmore under leaden skies in groups of four, to make individual short and vertical landings before the assembled crowds. At 1440 hrs Cottesmore's Station Commander brought the last Harrier back for a final bow and then touched down (vertically of course), to mark the end of the very last operational Harrier sortie. Accompanied by a pipe band, the Harrier pilots then returned to their waiting families and with more than a touch of sadness and partial disbelief, the long story of Britain's association with the Harrier was effectively over. Lieutenant Commander James Blackmore was Commanding Officer of No.1 Squadron's A Flight towards the end of the Harrier's service with JFH at Cottesmore, and in the following account he discusses some of his operational experiences with the Harrier GR9:

'As we now know, the Harrier GR9 was retired from service at the end of 2010 but I feel that my comments are a fitting tribute to the culmination of 41 years of VSTOL aviation, the numerous operations that Harriers have been part of, and all the personnel who have been part of a remarkable aircraft. This is my account of Operation Herrick and the GR9. After five years, 8,500 sorties and more than 22,000 hours airborne, the Harrier finally returned to the UK from operations in Afghanistan in July 2009. During this busy time for the Harrier, I was privileged to serve on two separate occasions on Operation Herrick with No.1(F) and No.IV(AC) Squadrons under the umbrella of Joint Force Harrier (JFH). I will focus on the capabilities of the Harrier GR9, our role in Afghanistan and JFH. It is my intention to concentrate solely on the Harrier GR9 here as this is the capability we eventually finished the operations in Afghanistan with and this variant is a very different beast compared to the GR7. Crucially, when compared with the Harrier GR7, the GR9 is essentially digitally wired, meaning that the pilot can communicate directly with the weapons on the pylons; consequently this has seen the introduction of the Paveway IV (PWIV) 500 lb laser and GPS-guided bomb along with a number of other significant upgrades. A brief description of the weapons or systems usually carried is as follows.

'PWIV – This weapon changed fundamentally the way the Harrier operates: not only can the bomb be guided to its target using a laser from either the aircraft, through the Sniper Advanced Targeting Pod, or from the ground, it can also be delivered on to precise GPS coordinates. At 500 lb

Vicon pod carried by Harrier GR7 and GR9. It provided daytime reconnaissance capability at low, medium and high altitude. (Photo: UK MoD Crown Copyright 2010)

A Harrier GR7 on a low-level mission with No.4 Squadron. The green camouflage scheme was a carry-over from the GR5 fleet and was swiftly replaced by grey colours. (Photo: No.4 squadron Association)

it is also a lighter weapon when compared to some of the more traditional 1,000 lb variants. This therefore gives the added benefit of reducing the overall launch and recovery weight of the aircraft; crucial when you consider CVS operations. The next advancement with this weapon is that the fuse is cockpit programmable, allowing the pilot to tailor the effect of the weapon depending on the target and the requirement of the soldier on the ground. It can, for instance, penetrate through layers of concrete before exploding, thus allowing the pilot accurately to target the precise part of the building to be destroyed. Sometimes we carried two more PWIVs replacing the CRV-7s, making the Harrier a true precision bomber. She's a big old girl when fully laden!

'CRV-7 – This pod contains 19 individual rockets, giving a total of 38 per aircraft. In many ways these mitigate against us having a gun (a subject which is open to a much bigger debate!) and with this standard of Harrier we can again make selections in the cockpit that allow us to fire one rocket, 38 rockets or any multiple in between. Once again this is crucial when considering the effect required on the ground and proportionality. Why fire 38 rockets when one, as a warning shot, would have the desired effect?

'Fuel Tanks – When fully fuelled the aircraft sat with 11,700 lb of fuel in the standard fit. Over Afghanistan this would often give us in excess of two hours airborne without the need to air-to-air refuel (AAR). With the AAR capability our time

on station could be dramatically increased, with sometimes missions lasting well over 6 hours.

'TERMA – This pod was a new addition to the Harrier for Afghanistan and provided us with many more defensive flares than the usual internal load; it also provides a missile launch cue to the pilot.

'Digital Joint Reconnaissance Pod (DJRP) – While many would imagine that our time in Afghanistan was all about dropping bombs, this couldn't be further form the truth; in fact the vast majority of the time we would be tasked with taking high resolution imagery for the ground commanders and their soldiers. This could be anything from looking at changes to patterns of life, building construction and layout, or in the hunt for Improvised Explosive Devices (IEDs). Crucially, carrying this pod does not affect our weapon load-out and therefore we could "swing" from either a reconnaissance mission to close air support at the drop of a hat depending on the circumstances and the requirements of the soldiers on the ground. Although the product is in black and white, the resolution is exceptionally high and, with correct equipment, 3D images could be developed and intricate graphics produced, thus providing an excellent tool for intelligence gathering.

'Sniper Advance Targeting Pod (ATP) – This replaced the TIALD 500 and offered a huge leap forward in capability. Essentially, Sniper allowed us to view the ground from altitude and stand-off with incredible resolution in both TV and infrared, which crucially allowed us to operate to the same effect at night. With the ability to zoom, the pilot has the potential to observe persons on the ground and in some cases distinguish between adults and children. Other enhancements on the pod allow the pilot to generate GPS coordinates from what is viewed or fire a laser to guide bombs to their point of impact. At night an infrared pointer allows the aircraft to operate together and point out ground features to each other; rather like using a Star Wars-style light sabre when viewed through night vision goggles! Finally, we were able to broadcast the

image we see directly to the soldier on the ground or back to the operations centre; crucial when having to make quick decisions. All of this imagery was recorded for analysis after the mission and also afforded us a second reconnaissance sensor, again increasing the ability of the aircraft to gather intelligence.

'Finally, moving on to the pilot and the cockpit. For the final six months we operated with a Helmet Mounted Cueing System (HMCS) which allowed the pilot quickly to identify coordinates on the ground using a red diamond that is projected over it on a reticule placed over the right eye. This is an excellent tool in increasing spatial awareness and takes away the need to spend vital minutes using binoculars to identify features from a map. Equally, in reverse, the pilot is able to look around the battle space and if he sees something of interest, he simply looks at it, designates it using controls on the throttle and immediately the Sniper ATP will move to look at that same point on the ground. At night, the pilot wore NVGs (Night Vision Goggles) and these were fully integrated with all the systems, meaning that the way we did business by night was exactly the same as during the day, including flying at low level, something the Harrier force was well trained in and extremely proud of. The cockpit itself continued to be busy with two TVs displaying anything from Sniper imagery, through to weapon programming, engine performance data or a moving map. We simultaneously used two radios to keep in contact with the ground forces, our wingman or the various control agencies that help make the tactical decisions. We also carried many maps to help us orientate ourselves with the forces on the ground or to find points of interest. Put simply, we were the Pilot, Navigator, Engineer, Communicator, Weapons Officer and Lawyer while operating the Harrier; this certainly is testament to the training each pilot was given.

'Joint Force Harrier (JFH), a combined Royal Air Force and Royal Navy Fleet Air Arm unit, first deployed to Kandahar AF in 2004 in support of the NATO led International Security Assistance Force

Harrier GR9 venting fuel from the wing tips for the benefit of the cameraman. In addition to external fuel tanks, Sidewinders and two SNEB 68 mm rocket projectile pods are carried externally. (Photo: UK MoD Crown Copyright 2010)

Harrier GR9 from No.20(R) Squadron performing a hovering 'bow' for air show crowds at Biggin Hill. Exhaust buckets are deflected down and the intake doors are fully open. (Photo: Tim McLelland)

(ISAF). Under this umbrella Harriers operated continuously day and night over five years and the Harriers' contribution of close air support and reconnaissance has been crucial to the ISAF mission. During this operational period JFH provided eight Harriers continuously available in theatre with 11 pilots and around 100 engineers and support staff. We always planned and flew missions in pairs, with two pairs being tasked during the day and a pair at night. Equally, during the day we kept two further Harriers at Alert 30, i.e. 30 mins notice to get airborne, and at night this was

Harrier T12 ZH663 pictured at low level during a training sortie. The re-designed forward fuselage of the twin-seat second generation Harrier afforded the instructor (in the rear seat) excellent all-round visibility. (Photo: UK MoD Crown Copyright 2010)

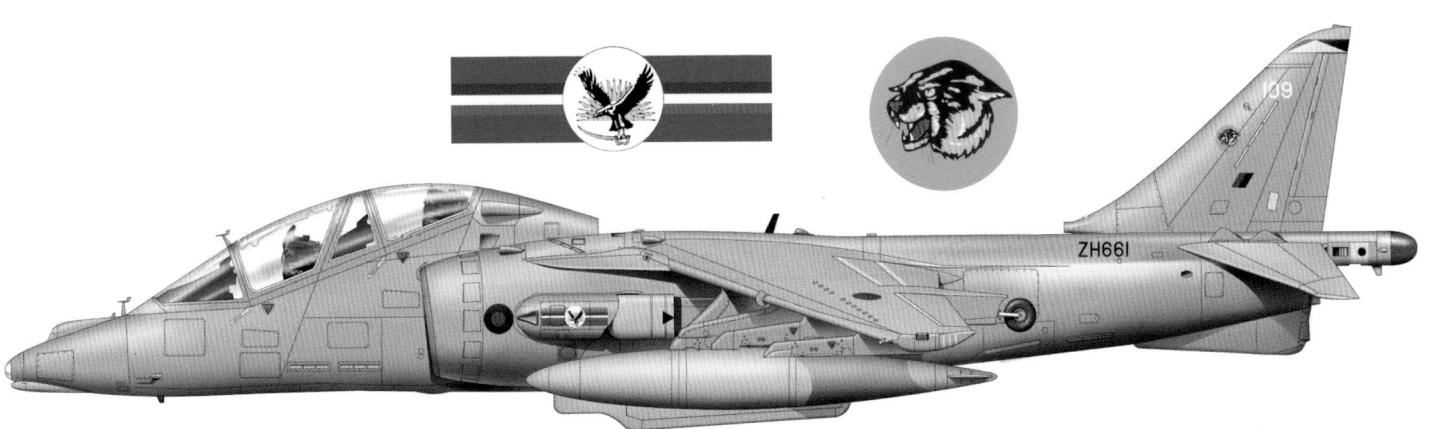

BAe Harrier T Mk.12, ZH661/109, No. 20 Squadron (230 OCU), October 2009
Camouflage Grey BS381C 626 overall; Blue/Red roundels on air intake fairings, above port and below starboard wings. Black serial, white code; markings on fin consisting of red/gey/yellow/black flash and Welsh Wild Cat over a pale blue disc. 20 Sqn badge, flanked by blue/red/white/green flash on air intake fairings aft of roundel

extended to Alert 120, although the CAOC (Combined Air Operations Centre) could reduce those times depending on the tactical situation; quite often aircrew would be airborne in well under these times. This stance was maintained throughout the five year period.

'Harriers never once lost a mission due to an unserviceable aircraft; often there would be numerous spare aircraft if one unusually developed a problem on start. The only times that the Harrier failed to get airborne in the five years of operations was if the weather curtailed flying operations.

'Unique to the Harrier is (or was) its short field capability. This proved to be extremely worthy throughout the five-year period. When Harriers first deployed, the runway at Kandahar AF was a narrow 3,000 ft strip only suitable to the VSTOL aircraft. Latterly, there were times when the runway became blocked and only a few thousand feet were available, not enough for the other fast Air to operate from. This occurred during one of my day missions when, crucially, the US carrier with its F/A-18s was in port, thus unable to get airborne, and Bagram and Kabul airfields were iced in; as such the Harriers were the only aircraft helping to support the troops at this time, utilising their unique short field capability to get airborne. The main area of operations for the Harrier was over the Helmand Valley supporting the UK Army and Royal Marines as well as all the other coalition troops. At 90 nm from KAF, flying time was usually about 15-20 minutes. However the Harrier was

ZH663 in a steep climb for the photographer. Unlike the first generation dual-control variant of the Harrier, the T12 featured only a redesigned forward fuselage and an enlarged tail fin. The rear fuselage structure remained unchanged. (Photo: UK MoD Crown Copyright 2010)

role of NTISR (Non-Traditional Information Surveillance and Reconnaissance) and in this respect we would use our sensors to provide an overview of the battle space. Equally it may also have been appropriate to provide a 'Show of Presence' where the aircraft were positioned such that a visible or audible presence would be observed on the ground. Finally, if the situation dictated, a deliberate "surgical" strike could be called for in order to provide ground forces with a tactical advantage. Clearing was where we brought the Harrier into the Close Air Support (CAS) role providing Armed Overwatch. Utilising "Shows of Force" – the aim was to deter or disperse insurgents and if that failed then a kinetic response could be brought to bear. The important point to stress at this juncture is that this effect had to be Precise, Discriminate and Proportional, something that the Harrier became known for. If an effect could be achieved through firing one rocket, then that was what was delivered; equally, if soldiers lives were at risk, then a PWIV might equally be the most appropriate weapon. Holding is, in many ways, similar to Shaping – seeing the pattern of life monitored as well as a continued presence being maintained both audibly and visually. Equally the continued hunt for IEDs would be undertaken whenever the sensors could be spared, all ensuring that the key ground gained was subsequently held.

'Building was through support to the local populace, which could include providing presence on voting days, deterring the placement of IEDs and a demonstration of a continued commitment by maintaining presence overhead both audibly and visually. Looking back after nearly a year, I can honestly say that JFH made a huge difference on Operation Herrick; undoubtedly the lives of many Afghanistan civilians were saved along with the lives of our own and coalition troops. In many ways, the JFH statistics for Operation Herrick speak for themselves: Missions Flown – approx 4,500; Sorties – 8,557; Hours – 22,771; Average sortie time – 3 hours; Close Air Support missions – 2,000.

'I was fortunate to fly the last mission for JFH over Afghanistan, a Night into Day sortie, and then fly one of the aircraft back to the UK – aircraft 13, ZD346, which I subsequently had my name on. I feel extremely privileged to have served in and over Afghanistan on Operation Herrick. Over my

A pair of Harrier GR9s from No.4 Squadron pictured during a refuelling rendezvous at 20,000 ft, with a VC10 tanker from No.101 Squadron. (Photo: UK MoD Crown Copyright 2010)

often tasked or re-tasked all over the country with jets operating over places such as the Khyber Pass and alongside the neighbouring countries of Pakistan, Iran, Turkmenistan and Uzbekistan, showing the full potential and reach of the aircraft. As for the role that Joint Force Harrier undertook, it could perhaps be summarised as Shape, Clear, Hold and Build and this was achieved through a graduated response. It must be stressed at this stage that this was through a mixture of kinetic and non-kinetic effects; indeed the latter was how the pilot often tried to resolve any situation. Shaping could best be described as missions that undertook the last few months we started a period of regeneration where the force focuses on regaining many of the skills that were put on the back burner. For example, Night Low-Level Flying, consolidated periods on-board the CVS and Operational Low-Level Flying at 100 ft to name but a few. As all will be aware, the more recent Defence announcements led to a downsizing of the Harrier force to two front line squadrons. The two Cottesmore-based squadrons were all to migrate south down the A1 to form up at RAF Wittering alongside the OCU. No.IV(AC) Squadron had been disbanded as a front line unit and re-formed as No.IV(R) Squadron in place of No.20(R) Squadron as the OCU. Consequently No.1(F) Squadron RAF and 800 Naval Air Squadron formed the two front line Harrier squadrons under the umbrella of the Joint Strike Wing within JFH. Each front line squadron was be equipped with 10-12 aircraft, approximately 14 pilots and in the region of 140 engineers. During this period we saw the last of the GR7s upgraded and we were an all GR9 fleet with, hopefully, enough of the large Mk.107 Pegasus engines fitted to each aircraft. While initially this looked quite disappointing, our focus was now on becoming a leaner but more capable force, able to deliver effective Day and Night capabilities from afloat or ashore in all weathers, with the ultimate goal still firmly being a transition to the F-35 Joint Strike Fighter in 2018. This transition is still the ultimate goal even though the Harrier force has now been withdrawn prematurely.'

Paul Tremeling's experience with the first-generation Harrier (as described in the previous chapter) was succeeded by a tour flying Harrier GR7s with JFH. Here he recalls his own experience of operations in Afghanistan:

'Whilst I was unfortunate enough to be delayed in getting to the GR7 due to the minor inconvenience of a staff tour, I did get there eventually. At the time the Harrier force had been deployed to Afghanistan for three years with each squadron manning the detachment for a four-month period before having eight months at home to rest, sharpen up again and redeploy. The war had been cruel and kind to the Harrier. By the time we left the theatre, the upgrades afforded to the jet had seen it become one of the world's best CAS platforms, period. Some would favour the A-10 or maybe AV-8B, but the GR9 was arguably as good as either of them. Medium level CAS, with some low level work became the norm and other tasks had to take a lower billing. The jet itself had its strengths and weaknesses compared to the Sea Harrier FA2. It was easier to fly in most regimes. It was incredibly stable in VSTOL, something that I actually found annoying to start with, preferring my old sports car to this lumbering bus. It was far more docile in combat and any departure was telegraphed well before you were bitten. Large flaps made short field work a doddle and launches that I considered the norm in the FA2 were seen as

emergencies on the Harrier 2. Lastly, the kit was vastly superior. That is, the kit that was there. I always felt naked without the radar and how the RAF had come to buy an aeroplane with no radar and no data link was beyond me. Any argument about the radar not being required came from people who had never seen one; any argument about other kit in the nose being better for bombing came from disinformation at best, unadulterated lies at worse.

'Having said that, the rest of the kit made the GR7 and latterly the GR9 very easy to operate. Your missions were planned and loaded into the aeroplane using a computer which put its data on a brick, you had a moving map, a fuel system that told you when to go home, a computerised weapons page, a wing that actually gave you lift. The kit could accept all manner of inputs, from a change in the mission time to moving one of the many waypoints, with consummate ease. It told you if you were early or late, it had a clock in the HUD, it was all very well thought out. It was an aeroplane built from the wheels up to allow a reasonable standard of pilot to use it effectively, primarily as a CAS platform but for strike and CVS ops as well. Afghanistan, like the GR7/9, was all about CAS. The war and the aeroplane suited each other perfectly. Life in Kandahar was simple. You got up in the dark and went to work. You planned a mission which would take about 15 minutes for a CAS mission, maybe about 45 for a recce mission. The brief initially took 30 minutes but we soon had it down to around 15. We started out-briefing an hour before launch, but got this down to 45 minutes quite quickly. So within a couple of weeks, from not knowing your task to being airborne, was possible in 1 hour and 15 minutes. This might sound a bit superficial, but bear in mind that we often got re-tasked when airborne, so there was no time to plan or brief. Equally, from Ground Alert Close Air Support (GCAS) we would be on a 30 minute alert and would be expected to be airborne within 30 minutes of the call, with no planning whatsoever. And we never took 30 minutes, we took about 16, the record being about 11 minutes. Not bad considering that the scramble involved a 2 mile drive.

'Once you had flown your mission for the day, or sat on alert for 12 hours, then the time was yours and this invariably meant a trip to the gym and some food. We repeated this pattern until someone was kind enough to send us home.

'Life at Kandahar was not without its hazards. The dust made your nose bleed, at times boredom was a crafty enemy and, despite what everyone says about the place being comfortable, westernised and "unwarlike", it attracted about 90 per cent of all Indirect Fire attacks in Afghanistan in 2008. The role of CAS aircraft in Afghanistan at a rudimentary level was simple. Help the ground forces do their job. Provide whatever effect they require, be it looking ahead with a targeting pod,

A Harrier waits fully armed in its shelter at Kandahar, Afghanistan, in June 2009. Harrier operations in Afghanistan ended in this month after five years of activity in the area, as part of Operation Herrick. (Photo: UK MoD Crown Copyright 2010)

getting pictures with a recce pod, putting noise down from medium level, putting lots down from low level. Then came the high order stuff, kinetics. We would provide the firepower the ground troops wanted, when organic fires were either impossible or simply wouldn't cut it. This is what we all lived and hoped for. The bones of the missions were simple. The Air Tasking Order told you when to go and what task to do. The Joint Air Request told you who to talk to, on what frequency and what they wanted. We left KAF, as Kandahar was known, using the Tesseral departure to stay in the MANPADS threat for as short a time as possible. The airfield was high so the air very thin. Indicated air speed was about thirty knots below ground speed on take-off, so the 144kts of Bernoullis we needed made about 175kt across the ground. The tyre limiting speed is 180, so fairly marginal, particularly in hot weather. The STO was done at full power using STOL flap, snatching 40 nozzle at the planned take-off speed. We would then level at 100 ft over the desert and accelerate to 400kts. You were allowed to turn once you were at 300kts. The excellent bubble canopy gave you a massive ground rush at these altitudes. Both fighters went outbound through different sectors to avoid the enemy being alerted by the first

and targeting the second. The climb to cruising altitude was made very quickly from these speeds and we dispensed countermeasures pre-emptively as we went. We spoke to KAF approach and then to C2, call-sign "Crowbar", told him where we were off to and what airspace we needed. The country, indeed the whole world, is divided up into usable chunks using the CGRS or "kill box" system. Each thirty minute-by-thirty minute box is called a kill box, each one broken down into 9 keypads, numbered 1-9 like a telephone. So you would book the keypads with "Crowbar" at your operating height and then "push tactical" or talk to the Joint Terminal Attack Controller. The weather varies massively in theatre, but on most days we had only brilliant blue skies to operate in. We had horrendous dust clouds that masked the runway and awful sandstorms. You could do an approach to the runway in some conditions using the FLIR, displayed on the starboard screen – these guys had thought of everything. The runway usually stood out boldly on FLIR even through the dust.

'The vast majority of the time would be filled using the excellent Sniper pod to move ahead of friendly troops or keep eyes on areas of interest for them. The Harrier was superb at this. We could maintain a very tight wheel above the target and with the Sniper downlinking to the JTAC he could see exactly what we did. We used the pod on either screen, slewing it around with our left thumb, zooming in and out via a wheel on the throttle and using other HOTAS to focus and track targets. When the enemy began to operate the first signs were usually hearing about it from the JTAC whose interpreter was listening in to the Taliban communications nets. It is an odd way of fighting at times. Below you are the real heroes of the fight, yet up at 16,000 ft, or so, you were there in a fully tooled up warplane waiting to help. The view out of the cockpit was excellent and we always carried binoculars for old-school "out the window" talk-ons. The rest of the time we used the pod. The two highlights were Shows Of Force and weaponry, or kinetics. For a Show Of Force you just needed a grid and a Line Of Attack: one aircraft would go outside visual range and then descend as rapidly as possible to be level below 150 ft running towards the target with at least 7nm to go. This was great fun. Head on a swivel for the AA threat in whatever guise, and hand on the countermeasure dispense button. You would give the JTAC a 60 seconds, inbound call and scream over the required position. Your flight path over the desert was marked by the velocity vector in the HUD which you moved smoothly to maintain the minimum we were allowed to go, 100 ft. The bombs topped out at 495kts, so we used to come in at about 490kts. Sometimes the target was enemy or suspected enemy, our SOF supposed to scare them off, sometimes 'friendlies' in order to warn the enemy that these guys had friends in high places.

'The kinetics were very exciting and fraught with anxiety. CAS with an LGB when the JTAC can see the pod picture via downlink. This is less worrying in one respect as target ID is given, but the thing still has to work. From our operating height the weapon took 25 nervous seconds from satisfying metallic "clunk" to incredibly satisfying impact; enough time to worry a lot about what would happen in the event of a malfunction. Dynamic aiming of weapons through the HUD was more exciting and you had to be doubly sure that the target you had in your sights was the correct one; sometimes the talk-ons were fraught as pilot and JTAC strove to marry up what a building looks like from the ground and what it looks like from the air. High above the target you confirm with the JTAC that the target is allowed

to be attacked under your ROE. The attacks would all start with a nine line. Nine mandatory pieces of information that you had to be told; you wrote them all on your right knee board as the autopilot flew the aeroplane for you. You then read them straight back to the JTAC and pointed the jet towards the correct bit of sky. Having punched the information into a waypoint you were in a position to ask for a talk-on if you needed one, or confirm any details you weren't sure about. After that you made your run in, probably with your weapons page on one screen and the Sniper picture on the other. Very high octane stuff and enough to get the heart racing. For an LGB drop you would fire laser at the target, using yet another small button on the throttle, making the target solution more accurate. You had to call the JTAC to say you were "In Hot"; in return, he would clear you to attack. The attack was then automatic for legacy Paveway or you pickled the weapon off once you got the correct indications for a GPS-guided weapon. You then went back to the pod and ensured the laser was firing. If for whatever reason it didn't – you got your wingman to fire his. All our bombs hit, which

No.1 Squadron Harrier GR9s high over Chicago towards the end of a long ferry flight to the USA for participation in an exercise, each aircraft carrying four external fuel tanks and centreline-mounted luggage pods. (Photo: Andy Townsend)

Pilot's-eye view of a Harrier mission from the rear seat of a T12. The HUD confirms the aircraft's height (1,300ft) and speed (355 knots). (Photo: UK MoD Crown Copyright 2010)

is testament to the arming teams and weapon supply. It was great to be up in that deep blue sky throwing high tech weapons at the enemy from such a well integrated machine. The easiest attacks, with no coordination required, were the ones where you simply did everything yourself, from getting a coordinate from the pod, putting it into the bomb, releasing the weapon and lasing until impact.

'The dynamic attacks were probably more fun. Using simple but accurate sights, we dropped 540 lb bombs and fired CRV7 rockets at the enemy in 30 degree dives, aiming for weapon release at 450kts. With the advent of the GR9 and Paveway 4 we changed our load to all jets carrying solely

A magnificent head-on view of the Harrier GR9, armed with SNEB pods, ADEN cannon (non-functioning) and Sidewinders. (Photo: UK MoD Crown Copyright 2010)

Harrier GR7 ZD407 pictured during circuit training at Wittering, proudly displaying the markings of No.20(R) Squadron. (Photo: Tom Cheney)

A Harrier pictured firing CRV-7 rockets. Each pod housed 19 rounds, fitted with high-explosive or armour-piercing warheads. With a high impact speed the rockets could be launched from a range of up to three miles. (Photo: No.4 Squadron Association)

PW4 and rockets, so flexible was that weapon load. We always tried to work as teams however. Each of us carried cards to read to the other before an attack, to confirm that everything was in the correct position. With that last check complete and with the JTAC's clearance you would haul the aircraft across and down to a point at a position below the target before bringing the sight up under positive g. The bombs left with a comforting "clunk", the rockets zipped out of their pod right on the edge of visual perception – they travelled so fast. Off target we would pull up out of the threat and away from our own weapon, dispense flares, then make the switches safe, ready for an immediate re-attack or other task, and listening intently for Battle Damage Assessment. As with all wars the warriors have always been keenly interested in their effect on the enemy, and whilst we don't count the kills in a Battle Of Britain way, you are aware of what you have done. Once off task we would head back to KAF, or join on a tanker for more gas followed by more trade. The arrival at KAF was fun. After you gave C2 your mission report you went over to KAF approach who cleared you into the overhead. KAF tower then told you when you could descend. Down you came from 20,000 ft at 50 or 60 degrees nose down, using nozzle to slow you down and to position yourself at the end of downwind at about 3,000 ft QFE for a sweeping finals turn. So long as you knew what you were doing with the air speed and nozzle combination you could come in steeply, thereby avoiding any threat and not exceed 165kts, the speed at which your flap came back up automatically. If this happened the results were likely to be eye watering. As with all aviation events there are many ways of arriving at a given parameter, but the margin for error decreases with time available. This was true of

the Tesseral recovery; you could be as steep as you liked, but you had to be in good shape, within engine performance and below 165kts when you crossed the airfield boundary, adopting the landing attitude to present all five tyres to the ground at once. Back on the ground we used a bit of braking stop, nozzles all the way forward, to stop and roll off amongst all the other fighter, helicopter and heavy traffic that called KAF home.

'What could be better? Flying a fully integrated jet, in support of coalition troops fighting for their lives in such a hostile environment. Joint Force Harrier saved lives in theatre and did some serious damage to the enemy. I would be amazed to hear a JTAC speak ill of the service we gave in our five years in Afghanistan.'

Above and top: Harrier GR7 ZG589 received a very unusual shark mouth marking during its stay at Ahmed al Jabar in Kuwait, whilst participating in Operation Warden (the British component of Operation Iraqi Freedom). (Photo: No.4 Squadron Association)

Harrier operations in support of commitments in Iraq, the Balkans and Afghanistan, often resulted in the appearance of traditional 'kill' markings which were applied on the aircraft's nose under the cockpit. This aircraft displays four LGB mission kills. (Photo: Tom Cheney)

Harrier T10 ZH665 in company with a GR7 from No.4 squadron, high over the North Sea during a refuelling rendezvous in October 2004. (Photo: Philip Stevens/TargetA Photography)

A Harrier turns away from the cameraman to reveal a pair of white-painted Maverick missiles. This air-to-surface weapon was introduced following experience in Kosovo in 1999 when poor weather often degraded the effectiveness of attacks. (Photo: UK MoD Crown Copyright 2010)

Harriers at Gioia del Colle in Italy, during assignment to Operation Allied Force in 1999. (Photo: UK MoD Crown Copyright 2010)

Harrier GR9 up close, illustrating the ARBS (Angle Rate Bombing System) laser seeker and the Forward Looking Infra Red (FLIR) sensor above it. Below the nose are the Zeus ECM sensors. (Photo: UK MoD Crown Copyright 2010)

ZD406 pictured firing a salvo of SNEB rockets whilst serving with No.20(R) Squadron, the RAF's Harrier Operational Conversion Unit. It later became well known as the wearer of the FAA's '100 Years of Naval Aviation' specially-painted tail. (Photo: UK MoD Crown Copyright 2010)

A close-up view of a Harrier from No.20(R) Squadron. Visible here is the small yaw vane attached to the upper nose ahead of the windscreen. This enabled the pilot to maintain directional stability - vital during hover manoeuvres. (Photo: UK MoD Crown Copyright 2010)

A Harrier GR9 high over Afghanistan, deploying flares as part of the ARI23333/1 Zeus ECM system fitted to the fleet. Chaff and flares were fired automatically by the system as required. (Photo: UK MoD Crown Copyright 2010)

An RAF Harrier GR7 pilot wearing (in daylight for the cameraman) the NVG (Night Vision Goggles) utilised for routine night time Harrier operations. (Photo: UK MoD Crown Copyright 2010)

Simultaneous flare activation by a pair of RAF Harriers, captured on camera over Afghanistan. (Photo: UK MoD Crown Copyright 2010)

A typical Afghanistan scene as a Harrier GR7 gets airborne, armed with a laser-guided bomb. (Photo: UK MoD Crown Copyright 2010)

An unusual image of the Harrier GR9, as seen from the refuelling station of a USMC KC-130 tanker. USMC units were occasionally tasked with the refuelling of RAF aircraft during operations in Iraq and Afghanistan.

(Photo: UK MoD Crown Copyright 2010)

A pair of Harrier GR7s painted in temporary grey camouflage for operations over Iraq. CRV-7 rocket pods are carried under the wings. Also visible is the BOL300 chaff dispenser on the adjacent weapons pylon.
(Photo: UK MoD Crown Copyright 2010)

ZD320, the first Harrier GR9 pictured during trials at Warton. Visible under the fuselage is the Lockheed AN/AAQ-33 Advanced Targeting Pod, deliveries of which were completed in June 2007. (Photo: BAE Systems)

Harrier GR9s from No.800 NAS pictured at altitude during a long-range ferry flight. Each aircraft is carrying four external fuel tanks plus under-fuselage baggage pods. (Photo: Andy Townsend)

Harrier GR9s pictured during a deployment to HMS Illustrious. Each aircraft is clean of external stores, other than BOL300 chaff dispensers. (Photo: UK MoD Crown Copyright 2010)

Composite digital photograph illustrating a pilot's-eye view of the Harrier GR9, positioned ready for take-off from HMS Illustrious.
(Photo: UK MoD Crown Copyright 2010)

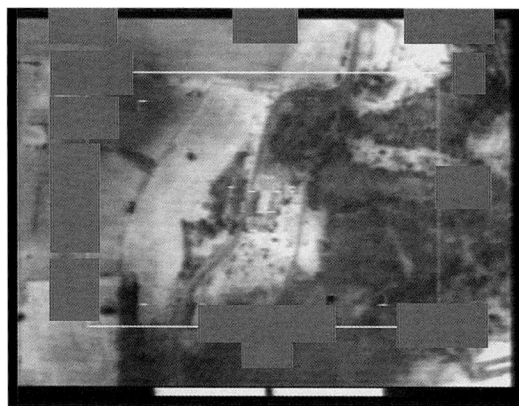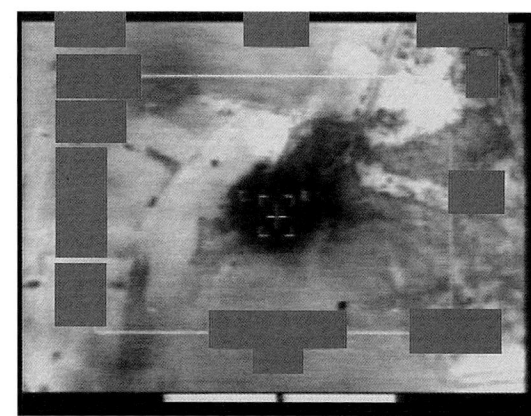

Reconnaissance imagery of a Harrier-launched LGB (laser-guided bomb) attack on a target in Iraq.
(Photo: UK MoD Crown Copyright 2010)

Close-up of the Zeus ECM sensors under the nose of a Harrier GR9. The central glazed panel houses the target seeker and tracker for the AN/ASB-19(V2) Angle Rate Bombing Set (ARBS). (Photo: UK MoD Crown Copyright 2010)

A close-up view at typical Operation Warden Harrier armament comprising a 500 lb laser-guided bomb, AIM-9L Sidewinder AAM and BOL300 chaff dispenser. (Photo: UK MoD Crown Copyright 2010)

Sniper pod and DJRP (Digital Joint Reconnaissance Pod) under the fuselage of a Harrier GR9. (Photo: BAE Systems)

Like other RAF Harrier units, No.4 Squadron decorated a number of Harriers with unit markings across the tail surfaces (usually applied to the CO's aircraft), this GR9 being the Squadron's last Harrier to receive such treatment, pictured taxying for take-off at Cottesmore in 2010. (Photo: Rich Pittman)

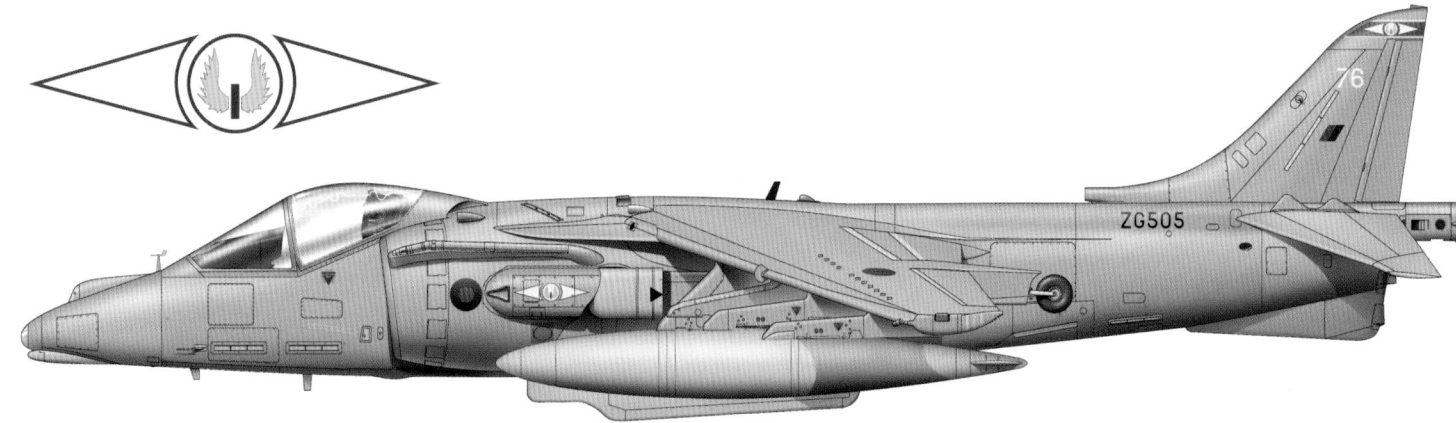

BAe Harrier GR Mk.9, ZG505/76, No. 1 Squadron, September 2009
Camouflage Grey BS381C 626 overall; Blue/Red roundels on air intake fairings, above port and below starboard wings. Black serial, white code; unit badge within a white disc flanked by two white arrowheads, all outlined in red. This marking repeated on top of fin over a red band, outlined in white

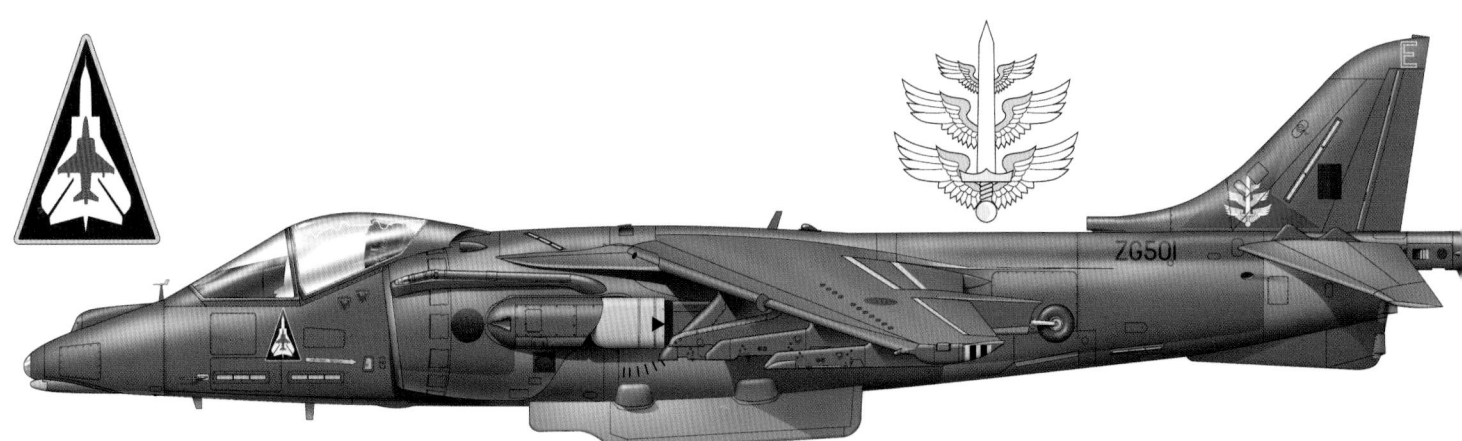

BAe Harrier GR Mk.9, ZG501/E, SAOEU,1996
NATO Green BS 381C:285 upper surfaces with Lichen Green BS 4800:12-B-25 undersides; blue/red national markings. Blue flash on fin with 'winged sword' marking; unit badge on nose. Black serial, code 'E' in yellow outline on top of fin

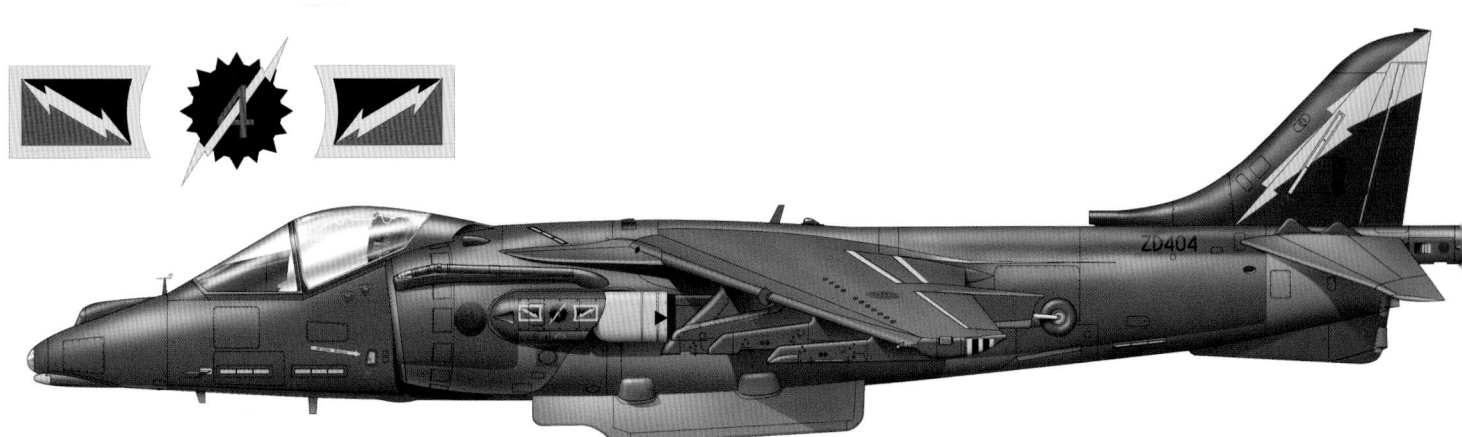

BAe Harrier GR Mk.7, ZD404, No. 4 Squadron, 1989
NATO Green BS 381C:285 upper surfaces with Lichen Green BS 4800:12-B-25 undersides; blue/red national markings (fin flash thinly outlined in black). Black serial; black/yellow/red fin. Unit marking with yellow/black/red flashes on air intakes

ZG858 pictured during a stop-over at RNAS Yeovilton. Unusually, the non-functioning ADEN cannon pods are not carried, and under-fuselage strakes have been fitted in order to restore the residual amount of jet lift available from the engine exhaust whilst in 'ground effect' in the hover. (Photo: Rich Pittman)

ZG512, a Harrier GR9 from No.1 Squadron, pictured at low level over the snowy hills of Wales during a training sortie in 2010.
(Photo: Rich Pittman)

ZD347, operated as part of JFH by No.800 NAS, received unusual tail markings which recall the unit codes worn during World War Two. The bolt-on refuelling probe is in the extended position. (Photo: Rich Pittman)

A Harrier T1 of No.800 NAS up close, illustrating the much-enlarged forward fuselage of the dual control variant, and the significantly raised cockpit position for the instructor. (Photo: Rich Pittman)

No.4 Squadron's ZD346 pictured seconds before touch-down at Cottesmore, just weeks before the type's retirement in 2010. (Photo: Rich Pittman)

CHAPTER NINE

USMC in the Cockpit

ALTHOUGH the Harrier's long and distinguished years of service with both the Royal Air Force and Fleet Air Arm are now ended, it would be wrong to imagine that the Harrier is consigned to history. The very fact that Harriers continue to equip the air arms of India, Italy, Spain and Thailand in only relatively small numbers might imply that the aircraft is no longer an aircraft which can be seriously equated with more modern and sizeable fleets of high-tech warplanes. But this would be an erroneous assumption. In the United States, the Harrier is still very much in business, active in substantial numbers, and destined to remain at the forefront of the United States Marine Corps' offensive capability until the eagerly-anticipated and continually controversial F-35 is brought into service. The Harrier is undoubtedly ageing but it is also a tried and trusted weapon of war which the USMC is in no hurry to relinquish. In order to explain in fascinating detail how the USMC operates the Harrier (the AV-8B) and to illustrate what Harrier operations are really all about, Captain Nicholas Dimitruk, an experienced Harrier pilot and USMC aviator, describes first-hand the world of operational Harrier flying from the pilot's perspective:

'The Harrier serves many different roles within the United States Marine Corps, but it is primarily used as an air-to-surface weapons platform. Most would say that within the air-to-surface realm, the Harrier focuses on the role of close air support. Close Air Support, by definition, is the exertion of

air action by fixed- or rotary-winged aircraft against hostile targets that are positioned close to friendly forces, requiring detailed integration of each air mission with fire and the movement of these forces. Other missions that the Harrier can support include Air Interdiction, Armed Reconnaissance, Strike Coordination and Reconnaissance, Air-to-Air, Anti-Air warfare and Forward Air Controller (Airborne). Any Harrier mission can involve any combination of these missions, but as noted, Close Air Support is the focus, and the most prevalent mission in today's warfare. As a pilot in a Harrier Squadron, you will generally know what type of mission you will be flying as much as a week in advance, but of course you can be scheduled on the spot because you are always expected to be able to execute any type of mission that you are qualified to perform. Generally, but depending on the complexity of the mission, planning for a mission begins several hours prior to the brief time. The Harrier has two computer screens called Multi-Purpose Control Displays that sit side-by-side and provide several different functions for different portions of the flight, but most notably they contain a moving map and compass rose, both of which are key to giving the pilot complete situational awareness. During the planning stage, most of the map that the pilot will see in the flight is first built-up using computers in the planning room. You have the ability to select accurate waypoints, build routes, create map overlays, satellite imagery, calculate times, build weapon envelopes and so on. The computers can also help calculate weights and drag,

AV-8B Plus releasing a shower of flares from its ALE-29 dispensers. (Photo: USMC)

plug in frequencies into preset channels, and 'weaponeer' diagrams help give the pilot a visual representation of how an attack will be conducted. Almost all aspects of the mission can be pre-planned and plugged into the computer, which can then be transferred to the jet. We always like to have paper copies to back up the plan should the computer fail, so we will often have waypoint locations, radio frequencies, weaponeering diagrams, weights and drag and so on, that can be manually fed into the jet

if necessary. This of course is the backup plan and can be very time-consuming, and as any pilot knows well – time equals fuel. Once we build our missions and save them to a disk, we will usually get another weather update and check the notices to airmen (NOTAMS). After several hours of pre-flight planning, we are then ready to conduct the brief.

'Briefs always begin exactly on time, and the first item of business is to conduct a "time hack". We work backwards from when we need to have

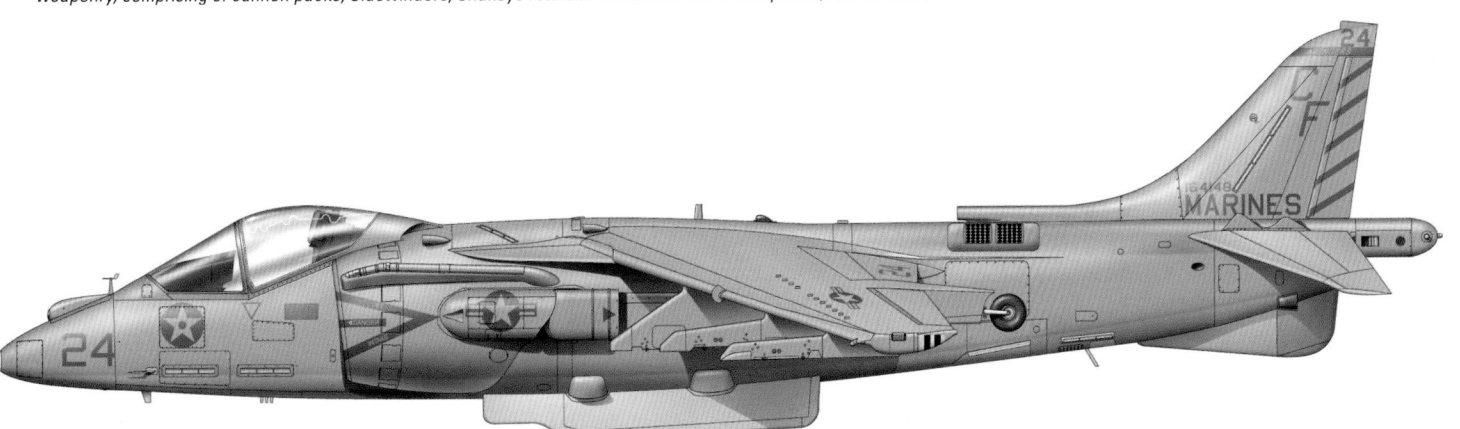

A pair of AV-8B Harriers from VMA-211, the 'Wake Island Avengers.' Together, the aircraft are carrying a wide range of standard weaponry, comprising of cannon packs, Sidewinders, Snakeye retarded HE bombs and rocket pods. (Photo: USMC)

McDonnell Douglas AV-8B Harrier II, 164148/CF-24, VMA-211 'Avengers', US Marine Corps
Upper surfaces in FS.36231, undersides in FS.36320; markings in dark grey

AV-8Bs from VMA-223 receiving attention between sorties. The aircraft in the foreground has been painted with a special anniversary tail marking which refers to the unit's history, and its previous incarnations as VMF-223, when it operated Skyhawks and Hellcats. (Photo: USMC)

the bombs on target. This allows us to know when to take off, when to taxi, when to check in, when to start the jets and so on. These time hacks are essential for us to manage timelines in such a manner. Following the time hack, we conduct a product inventory to ensure every participating pilot has the proper products to aid him in the flight. This includes maps, imagery, and what we like to call "smart packs" which include all necessary information pertaining to the flight. Following this, we conduct a sortie overview and outline our main objectives. This allows everyone to see the big picture before we start getting down to the exact details of each part of the mission. Intelligence will brief us on enemy and friendly dispositions, allowable risk in regards to threats we might face, threat specific details such as the envelopes in which the enemy can engage us, or what indications our cockpit would give us if we were to be engaged by a surface-to-air missile, etc. Following an Intelligence Report, we tackle the administrative portion of the flight. This includes current and forecasted weather, call signs, aircraft assigned, block altitudes assigned to each aircraft for de-confliction, the succession of leadership should the lead jet break down, what ordnance our aircraft will have, how much fuel, how heavy we expect to be, what our drag will be, and what we can expect in regard to back-up jets should our jets break down. Next we will go over our VSTOL capabilities. The ability to hover, or any nozzle usage other than when directed aft, relies on our aircraft weight, expected weather, and elevation (altitude). For weather, the colder the temperatures and the higher the altimeter setting, the more thrust our engine will produce and the more likely we will be able to hover. The same applies for elevation – lower elevations allow greater engine performance. Added to this, the aircraft's gross weight has to be sufficiently low enough to hover. For the pilot, hover weight is generally achieved by burning gas down to an acceptable level and hopefully returning without any heavy ordnance. In the jet, our computers calculate how heavy the jet is and provide us our hovering capabilities in the form of fuel levels. In other words, it will tell us at what fuel level we need to be at before we can start hovering with the current aircraft configuration. If it spits out 4.5, for example, then I will need to burn my gas down to 4,500 lb before I can expect to be light enough to hover. If it gives me a number close to zero, or a negative number, then I am being told that under the current aircraft configuration and

weather, my aircraft will not be able to hover. So during the VSTOL part of the brief, we like to get an idea of whether we will have VSTOL capabilities, and if we don't, what methods we can use (such as jettisoning bombs) to reach hover performance in case we need to do so in an emergency. If we are away from home base, we usually reserve this portion of the brief also to go over other such variables that may affect both our departure and arrival into a foreign field. Such variables include field elevation, runway distances available, what speeds we can reach on the runway before we are no longer able to abort the take-off, whether there is concrete available should we have to perform a vertical landing (our exhaust is so hot that asphalt will melt, thus requiring concrete for vertical landings) and so on. We next cover fuel management. We usually designate three fuel levels that we can programme into our jet. Upon reaching that fuel level, the jet will give us both an audio and visual alert. We begin with "Tiger" fuel, which we usually designate as the level of fuel at which we can afford one more attack or manoeuvre specific to the mission. Next we have "Joker" fuel, which usually designates enough fuel to stop the tactical portion of the flight, join up, and go home. The last fuel state is "Bingo" which is the fuel level that means we need to be pointed at home base immediately. We will also use this portion of the brief to discuss details concerning the refuelling tanker should we be requiring in-flight refuelling. For instance, we'll discuss the tanker times, what sequence different sections are going to rendezvous the tanker, and any other fuel related administrative briefing items.

'Next we cover communications. We will cover what frequencies we are likely to use, which preset channels (1 through to 99) that we have assigned each UHF frequency, what frequency we will use

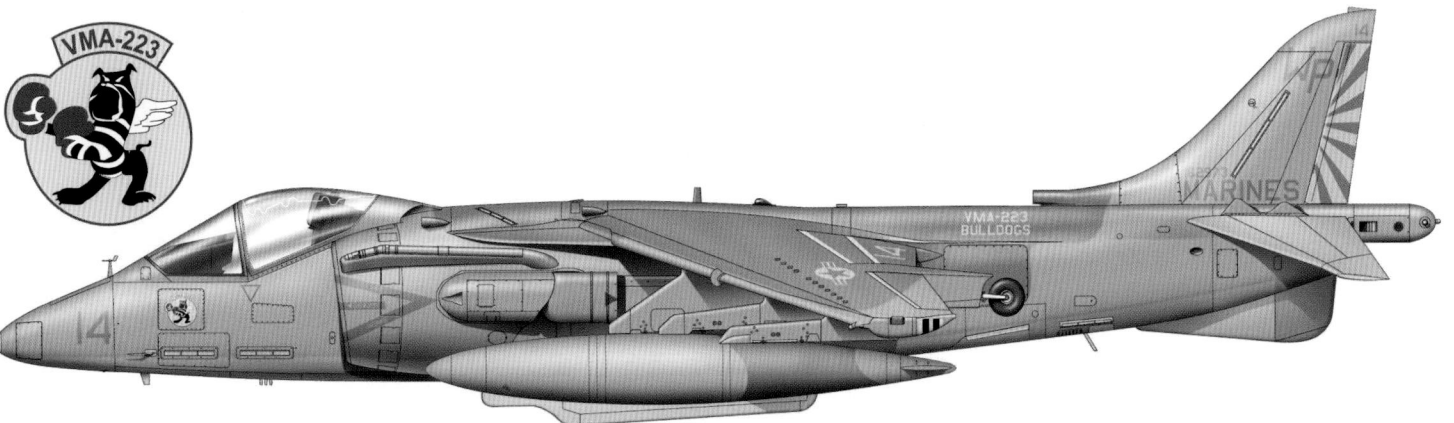

McDonnell Douglas AV-8B Harrier II, 162973/WP-14, VMA-223 'Bulldogs', USMC, 1997
Upper surfaces of wings and fuselage spine in FS.36118; fuselage sides and top of horizontal tail surfaces in FS.36231, undersides in FS.36320. Unit insignia on nose; '14' repeated on nose, top of fin and above wing flaps

for inter-flight communication and what frequency we will hop to should we have no luck on that frequency (referred to as "chatter mark" frequency). We should normally have two working radios, one for inter-flight communications and the other used primarily for external agencies. Sometimes one of the radios might not work, so we have to cover how we will handle this particular contingency.

We will also cover the plan should we lose communications altogether. Next we cover navigation and we usually cover our waypoint plan at this stage. We use waypoints to mark our home field as well as alternate airfields, points of interest along the route, locations where we would like to filter through to both begin and end an attack, and of course the targets themselves. We will usually print out maps of several scales to give us better situational awareness of where the waypoints are located. We also like to use satellite imagery to find good geographical reference points which serve to help talk each other on to targets visually. We will discuss our sensors and how effective they will be given the time of day and the environmental conditions. We have many sensors that can be used both by day and night including a forward looking infrared pod, radar, camera, and night vision goggles. We have two FLIR (Forward Looking Infra Red) systems, one of which is internal to the jet and used primarily for navigation. The other is located in a targeting pod that is hung off our wing. As the name suggests, this FLIR is used primarily for reconnaissance and targeting. Unlike the FLIR internal to the jet, this FLIR can be slewed about its axis. Environmental conditions such as visibility, humidity, time of day etc., greatly affect how well these sensors can operate. For instance, the position of the sun greatly affects our ability to see targets, especially when it comes to shadows. Similarly, the position of the moon greatly affects our ability to

see at night. We will have dedicated weather personnel send us over a report that details how well our sensors are expected to work that day and how far we can expect to see, given the variable conditions. We will then go over our weapons loads and how we need to set them up and employ them so we maximize our ability to accomplish the mission. This is a very detailed process with many moving parts, and any kink in the chain could result in "duded" (non-functioning) bombs or unsafe attacks. We will go over how to pre-flight each weapon, the limitations of the weapons themselves and the limitations that these weapons place on the jet. Each weapon and external store configuration limits how fast we can go, how fast we can release the weapons, what Gs we can pull, how steep we can dive, whether we can dive at all, and so on. It is also important to cover how many weapons we can release at any one time and the time intervals between each release should we choose to drop multiple weapons. We calculate the distance between where each weapon will impact the ground, and what will maximize the probability that the specific target will be destroyed. Discussion will cover not only how we will deliver the ordnance, but also how we will fuse it. How long, from the time the weapons fall off our jet, do we want until the fuse arms the bomb? Do we want the explosion to happen upon impact, or do we want there to be a delay so that the weapons can penetrate a roof top for example? As with most aspects of flying, we always like to plan for contingencies and worse case scenarios. What happens if the bombs fail to come off the jet? Will we be too heavy to vertically land? Will we be too heavy to land at all? What happens if only the bombs on one wing come off, leaving us with an asymmetric load? Will we have enough aileron control authority to keep the jet controlled? Will the puffer ducts on the wing tips have enough thrust to keep the jet upright should we need to use our VSTOL capabilities and we happen to be asymmetric? What do we do should our gun misfire, or we have hot round in the chamber? As you can see, you can never plan enough, especially with the endless possibilities that come with the task of delivering ordnance.

'Much like we can input fuel levels to alert the pilot, we can also input altitudes to give us more situational awareness. For each type of delivery, we can input an altitude that will flash a warning light and audio tone to alert us when we pass through that altitude. When we dive deliver a bomb, we will usually use this feature to mark the minimum altitude in which we can make a safe recovery. In other words, when we hear what we refer to as "bitching betty" saying "altitude, altitude", it means we need to start pulling up now before we hit the ground or "frag" ourselves (fragmentation damage) with our own bomb. This can be a real life saver especially at night when we are diving into pitch black. We can also input an altitude into the computer that gives us a visual cue in our heads up display to show whether the bomb will dud or not. As we dive towards the ground we lose altitude, which means when the bomb leaves our aircraft it

has less and less time for the fuse to arm the bomb. Eventually, at a given altitude, there will not be enough altitude for the fuse to arm the bomb, and as a result the bomb will fall harmlessly and dud. So we will discuss what altitude we need to input into the system, given our calculations, so that we get an accurate visual cue in the HUD that notifies us when our bomb will dud. Finally, given all these variables, we will go over the numbers of each type of attack to include altitudes, speeds, dive angles, etc. The Harrier is armed with the ALR-67, a passive detection system designed for both airborne and ground threats, and we will set up this system. Do we want the computer to prioritise air threats or ground threats? Do we want to display all threats or do we want to prioritise only those threats most dangerous to us? We are also armed with an ALE-39 which is a system that dispenses flares, chaff, and jammers (expendables). We use the heat from flares both as a pre-emptive and a reactive way to decoy infrared-guided missiles. For both radar and radar-guided missiles, we use chaff as a decoy. Finally, we can expend jammers that will jam specific radars and radar-guided missiles. During the brief, we need to know what and how many expendables we have and how we plan to set up them up. When we activate the flare switch, for

AV-8B 162966 (NWC-87) pictured at China Lake NAS in April 1989 during night-attack systems trials. (Photo: US Navy)

Visible in this photograph is the installation of the GAU-12/U Equaliser 25 mm cannon under the fuselage. The gun is carried in the port pod with 300 ammunition loaded into the starboard pod (transferred to the gun by a feed system). (Photo: USMC)

instance, how many flares do we want to go off, what time interval between each flare do we want, when should we activate this switch both pre-emptively and reactively, etc., and then we will discuss the same in regard to chaff and jammers. After these systems discussions, we then talk about how we plan to taxi, what type of take-off we want, the departure, arrival and landing that we plan to do. What formations do we plan to be in during each portion of the flight? How fast, and at what altitude do we want to be? What approaches at each airfield are available to us should the weather go bad. We will then discuss what external assets are available to us for the mission. Will we have tankers for in-flight refuelling, will we have EA-6B Prowlers to jam enemy radar, will we have AWACS to provide us de-confliction and be our eyes in the sky, will we have a forward air controller on the ground helping us guide our bombs to their intended target, and so on. Lastly, we will go over all the possible emergencies we could encounter from weapons malfunctions to bird strikes, engine fires, oil failure, mid-air collisions, ejection procedures etc. We will also discuss what our game plan will be

for each emergency. We will explore what particular rules we have to help mitigate any of these emergencies. Every particular type of mission, whether it be close air support, low altitude training, air-to-air combat, air-to-surface or anything else, has a set of rules that we legally have to verbalise before we can fly that type of flight. This covers the administrative and tactical administrative portion of the brief. Everything discussed above should typically take fifteen minutes of the brief. As you can see, it is a lot of information to be passed in such a small period of time. This is why, as I stated before, flight leads are trained to be extremely articulate and well spoken. The majority of the brief is left to the tactical portion of the brief. This tactical portion will discuss in minute detail every manoeuvre we plan to do during the actual attack phase of the flight.

'The many different types of attack we can do would be difficult to summarise succinctly. The tactical portion of the brief usually concentrates on specific attacks we plan or are likely to conduct during the flight. The flight lead will first cover the goals of the mission that determine mission success. The flight lead will go into minute detail covering every second of the attack timeline. He will discuss every altitude, position, heading and airspeed he expects every member of the flight to be in throughout the entire course of the attack or manoeuvre. He will discuss every check each pilot needs to do, what the pilot should see in his head up display, and what he should see in his computer screens below. He will discuss common mistakes and how to correct these mistakes. He will go over required communication, expendable usage, and all details pertaining to the attack. The flight lead will have every attack drawn up on the board and will likely use plane models as a visual aid. We try to be as standardized as possible, which means every word uttered by the lead must be in accordance with what the tactical manual says. The lead must even use the proper colours when drawing attacks up on the board. Every mis-speak will likely be debriefed, especially if there is a weapons and tactics instructor present during the brief (WTIs are the weapons and tactics experts who have considerable flight time and have been through a very gruelling and extensive several-month course in weapons and tactics training). Following the brief we get one last out-brief from the duty officer. This duty officer (always a pilot) will provide a final report on weather and any significant details concerning the airfields we plan to use. He will make sure we have jets assigned to us and that they are ready to go. He will make sure we understand all the risks pertaining to the flight and that we have read all current squadron policies. Lastly, he will run down a quick checklist to make sure we have accomplished all basic items required for the flight. The next order of business is to walk to maintenance control and sign the jet out. Every jet has a history of what maintenance it has received recently, and it is essential that each pilot has an understanding of what unique characteristics and discrepancies are associated with that aircraft. This is also an opportunity for the pilot to raise any questions before he finally signs for and takes full responsibility for that aircraft. We will also be able to confirm at this stage that our aircraft has the proper ordnance and external stores loaded. Following this we will suit up. Our equipment includes a g-suit, harness, survival vest, and helmet (with or without NVGs). As we suit up we are performing a quick inspection of the equipment. Are there any holes in the g-suit? Is the harness twisted? Do we have all required survival items in the vest? If we were to use NVGs, we would use this portion of the flight to adjust and focus them. The Flight Equipment room has a special dark box with an eye chart that allows us to properly focus the NVGs.

'It is then time to walk to the jets and conduct a pre-flight inspection. The aircraft at this point has been heavily prepped by the plane captains and maintenance personnel, and the pilot's pre-flight is just one last check to make sure the jet is ready to

be taken into the air. The pre-flight is designed to be one single walk around the jet, checking that all external probes look like they are in functioning order, that panels are secure, no bolts are missing, control surfaces and puffer ducts look to be in working condition, intake and exhaust ducts are clear of any foreign objects such as tools and debris, the aircraft has sufficient oil levels, the tyres are in good shape, and so on. We will also do a quick foreign object sweep in front of the aircraft and then climb the access ladder to begin strapping in. Before we climb in the cockpit, we check the seat to make sure all safety pins have been removed (so that the seat can eject), make sure all the straps are good, switches are in the correct initial position, and tapes and cards (which hold the mission plan much like a CD) have been inserted and are ready to go. We climb in, strap in, and prepare the cockpit for start-up. In tactical aviation we test our systems using what we call BITS (Built-In Tests System). With the flick of a switch we can perform BITS which will help to show whether the system is performing as it should. If the system is not performing properly, then we will be given a certain indication as to what is wrong with it. We perform a BITS check on almost all of our systems. Once the cockpit is prepped for start-up, we check our watches and start the engines at the precise briefed time. We flick the engine switch to start, watch as the RPMs (Revolutions Per Minute) creep up, and with sufficient initial RPMs, we push the throttle up a little to introduce fuel into the combustion chamber. The RPMs continue to creep up along with the engine temperature, and we are looking for the engine not only to light off in time, but to reach a specific RPM at or below a specific temperature. If we see any abnormality in the start that exceeds a specific value (for instance the temperature of the engine during start exceeding 475 Celsius) then we will immediately cease the start process and try to troubleshoot the cause of the problem. With a good start, we can continue the process of getting the jet ready to fly. We test the hydraulic system, make sure all the lights work properly (such as warning and caution lights, or gear down/unsafe lights), we check the engine numbers, load the mission planned data into the plane's computer, turn on the aircraft's navigation/communication and other electrical systems, perform tests on the fuel system, the electrical system, the water system, check the trims, the standby instruments (which are the traditional

A fascinating sequence of stills showing a TAV-8B making a very unconventional landing. After suffering technical difficulties which prevented the undercarriage from extending, the pilot elected to land the aircraft vertically with the gear retracted, aided by a hastily-collected pile of mattresses to soften the landing. As can be seen, the aircraft touched down safely without any injury to the pilot (or aircraft!). (Photos: US Navy)

An in- flight view of an AV-8B from VMA-211, carrying an inert LGB training round. Visible on the upper fuselage ahead of the fin is the ALE-29 flare dispenser. (Photo: Gary Wetzel)

VMAT-203 TAV-8B getting airborne at Cherry Point. All USMC Harrier conversion and training is undertaken by VMAT-203. (Photo: Lance Pawlik)

AV-8B Plus wearing unusual 'special' markings of VMA-214 'Black Sheep'. This unit was the first to re-equip with the night-attack-capable AV-8B. (Photo: Gary Wetzel)

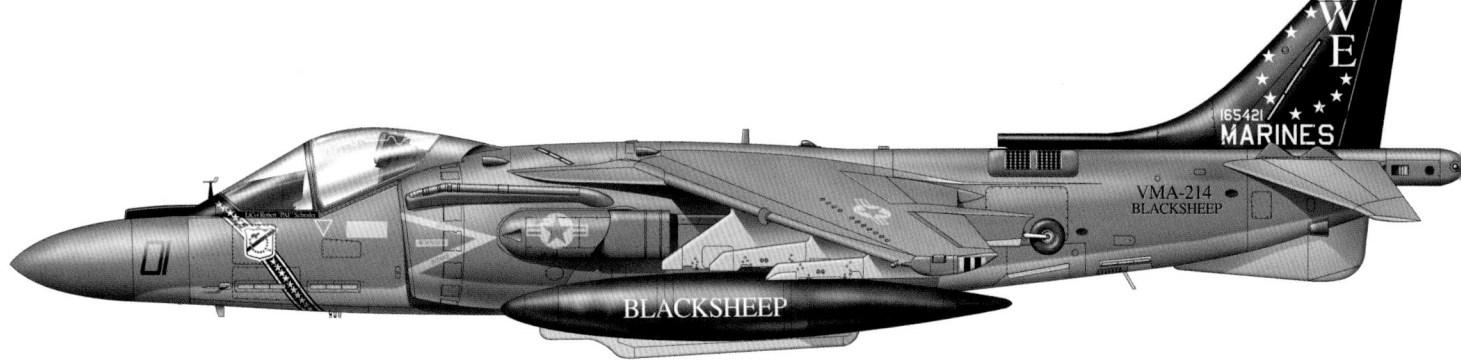

McDonnell Douglas AV-8B Harrier II Plus, 165421/WE-01, VMA-214 'Blacksheep' USMC, 2010
Gunship Gray FS.36118 upper surfaces with Blue Gray FS.35237 undersides; general markings are in reverse colours. Black/white decorations to nose and fin/rudder; black '01' on nose. 'Marines' in black above starboard wing; legend on rear fuselage in black with white drop shadow

stem gauge instruments provided for if our electrical ones should fail), the oxygen system, and the flaps system. We cycle all of our controls to make sure they move properly and that there is nothing binding them, and we conduct a mass BITS check that pretty much tests all other systems to make sure they are functioning properly. After making sure the jet is ready to fly, we then prepare it to make sure it is ready for combat. We check that

we have proper GPS time loaded, we make sure the aircraft computer knows what weapons it has loaded, what fuse times we want for each weapon, what system we want to utilise to drop the weapon, etc. We will double-check that our GPS is operating at a sufficient level, that the targeting pod is properly calibrated, and that our expendables are properly loaded (chaff, flares, jammers). We check within each of us in the flight that all our radios work properly. Once the jets look to be in good shape and all weapons are set up sufficiently and armed by the ordnance personnel, the lead aircraft will communicate with ground that we are ready to taxy, and we are then ready to leave the flight line. We will almost always taxi sequentially and with a considerable distance between each other ("considerable" meaning more than in other tactical jet aircraft). As mentioned before, we are very wary of foreign objects (such as rocks and debris) and the risk of such items entering our intakes and damaging the engine. As you will know, the Harrier has very large intakes, so more than most aircraft it is very susceptible to foreign object damage. We taxi very far apart to prevent another aircraft's exhaust from blowing debris down the trailing aircraft's intake. As we roll towards the runway, we will conduct our final checks to prep the aircraft for take-off. Part of this means checking (given the current weather conditions) what speed we want to throw our nozzles down to jump off the deck successfully and what angle we want the nozzles to be at to maximize our lift (we have a stop near the nozzle lever that can be moved to a particular nozzle angle so we can quickly throw the nozzles to this position). We set our trim to the proper settings, check our flap setting, and double-check we have no warning/caution lights. When we are ready to take the runway, we notify lead that we are "up and ready" and he will call the tower to take position on the runway. We position ourselves on the runway usually with the same spacing as before (for FOD reasons), and the wingman notifies lead that he is "one finger checks complete." This is terminology to signify that he is ready to run his engine up. Lead calls for take-off clearance and tells the flight to run up the engines. This is our final check before we go airborne. We run the engines up to 60 per cent and check that the engine accelerates properly and that all the moving surfaces internal to the engine move to the right position (we have an engine page on our computer displays

Approaching the hover during deployment to MCAS Yuma, an AV-8B from VMA-214 'Black Sheep'. The unit first acquired the AV-8B in 1989. Unusually, the unit's familiar ram's head motif is not carried on the nose. (Photo: US Navy)

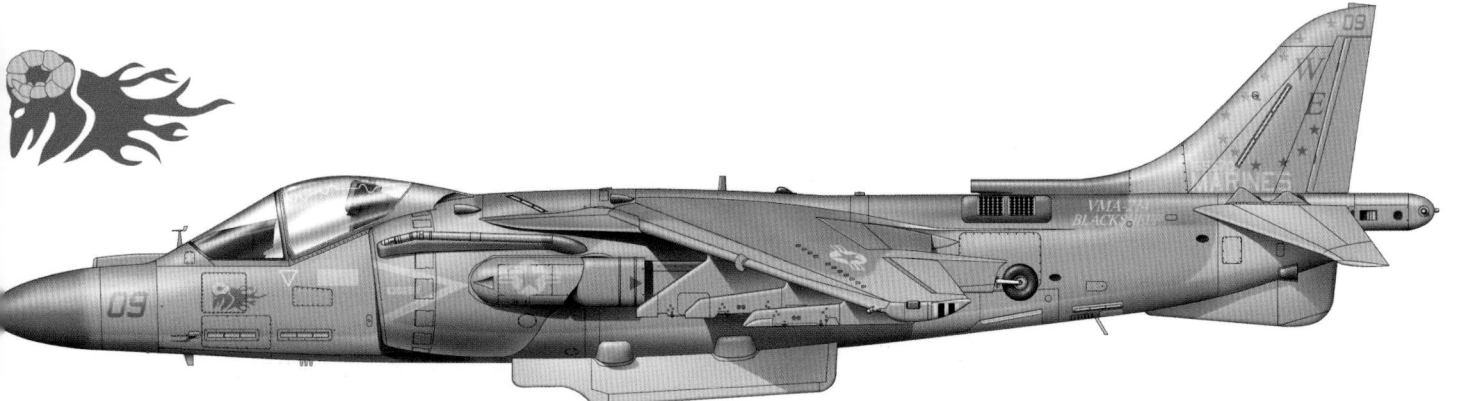

McDonnell Douglas AV-8B Harrier II Plus, 165570/WE-09, VMA-214 'Blacksheep' USMC, Al Asad AB, Iraq, 2004
Dark Compass Gray overall with Gunship Grey top fuselage and wing decking, and Light Compass Gray undersides; markings in a mix of the same three colours. Unit badge on nose

VMA-414 AV-8B Plus pictured during a short take-off from the USS Boxer (LDH-4) (Photo: USMC)

Impressive head-on view of an AV-8B Plus assigned to VX-31 at NAS China Lake.
(Photo: Gary Wetzel)

AV-8B Plus Harriers on VMA-542's flight line. The 'Flying Tigers' were the first to
convert onto the AV-8B Plus variant, deliveries beginning in July 1993.
(Photo: US Navy)

As the VMF-414 AV-8B Plus moves down the flight-deck of the USS Boxer, this view illustrates the second generation Harrier's large wing area, and the leading edge root extensions.
(Photo: US Navy)

that provides all of this engine data), we throw our nozzles to the position we want for lift-off to check the nozzles and nozzle indicators work, that the flaps programme properly alongside the nozzle movement, and that engine duct pressure going to our puffer ducts is sufficient. We throw the nozzles forward again and tell our lead we are 'two finger', which means final checks are complete, and that my jet is ready to be airborne. Lead will roger up this call and say he's rolling. Lead conducts his take-off and as soon as the lead aircraft breaks the deck, the wingman is then ready for his take-off. For take-off, we hold a button to command proper take-off steering, we release the brakes, and slowly and smoothly add full power. Initially the engine will spin up relatively slowly, but as the engine speeds up it will accelerate very suddenly. The pilot will experience this very sudden acceleration which, when experienced for the first time, is an amazing rush. Not many (if any) aircraft can replicate the Harrier's ability to accelerate below 10,000 ft. As the engine reaches full speed, we check that the engine is operating within its RPM and temperature limit. If there is a problem, it is most likely too late by now to abort. Because the engine accelerates the aircraft at such a rapid rate, the aircraft will be too fast to abort successfully.

It is usually more appropriate to take the aircraft into the air at this point and troubleshoot the problem airborne, rather than trying to control and brake the aircraft within the remaining runway length without blowing the tyres and losing

control. That being said, we would have to abort should the emergency prevent us from flying (such as a complete hydraulic failure). With the engine spooled up and the aircraft accelerating down the runway, we very quickly hit the velocity (calculated before by our flight computer) that we take our nozzles from fully aft to the specific angle calculated before. As the nozzles are thrown down, the aircraft literally jumps off the deck like a bottle rocket, aided by some of the aerodynamic lift from the speed that we already have under our wings. The next process is a gradual trade-off of vertical force between the nozzles blowing exhaust downwards and the lift created by our wings. As we creep the nozzles back to their aft position, less thrust is vectored downward so we lose this lifting force. On the other hand, as we push the nozzles to the rear more force is vectored horizontally, accelerating our aircraft and causing the wings to produce more lift. So as we are losing the jet-borne vertical component of force, we are gaining more lift through the wings. As stated before, this is a careful trade-off to keep the aircraft airborne and in control, and a trade-off that is 100 per cent under the control of the pilot. If done too quickly, the lift from the wings will not be sufficient to compensate for the loss of downward thrust from the nozzles, and the aircraft will descend and possibly hit the deck. If done too slowly, the aircraft will remain in a limbo of jet-borne and wing-borne flight which can overheat the engine and also cause the aircraft to linger at a low and dangerous altitude.

An unusual angle on a quartet of AV-8B aircraft, illustrating the distinctive nose profile of the radar-equipped AV-8B Plus variant as compared to the AV-8B(NA), one example of which (No.54) can be seen.
(Photo: US Navy)

'As we perform this slow and controlled acceleration, the pilot will lift the gear up before reaching 250kts, re-programme the flaps for conventional flight, and eventually we will be flying like any other conventional aircraft (nozzles fully aft and all controllability through our aerodynamic control surfaces). We run down to our to lead aircraft and pull up into formation. As we fly out to the tactical area, we start setting up our systems so we are ready to attack the given target. This involves arming up the system, changing our head-up display image to the air-to-surface mode (or air-to-air mode given the mission at hand), selecting weapons and checking the right settings, un-stowing our targeting pod and checking that the display is clear and properly focused, and then arm

our flares/chaff and jammers. We access the environmental conditions such as the visibility and the wind condition at altitude. The wingman will pull up next to lead and both aircraft will expend a single flare/chaff and jammer to verify the system is working properly. Next the aircraft will perform a couple of high G turns (called a G-warm) to make sure that the pilots are in a proper physical condition to take Gs and that the aircraft itself is in good condition to pull Gs. Next we will test the laser located in the targeting pod. The laser has many uses. It is used to calculate very accurate target elevation (one of the most important and difficult variables when trying to generate the precise location of a target), it helps guide bombs to the target (i.e., a laser detector located in the nose of certain bombs hones towards the target that the laser is pointed at) and it also acts as a laser pointer to help steer your eyes towards the correct target. To test the laser, one aircraft will fire the laser while the other aircraft's laser detector will pick up the energy and point the targeting pod to where the laser energy is coming from. When both pilots confirm that the laser works and it is pointing to the desired location, the planes will switch roles to test the other aircraft's laser. Following this, we perform final checks on the targeting pod, check our lighting package (securing external visible lights especially in combat) and double-check the weapons and expendables. At this point we will notify our flight lead that the aircraft is completely set up and ready for the tactical portion of the flight.

'During the outbound leg to our assigned area of operations, we will go through several controlling agencies. We pass them information about our flight (such as the ordnance we are carrying) and they filter us down eventually to the unit they want us to support. As stated before, it is usually known in advance which area or unit we have been assigned, but we are always ready to be on call for whoever needs us. Eventually, for a Close Air Support Mission, we will be in a holding stack above our assigned area and be in contact with our eyes on the ground (in the USMC this will usually be a Forward Air Controller – another "Winged Aviator"). After checking in with the FAC and providing him with pertinent information concerning the flight, he will give us a quick update on the situation on the ground. This usually consists of both the enemy and friendly location and situation. Following this, and should the Marines on the ground need it, we will begin setting up an attack. The Marines, as well as all of the other services, have a very standardized way of setting up a CAS attack. The FAC on the ground will pass all key details of the attack in what is referred to as a "nine line". The nine line is essentially nine pieces of information needed to conduct the attack. The Harrier has a CAS page in its computer devoted to this nine line. The nine line consists of the following – the location to begin the attack, the bearing and distance from this location to the target, the elevation of the target, the description of the target, the exact coordinates of the target, how the FAC will possibly mark the target (laser/smoke), exact location of the 'friendlies' and, finally, the route we need to egress the target area. Following this, he will give us the time he wants the ordnance to hit and the heading he wants us to attack from. Following the nine line, we must legally read back the target elevation, location, the final attack heading and any restrictions he gave us. Once we are confident our system has what the FAC has passed to us, we input the information and load it into our maps. The digital maps will automatically provide a display showing the location to begin the attack, the target and egress route, the attack heading, and the location of the friendlies. All the aircraft in the flight will make sure everybody is working in unison ("looking at the same sheet of music"). The lead will describe where he sees the target in relation to the digital map, the bearing and distance to the target, the speed required to hit the target on time, what attack and what weapons he proposes to use, what time the flight will actually push to the target, and, finally, the flight will physically plot the target on a map and describe what they see. This entire process is to make sure everyone is on that same proverbial sheet of music. Once the flight is confident of this, the aircraft can snap the targeting pods so that each pilot can see the target given by the FAC on their computers. At this point the FAC will help talk us

on to the specific target he needs to be attacked. Though coordinates can be very accurate, we always make sure that we have the right target and a FAC "talk on" is just another way to ensure this. Once we are absolutely sure we have the correct target, the flight will push to the initial position from where the attack will commence.

'The Harrier has many different types of attack catered to both the types of situation and the type of ordnance carried. For laser-guided weapons, we have the capability as a single aircraft to both drop and laser a weapon to the target. If one of the lasers from the targeting pod is not functioning properly, we can have a wingman laser a bomb dropped from the other aircraft in the section. The laser designation can also come from another platform such as an attack helicopter or even the FAC on the ground. If there is a cloud deck, we also have the option of having an aircraft above the clouds drop on a coordinate that will put the bomb in what is referred to as the laser basket, and have another aircraft below the cloud deck with eyes on the target laser the bomb to the exact target. The other type of precision bomb we have is the Joint Direct Attack Munition (JDAM) which is essentially a GPS-guided bomb. With our targeting pod, we can laser and generate very accurate coordinates that can be transferred directly to the JDAM. Once we fly into the weapons envelope, we can release the bomb and it will guide itself accurately to the target. Both the JDAM and the laser-guided bombs are usually dropped from

This Harrier from VMA-231 wears the short-lived light grey/blue camouflage scheme which was applied to the unit's aircraft during the Gulf War. (Photo: Mick Roth collection)

Whilst deployed as part of a Marine Expeditionary Unit, the AV-8B units are normally re-assigned to a composite reinforced helicopter squadron. In this image a pair of 'Black Sheep' aircraft can be seen wearing temporary HMM-163 titling, whilst deployed on the USS Boxer.
(Photo: US Navy)

straight and level flight. For general munitions (dumb bombs, as we like to call them), we will usually dive deliver. Though the bomb is literally just a free-falling piece of explosive, we can still utilise our targeting pod to enhance its accuracy. The mechanics of finding a target and lasing it for precise coordinates are the same as those for the precision-guided munitions. These precise coordinates are fed into our head up displays so that we get an accurate visual representation and cue as to the exact time and position to drop the bomb. Though less accurate than the LGB and JDAM, it still provides very accurate delivery. We can also use cluster bombs and firebombs which are delivered very similarly to the dumb bombs. For forward-firing ordnance, we are armed with a 25 mm Gatling gun and 2.75 to 5 inch rockets. This type of ordnance is delivered in a simple ramp down attack with the nose pointed at the target and firing at a specified altitude. We also have the LMAV, a laser-guided forward-firing missile for surface targets (very useful for moving targets). For air targets, we can carry an assortment of air-to-air missiles to include the AIM-9 (IR missile) and the AMRAAM (radar-guided missile).

'As we push from the initial position to the target, lead notifies the FAC that the flight is inbound. The flight begins a set of manoeuvres designed to accomplish the lead aircraft's scheduled moves. For instance, should the lead aircraft want two bombs dropped with a minute interval, the wingman needs to fly a separation manoeuvre to make this happen (using geometry and timed turns). Along with these manoeuvres, both aircraft are busy manipulating their targeting pods so that the most accurate target coordinates are being fed to the system each second. As each aircraft completes all the final checks to make sure the system is set up and as the aircraft nears the point of ordnance delivery, both aircraft will confirm they are visual the target and their laser is firing. Whether it be a straight and level or dive delivery, each aircraft will call "in" with a heading. This call tells the FAC that the aircraft is ready to employ ordnance from the correct heading given in the

nine line. Ordnance delivery all rests on the FAC giving either the "Cleared Hot" or the "Abort" Call. With a cleared hot, the pilot's thumb presses the firing mechanism for the specified weapon. The other aircraft will always have his targeting pod in the area to assess the hit of the other aircraft. Once the aircraft have employed their ordnance, they will meet up at either a higher "sanctuary" altitude or just "low and away" from the target and either return home or set up another attack. Following the tactical portion of the flight and during the return to base, lead will call the flight to "fence out". This command requires both aircraft to secure their Master Arm switch, switch from their "air-to-ground" tactical display in the HUD to the navigation mode, deselect any weapons, secure the targeting pod, and turn the expendables off. Lead will then clear the wingman into a close formation and, provided all his weapons are secure, a battle damage assessment will be conducted. Both aircraft will take turns inspecting each other for any damage that might have occurred during the mission. Most likely you are looking for loose or missing panels, possible bird strikes, and possibly any combat damage inflicted by the enemy. While this occurs, lead is performing and delegating administrative tasks such as passing on mission reports and intelligence to the airspace controller, giving a battlefield turnover to the flight that takes over, checking up on the weather at the destination, and checking the fuel level required for aircraft to possibly land vertically, etc.

'Before or after the tactical portion of the flight, the Harrier has the capability to refuel whilst airborne. The tanker usually has a pre-planned refuelling track, and the flight approaches this tanker track from below to ensure altitude de-confliction. After locking up the tanker on the radar, and having the tanker clear us aboard, the flight joins the tanker from below and to the left. Each flight member prepares the cockpit for refuelling. The Harrier, like most tactical jets, does not favour slow flight. Unfortunately, because many tankers fly in the low "two hundreds" for airspeed, we are forced to fly the same airspeed if we want to refuel. To help the jet fly comfortably at this speed, we will usually choose a flap configuration (primarily used for landing) to maximize our lift at this slow speed. We extend our fuel probe and check the aircraft is flying in coordinated flight (the fuel probe can significantly change the aerodynamics of the Harrier, especially in yaw, so significant rudder trim is required to accomplish coordinated flight). Once the aircraft is ready to accept fuel, the tanker will clear us in. Unlike many aircraft, the Harrier has a fuel probe that extends from the left of the aircraft (rather than emerging straight out in front). As a result, it takes some practice to steer the probe into the basket. We often approach the basket looking straight ahead and use our peripheral vision to place the probe near the basket. If we were to stare at the probe, we would

likely create pilot induced oscillations. This is a phenomenon whereby, as the basket naturally sways to and fro in some direction, the pilot over-corrects to keep the probe aimed towards the basket. These over-corrections usually result in counter oscillations, making successful contact with the basket near impossible. Our peripheral vision is less susceptible to this, so with the unique location of our probe, this is what we use to initially guide the probe to the basket. As we approach the basket from the side and it is no longer visible in our periphery, we take a quick glance at the probe and make a last minute correction if needs be, to put it in the basket. With successful contact, we push the hose in to initiate fuel flow to the aircraft. Once we have filled up, we tell the tanker we are satisfied and he clears us to break away (we then move aft until the probe unsticks from the basket) and form the flight high and to the right. Following everyone's successful refuelling, we are cleared to break away and conduct the next portion of the flight. Once both aircraft have completed all of the administrative tasks, and the flight nears its destination (a ship in this case), both pilots ready their cockpit for landing.

'The typical landing at the ship will have both aircraft flying a tight formation at 350kts overhead the ship at eight hundred feet. As the flight continues a couple of miles past the ship, the lead will give his wingman the signal that he is going to break, and will usually give the signal for the break

interval, which is generally two seconds. As lead banks his aircraft sharply and turns, wingman counts a couple of seconds and does the same. We bank our aircraft to near 90 degrees, pull our throttle to idle, extend the speed brakes (a switch on the throttle will open up a flap door on the base of our aircraft to create drag and help slow down the aircraft), and pull approximately 4Gs. The aircraft will slow down quickly, and as we complete 180 degrees of turn we can generally expect the aircraft to be below 250 knots (the max speed that we can pull the gear down). We throw down the gear handle, switch the HUD to the VSTOL display (a display that provides us with all the critical information to safely perform a landing), switch our altitude display from barometric to radar (which gives us height above the actual ground rather than sea level), and at this point we are ready to utilise the Harrier's unique VSTOL capabilities. As we ease the nozzles from the aft position, we switch to a flap programme that allows us to maximize the ever-decreasing lift from the wings as we reach speeds at which most tactical jet aircraft would stall. We approach abeam the ship and notify the LSO (Landing Safety Officer) that our gear is down and locked, we notify him of what the required fuel level is for our aircraft to hover, and what our actual fuel level is. The LSO, once he is satisfied that our fuel levels to hover are correct and we have the sufficient engine performance to do so, will clear us to continue. At this time, our nozzles

Pictured at El Centro NAS, this angle on the TAV-8B illustrates the unusual proportions of the type's tail fin. Unlike the first generation T2/4 which incorporated a longer tail boom and taller fin, the TAV-8B incorporates a broader chord and higher fin with a downward-stepped leading edge. (Photo: Gary Wetzel)

Basking under the Arizona sun, an AV-8B(NA) from VMA-223 wearing one of the USMC's more recent camouflage schemes adopted by the Harrier fleet, with dark grey upper surfaces and light blue markings.
(Photo: Lance Pawlik)

View from the refuelling position of a KC-10 Extender tanker aircraft as a pair of AV-8B Plus aircraft take on fuel during a mission over Iraq.
(Photo: US Navy)

Not normally captured on film, an image of typical night operations on board the USS Iwo Jima (LDH-7) as an AV-8B(NA) prepares to get airborne. (Photo: US Navy)

are pointing 60 degrees down, and we arm the water injection switch. In short, the water switch allows 500 lb or 90 seconds of water to be sprayed into the engine to cool it off. The maximum thrust our engine produces is either limited by temperature (most likely on a hot day) or RPMs. The water switch, should the engine pass a particular threshold, will allow water to be sprayed into the engine to cool it down. As a result, we can operate the engine at faster RPMs (6-7%) to take advantage of the cooler engine temperature. The end state is that, should we need it, we can achieve considerable additional power to help the aircraft hover. Additional power from the water switch can be utilised both with landings and take-offs. We throttle-up the engine to full power so that the engine passes the threshold for water to flow into the engine, and check that the water gauge ticks down and the water light turns on. The LSO will note that water is flowing into the engine because the exhaust will become very noticeably black. Once the pilot has verified that water has successfully flowed to the engine, he eases back on the power so that the water ceases to flow (we need to save this water for when we really need it). We continue our descending turn so that we line up with the axis of the ship. By this time we should have conducted our landing checklist. Gear is

down, flaps are in the correct position, the stop we use to help place our nozzles to a precise angle is completely aft allowing full use of the nozzles, the duct pressure shows that air is getting successfully blasted to the puffer ducts which allow us controllability in the hover, we press on the brakes and check the brake pressure is sufficient, we check that we have no warning or caution lights, we double-check that the water switch is armed should we need it and, lastly, we check our landing light is on. We slowly turn towards the ship with our landing spot in sight. As we get to the proper distance and the proper altitude window we advise the LSO that we are going to throw the nozzles from 60 to the full vertical position. The LSO will roger up this call and make us verify one more time that we have armed our water switch. As we throw the nozzle lever back and push all our exhaust directly down, it feels much like the aircraft is jammed on the brakes a little too hard. The pilot will lurch forward and the speed will drastically tick down. The most important and often most perilous portion of VSTOL flight is transitioning from wing-borne flight to jet-borne flight. It is a careful balancing act as we pass through speeds that, should we not be riding a column of air, would make any other aircraft drop out of the sky. Our wings gradually become useless, and all that is keeping

A familiar sight for air show enthusiasts, as an AV-8B from VMA-542 enters a steep vertical climb during a performance at Cherry Point. Water injection results in a sooty trail of exhaust from the hard-working Pegasus engine. (Photo: US Navy)

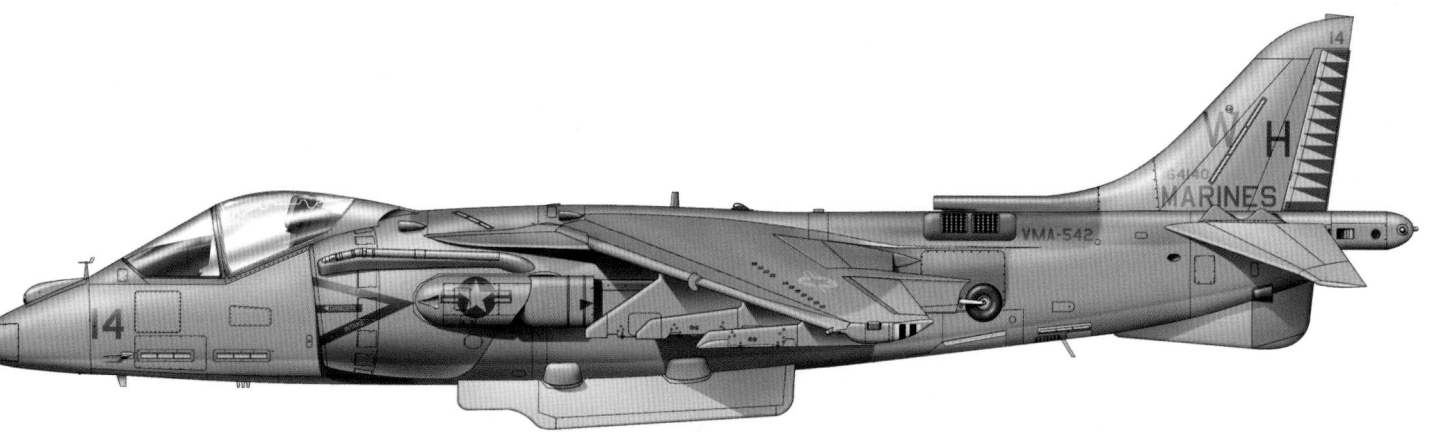

McDonnell Douglas AV-8B Harrier II, 164140/WH-14, VMA-542, US Marine Corps
Upper surfaces of wings and fuselage spine in FS.36118; fuselage sides and top of horizontal tail surfaces in FS.36231, undersides in FS.36320. Markings and lettering in dark grey; fin in dark grey with yellow motif. '14' repeated on top of fin

the aircraft aloft is this column of air and the controllability from the puffer ducts.

'Every Harrier pilot is schooled from the very beginning that successful VSTOL flight relies on a strict adherence to what many call the 'death equation'. The death equation is airspeed x sideslip x angle of attack. If this equation has any value other than zero, then our jet can possibly lose control. If the angle of attack is too high, our wing can stall before we can rely on the jet exhaust to keep us airborne. If we have enough airspeed to create lift on the wings, and we have too much

sideslip (imagine an aircraft skidding through the air) then one wing will produce more lift than the other and the aircraft could possibly flip over. So we must have one of these values at zero to make the equation zero. Of course we can't always have airspeed at zero because there is the transition phase from wing-borne to jet-borne flight. Angle of attack is rarely zero either (this is the angle at which the relative wind hits our wings). The only value we can realistically zero out to perform successful VSTOL flight is sideslip. On the nose of our aircraft we have a weather vane that shows the

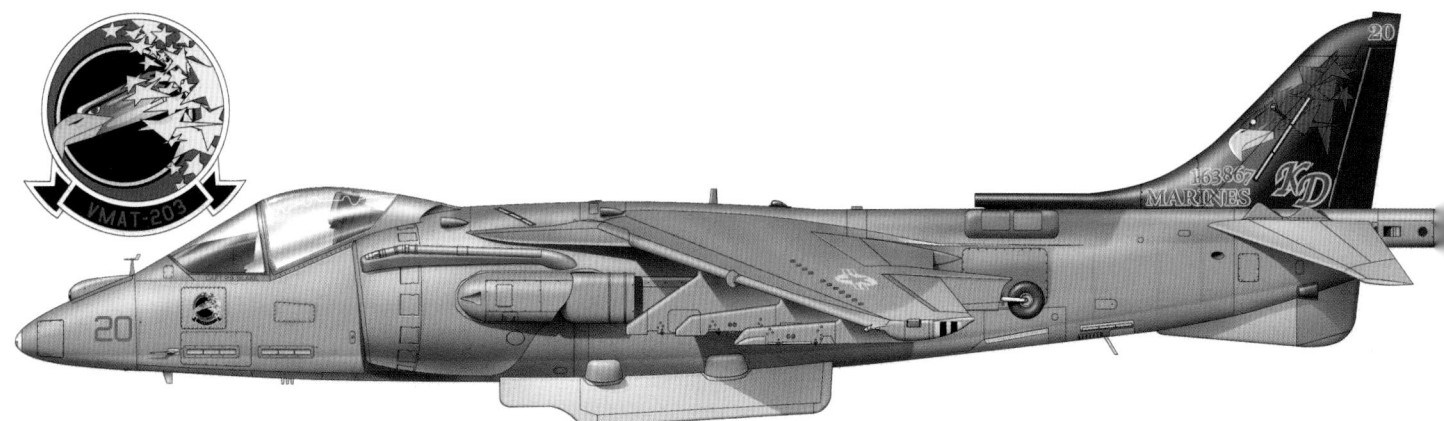

Although VMAT-203 is more generally associated with the dual control TAV-8B (as the USMC's Harrier training unit), a number of single-seat AV-8B aircraft also operated by the unit, including this specially marked machine with a celebratory tail decoration. (Photo: Lance Pawlik)

McDonnell Douglas AV-8B, 163867, KD-20, VMAT-203, US Marine Corps, 2007
Upper surfaces of wings and fuselage spine in FS.36118; fuselage sides and top of horizontal tail surfaces in FS.36231, undersides in FS.36320. Black fin and rudder with lettering in red, outlined in yellow; unit badge on nose

relationship between our aircraft's nose direction in relation to where the relative wind is coming from (sideslip). Our goal throughout the hover is always to have the relative wind and the nose of our aircraft at parallel. As we throw the nozzles to full hover stop, and the aircraft rapidly decelerates to zero airspeed, the pilot will dance on the rudder pedals to keep the wind vane centred. Passing through 60 knots the pilot checks the engine

performance to make sure that, as we lose the final bit of lift from our wings, we have enough engine performance for the aircraft to rely solely on exhaust gas to keep us airborne. If not, we must make a hasty transition back to conventional flight before we drop out of the sky. The aircraft slowly approaches zero airspeed alongside the ship's landing spot. The LSO clears us to transition sideways above the ship. Aboard the ship, there is a system of lights that cue the pilot to his exact fore, aft, and vertical position above the intended point of landing. The pilot can easily figure out his side-to-side position above the spot using the 'tram line' that extends along the longitudinal axis of the ship. In simplistic terms, once the pilot is cleared to land, he uses the lights to guide him down to a precise touchdown point. As he nears the deck the LSO will call the pilot to pull the throttle back to idle. The pilot will pull the throttle back, put his feet on the brakes, place the nozzles back to aft, and secure the water switch.

"The taxi back is very much similar to the taxi out. We conduct engine shutdown procedures, record pertinent engine and aircraft data for the maintenance crew, and post-flight the aircraft. During post flight, we are generally looking for damage and missing panels. We check for things such as leaks or any damages/nicks to the engine blades. After a quick post-flight, we will go straight to Intelligence, while the mission is fresh in our minds, and debrief what we saw, what we attacked, and the damage we inflicted. The Harrier can record everything seen in the Head Up Display and what was seen in the targeting pod. We will use these videos both during the intelligence debrief and the flight debrief. For the debrief, we always begin with safety of flight. In other words, did anything happen during the flight that was deemed unsafe? Next, we will debrief the administrative portion of the flight. We generally concentrate on what we did wrong or what we could have done better. After this, we concentrate on the tactical portion of the flight. This is where the HUD and targeting pod video come in handy. Almost every second of the video is critiqued with the same questions in mind. What did we do right? More importantly what did we do incorrectly? How could we have done things better? The flight lead will write up a matrix with his individual mission goals and discuss (with check marks or Xs) whether they were successfully accomplished. Much like the brief, the debrief is covered extensively (especially the tactical portion which is debriefed by the second). Following the debrief, the wingman will type up a report of lessons learned during the flight and send it to the flight lead who will then add his thoughts.

'This sums up a typical flight in the Harrier Community. As stated before, the Harrier is also capable of flying an assortment of missions outside of CAS. The overall planning, execution, and debrief occur in quite the same fashion though. I would lastly like to add that the Harrier mission is constantly evolving. Though it is deemed as an older generation aircraft, the platform has done an outstanding job in maintaining state of the art technology – specifically our targeting pod and

This image of a VMA-231 Harrier getting airborne from the USS Iwo Jima illustrates the power of the Pegasus engine, clearing standing water from the deck as the aircraft thunders forward along the soggy deck surface. (Photo: US Navy)

A magnificently-marked AV-8B Plus from VMA-542 'Flying Tigers' seen high over the Arizona Desert. The aircraft is carrying an AN/AAQ-28(V) LITENING targeting pod. (Photo: Gary Wetzel)

An AV-8B 162722 from VMA-331, wearing Gulf War grey/blue camouflage. The unit flew some 242 combat sorties during Operation Desert Storm.(Photo: Mick Roth collection)

advanced weaponry. As we maintain our technological prowess, commanders in the field still discover many new uses for the Harrier's unique capabilities.'

While retaining standard USMC camouflage colours, this AV-8B Plus from VMA-223 displays flamboyant markings on its tail. Despite being a much-modified second-generation Harrier, the tail fin remains identical to the proportions of the P.1127 from the 1960s. (Photo: Lance Pawlik)

A comparison view of the AV-8B(NA) single-seater and TAV-8B twin-seater, both aircraft from VMAT-203 at Cherry Point. (Photo: Lance Pawlik)

A close-up view of the AV-8B Plus in flight, illustrating the outward bulge of the AV-8B's much improved canopy which affords the pilot excellent all-round visibility. (Photo: Gary Wetzel)

The most recent standard for USMC Harrier camouflage colours is slowly spreading across all Harrier units as aircraft are re-painted during servicing. This TAV-8B from VMAT-203 is pictured shortly after repaint in the latest dark grey camouflage. Note the luggage pod carried on the wing pylon. (Photo: Lance Pawlik)

McDonnell Douglas TAV-8B Harrier II, 162747/SD-626, USMC, NATC Patuxent River, 1988
Wrap-around camouflage in FS.36320 and FS.36009. All markings and lettering in black.

VMA-223 AV-8B Harriers pictured during a training detachment to NAF El Centro. (Photo: Lance Pawlik)

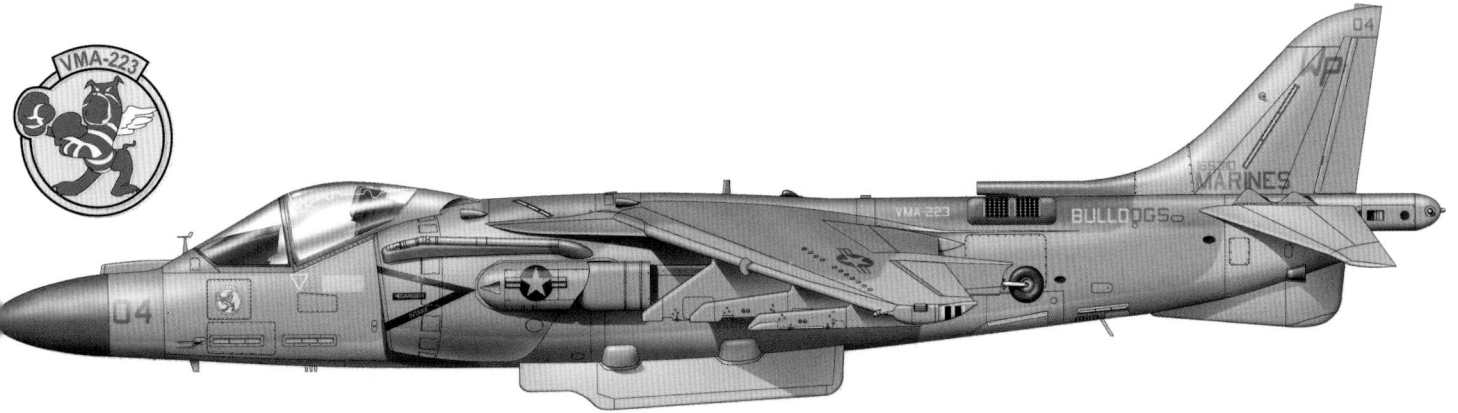

McDonnell Douglas AV-8B Harrier II Plus, 165310/WP-04, VMA-223 'Bulldogs' USMC, 2007
Dark Compass Gray overall with Gunship Grey radome, top fuselage and wing decking, and Light Compass Gray undersides; markings in a mixture of same colours. Low-viz version of unit marking on nose

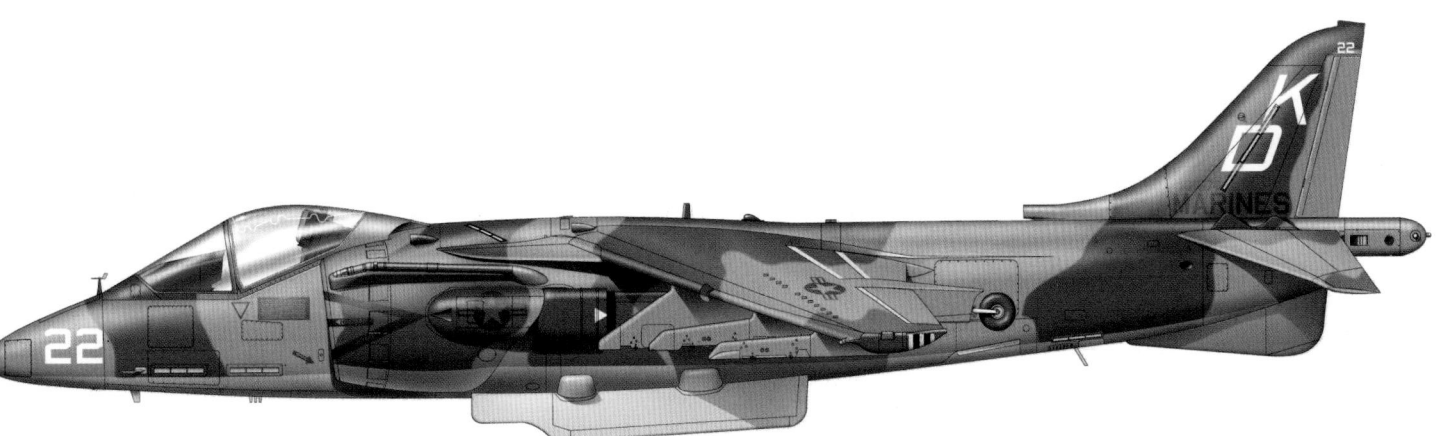

McDonnell Douglas AV-8B Harrier II Plus, 165310/WP-04, VMA-223 'Bulldogs' USMC, 2007
FS.34064/FS.36099 upper surfaces with FS.36440 undersides; all markings in dark grey, except for '22' on nose and fin which are in white

McDonnell Douglas AV-8B Harrier II Plus, 165006/CF-01, VMA-211 'Avengers', 2004
Dark Compass Gray overall with Gunship Grey top fuselage and wing decking, and Light Compass Gray undersides. Red/white rudder; unit marking on nose. Lettering in black; blue stripe across fin with 'Avengers' in white

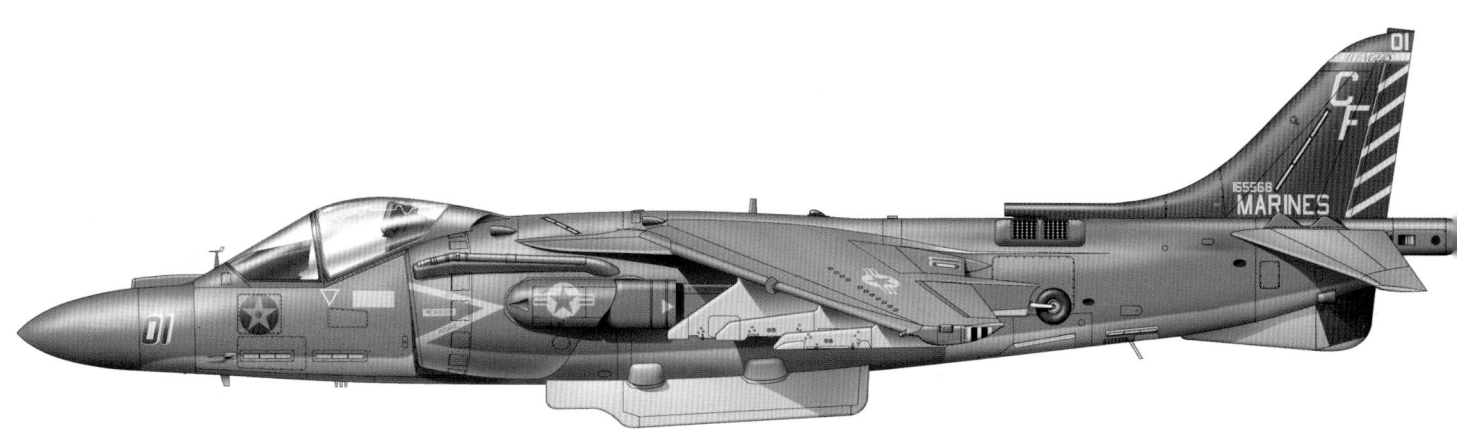

McDonnell Douglas AV-8B Harrier II Plus, 165568/CF-01, VMA-211 'Avengers' USMC, 2010
Gunship Gray uppersurfaces with Blue Gray undersides; general markings in reversed colours. Matt red vertical tail surfaces and rear section of ventral fin with yellow markings; red '01' on nose with yellow drop shadow

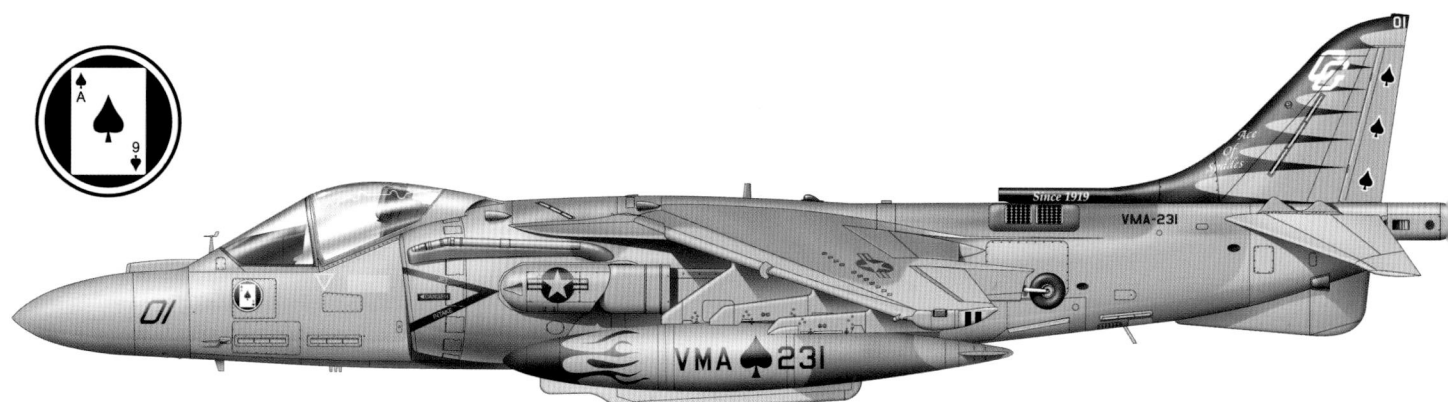

McDonnell Douglas AV-8B Harrier II Plus, 164570/CG-01, VMA-231 USMC, 2006
Dark Compass Gray overall with Gunship Grey top fuselage and wing decking, and Light Compass Gray undersides. Black white trim on fin, rudder and front of underwing tanks; lettering in black except 'CG' on fin which is white. Black/white unit marking on nose

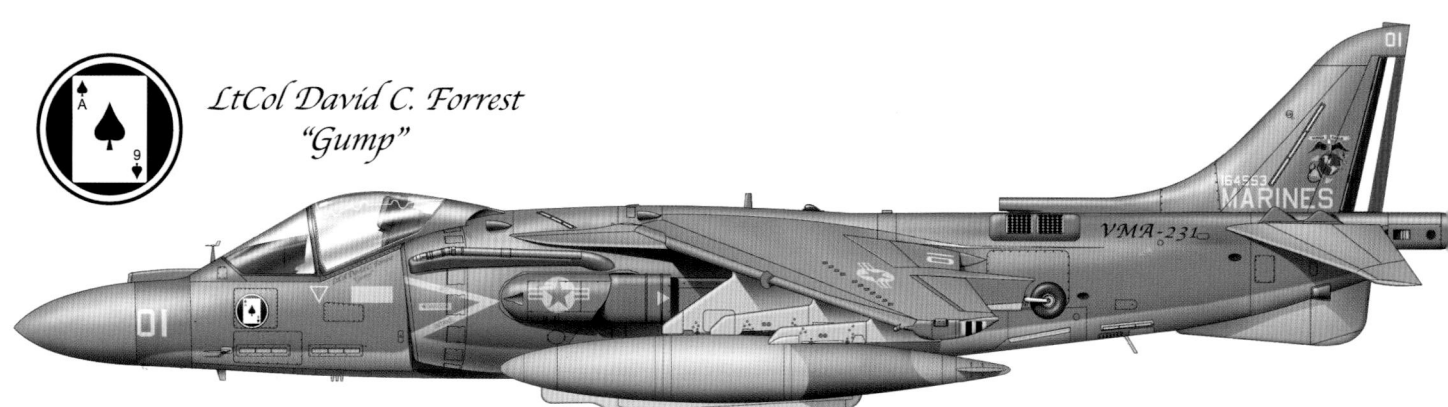

McDonnell Douglas AV-8B Harrier II Plus, 164553/01, VMA-231 USMC, 2009
Upper surfaces in Gunship Gray with Blue Gray undersides; general markings in reversed colours. Blue/white/red rudder; USMC badge on fin, unit badge on nose. Vertical tail surfaces appear to have a high gloss Gunship Gray finish

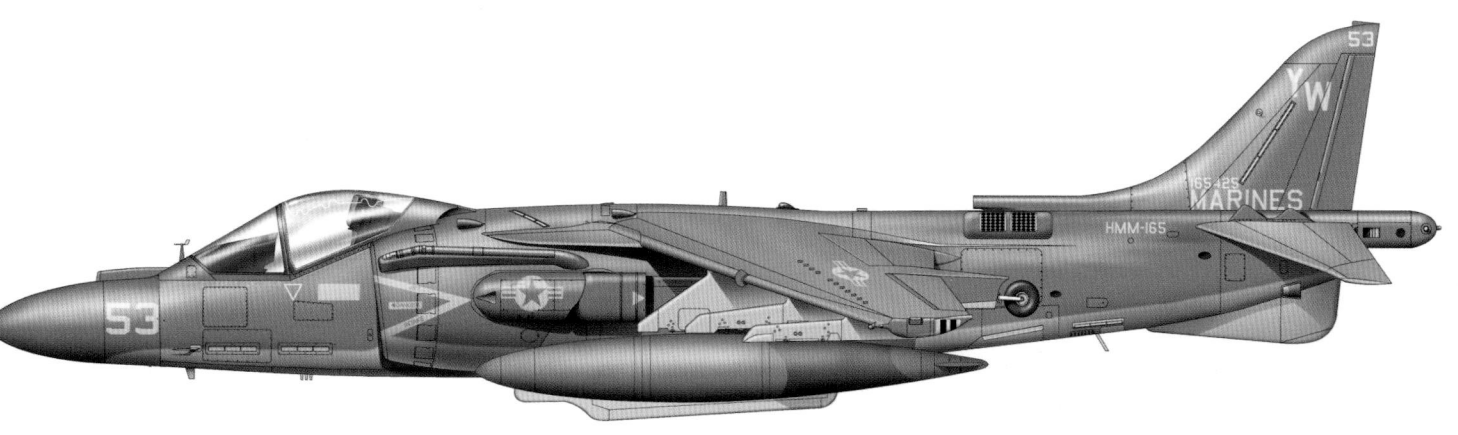

McDonnell Douglas AV-8B Harrier II Plus, 165425/YW-53, HMM-165 USMC, USS Peleliu, 2010
Gunship Gray FS.36118 upper surfaces with Blue Gray FS.35237 undersides; markings are in reverse colours

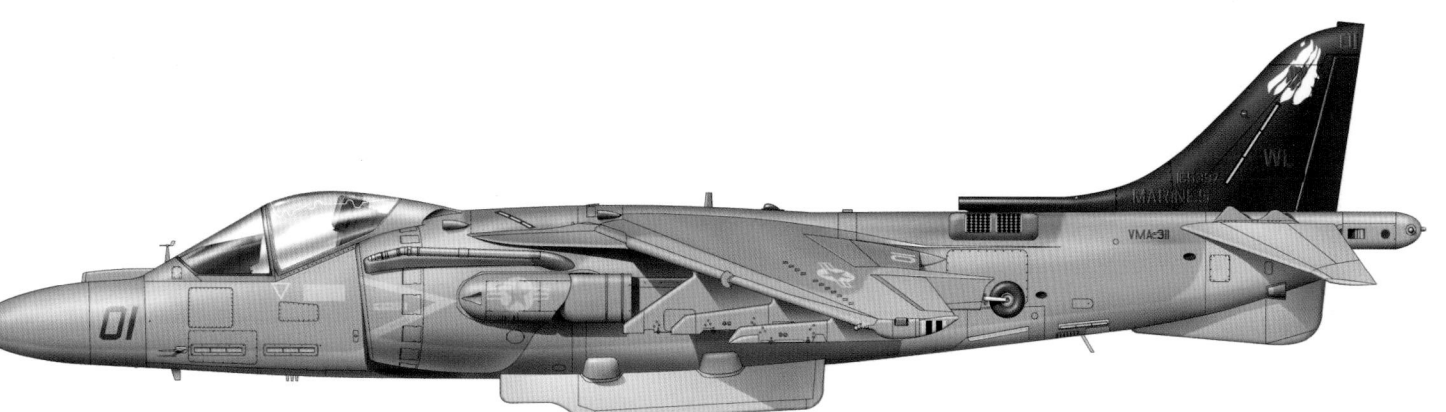

McDonnell Douglas AV-8B Harrier II Plus, 165397/WL-01, VMA-311, 2007
Dark Compass Gray overall with Gunship Grey top fuselage and wing decking, and Light Compass Gray undersides; matt black vertical tail surfaces with white/red motif. Lettering on fin in red

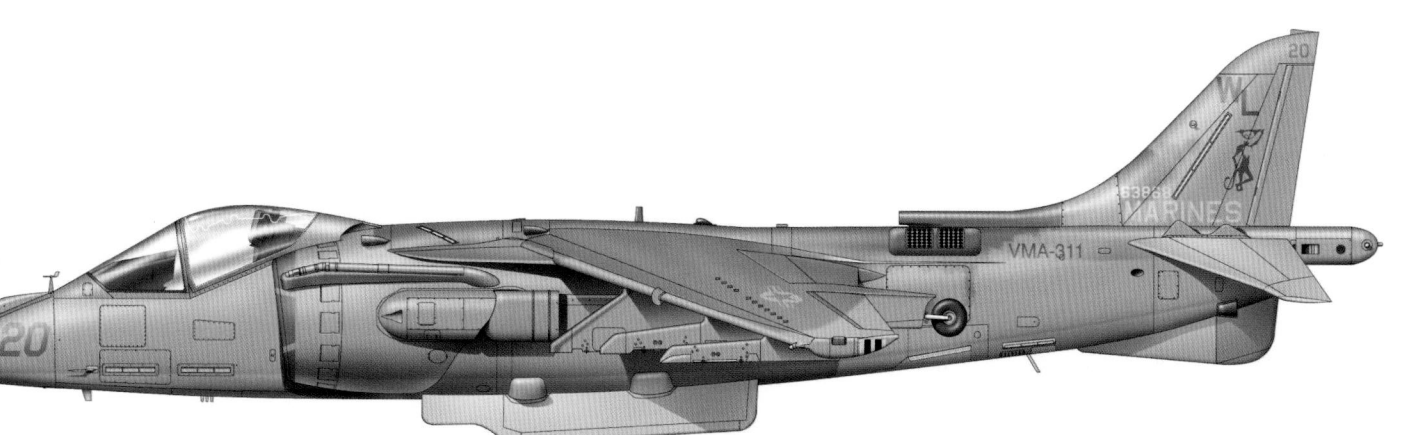

McDonnell Douglas AV-8B Harrier II, 163868/WL-20, VMA-311, US Marine Corps, 2007
Upper surfaces of wings and fuselage spine in FS.36118; fuselage sides and top of horizontal tail surfaces in FS.36231, undersides in FS.36320. Markings are in a mix of dark light grey; note dark grey motif around air intake

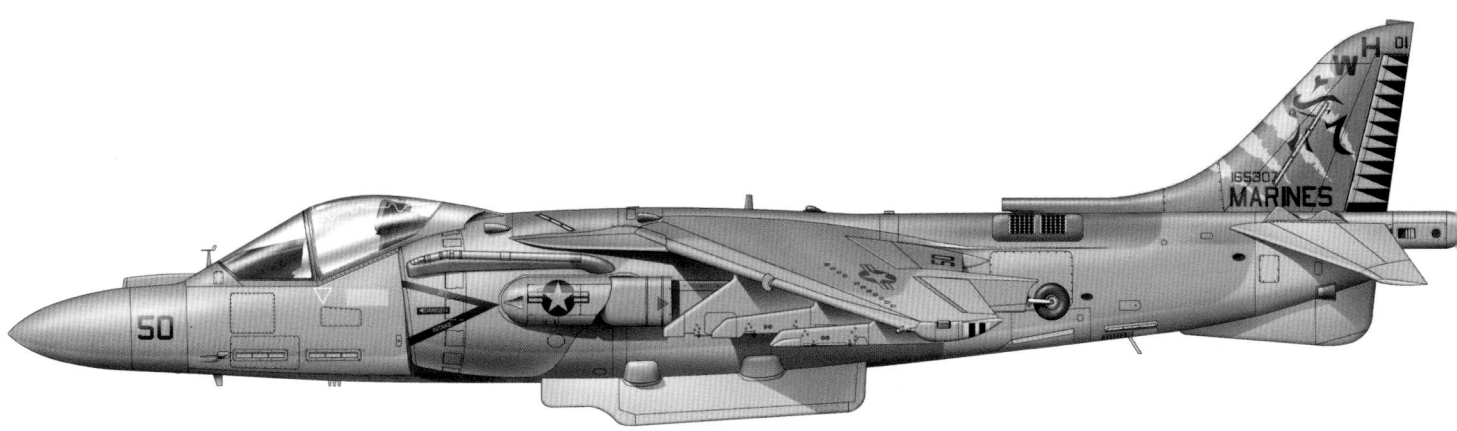

McDonnell Douglas AV-8B Harrier II Plus, 165307/WH-50, VMA-542 USMC, 2007
Dark Compass Gray overall with Gunship Grey top fuselage and wing decking, and Light Compass Gray undersides; black/yellow rudder. Unusually, fin is in Gunship Gray with Light Compass Grey 'scratches' and black lettering. Note wrong Codex on fin (01)

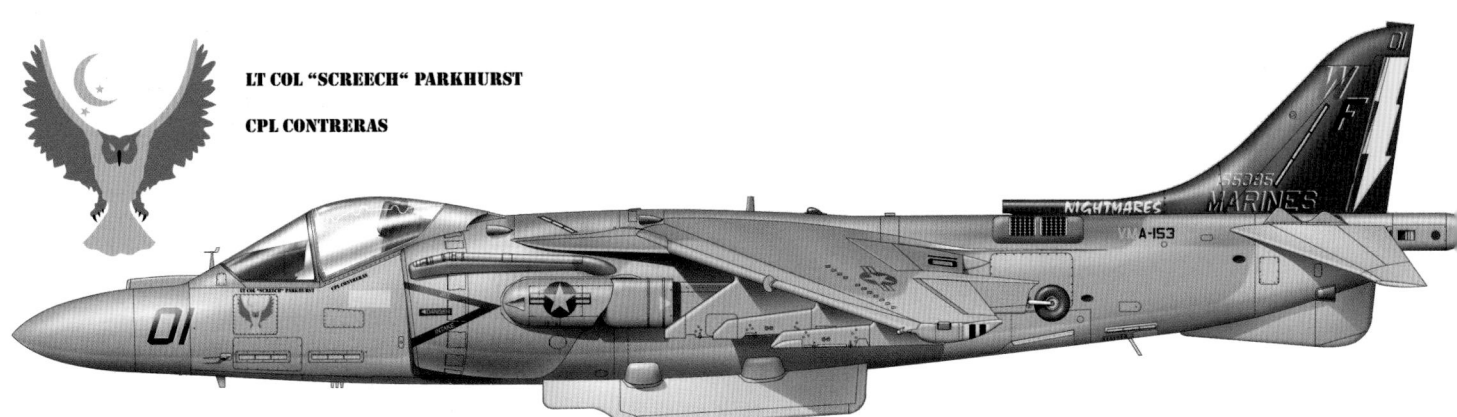

McDonnell Douglas AV-8B Harrier II Plus, 155385/WF-01, VMF-513 USMC, 2008
Dark Compass Gray overall with Gunship Grey top fuselage and wing decking, and Light Compass Gray undersides; Blue vertical tail surfaces with yellow flash on rudder. Lettering on fin in black with yellow drop shadow, except for 'Nightmares' which is yellow; unit badge on nose. Names below windscreen and canopy are in black

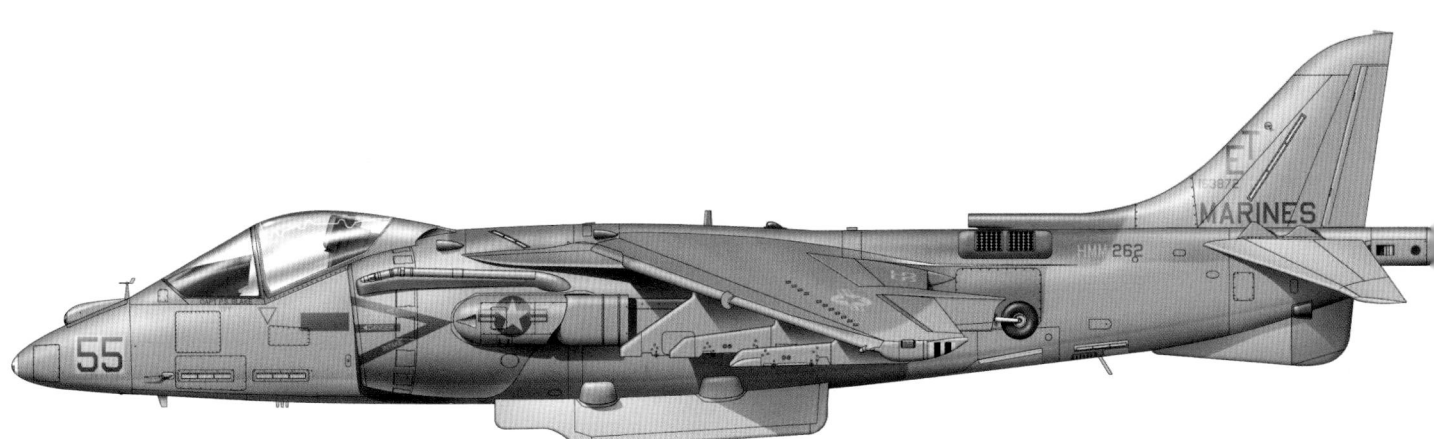

McDonnell Douglas AV-8B Harrier II, 163872/ET/55, of HMM 262, US Marine Corps, on board USS Belleau Wood
Upper surfaces of wings and fuselage spine in FS.36118; fuselage sides and top of horizontal tail surfaces in FS.36231, undersides in FS.36320. Markings are in a mix of dark light grey; Flown by Capt P.S. Blake 'IVY'

CHAPTER TEN

Reflections

THIS book started with the author's description of a 'civvy's view' of flying the Harrier. To end this celebration of the aircraft, we return to the 'Home of the Harrier' at Dunsfold where Andrew Lawson developed a long and fascinating association with the aircraft:

'My father had been an assistant foreman at Dunsfold Aerodrome since I could walk and talk. I used to go around with him and his chums when he played golf on the quite good nine-hole course around the field. There were quite a few people with fantastic careers, but all too often I only found out during their retirement speeches. I had done well at school, and through the persuasion of my father went into the 'engineering stream' which was quite a big thing in those days of 1974-77. When I got to the apprentice school at Kingston I hated every second, not least because I was in unfriendly lodgings. My fellow lodger Nigel, a Technical Illustrator with BAe who was also a lead guitarist in a band, was a good chum but the apprenticeship was not for me – mainly, I think, because I was immature, it was my first time away from home, and the 'Londoner' Kingstonians seemed to regard anyone from Dunsfold as an enemy. This was to persist throughout my years at Dunsfold. I was good at the academic side but struggled with the manual, such as filing patterns to four-thousands of an inch; when I finally got it right, the instructor accused me of breaking into his safe (yes, a real bank-type safe) and filing around the master template! I carried on, but I and the training centre both realised I wasn't cut out to be a Fitter; frankly if I

could have won 'Apprentice Fitter of the Year' Award' I'd still have walked. Then I was hauled into the office of the boss of the Apprentice Training Centre, Rex Harrison, who asked if I would like to be a Technician Apprentice at Dunsfold Photographic, as they needed a cheap assistant, and it was where I wanted to be, wasn't it? I knew a bit about photography, having dabbled in it, but nothing technical. I presumed on the spot, rightly as it happened, that I'd be taught. I was on my way to Dunsfold!

'It may have been the job of a lifetime, but it was pretty hard to do it well – I'd like to think towards the end I was getting it mostly right; but by then I couldn't stand what was happening to Dunsfold, as it was like seeing an old friend with a bad illness; so I took voluntary redundancy. I will always be grateful for the practical and academic engineering basis though, as it equipped me well as a technical photographer and through life. Dunsfold was a fascinating place during the many years in which Harrier development was our main task. I remember a Monday in 1982; we arrived for work as usual in the Experimental Hangar, to find it virtually empty. Our development Sea Harrier FRS1s, XZ 450, 438 and 439 plus our T8M Hunter XL602 (with Sea Harrier Blue Fox radar) were all gone. The Experimental Manager, John Kimberley, assembled us all and gave a little speech to the effect of, "You all know what's been going on about the Falkland Islands. Well, the Navy have been in here for their planes over the weekend because they're assembling a task force, which is sailing to the

*G-VTOL, Hawker
Siddeley's company-
owned demonstrator,
pictured whilst
undergoing ski-ramp trials
at RAE Bedford. At the
time the aircraft was
painted in two-tone
brown camouflage and
allocated a temporary
military serial as ZA250.
(Photo: BAE Systems)*

South Atlantic as I speak. They've also grabbed back Taylor Scott," he mentioned, though knowing Taylor, I don't think anything could have kept him away. This Navy Test Pilot, seconded to Dunsfold, had carried out the recent trials on the new AIM-9L model Sidewinder, capable of engaging enemy aircraft from ahead rather than just the rear-aspect of earlier versions, and he made strenuous efforts to make sure the task force had this model with it (it was supplied discreetly by the US). I imagine much to his chagrin, Lt. Cdr. Taylor Scott was kept at Yeovilton training up the service pilots, and did not get to the Islands until it was all over, joining the *Illustrious* in charge of her air group. It is a cruel twist that Taylor, a true "gung-ho" Fleet Air Arm pilot, was later killed in an RAF GR5 (ZD325) on a quiet evening routine test-flight on 22 October 1987. After climbing to 30,000 ft from Dunsfold a little after 17.00 hrs, radio contact had been lost half an hour later. Search and Rescue procedures were launched and a westbound USAF C-5 was vectored on to the aircraft, and intercepted it some 140 nm west of the southern tip of Ireland. To the astonishment of the USAF crew, they reported that the Harrier was flying pilot-less and escorted it for

a further 260 nm. Sometime later (when it ran out of fuel), the Harrier entered a gentle descent and crashed into the sea. Scott's body was later found just five miles from Boscombe Down and, after a thorough investigation, it was concluded that a loose object (probably the 'wander lamp' attached to a cable in the cockpit) had become lodged under the side of the ejection seat. Scott had presumably lowered his seat (he was heading west into evening sun and would have been concentrating on the aircraft's instruments) and this caused the seat's parachute cartridge to be fired accidentally, pulling the parachute and Scott from the cockpit. It was a tragic loss caused by a simple accident that couldn't have been foreseen. In the pub outside Dunsfold Aerodrome ("The Three Compasses") a simple brass plaque on a beam is now dedicated to him.

'Dunsfold was of course very busy indeed during the Falklands conflict. We had a rash of bright ideas from the Kingston design office to help our guys. Among these was an ALE 40 chaff and flare dispenser – this had not been budgeted for previously, and all the Harrier pilots could rely on in the meantime was a bunch of tin foil stowed above the airbrake, giving a vague "one-shot" chaff

G-VTOL made a media appearance during the public sell-off of British Aerospace, suitably decorated with the initial share price under her wings. (Photo: BAE Systems)

option when the air brake was opened. After urgent requests, the modification schemes also came up with larger drop tanks, 190 as opposed to the original 100 gallons, and a fit for four rather than two Sidewinders. We also arranged an AIM-9L Sidewinder fit for the RAF GR3s and, in a marathon effort, nine of them flew non-stop (with in-flight refuelling) to Ascension Island, where six were loaded on to *Atlantic Conveyor*, and three remained as guards for the outpost at Wideawake, as there was a perceived threat from Argentine aircraft – albeit slight. Eight Sea Harriers from 809 Squadron were also loaded on the *Atlantic Conveyor*, along with helicopters. The Harrier GR1 originally had the option of extended wing tips for ferry flights, though I never saw these used, and they were limited to 3g in any case which made them less than useful. More important to Falklands deployment was the topping up of the engine oil to the higher ferry level for sustained endurance. Perhaps more difficult to sort, the Sea Harrier navigation system (NAVHARS) had to be persuaded it was South of the Equator, as nobody had considered trying this on trials (or maybe they thought the expense wouldn't allow it) and

consequently the system usually toppled. If you ever see any cockpit HUD film (Pilot Display Recorder) of the time, you'll see the compass heading stays on zero. As the GR3s had never expected to go to sea, a system was quickly devised to align their inertial platforms while on the carrier. It's remarkable how the UK military seems shambolic at times, but when pressed it seems to have a "plan B" for most situations somewhere up its proverbial sleeve!

'Despite feverish activity night and day, we were later told by Navy test pilot Steve Thomas that none of the Sea Harrier modifications reached the front line before it was all over. He also told us of his first two of three "kills" in the Falklands stating that he "… had read a book on Vietnam where the pilots had learned to invert and look down every thirty seconds or so. As I did this, I saw two Mirages going for the fleet, and dived, calling "Tally-Ho" to my leader, Sharkey Ward. I got behind the first one, and gaining a tone on my Sidewinder, I let it go… with unfortunate results for the Mirage. The missile went up the jet pipe and blew the plane apart. The Mirage flown by Miguel was by now generating a lot of heat, so I had to get past the fireball before I could lock on to his wingman Carlos and blew his

A rare photograph of
G-VTOL over the landing
pad at Dunsfold, suitably
signed by test pilot,
Heinz Frick, in
celebration of 25 years
of Harrier flying.
(Photo: BAE Systems)

25 YEARS OF VERTICAL TAKE OFFS

which are supposed to be empty can siphon back from the wing tanks over a period of time – my father discovered this after a lunch break – so maybe that's what happened to 438. The pilot ejected safely, though I met a member of the ground crew who was watching, and he'd realised that there was a problem and ran for the ATC door, just closing it behind him when the main undercarriage leg hit it! Meanwhile, all Sea Harriers were being given low-observability overall grey RAM (radar absorbent material) paint schemes, which also helped reduce their radar signatures. Every FRS1 in original blue and white livery which landed at Yeovilton was immediately descended upon by a gang who rubbed down the paint, prior to application of the new scheme. Unfortunately, our remaining development FRS1, XZ440, was visiting Yeovilton at the time and as our pilot landed, this gang appeared, and despite all his frantic signalling from the cockpit they proceeded to destroy the paint finish. Funds being what they were, 440 stayed like this for years, and although it was a favourite aircraft of mine, I sighed with despair whenever I heard that I had to do a photo-assignment with it.

'When the shooting war started, the first casualty was Lt. Nick Taylor in XZ450, brought down by damage to his Harrier's wing leading edge, and though some earlier reports reckoned it was a result of AAA, it seems that a Roland SAM may also have been responsible. This was obviously a tragedy in human terms, but also a waste of a special aeroplane; XZ450 was the first Sea Harrier to fly, in August 1978, and had been with us at Dunsfold for development work ever since. It had taken thirteen months to instrument this aircraft for the Sea Eagle sea-skimming anti-ship missile, yet the Navy used it on a standard iron bomb raid on Goose Green. The only good thing to come out of it, as related by John Farley, was that the Argentinians found the missile control panel in the wreckage, and thought *"Christ, they've got Sea Eagle operational already"* thus contributing to their inclination for keeping their ships in port. Personally, I can't help thinking our subs were more a part of the equation, but it's a nice idea that Lt. Taylor's sacrifice may have borne some fruit. Air strikes on the Argentinian fleet (even in port) were indeed planned at one stage. But they were never deemed necessary. A little while later, in more peaceful times, I was hanging cine cameras on XZ440 for the first Sea Eagle firing; in typical fashion, we were stationed at Hatfield, while using the Aberporth range all the way over in Wales. We were using a centre-line camera pod built at Boscombe Down which, while streamlined, had a few shortcomings. For one, it ran from a huge self-contained battery which weighed ninety-six pounds and nearly killed me every time I had to take it out for recharging at the battery bay. The installed Telford cine cameras were also rather restricted in their angle of view, but overall it worked, and like some of our later films, the results

wing off." At the time I assumed these were stereotypical names, but it transpired the pilots had all survived the conflict and all three had been out for meals together! The Dunsfold guys also completed the last feasibly useful Sea Harrier in record time so that it could also be sent to the South Atlantic. I remember Mike Snelling took off, and did a tight circuit at what seemed full power. He buzzed the production hangars at very high speed, waggling the wings in a thank-you to the workers who had put so much effort in, before heading full-bore for Yeovilton. This was a very out-of-character performance for a remarkably restrained flyer. His nickname, of which he was quite proud, was "Snagger." At Yeovilton it was organised chaos of course, and two events spring to mind. One of "our" (actually Ministry) development Sea Harriers (XZ438) was being used for ski-jump training, and during one sortie, due to human error, only one drop tank was filled with fuel. There are no gauges to inform the pilot of this asymmetric state, though a careful tapping on the walk-round might have revealed a lot, and as soon as it left the ski-ramp it yawed violently out of control. I understand it's possible that drop tanks are still used on the "*Discovery Wings*" satellite television channel for trailers. At least whoever designed that pod had the sense to put an "eye-lid" covering over the forward facing camera; the dirt thrown up by a Harrier nose wheel, especially on rough ground, can make short work of any lens. Some manufacturers of reconnaissance pods would have done well to have thought of that. It was not unknown for pilots to forget to arm the cameras on a weapon firing, especially dive attacks, but then they had a lot to think about! Jim Moore – my boss at Dunsfold Photographic – had a typically RAF expression to use if results turned up blank… "*Camera switched on – pilot not switched on.*" Later, on the development GR5s, the Instrumentation Department came up with a computer-controlled keypad in the cockpit so we could pre-programme the duration, running speed etc., of the cameras to commence as soon as the pilot touched the appropriate HOTAS (Hands-On Throttle and Stick) buttons for the firing or release of whatever item was supposed to drop off the aeroplane.

'The purpose of our film data was to check the release trajectory of the weapon, drop tank or whatever store was being carried, and make sure it released cleanly, not risking hitting the aircraft. At high speeds especially, even iron bombs have been known to "float" in the slipstream of aircraft and take a wing or tail right off – as some American trials on other aircraft found out the hard way. All drop tanks or bombs and other stores are pushed from the pylon by two explosive cartridges known as ERUs – Explosive Release Units. The power of these charges is carefully selected, in what's known as "throttling" – usually the more powerful one at the nose of the weapon or tank, to give a pitch-down effect. The firing sequence is controlled from the cockpit in what is known as "patching", though in modern Harriers the SMS (Stores Management System) is programmed to sort this out for itself, once the pilot tells it what the pylons are carrying in his pre-start routine. More recently this was done by inserting a data cartridge from his briefing. Wire lanyards are also connected to the pylons, to SPEMs (Secure Points Externally Mounted) which control such things as bomb tailfin deployment etc.

'Meanwhile, on the good old FRS1, Mike Snelling was the pilot for the Sea Eagle missile firing: on test ranges, the pilot performs a "dry run" to get the alignments okay, then will come back in under range control for a "hot run" to fire. On this occasion, Snelling had completed his dry run and was cleared "in hot." He acquired a target in about the right place and prepared to loose off the Sea Eagle. With a few seconds to go, he thought the angle looked slightly unusual, so he aborted. The contact turned out to be a fishing boat! This would have been ironic as he ran a fishing boat of his own out of Brighton in his free time. I once saw a letter written by him to the *Times* along the lines of "we poor fishermen…", forgetting to mention he was also a test pilot!

'One test pilot who should not go unmentioned is Graham Tomlinson, or as we knew him, 'GT'. He's the chap in the well-known photo of the Harrier GR5 in the dust on the Rough Ground Trials; they were quite high-risk tests, because if an outrigger had gone, it may well have been curtains, but only wimps like me ever ventured to ask where the rescue cover for the trial was. Some pilots have been known to put a Harrier wing tip between the hangars at West Freugh during trials up there (I know of one other service pilot who came back to photographers later with a quiet request to "lose" the films), but GT was far too professional to indulge in such hooliganism. When the GR5, with its Digital Engine Control System (DECS) was quite new, GT was taking off one day when the engine stopped at only a few hundred feet. The drill was, of course, to get out, but Graham stayed with it, worked out that the LP cock micro switches had disengaged, and did a complete restart all in the space of a few seconds – which is about all he had available to him. I also remember attending a lecture by test pilot John Farley, after he'd been helping out in the United States with the first AV-8Bs. At the time there was a surge problem, thought to be caused by airflow disturbance from the bulged canopy around the intakes. John had at that point amassed no less than two hours gliding – yes, gliding – the Harrier II. As I recall, the glide rate of a Harrier II (infinitely better than the original Harrier series) decrees that for an engine-out landing – not recommended – one needs to be at least 4,000 feet up at one mile from the threshold. John Farley's input cannot be overstated, both as a demonstrator of the aircraft for sales, and extremely risky development flying overcoming such things as the Intake Momentum Drag Yaw problem. This effect occurs when a Harrier hovers with the slipstream stronger on one wing than the other, creating more wing-lift that side. The result could be a catastrophic roll. There's a flight test film of a US Marine pilot, Major Chuck Rosberg, testing a Harrier GR1 at Dunsfold who fell victim to this phenomenon. He ejected, but hit the ground. He was nursed by Duncan Simpson and his wife en route to hospital, but did not make it. John Farley deliberately went into this part of the flight envelope repeatedly, right on the edge, and eventually a system was designed to counter it – more powerful reaction ducts, and sensors to detect yaw onset, causing the appropriate rudder pedal to shake, alerting the pilot to "boot" it.

'In the early days of P.1127 development, Hugh Merewether had his engine explode at high altitude over West Sussex. He spotted a gap in the cloud over Tangmere and went for it: there's a famous voice tape with him calmly saying "*I'm going in now…*" before making a heavy, but survivable, arrival. He managed a dead-stick landing at very high speed, and the evidence gave rise to the discovery of titanium fires. I had an interesting moment at Boscombe Down: we had two

QinetiQ's VAAC (Vectored Thrust Aircraft Advanced Flight Control) Harrier pictured during carrier trials. Although equipped with modified systems, the aircraft remained externally unchanged as the T2 second prototype and was the oldest active British Harrier. (Photo: QinetiQ)

XW175 ended operations in support of systems development for the F-35 programme in 2009, although the aircraft remains in storage at Boscombe Down and may be used for further testing. Pictured at Boscombe Down, the main runway and the historic site of the former TSR2 test area is visible in the background. (Photo: QinetiQ)

Aa artist's impression of
Harriers utilising the
proposed 'Skyhook'
concept. Developed by
British Aerospace and
Dowty Boulton Paul, the
system enabled Harriers
to be recovered and
launched by crane,
allowing the aircraft to be
operated from small naval
vessels which could not
support full-sized flight
decks. Although the
system was tested and
demonstrated, no interest
in the proposal emerged,
largely because the
concept of operating a
very small fleet of Harriers
was thought to be
logistically and financially
impractical.
(courtesy BAE Systems)

development GR5s (ZD318 and ZD319) which could mount up to sixteen cine cameras (Photo-Sonics 1VNs) capable of up to two hundred frames per second, as used in the film *Top Gun*, but this time without the make-up! We could have three cameras on a pylon each side in adapted CBLS200 practice bomb-carriers, two at wide angle, by the airbrake facing forward, and four in each dummy (mahogany!) gun pod. Of these, three were facing outboard, and one in each gun position, pointing forward, to observe missile launches and so on. As it turned out, this maybe should have been a standard fit, as it was a lot more useful than the

25 mm ADEN cannon – a gun whose main threat was that it might hit its opponents with its own innards. The "gun pods" are used for other purposes now, but I always thought the Gatling gun – as in the GAU-12 used by the American AV-8B, with the gun one side and ammunition the other – was designed like that for a reason (barrel cooling) and the geniuses at Royal Ordnance had tried to bypass the laws of physics. The original 30 mm ADEN on the Harrier GRI (plus the Sea Harrier and GR3), while not trendy in modern terms, at least did its job! At this stage, the gun pods also had strakes underneath to aid lift in the hover; it was a tight squeeze to get under there and work on the cameras – you could not get in under the centre line from aft because of the main wheel leg, or from forward because of the LIDS (Lift Improvement Devices) dam. I remember having to roll under there in snow, as the "powers that be" were bright enough to book a photo-dependent trial in mid-winter up in Scotland. This was not unusual. I'm sure they got an "off season" discount or some other benefit. After a part of the Rough Ground Trials at Boscombe Down, I was panelling up the camera bays, between the gun pods. I knew the pilot was in the cockpit, but thought he was just aligning his navigation system (the notorious Ferranti 1097 inertial platform, not their best

Sea Harrier FRS1 XZ438 was a long-term resident at Dunsfold and assigned to test duties. It is pictured during Sea Eagle trials, illustrating to good effect the Harrier tail plane's cranked leading edge and RWR fit on the fin leading edge and tail boom. (Photo: Andy Lawson)

The first Harrier GR5 pictured at Dunsfold during short take-off trials. Note that the rear fuselage is temporarily painted cream and the undersides of the wings (and hard points) are painted light blue, presumably in order to aid photography during weapons release trials. (Photo: Andy Lawson)

product – thank Heavens for the installation of GPS!), when I heard the engine igniters click and the main engine (rather than APU) starting up! I was obviously hidden from the view of the crew chief, and some communication snag meant nobody had told him I was there. I happened to know from a previous conversation with Flight-Test that start-up took nine seconds, so I was able to do up the last two fasteners in world record time before rolling out with haste to a very surprised and apologetic supervisor! We've seen a scheme published recently whereby members of Special Forces units or downed aircrew etc., may be inserted or recovered in pods under a Harrier pylon. I have to say I'd have to really want to travel to use that method!

'Another fun job Jim Moore and I had was to photograph the two-seat demonstrator Harrier G-VTOL from beneath while it hovered. The trials were to test handling with asymmetric loads, for example with Sea Eagle one side, drop tank the other, etc. However, Harriers rarely hover on the spot if they can help it, but prefer to creep forwards at around five miles an hour to minimise hot gas re-ingestion. I soon found out that the practice was to walk forward towards the Harrier nose as far as one's nerve and ear defenders would allow, then start smartly walking backwards while taking shots upwards. Jim swears that Heinz Frick chased him around the airfield in the hover, and knowing both of them it sounds about right! During the development of the "Skyhook" – an idea of Heinz Frick's, whereby a space-stabilised crane arm could pick up a Sea Harrier for launch or recovery from small warships – Kingston Photographic had the brilliant idea of

placing an array of stills and cine cameras right under the spot, facing upwards. We at Dunsfold had our doubts that the average tripod or lens was designed to take 23,500 pounds of thrust ("officially speaking" that is - and read that as you will, as the then-current Pegasus was meant to produce a max of 21,500 lb thrust) and I suspect we were vindicated by the multi-thousand pound repair bill and zero footage! It was one moment I did enjoy especially though. We were on a trial for future FRS2 (as then) development at the West Freugh test range in Scotland. The pilot of the moment was a rather abrasive Navy guy who still thought he could treat everyone as dirt, which is no doubt how he'd behaved in the services. At this time, there was a union dispute on, and we "technical staff" had to support the aircraft without any ground crew. This was fine and within the rules, as long as we stayed within certain limits, one being

Although the PCB (Plenum Chamber Burning) development of the Pegasus engine was pursued by Rolls Royce for many years, the engine was never incorporated into an operational design. Much of the engine-testing was performed at Shoeburyness, using a composite Harrier GR1 airframe. The carcass of this aircraft is now preserved at Kemble. (Photo: Rolls Royce)

A former Development Batch Harrier and an ex-FAA Harrier T8 were placed on display at Wittering after withdrawal from use. With flying operations at Wittering ended, the future of these airframes remains uncertain.
(Photo: Tim McLelland collection)

that any work on the aeroplane had to be capable of being carried out by the pilot "in the field." As a consequence of this, the pilot had been warned only to use water injection as an emergency measure. As he came in to land after his dummy bombing runs, ATC let him know there was a bunch of visiting schoolgirls watching. He could not resist the full hover routine, complete with a nod to the crowd; the Flight-Test engineer next to me groaned "*He's got to have full water on for that...*" The end result was a not-so glamorous pilot sat astride the fuselage in the hangar with a jerry-can… "*Sorry we'd love to help you, but it would break the rules…*" Fifty gallons later he'd probably got the message. When my father, "Stan" Lawson, was crew chief at the Paris Salon Air Show (XZ439, piloted by Heinz Frick, and aircraft now flying in civilian hands in the USA) his request for fifty gallons of distilled water a day was met with incredulity – "*Sacre Bleu! The thing runs on water!*" was the usual reaction from our French hosts.

'There was an amusing ruse pursued by John Farley and Mike Snelling. In the early days of development, when hoping to get the US Marines to buy the aircraft, they had hosted a high-ranking member around Dunsfold, ending back at the Pilots' Office in the 1942-vintage Control Tower. This chap made a comment along the lines of "*Gee, I think the Harrier's great, but I can't believe you build that aircraft in such a rustic little place as this…*" and so on. Mike Snelling, catching Farleys' eye, instantly replied '*Oh, well you obviously don't have clearance to*

see the underground production facility.' The American was outraged; '*I have the highest clearance, show me it now!*' I suppose that's just the sort of thing the Americans would have, but things were rather more basic and British at Dunsfold. In the 1980s we were having a sales push at the US Navy. Farley took up an Admiral in G-VTOL. It was filthy weather and, in an unusual move, John taxied back to the hangar to get the Admiral out of the cockpit in the dry. I had to be there poised with my camera. J.F. slung the canopy open, and grinned back at the Admiral saying, '*Accelerates well, doesn't it?*' The Admiral looked like he'd done several rounds with Mike Tyson, and was in no state to argue. But he got his own back against the "limeys" later on during his tour when recovered. He had a glamorous female assistant, and when shown the Harrier simulator she was asked rather patronisingly if she'd like to have a go. She calmly took the controls and executed a perfect flight, much to the amazement of the technician standing by. "*Yeah, she's got four thousand hours on helicopters,*" the Admiral casually mentioned, with a very restrained smile. I tried flying the GR5 simulator one day. It was fine whizzing about at altitude; after all I'd played "Space Invaders" enough. Then the Flight-Test engineer who was giving me the go (Dave Byford) said, "Let's try a vertical take-off… now mind, this will be sensitive…" I thought, *Yeah, I know fighters are sensitive…* On lift-off from the runway, the HUD said I was slightly nose down as I ascended. I gave the merest back-pressure possible on the stick – and

Harrier GR5 ZD310 emerges from the assembly shed at Dunsfold to begin test-flying. Much of the airframe remains unpainted in yellow primer.
(Photo: Dave Bullock)

Sea Harrier T.Mk.60 for the Indian Navy, pictured at Dunsfold prior to delivery with underwing 'ferry' tanks fitted in preparation for the long journey to its customer. (Photo: Andy Lawson)

Below and opposite page: A specially-painted Harrier GR9 ZG506, which performed the final operational Harrier landing at Cottesmore on 15 December 2010. (Photo: Rich Pittman)

Typical of the JHF concept, HMS Illustrious pictured from the air, with a mix of Harriers on board comprising Sea Harrier FA2s and Harrier GR7s from No.4 Squadron. *(Photo: UK MoD Crown Copyright 2010)*

television programme and, at the time of writing, plans continue for the historic airfield to become the home of a major housing development. To the west, RNAS Yeovilton's Harrier ramp has long since been dismantled. RAF Wittering's flying days are ended and Cottesmore said farewell to the very last Harriers early in 2011. Over in Germany, Gütersloh still remains intact but no longer an active airfield, while Wildenrath has been obliterated and now provides the home for a tramway test track. The Royal Navy patiently waits for its new carriers (in effect just one carrier, as only one will be in service at any given time) and its fleet of F-35C jets which will be operated at sea. The RAF anticipated its share of the F-35 order too, and when – or if – the aircraft finally enters service, it will join the Typhoon as one of only two aircraft types equipping the RAF's front-line offensive and defensive order of battle. By then the Harrier – and the concept of VTOL – will doubtless be forgotten. It might be imagined that the Harrier and its revolutionary abilities were simply an interesting, but ultimately pointless, episode in Britain's military history, but this would be a clumsy misunderstanding of the Harrier's contribution. The Harrier was created through a muddled process of confused political will, constantly changing military requirements, and continually developing technological advances. It emerged initially without any clear purpose, but by the time the aircraft's abilities were fully understood, its value was only too clear. Through the long, dark years of the Cold War, Britain relied upon deterrence to stay alive. Deterrence relied upon credibility, particularly the ability to demonstrate that the UK had the will and the means to defend itself. The Harrier was fundamental to this posture. While the Soviet Union retained the capacity to destroy NATO's airfields almost at will, the RAF had a unique ability to take at least part of its air power away from the vulnerability of these sites, ensuring that it (and therefore the ground forces which it supported) remained sure of their survivability. This was a vital capacity which could only be provided by the Harrier. Nobody should underestimate the importance of this remarkable aircraft. But the Cold War is gone and with it, the Harrier's *raison d'être*.

Across the Atlantic, however, the Harrier remains very much in business. It will remain so until the F-35 reaches service with the USMC. The Marines understood the value of VTOL and today they still do, and it seems likely that if the F-35B is developed to production status, the Marines will get themselves a STOVL aircraft which is even more flexible and versatile than the Harrier. For Spain, Italy, India and Thailand, the Harrier is also still a vital asset, able to operate from modestly-sized carriers at sea, and each of these countries is in no hurry to dispose of what – by any standards – must be seen as a very good buy indeed. But no matter how brilliant the Harrier undoubtedly has been, it

the next thing I knew it was on the ground, inverted with its wheels in the air. And that was a "user-friendly" Harrier II!

British Aerospace sold off Dunsfold in 2002 (the famous Kingston site was vacated in 1994) and now the airfield is mostly silent. The site where Harriers were once prepared for test-flying is now better known as a studio for the BBC's '*Top Gear*'

An unusual pilot's-eye view of USMC operations from the USS Kearsarge (LHD-3), the deck shrouded in sooty smoke as an AV-8B gets airborne with the aid of water injection. (Photo: USMC)

cannot last forever. It was a 'Sixties' machine built for, and operated right through, the Cold War. It reappeared in its second-generation guise to embark on a new service life but now, after almost fifty years, it is inevitable that the Harrier is approaching the end of its illustrious career. Whilst commentators in Britain might question the wisdom of withdrawing the RAF's and Navy's Harriers so prematurely, it must be accepted that the aircraft was to be retired eventually in any case,

and the surprise, bitterness and anger which greeted the announcement of the Harrier's withdrawal does therefore seem a little disproportionate. But, of course, the news of the Harrier's early retirement was not just about defence needs and cost. For those who flew, maintained, designed, manufactured and supported the Harrier over successive decades, it was about emotion, respect and admiration for a shining example of British design and engineering brilliance.

At the time of writing, the F-35's troubled developmental programme continues and the aircraft is still expected to enter USMC service as the Harrier's replacement. With the RAF Harrier fleet now withdrawn, the UK is without any fixed-wing carrier capability until the F-35 enters service in 2015-16. (Photo: Lockheed Martin)

Although the F-35B was to have been adopted for British service, at the time of writing, the conventional F-35C is being pursued. Consequently, following the retirement of the Harrier fleet, Britain is no longer in the VSTOL business and will remain so – a sad outcome for the country which developed this unique capability. (Photo: Lockheed Martin)

Harrier GR9 ZG477 pictured shortly before retirement, specially marked in the colours of No.1 Squadron. This aircraft performed the very last Harrier take-off from Ark Royal a few days previously.
(Photo: Chris Sandham-Bailey)

Harrier sunset: A Harrier GR9 makes a late afternoon approach at RAF Cottesmore, just days before the type was withdrawn from RAF service.
(Photo: Rich Pittman)

Evocative view of the Harrier performing for the public. The Harrier's unique capabilities made the aircraft a star performer wherever it appeared and although the aircraft will doubtless continue to impress at events around the world, its absence from the UK air show scene will be very evident.
(Photo: USMC)

An eye-catching quartet of specially-marked Harriers captured in flight on 14 December 2010. The lead aircraft is painted in a special scheme reflecting the original post-delivery finish applied to RAF Harriers, and is joined by aircraft from the last Cottesmore units – No.1 Squadron, No.4 Squadron and 800 NAS. (Photo: UK MoD Crown Copyright 2010)

Out over snowy Lincolnshire, JHF Harriers gather in a 16-ship formation in preparation for the Harrier's farewell on 15 December 2010.
(Photo: UK MoD Crown Copyright 2010)

Farewell to RAF Wittering as the JHF Harriers fly over the base for the last time on 14 December 2010, half a century since the Harrier first entered RAF service there.
(Photo: UK MoD Crown Copyright 2010)

All aboard for the last time: 16 Harriers from Cottesmore assemble over Lincolnshire to commemorate the Harrier's withdrawal. Sadly, the flypast was scrubbed on the official day of retirement because of poor weather. (Photo: UK MoD Crown Copyright 2010)

Harrier Variants

P.1127

Experimental STOVL project manufactured in accordance with specification ER.204D
11,300-12,000 lb Bristol/Bristol Siddeley BE/BS.53 Pegasus 2
12,000-13,050 lb Pegasus 3
XP831 & XP836

P.1127

Development batch derivative based on earlier prototypes
XP984 (powered by a Pegasus 5) became the Kestrel prototype
13,050 lb Bristol Siddeley BS.53 Pegasus 3
15,200 lb Bristol Siddeley BS.53 Pegasus 5
XP972, XP976, XP980, XP984

Kestrel FGA.Mk.1

Development of P.1127 as a preliminary ground-attack fighter for tripartite evaluation by UK, USA and FRG in accordance with specification FGA.236.
US and German airframes subsequently shipped to US, redesignated XV-6A
15,200 lb Bristol Siddeley BS.53 Pegasus 5
XS688-XS696

P.1127(RAF)

Development batch ground-attack and reconnaissance aircraft based on P.1127/Kestrel. Created in accordance with specification SR.255 & ASR 384
19,000 lb Bristol Siddeley BS.53 Pegasus 6
20,500 lb Pegasus 10
21,500 lb Pegasus 11
XV276-XV281

Harrier GR.Mk.1

Operational ground-attack and reconnaissance fighter for RAF
19,000 lb Rolls-Royce Pegasus 6/Mk.101
XV738-762, 776-810 & XW630

Harrier GR.Mk.1A

Operational ground-attack and reconnaissance fighter for RAF
GR.Mk.1 airframe with improved engine plus new-build aircraft
20,500 lb Rolls-Royce Pegasus 10/Mk.102
XW916-924 & XW763-770

Harrier GR.Mk.3

Operational ground-attack and reconnaissance fighter for RAF
Converted GR.Mk.1/1A and new-build
Uprated engine, LRMTS and RWR fit
21,500 lb Rolls-Royce Pegasus 11/Mk.103
XZ128-139, 963-973, 987-999 & ZD667-670

HS.1174

Development batch twin-seat ground-attack and reconnaissance fighter and trainer. Produced in accordance with SR(A)386
19,000 lb Rolls-Royce Pegasus 6
20,500 lb Pegasus 10
21,500 lb Pegasus 11
XW174 & XW175

Harrier T.Mk.2

Twin-seat ground-attack and reconnaissance fighter and trainer
19,000 lb Rolls-Royce Pegasus 6/Mk.101
XW264-272 & XW925

Harrier T.Mk.2A

Twin-seat ground-attack and reconnaissance fighter and trainer
Re-engined T.Mk.2 plus new-build airframes
20,500 lb Rolls-Royce Pegasus 10/Mk.102
XW926-927 & XW933-934

Harrier T.Mk.4

Twin-seat ground-attack and reconnaissance fighter and trainer
Converted and re-engined T.Mk. 2/2A plus new build airframes
LRMTS and RWR fit
21,500 lb Rolls-Royce Pegasus 11/Mk.103
XZ145-147 & 445, ZB600-603 & ZD990-993

Harrier T.Mk.4A

Twin-seat Active Control Technology aircraft assigned to MoD(PE)
Vectored thrust Advanced Aircraft Flight Control (VAAC) system
21,500 lb Rolls-Royce Pegasus 11/Mk.103
XW175

Harrier Mk.52

Twin-seat company demonstrator
21,500 lb Rolls-Royce Pegasus 11/Mk.103
G-VTOL or ZA250

AV-8A Harrier

Ground-attack and reconnaissance fighter for the United States Marine Corps (USMC)
20,500 lb Rolls-Royce Pegasus 10 Mk.102 F402-RR-400
21,500 lb Pegasus 11/Mk.103/F402-RR-401or 402
158384-395, 158694-711, 158948-977, 159230-259, 159366-377

AV-8C Harrier

AV-8A upgrade with improved capability and modifications
21,500 lb Rolls-Royce Pegasus 11/F402-RR-402
Converted from AV-8A airframes

TAV-8A

Harrier Mk.54
Twin-seat trainer for United States Marine Corps (USMC)
21,500 lb Rolls-Royce Pegasus 11/Mk.103/F402-RR-402
159378-385

AV-8S

Harrier Mk.55 'Matador'
Ground-attack and reconnaissance fighter for the Spanish Navy
Seven subsequently sold to Thailand in 1996
21,500 lb Rolls-Royce Pegasus 11/Mk.150
159557-562, 161174-178

TAV-8S

Harrier Mk.58 'Matador'
Twin-seat trainer for the Spanish Navy
Both aircraft subsequently sold to Thailand 1996
21,500 lb Rolls-Royce Pegasus 11/Mk.150
159563-564

Sea Harrier Mk.1

Development batch interceptor, reconnaissance and strike
fighter for the Royal Navy
21,500 lb Rolls-Royce Pegasus 11/Mk.104
XZ438-440

Sea Harrier FRS.Mk.1

Interceptor, reconnaissance and strike fighter for the Royal
Navy
21,500 lb Rolls-Royce Pegasus 11/Mk.104
XZ450-460 & 491-500, ZA174-177 & 190-195, ZD578-582 &
607-614, ZE690-698

Harrier T.Mk.4N

Twin-seat trainer for the Royal Navy
21,500 lb Rolls-Royce Pegasus 11/Mk.103
ZB604-606

Sea Harrier FRS.Mk.51

Interceptor, reconnaissance and strike fighter for the Indian
Navy
21,500 lb Rolls-Royce Pegasus 11/Mk.151-32
IN601-623

Harrier T.Mk.60

Twin-seat trainer for the Indian Navy
21,500 lb Rolls-Royce Pegasus 11/Mk.151
IN651-654

Harrier T.Mk.4(I)

Twin-seat V/STOL trainer for the Indian Navy
Converted T.Mk.4 airframes from RAF
21,500 lb Rolls-Royce Pegasus 11/Mk.151
IN655-656

Sea Harrier FRS.Mk.2

Development batch aircraft
Mid-Life Update. Converted from FRS.Mk.1 airframes
21,500 lb Rolls-Royce Pegasus 11/Mk.106
ZA195, XZ439

Sea Harrier FA.Mk.2

Mid-Life Update of FRS.Mk.1 fleet
Conversions and new-build airframes
21,500 lb Rolls-Royce Pegasus 11/Mk.106
ZH796-813

Harrier T.Mk.8N

Conversions of T.Mk.4/4N
Twin-seat trainer for the Royal Navy
21,500 lb Rolls-Royce Pegasus 11/Mk.106
ZB603-605 & ZD992-993

YAV- 8B

McDonnell Douglas conversion of AV-8A airframe
Prototype 'second-generation' Harrier for the USMC
21,180 lb Rolls-Royce Pegasus 11/Mk.105/F402-RR-404 or 404A
158394, 158395

AV- 8B Harrier II

Full Scale Development (FSD) aircraft for the USMC
21,180 lb Rolls-Royce Pegasus 11/Mk.105/F402-RR-404 or 404A
161396-161399

AV- 8B Harrier II

Second-generation Harrier, ground-attack fighter for the USMC
21,180 lb Rolls-Royce Pegasus 11/Mk.105/F402-RR-404 or 404A
21,450lb Pegasus 11-21/Mk.106/F402-RR-406 or 406A
162942-163852

EAV-8B Harrier II

AV-8B export aircraft for Spanish Navy
21,450 lb Rolls-Royce Pegasus 11-21/Mk. 152-42
163010-021

TAV-8B Harrier II

Twin-seat trainer derivative of AV-8B for the USMC and
Spanish Navy
21,450 lb Rolls-Royce Pegasus 11-21/Mk.106/F402-RR-406 or
406A
162747-164542
165036 (Spain)

AV-8B(NA)

Conversion of AV-8B airframe with FLIR & NVGs for night-
attack capability
Uprated engine from 15th airframe
One AV-8B converted as development aircraft (163853)
21,450 lb Rolls-Royce Pegasus 11-21/Mk.106/F402-RR-406A
23,800 lb Rolls-Royce Pegasus 11-61/F404-RR-408
163853-16547

AV-8B Harrier II+AV-8B development with radar

Conversion of existing airframes and new-build for USMC
Export aircraft for Italian Navy
23,800 lb Rolls-Royce Pegasus 11-61/F402-RR-408
164548-571 and 165001-006
164563-165019 (Italy)

**TAV-8B Harrier II+ Twin-seat trainer derivative of AV-8B+
for Italian Navy**

23,800 lb Rolls-Royce Pegasus 11-61/F402-RR-408
164136-137

EAV-8B Harrier II+ AV-8B Harrier II+ for Spanish Navy

EAV-8B conversions and new-build aircraft
23,800 lb Rolls-Royce Pegasus F402-RR- 408
163028-035

Harrier GR.Mk.5

Development Batch aircraft
Second-generation Harrier derivative for the RAF
21,750 lb Rolls-Royce Pegasus 11-21/Mk. 105
ZD318, ZD319

Harrier GR.Mk.5

Second-generation Harrier for the RAF in accordance with
ASR.409
21,750 lb Rolls-Royce Pegasus 11-21/Mk. 105
ZD320-330, ZD345-355, ZD375-380, ZD400-412

Harrier GR.Mk.5A

Harrier GR.Mk.5 conversions with night attack capability
Stored and converted to GR.Mk.7 standard before service
21,750 lb Rolls-Royce Pegasus 11-21/Mk. 105
ZD430-438, ZD461-470

Harrier GR.Mk.7

Harrier GR.Mk.5 development with night-attack capability
for RAF
Converted GR.Mk.5/5A aircraft and new build airframes
21,750 lb Rolls-Royce Pegasus 11-21/Mk. 105
ZG471-480, ZG500-512, ZG530-533, ZG856-862

Harrier GR.Mk.7A

Conversion of Harrier GR.Mk.7 with uprated engine
Subsequently converted to GR.Mk. 9A standard
23,800 lb Rolls-Royce Pegasus 11-61/Mk. 107

Harrier GR.Mk. 9

Development of GR.Mk.7 with enhanced weapons capability
and updated avionics
21,750 lb Rolls-Royce Pegasus 11-21/Mk. 105

Harrier GR.Mk 9A

Development of GR.Mk.7 development with uprated engine of
GR.Mk.7A and enhanced weapons capability and updated
avionics of GR.Mk.9
23,800 lb Rolls-Royce Pegasus 11-61/Mk. 107

Harrier T.Mk.10

Twin-seat ground-attack and reconnaissance fighter
and trainer for RAF
Second-generation Harrier trainer derivative
21,750 lb Rolls-Royce Pegasus 11-21/Mk. 105
ZH653-665

Harrier T.Mk.12

Development of T.Mk.10 with enhanced weapons capability
and updated avionics of GR.Mk.9
21,750 lb Rolls-Royce Pegasus 11-21/Mk.105

Harrier Exports

SPAIN

Spain was the first country to express serious interest in the Harrier during 1973. At that time, relations between the United Kingdom and Spain, which was still under General Franco's control, were poor and an arms embargo was in place which prohibited any direct sale of British-built aircraft to the country. However, an order was placed through the United States, and indirectly transferred to Hawker Siddeley. Six AV-8A (Mk.55 models) and two TAV-8A aircraft were initially ordered, designated as the AV-8A(S) and TAV-8(S), all of which made their first flights in 1976. Prior to delivery to Spain, the aircraft were air-freighted from the UK to McDonnell Douglas for final completion, and subsequently assigned to training with the USMC. For service with the Spanish Navy (*Arma Aerea de la Armada*) the Harriers were designated as the VA.1 and VAE.1 (the single- and twin-seat derivatives respectively) but the British-inspired name 'Matador' was never adopted by the Navy.

Five additional AV-8S aircraft were ordered in August 1977 and these were delivered during 1980, although these aircraft were delivered directly from the UK, with relations between the countries having been restored by this stage. The aircraft returned briefly to the UK for modification during 1987 when Sky Guardia radar warning receivers were fitted at Yeovilton. In March 1983 Spain ordered 12 AV-8B second-generation Harriers (designated as the VA.2) although these aircraft are referred to as the EAV-8B by McDonnell Douglas. Initially assigned to conversion training in the US, the aircraft were then flown directly to Spain during mid/late 1987. In 1990 Spain entered into an agreement with the US to produce the Harrier II+ derivative, incorporating APG-65 radar and night vision capability. From the existing fleet, ten aircraft were subsequently converted to this standard and a further eight new-build aircraft were ordered, enabling Spain to retire the first-generation AV-8S aircraft. Operating at sea from the Navy's carrier *Dedalo* until 1988, a new carrier (*Principe de Asturias*) entered service in 1989 with facilities to handle eight Harriers, including a 12-degree launch ramp from the outset (the previous carrier was never fitted with a ramp). Although the integration of modern weapons systems has been slow, the Navy's Harriers are arguably the most able aircraft in Spain's military inventory, and they look set to remain in service for many more years, with no plans for any replacement programme having yet been made.

Hawker Siddeley AV-8S Harrier, 01-804, Escuadrilla 008, Spanish Navy, 1994
Medium Grey upper surfaces with White undersides; all lettering in black. National markings in six positions; unit marking on nose, Spanish Navy marking on fin

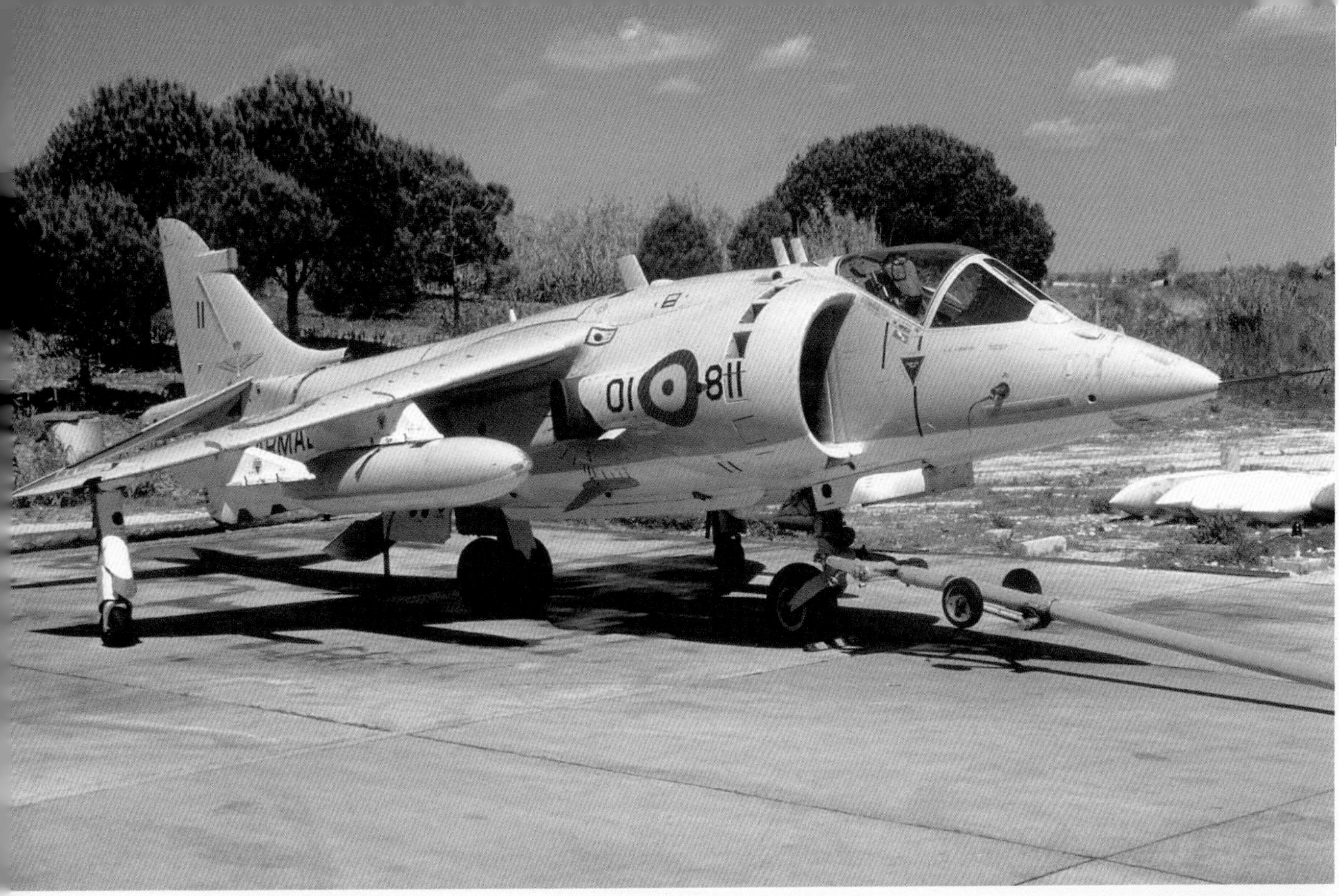
01 811

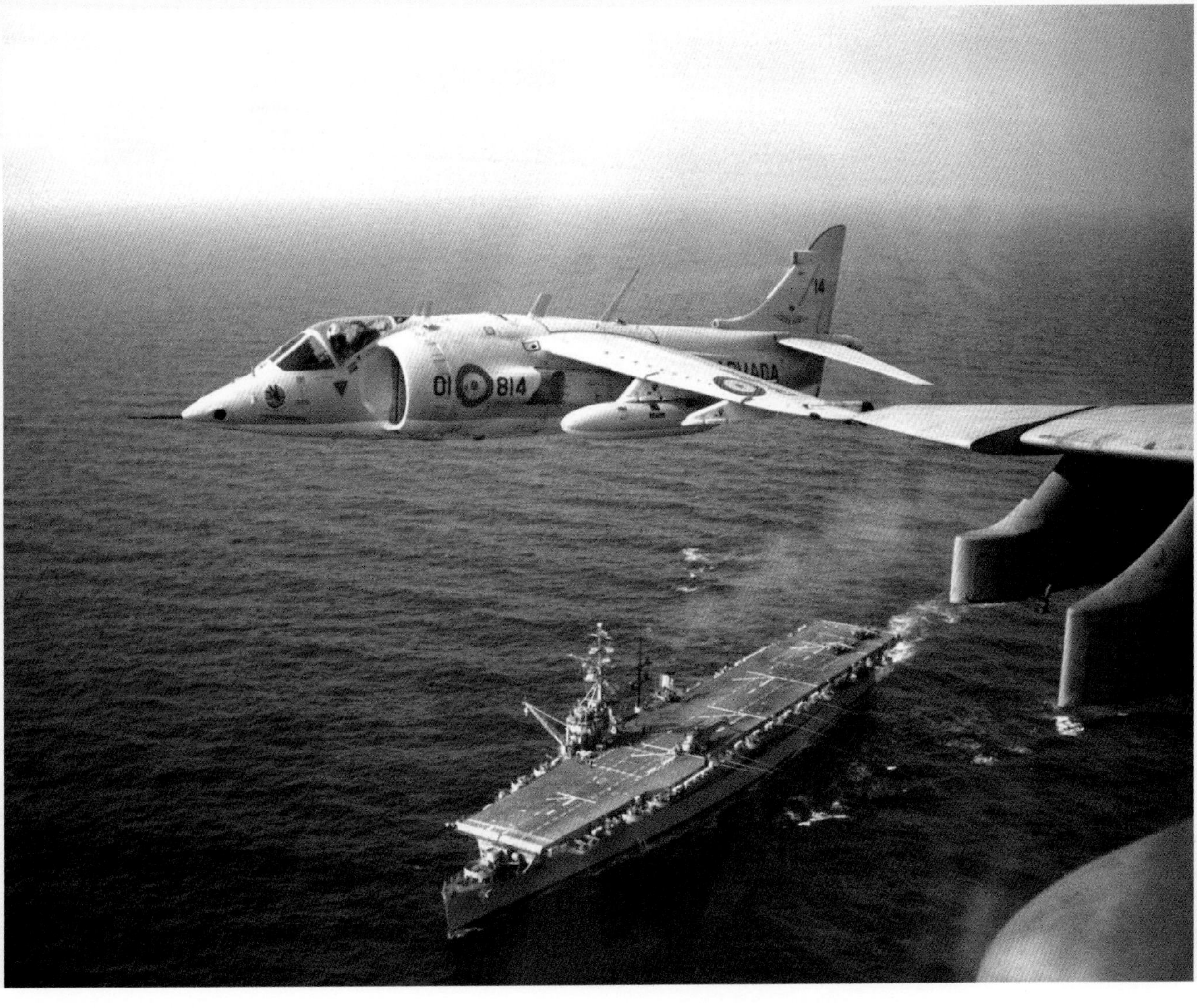
14
01 814

SPAIN

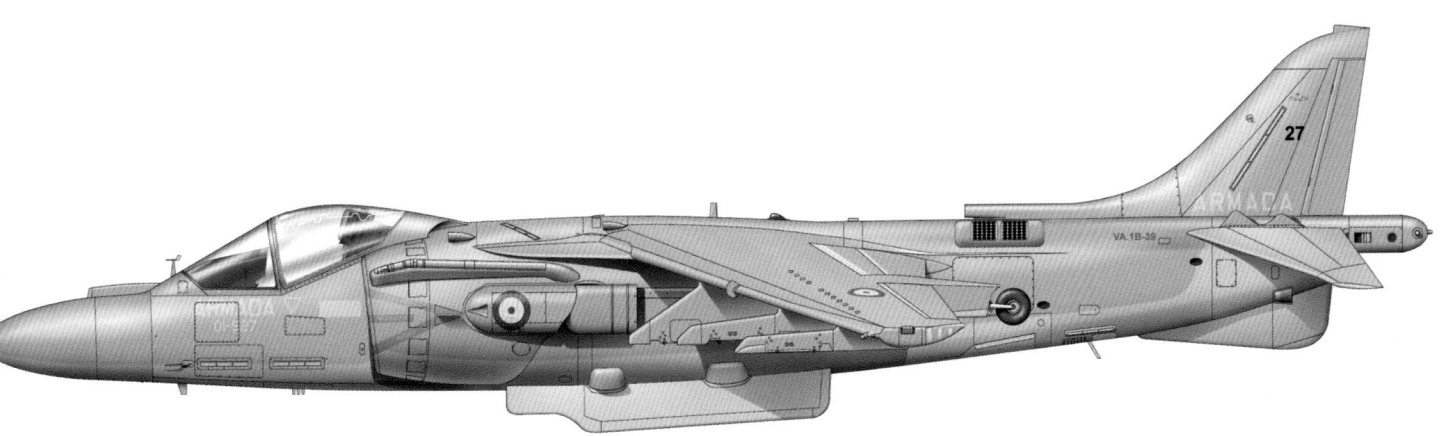

McDonnell Douglas VA.1B Harrier II+, 01-927/VA.1B-39, Spanish Navy, on board Principe de Asturias, March 2007
FS.36118 uppersurfaces with FS.36231 undersides; all lettering in lighter or darker greys except '27' on fin which is black

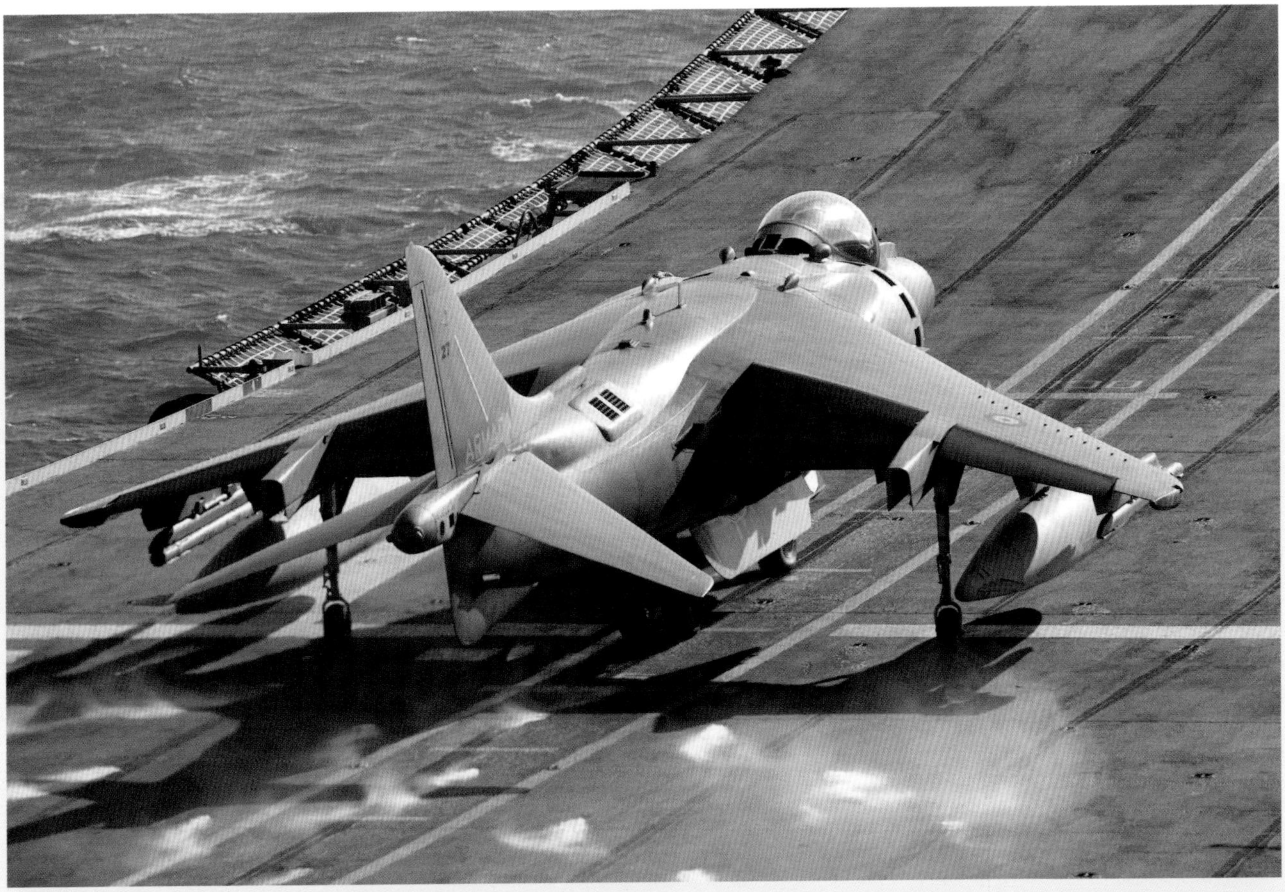

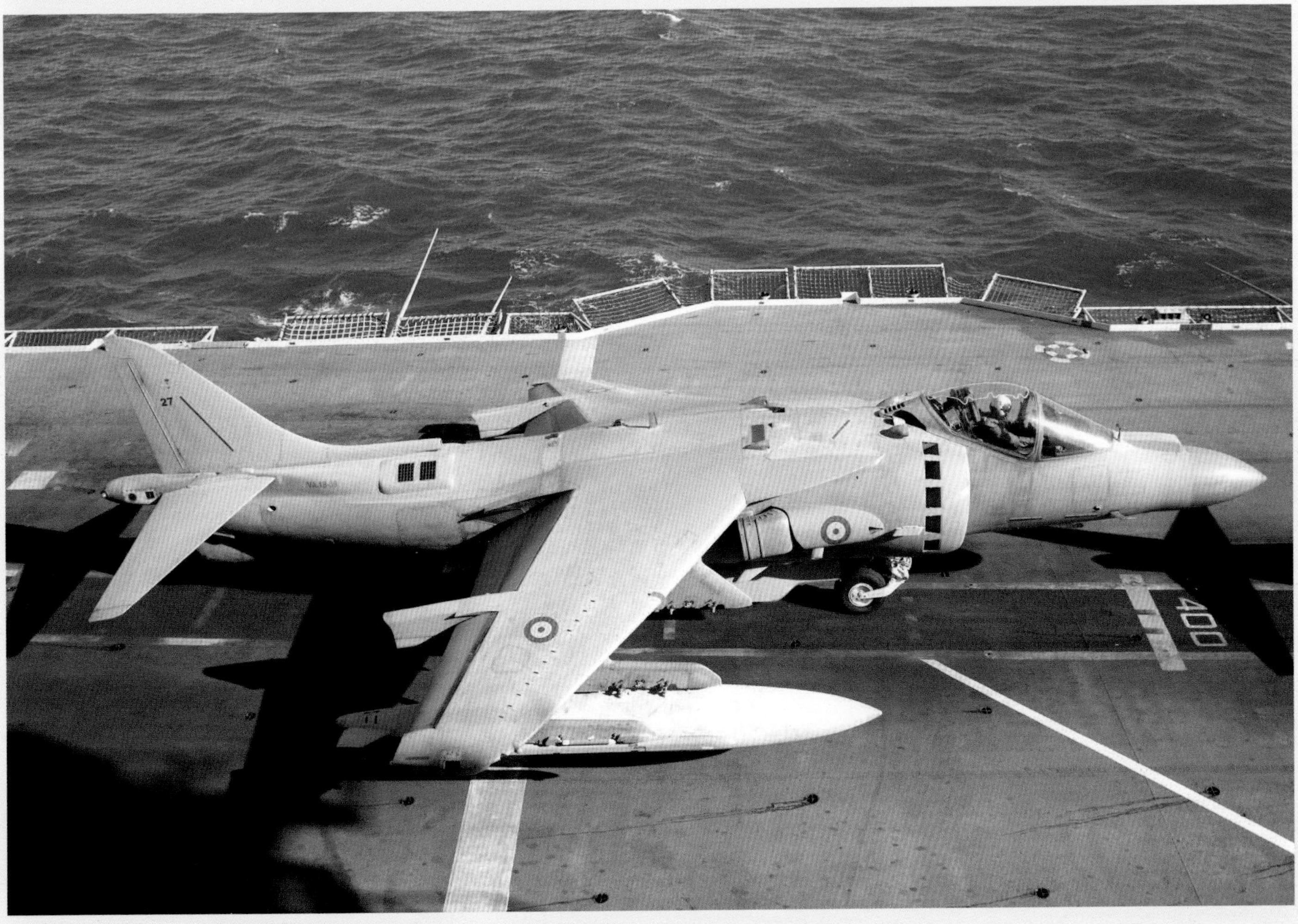
27
400

SPAIN

INDIA

India's interest in the Harrier emerged in 1978 when plans were drawn up for a modern carrier force which would be equipped with 48 Harriers, these being export versions of the Royal Navy's Sea Harrier (the Mk.51). The first six aircraft (together with a pair of T.Mk.60 trainer derivatives) were ordered in December 1979, the first aircraft taking to the air in August 1982. The new aircraft were initially delivered to Yeovilton where crew conversion training took place and the first three aircraft departed for India on 13 December 1983. The projected second order for an additional four aircraft was cancelled, but in November 1985 a further ten single-seat and a single twin-seat aircraft were ordered. A third batch of seven single-seat aircraft and another twin-seater was placed in 1986, bringing the total order up to 23 single-seat machines and four dual-control variants. India now operates the only surviving examples of the Sea Harrier, together with the T.60 trainers which were based on the RAF's T.Mk.4 airframe.

Two attrition replacements entered service in 2002, these being former RAF aircraft which were refurbished prior to delivery. Equipped with the Sea Eagle missile, the Sea Harrier provides India's Navy with an aged but effective fighting machine. Operating initially from both the *INS Vikrant* and the *INS Viraat* (better known as the British *HMS Hermes*), the former vessel was subsequently retired. Upgraded with a new Elta EL/M-2032 radar and Rafael Derby BVRAAMs, the Sea Harrier fleet is expected to be replaced by MiG-29K fighters, although no date for this transition has yet been established and the Harriers may be retained in service for many more years. Some interest was expressed in purchasing a batch of former Royal Navy Sea Harrier FRS2 aircraft, but no suitable deal was reached (it was reported that the sale did not include the aircraft's radar), and it seems unlikely that any additional Harriers will be purchased, now that eventual replacement by the MiG-29K seems certain.

(Photographs of Indian aircraft: BAE Systems and Simon Watson)

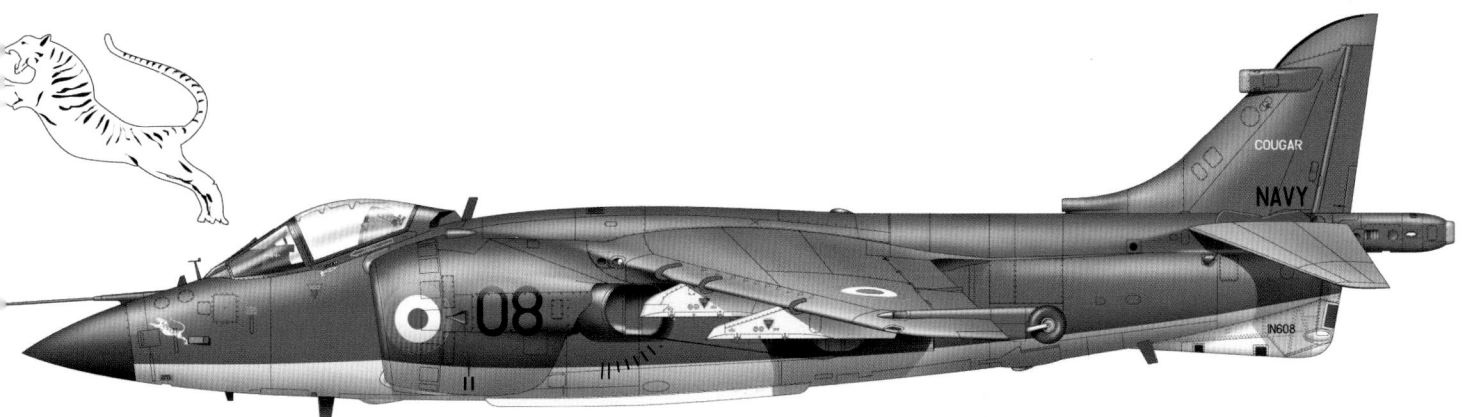

BAe Sea Harrier FRS.51, IN608/08, 'Cougar', No. 511 Squadron, INS Viraat (R22), Indian Navy
Extra Dark Sea Grey/White scheme with Orange/White/Green roundels in six positions; black serial, repeated below wings.
Black '08' on air intake and 'Navy' on fin (see detail of starboard side); white 'Cougar' on fin and white tiger on nose

INDIA

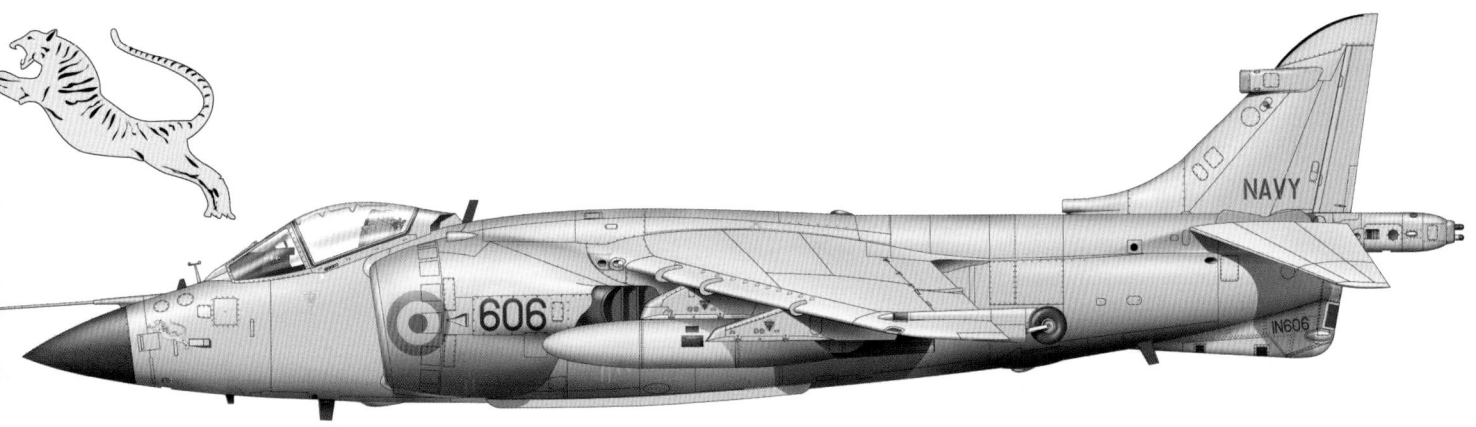

BAe Sea Harrier FRS.51, IN606/606, No. 300 Squadron, INS Viraat, Indian Navy
Matt Medium Sea Grey overall with all lettering in dark grey; Orange/MSG/Green roundels in six positions. 'White Tiger' marking on nose in grey/black

ITALY

Italy's purchase of the Harrier took place many years after some initial interest in the aircraft had been expressed back in 1967 when Hugh Merewether landed a pre-production aircraft on the Italian Navy's *Andrea Doria* helicopter carrier. It was envisaged that six Mk.50 aircraft would be purchased while a further 44 would be licence-assembled in Italy; however, cost considerations, combined with political opposition (compounded by a 1937 treaty which prohibited the Italian Navy from flying fixed-wing aircraft), eventually led to the abandonment of these plans. When a new helicopter carrier (the *Giuseppe Garibaldi*) was launched in 1983, it was clear that Italy still intended to acquire fixed-wing aircraft of some description as the vessel incorporated a 'ski jump' ramp

in its design. Following evaluation of both the Sea Harrier and AV-8B, Italy finally ordered two TAV-8B trainer aircraft in May 1989. Some 16 AV-8B+ aircraft were then ordered with options on a further eight machines. The first aircraft were taken from the USMC order and went directly to Cherry Point for conversion training, while later aircraft were assembled in Italy by Alenia. The Italian Harrier fleet continues to operate from the *Garibaldi* and exercises are frequently conducted with Spain's Harrier force. Together they are expected to remain in business for the foreseeable future with no replacement plans having yet been identified.

(Photographs of Italian aircraft: Mick Balter/ MBAviationImages and Andre Jans)

McDonnell Douglas AV-8B Harrier II Plus, MM7224/1-19, GRUPAER, Italian Navy, 2007
Dark Gull Gray overall with Dark Ghost Gray undersides. Light Grey lettering; black 'paws' and 'scratches' on rudder. Unit badge on nose

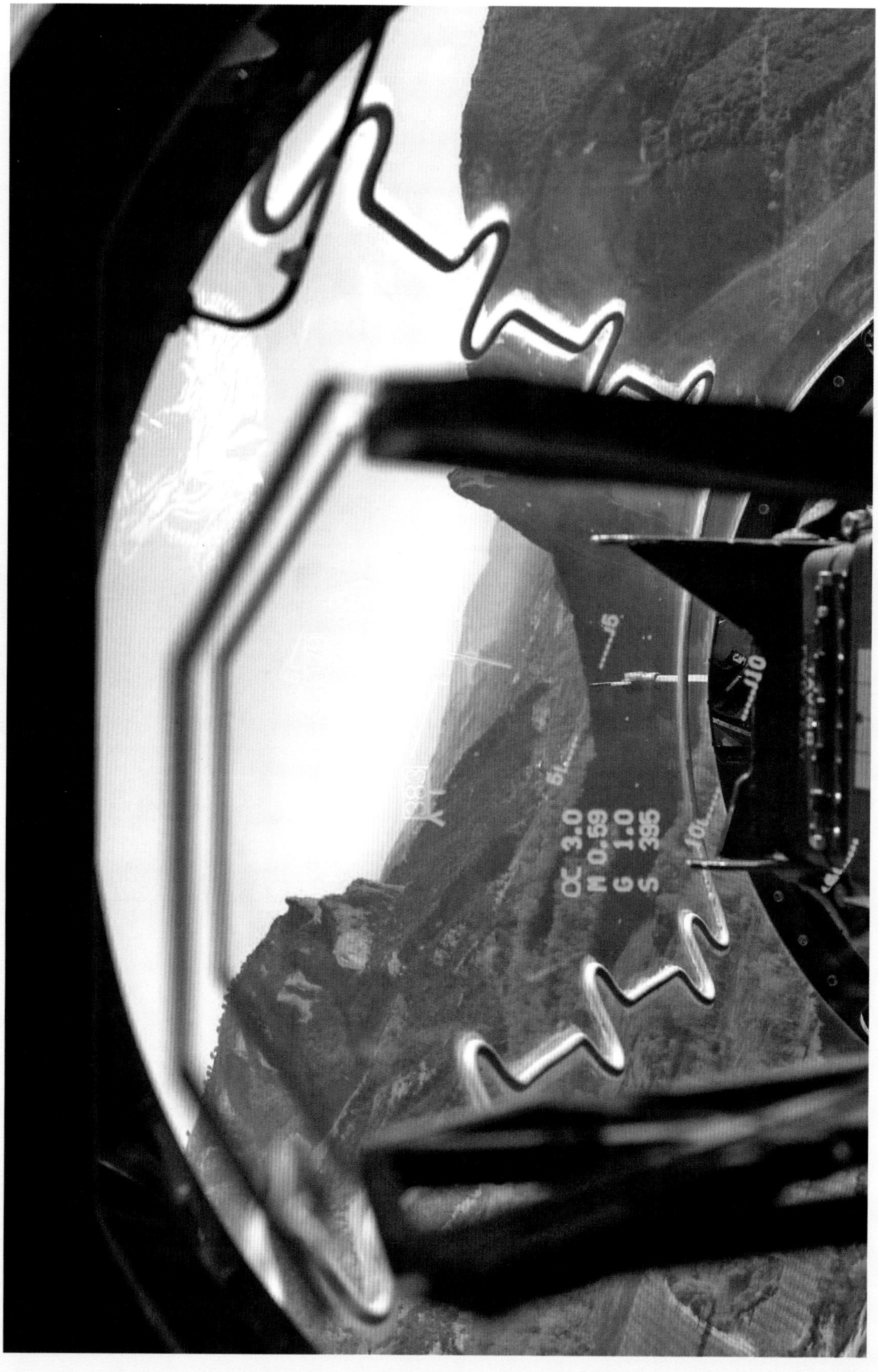

ITALY

(Photographs of Thai aircraft: BAE Systems and Y.Nisho)

THAILAND

Following the retirement of Spain's fleet of first-generation AV-8S aircraft, Thailand purchased seven aircraft plus a TAV-8S trainer from Spain in September 1997. Thai Navy pilots conducted initial training with the US Navy and converted on to the Harrier at Rota. After delivery, this small batch of Harriers was established at U-Tapao and the aircraft remain in service at this base, pending any decision on future requirements. Some interest was expressed in the purchase of former Royal Navy Sea Harrier FRS2 aircraft but, like the Indian Navy, the idea was not pursued. For deployment at sea the Harriers operate from OPHC-911, the *HTMS Chakri Naruebet*. With limited defence resources, it is unlikely that any re-equipment plan will be implemented for some years and in the meantime Thailand's AV-8S aircraft remain active as the last-surviving examples of the original Harrier design.

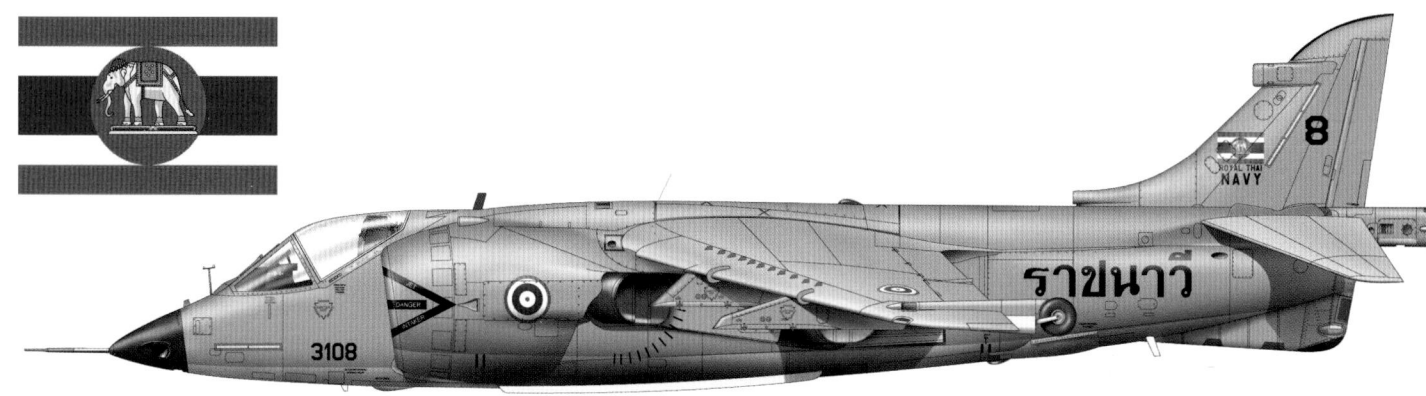

Hawker Siddeley AV-8S Harrier, 3108/8, Royal Thai Air Force, 2009
Medium Grey upper surfaces with White undersides; black radome and all lettering. National markings in six positions

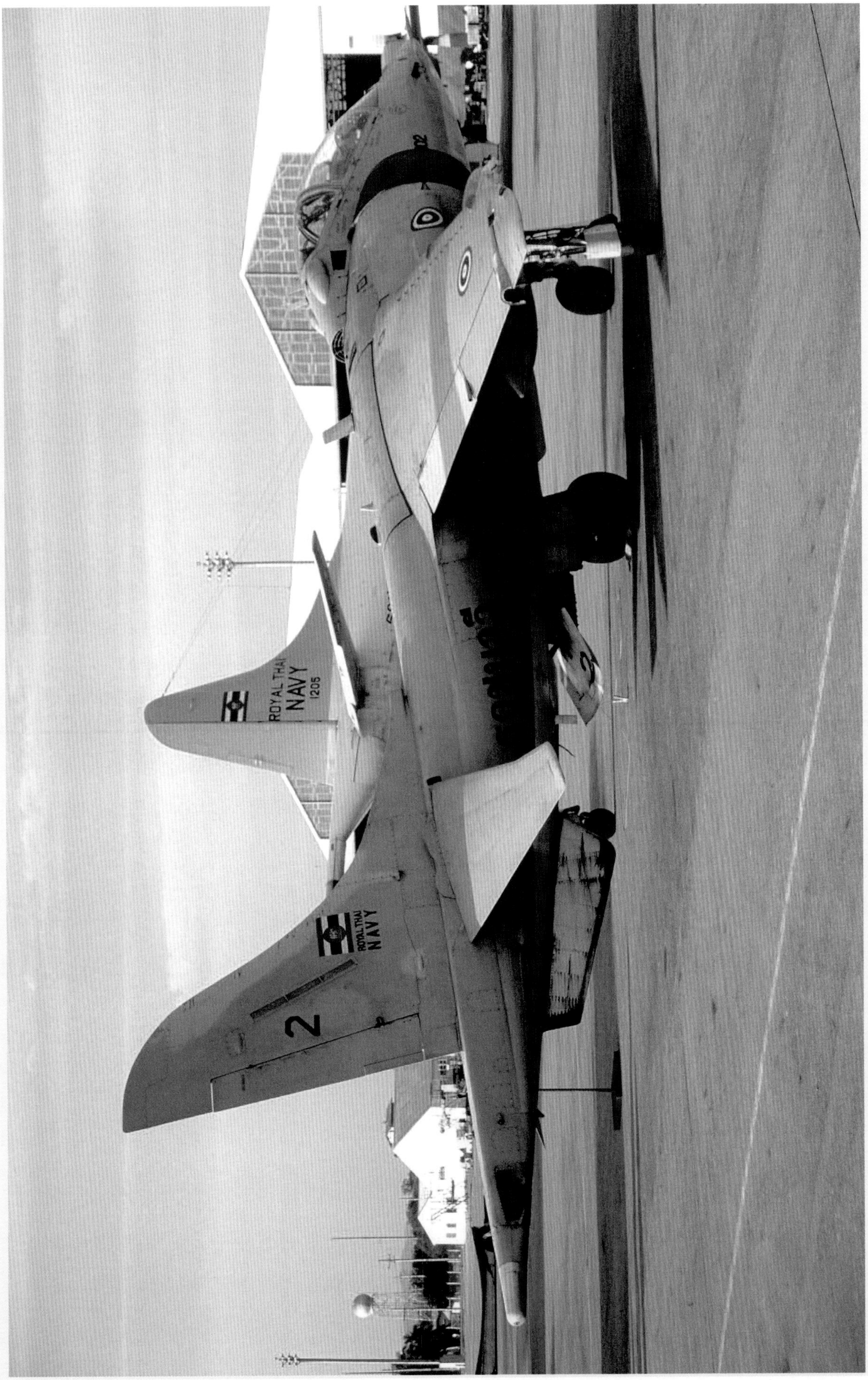
ROYAL THAI
NAVY
1205
ROYAL THAI
NAVY
2

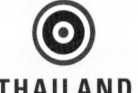

(iv) Engine Lights But Surges

The JPT limit can rapidly be exceeded. The HP cock/throttle must be set to HP cock off.

Warning

The engine normally starts well. If abnormal starting techniques are necessary, even though they are successful, the serviceability of the FCU is suspect and acceleration checks should be made.

Checks After Starting

3. Complete the Flight Reference Cards Checks After Starting.

Taxying

4. a. Paved Surfaces

(i) Since there is no differential braking, directional control on the ground at low RPM is wholly dependent on nosewheel steering. (At high RPM and with nozzles deflected to or beyond about 20° down, reaction controls are available). It is recommended that nosewheel steering is continuously engaged and the rudder used as required. If rudder is applied and the engage switch blipped, the handling advantage of the non-linear gearing incorporated in the steering at small rudder deflections is lost and the fatigue life of the system reduced.

(ii) Idling thrust is high and taxying speed will normally become excessive unless the nozzles are deflected or the brakes used. The brakes are designed for the limited needs of V/STOL operations and they will overheat more easily than those on most conventional fighter aircraft, if they are used frequently. The use of deflected nozzles, between 45° and 60°, is therefore recommended. When the nozzles are lowered, it is essential to hold or trim the stick forward of $+2°$ tailplane, to keep the front reaction control valve shut to prevent its very high velocity jet from blowing

(ii) Re-starting Shortly After Shut-down

(a) A minimum of 35 seconds must elapse between shut-down and restart.

(b) Delay opening the HP cock for 30 seconds after pressing the STARTER button, or until the JPT falls below 150°C, whichever occurs first.

Failure to Start

c.

(i) APU Does Not Light

Allow the automatic cycle to finish, switch the APU selector to OFF and then START, and try a second attempt. To avoid overheating the APU starter motor windings, APU starts should be restricted to 3 in any 20 minute period. An external power supply or the shedding of all internal electrical loads except the starboard booster pump will help if the reason for non-start is low battery voltage.

(ii) Engine Does Not Light

Select HP cock off. Recheck LP cock, booster pumps and ferry proportioner are on and check igniter operation by using the relight button. Try another attempt delaying opening the HP cock for 30 seconds after pressing the button. Be prepared for a hot start and a quick shut down.

(iii) Engine Lights But Stagnates at Sub-idling Condition

Operating the relight button may increase the fuel flow sufficiently to achieve normal Idling RPM. However, the aircraft should not be flown since sub-idling or stagnation conditions from which the engine cannot be accelerated may subsequently occur in the air.

debris into the engine intakes. If the nozzle angle exceeds 60° there will be an increased danger of blowing debris into the intakes and of overheating the tyres. Should the taxying speed become too slow (for any reason) whilst taxying with the nozzles deflected, the nozzles should be rotated aft before increasing RPM above Idling.

(iii) The nozzles should always be rotated fully aft immediately on stopping to avoid heating the main wheels. In addition if the surface is a bituminous one, it will be softened even at idle RPM if the aircraft is stationary with the nozzles deflected. A subsequent increase in RPM will then erode the softened area, deposit tar over the underside of the aircraft and permanently damage the ground surface.

(iv) Backward taxying should not be carried out because of the danger of reingestion.

(v) When taxying at low speeds, particularly when braking to a halt, marked brake judder may be experienced. If possible, brake pressure should be reduced to below the judder threshold (usually 300 to 400 PSI) to stop the judder. Prolonged judder adversely affects the undercarriage fatigue life.

(vi) Above 15 to 20 kt the anti-skid system operates and a characteristic tugging deceleration will be felt. Brake pressure at the wheels with full braking selected, will oscillate between 100 and 1,000 PSI approx and the green anti-skid light will flash until the speed falls below anti-skid drop out speed, when brake pressure can rise, as the brakes are applied, to 1,850 ±50 PSI. Care must be taken, below anti-skid drop out speed, to avoid locking the main wheels. At low speed there is no impression of wheel locking and it must be accepted that heavy braking will damage the tyres, especially at low AUWs.

(vii) For minimum radius turns reduce speed to a walking pace; the radius of turn increases with speed. At high speeds nosewheel steering should be used with caution since max nosewheel steering demand will cause a bank angle up to 5 to 7 out of the turn, heavily loading the outside outrigger, and especially on wet surfaces, may result in a breakaway of the main wheels.

b. Unprepared Surfaces

(i) On loose surfaces, RPM and nozzles deflection should be kept to a minimum to reduce the danger of debris ingestion.

(ii) On grass, directional control is good even if the nose-wheel digs a rut. The main unit sinks more than the nosewheel and the aircraft can be taxied with increased RPM, but otherwise quite normally, nozzles aft, on a surface too soft to support its parked weight. The use of nozzles up to 45° (stick forward of $+2°$) may reduce the extent to which the aircraft sinks in soft ground.

(iii) Snow should be treated as a combination of soft and loose surfaces.

Warning

If the aircraft becomes bogged while taxying, not more than 70% RPM should be used in attempts to free it (to avoid possible overloading of the undercarriage). The stick must be forward, to keep the front reaction control valve shut.

Checks Before Take-off

5. Complete Flight Reference Cards Take-off Checks.

Engine Handling on Take-off

Warning

A failure to understand the characteristics of the engine can easily result in the engine being over-temperatured and rejected

INTRODUCTION

1. The Harrier GR Mk.1 is a single seat, single engine, V/STOL strike/reconnaissance aircraft which can operate from small unprepared sites.

2. The power unit is a Pegasus 101 axial flow twin spool turbofan, rated at 19,000 lb static thrust at sea level. Water injection can be used to restore or improve thrust for take off or landing when the ambient temperature is high. The engine has four exhaust nozzles which can be simultaneously rotated to any position from fully aft to a braking position just forward of vertically down. The nozzles are controlled by a lever in the cockpit and this single lever gives the aircraft V/STOL capability.

3. Aerodynamically the aircraft is conventional, with a shoulder mounted swept wing and a swept slab tailplane. The wing has trailing edge flaps and its normal 'combat' tips can be exchanged for larger span 'ferry' tips to increase range performance.

4. The tailplane and ailerons are fully power operated, from duplicated hydraulic systems, and incorporate artificial feel for each control. A ram air turbine can provide hydraulic power to these controls in emergency conditions. The rudder is manually operated.

5. Control, while hovering or at low speed, is maintained by jet reaction controls. These are shutter valves at the nose, tail and wing tips to which high pressure air is ducted from the engine. The valves are interlinked with the flying controls with the exception of the nose valve: this is connected directly to the control column.

6. The low authority simplex autostabiliser is used, in the roll pitch and yaw axes, below 250 knots.

7. The retractable undercarriage consists of a steerable nosewheel unit, a twin wheel main unit in tandem with the nosewheel and an outrigger wheel at each wing tip. The main wheels have brakes which incorporate an anti-skid system.

8. An auxiliary power unit, using fuel and oil from the aircraft main supplies, provides a self contained engine start facility and electrical generation for operational standby periods, for servicing, testing and preparation for flight.

9. When the engine is running electrical AC supply is derived from two engine driven AC generators which also separately supply transformer rectifier units to provide DC. There are two service batteries, one in each of two sub-systems. A third battery can be used to maintain essential services in emergency.

10. Because fuel weights vary, these figures are simply a guide. Accurate figures are contained in an associated publication, the Operating Data Manual. The integral fuel tanks contain about 5,000 lb; additional fuel can be carried, on underwing pylons, in pairs of combat or ferry tanks, in conjunction with associated wing tips. Combat tanks increase fuel capacity to about 6,600 lb; ferry tanks increase fuel to about 10,500 lb. Drop tanks can be jettisoned or fuel from them, or from the main (wing) tanks can be jettisoned by selection. An air to air refuelling probe is an optional fit.

11. A retractable footstep gives access to the pressurised cockpit which is equipped with a Type 9A rocket assisted ejection seat. The cockpit hood is mechanically operated and slides fore and aft on rails. It cannot be jettisoned so it is fitted with miniature detonating cord (MDC) to assist ejection or for ground escape.

12. The airframe has a pylon attachment point under the fuselage and two similar points under each wing. In addition to a range of jettisonable, pylon mounted stores, gun pods each carrying one 30 mm Aden gun plus ammunition may be attached, one on each side of the lower fuselage.

13. The equipment fit includes an inertial nav/attack system, a head up display, TACAN, IFF/SSR, HF/VHF/UHF communications and a photographic reconnaissance capability.

14. Basic empty weight (combat tips) with pilot 12,150 lb.
Span 25 ft 3 in., combat tips, 29 ft 8 in. ferry tips.
Length 45 ft 7 in.
Height 11 ft 3 in.

15. This manual should be read in conjunction with the Harrier Aircrew Manual – Weapon System.

PART 3

CHAPTER 1—STARTING, TAXYING AND TAKE-OFF

Contents

Preparation for Flight

1. Complete the Flight Reference Cards External Checks and Pre-start Checks.

Starting the Engine

2. a. Complete the Flight Reference Cards Starting the Engine Checks.

b. (i) Starting Cold

Press the starter button momentarily (5 seconds maximum). The APU will then commence spin up electrically and its light up will be heard after 4 to 6 seconds. When the stick starts to move set the throttle to Idle. The APU will still be accelerating and the engine light up will be apparent by the JPT gauge registering after 12 to 15 seconds. Sharp pops

may be heard if the APU surges during acceleration. The JPT will rise slowly and progressively to 300 to 400°C and stabilised Idling RPM will be obtained in 40 to 50 seconds. If initial stabilised Idling RPM is below 25% open the throttle slightly to increase RPM then throttle back to Idling and check that RPM have stabilised within limits. If the JPT rises rapidly select HP cock off at 450°C max. During the start considerable tugging of the CWS may occur as the electrical generation system comes on line. The APU will shut down automatically after its cycle is complete. The APU selector should then be returned to OFF. In emergency the APU may be shut down prematurely by the same selection. With the engine running at Idling RPM and with the nozzles aft there is noticeable buffet and vibration due to efflux excitation of the tail.

6. a. The limiting JPT appropriate to any given thrust rating can be reached without exceeding the RPM limit. The result is, except under low OAT conditions, the limiting JPT will be reached *before* the limiting RPM, during sustained operation.

b. Due to thermal lag, when accelerating from low power the limiting RPM may be achieved without exceeding the limiting JPT, but this condition is not a steady state and the JPT will continue to rise at constant RPM. Using thermal lag, short lift thrust rating can be achieved for 15 seconds. Should it become vital to exceed the 15 second limit, the reduction in RPM necessary to maintain the engine at the JPT limit will reduce the thrust (630 lb in 40 sec).

c. From the above it is apparent that frequent monitoring of the JPT is vital to ensure that the relevant JPT limit is not exceeded. If it is exceeded, at best uneconomically high bleed life usage will occur and at worst the engine will be rejected.

d. Whilst RPM used is the major factor in deciding the JPT reached, there are three other very important factors which act to determine the final JPT/RPM relationship. These are bleed usage, recirculation and ambient temperature.

(i) Bleed Usage

Bleed usage can vary from 0 lb/sec with nozzles aft to a maximum of 18 lb/sec with nozzles deflected and a large reaction control demand. The rise in JPT is 5·5°C/lb bleed. Typically a hover will use 6 lb/sec and give a rise of 33°C whilst an accelerating transition will use 12 lb/sec and give a rise of 66°C. These typical values can easily be exceeded with extra control demands, e.g. coarse use of rudder to change heading in hover. The nominal thrust ratings assume a bleed usage of 9 lb/sec. Thus it will be seen that the use of higher values of bleed, like the 12 lb/sec transition quoted above, with its associated higher JPTs, will result in the JPT limit being reached in short lift before the end of 15 secs with the consequent need to throttle back and reduce thrust. (At lift rating 1·0% RPM = 12°C JPT and 380 lb thrust.)

(ii) Recirculation

Recirculation effects are negligible during a normal and into wind VTO. A no-go or excessively slow VTO, a downwind VTO, a VTO where the aircraft is allowed to move backwards or one where the nose is pulled high can result in recirculation JPT increases of over 100°C. There is no theoretical limit if all the adverse factors are taken together.

(iii) Ambient Temperature

There is a rise of JPT at a given RPM of 1·3°C (JPT)/°C (ambient) increase.

e. Under low OAT conditions the non-dimensional fan speed $(N_F/\sqrt{T_1/288})$ can easily exceed the limit of 106·5% (N_F is the % indicated fan RPM and T_1 the air intake temperature in °K). If the non-dimensional fan speed limit is exceeded, the engine may surge. It is therefore vital that the corresponding fan RPM limit for the ambient conditions is known before flight and that this overriding limit is observed by the pilot. The FCU will not give automatic protection against this limitation below 10,000 ft.

f. Correct take-off performance planning is vital to ensure that the engine limits will not have to be exceeded shortly after unstick to complete the take-off to wingborne flight safety. Correct planning allied to the handling techniques quoted in the relevant take-off paragraphs will ensure operation within engine limitations.

g. Notes on JPT Limiter Operation

(i) The JPTL will throttle back the engine as short lift limiting JPT is reached when the nozzles are deflected 10 to 15° or more and/or the undercarriage is selected DOWN. It will not control the engine at the normal lift rating and it will still be necessary for the pilot to throttle back the engine to enter normal lift rating from short lift operation. Allowing the engine to continue at the short lift JPTL setting will double the life count during the period. There will also be a reduction in thrust due to the JPTL controlling at the limit (see para. 6. b.).

(ii) Except during a conventional take-off the JPTL will throttle the engine back to the max thrust rating when the undercarriage is locked up and the nozzle angle becomes less than 10 and 15°. This large and sudden reduction in thrust may be disconcerting until experience is gained.

(iii) Should the JPTL fail it could involve a sudden and large thrust reduction of 32·5% RPM. Manual control of JPT can be regained by selecting full throttle and pushing hard to trip the **Limiters off** switch.

Use of Water Injection on Take-off

7. a. The water injection system is armed when required during the Engine Checks before Take-off. Its use does not change engine handling techniques but the following points should be noted.

(i) The water flow green light should appear between 94 and 96% RPM. If it does not, water is not flowing and the governor datum reset will allow up to 3% higher RPM if the fault is not a failure of the arming circuit.

(ii) If the water contents become exhausted, the JPT/thrust changes that will occur will depend on the conditions at that time. If the engine is already running above the SLD datum, the JPT will be reduced by the JPTL to the SLD datum and the thrust will fall accordingly. If the engine is running below the SLD datum, the JPT will rise in the absence of water. If the rise reaches the SLD, a small reduction in thrust may occur when the JPTL operates. Regardless of conditions, when water ceases to flow, the pilot can maintain existing RPM at the expense of JPT by overriding the limiter switch; thus, in emergency, full wet RPM can be obtained without the presence of water, providing the arming switch is left on. The engine is almost certain to be over-temperatured in this case.

b. Water flow may be cancelled at any time by throttling back below approximately 94 to 96% or by selecting the arming switch off. If it is desired to conserve water, selecting the arming switch off during a take-off can be done earlier than a throttle reduction to approx 94 to 96%. Whenever the arming switch is put off above approx 85% RPM, and whether or not water is flowing at the time, there will be a reduction in RPM due to governor datum reset. This will normally be about 3% but can vary slightly with ambient conditions.

c. The adjustable full throttle stop values will be increased with water armed. Up to 4% RPM more than set may be achieved depending on circumstances.

d. If it is desired to use up the water after take-off, rather than select jettison, the remaining water should be used at as low an RPM as will keep it flowing. This will reduce engine wear effects, caused by some turbine stators being cooled less than others when water is flowing.

e. The use of water injection will reduce the JPT and save engine life for a given take-off AUW. If however, water injection is used, not to suppress the JPT but to increase the thrust (i.e. a wet rating is used), the increase in JPT will result in very high Engine Life Recorder (ELR) counting rates. Typical figures are as follows:

JPT °C	*Rating*	*Counting RATE/MIN*
640		4·6
650	NLD	10
660	SLD	21
670	NLW	44
680	SLW	110

It will be noted that engine life is being consumed at 680°C about 25 times as fast as it is at 640°C.

Sideslip in Jetborne and Partially Jetborne Flight

8. a. Limitations

Part 2, Chapter 2, details handling limitations when in jetborne and partially jetborne flight. These limitations are imposed largely because of the difficulty in minimising sideslip at speeds below 120 kt and because of the dangers that can arise if sideslip is allowed to develop, particularly at airspeeds between 30 kt and 90 kt.

b. Directional Stability

When the aircraft is fully wingborne, the fin ensures directional stability in the normal manner. However as speed is reduced the stabilising force produced by the fin is reduced and is clearly zero at zero airspeed. Intake momentum drag which acts parallel to the relative airflow, at the intakes and so ahead of the CG, produces a force opposing the fin. Thus the aircraft is directionally unstable in the hover. The cross-over point, where the contribution from the fin exceeds the contribution from the intakes, so establishing directional stability, is not a fixed IAS, but one which varies, depending upon the RPM in use and the ambient conditions. This speed is of academic interest only, since there is a band of airspeed above it in which the effect of the fin is only slightly greater than that of the intakes, and the pilot must still act to assist this weak directional stability. Broadly, as reflected by the limitations, below 120 kt the pilot must act if sideslip is to be kept small. Below 90 kt it becomes vital that he does so.

c. Rolling due to Sideslip

As in any aircraft having a dihedral effect, should sideslip develop, a rolling moment will be produced requiring aileron to be used to keep the wings either level, or at a constant bank angle if turning. This rolling moment due to sideslip becomes critical only if it is so large that it exceeds the rolling moment available to the pilot from the stick. In this case roll control is lost. *The size of the rolling moment due to sideslip is ultimately determined by the product of three quantities, namely, ADD, IAS and Sideslip Angle.* In wingborne flight, regardless of ADD and IAS, the fin produces such a large stabilising effect, that sideslip cannot reach the value where the rolling moment exceeds that available to the pilot from the ailerons, even if large rudder inputs are made. Lateral control is therefore never at risk. However as IAS is reduced below wingborne speeds, and the fin produces a smaller margin of stability, it is possible to increase the amount of sideslip either by pilot rudder inputs or the effects of directional instability, so that the final product of ADD, IAS and sideslip produces a rolling moment in excess of that available to the stick from the reaction controls and the ailerons. Lateral control can then be lost. It is important to realise that a dangerous rolling moment due to sideslip can arise from different combinations of the three terms, giving very different looking situations to the pilot. Thus, say, a combination of high IAS (120 kt) and high ADD (15) requires only a relatively small slip angle to generate a large rolling moment; whereas a low IAS (40 kt), low ADD (5) situation will require a very large sideslip angle indeed to generate the same rolling moment. When flying so that any two of the terms have high values, only a small third term is needed to produce loss of control.

d. Rate of Onset of Difficulties

The rate at which the dangerous level of rolling moment can be reached clearly depends on the rate at which the terms are increased. In this connection it should be noted that whilst IAS and sideslip can be changed fairly quickly, it is usually reasonably clear to the pilot that this is happening. The same is not true of ADD. ADD can be increased rapidly by stick application, but more dangerously, it can be increased very rapidly with sink rate: finally, and perhaps most dangerous of all, it increases instantly by banking if there is sideslip present at the time. (If this is difficult to realise remember ADD is related to the amount of the undersurface of the wing seen when looking *along* the line of the relative airflow *towards* the wing. Then, using a model, consider the view seen by the relative airflow of the underside of a wing at about 10 ADD. Then add 30 degrees of slip from the right to the same ADD. Finally bank the wing 40 degrees left, away from the relative airflow and immediately a much increased view of the underside of the wing results; i.e. the ADD has increased).

e. Misleading Visual Cues

As height is increased from low level it is easy to have considerable airspeed, due to a combination of ground speed and wind speed, even though the aircraft appears to be hardly moving. The higher the aircraft, the harder it becomes to judge changes in ADD and sideslip without continual reference to the vane or the ADD indicator. Jetborne flight therefore should never be carried out higher than necessary.

f. Effect of RPM

Low RPM reduce reaction control duct pressure and reduce the control available, whereas high power has the opposite effect and is therefore beneficial. Note that a typical overshooting decelerating transition will require a reduction of power and increased ADD thus making it important to keep sideslip small. An increase of RPM will not only increase control power but will reduce ADD due to the flight path changing even at a constant attitude.

g. Use of Vane, HUD and Rudder Pedal Shakers

(i) From the foregoing it can be seen that providing slip is kept zero there can be no tendency for the aircraft to get out of trim laterally and start rolling. The vane or the HUD should be used, in conjunction with the rudder pedal shakers, to keep sideslip so small that the final product of the sideslip, ADD and IAS combination is insignificant.

(ii) To interpret the sideslip vane correctly, consider it as an arrow pointing into the relative wind. As such, it points both in the direction of nose movement required to zero slip and to the rudder pedal needed to achieve this.

(iii) To interpret the HUD sideforce symbol correctly consider the gap in the bar as showing the side from which the relative airflow is coming, and proceed thereafter as with the vane. (In this respect the gap in the bar corresponds to the conventional "ball" of a slip indicator).

(iv) To interpret the RPS correctly, push the rudder pedal that is shaking. The level of sideforce at which the RPS have been set to operate is relatively low and they can be expected to operate before lateral control difficulty is experienced. Whilst the operation of the RPS should never be disregarded, it is not expected that violent recovery action, necessitating aborting the manoeuvre in question, should be necessary. Rather, the operation of the RPS should be likened more to the indication of buffet in normal wingborne flight, i.e., it provides some feel that the manoeuvre has reached a certain stage, in this case that the directional trim of the aircraft is starting to become poor. Further, as with buffet, experience of RPS operation will be found to vary, depending upon the circumstances, from the occasional transient shake to continuous operation. The most likely reason for transient operation will be the use of high roll rates and the presence of turbulence, in which cases coarse recovery action is certainly not called for from the pilot.

(v) In all cases of operation of the RPS the vane should be immediately cross checked as this will give extra guidance as to the severity of the directional out of trim that exists.

NOTE: The importance of the vane as a reliable cross check on the operation of the HUD and RPS systems is stressed. In any case of conflicting evidence from the three sources of information the vane is clearly the most reliable one.

h. Recovery

If the limitations referred to in sub-para. a. above are exceeded, and roll control difficulties experienced, the following recovery action must immediately be taken in order to return within the limitations as quickly as possible.

Normally when flying with ADD above 0 units

Simultaneously apply:

(i) Tailplane to reduce ADD
(ii) Rudder to zero the vane
(iii) Aileron as required to level the wings.
(iv) Full power.

NOTE 1: It should be noted that rudder alone should not be used in an attempt to recover since it will only have a rapid effect if the slip angle was the last of the three terms (IAS, ADD and sideslip) to increase and cause a critical situation. If control was lost because ADD was doubled in the presence of some existing slip, then recovery by rudder, without reducing incidence as well, will require a much greater reduction of slip, and take longer than if incidence was reduced at the same time. Also, the use of rudder alone may momentarily make control of bank worse since the large reaction control flow through the yaw shutter valve will slightly reduce the overall pressure in the system causing a reduction in existing aileron response. It is important that such an effect, if observed, should not lead the pilot to mis-believing the vane and thinking that he has used the wrong rudder.

NOTE 2: In exceptional circumstances, it is possible to fly the aircraft so nose low that the wing is at a negative ADD. If lateral control difficulties are experienced in these conditions the recovery action quoted above should still be applied, but in this case the stick will need to be pulled back, not pushed forward. The rudder used will be opposite to the aileron (although still in the same sense with respect to the vane, RPS and HUD).

Vertical Take-off (VTO)

9. a. Solid Surface VTO

(i) Having completed the Checks before Take-off, hold the aircraft with the toe brakes and set 55% RPM with nozzles aft. Check IGVs move to about 18°. Lower the nozzles to at least 20° and check the duct pressure rises off the stop and the RPM reduce slightly (up to 2%). Then without delay, move the nozzle lever to the hover stop and immediately select full throttle, allowing the stick to remain in the trimmed position. The engine should accelerate very rapidly, in 2 to 3 seconds. The aircraft will become comfortably jetborne in less than 5 seconds from selecting the throttle open. As soon as the aircraft is clear of ground effect (at 10 to 15 ft), reduce RPM as necessary to observe the planned JPT limit and continue the climb as required. Release the toe brakes.

Warning

Should the engine not seem to accelerate very rapidly, or should the RPM become stabilised with the aircraft on the ground, immediately throttle back to Idling, select nozzles aft and if possible taxy a short distance forward to clear the hot surface. A second attempt to take-off should only be made if reasons for the first failure can be found and corrected.

(ii) A slow increase of RPM and gradual lift off the ground is not recommended since there will be higher JPTs, an increased chance of recirculation, ground erosion, greater heating of the tyres and the braking system and an increase in ELR counts, compared with the rapid lift off techniques.

(iii) An alternative method to the use of full throttle and then reducing RPM shortly after take-off, is to set the adjustable full throttle stop. Whilst a perfectly feasible technique, this does not take full advantage of the high thrust available during the engine thermal soak period, and generally for a given AUW will result in slightly more ELR counts being obtained. However, when used with very high thrust/weight ratios, the technique does have advantages for training purposes using the adjustable stop at say 96·5% to represent full throttle. The associated slower climb and accelerating transition following a low thrust/weight ratio take-off can then be experienced without the high bleed usage of the actual heavy weight manoeuvre.

(iv) To ensure that the ELR count penalties of a slow and protracted lift are avoided, a VTO should not normally be attempted with a thrust/weight ratio of less than 1·08 (see Operating Data Manual for effect of stores).

(v) In general, rate of climb close to the ground will be increased with a slight lowering of the nose and reduced with an increase of pitch attitude. An improved performance will also be achieved if the STO stop, set to 75°, is used instead of the hover stop. In this case some forward movement will occur when getting airborne.

b. Mat VTO

(i) Use the technique of sub-para. a. (i) above for solid surface, but additionally note the importance of ensuring a rapid clean lift-off since it will not normally be possible to reposition on a mat following a no-go. Further, due to the restricted site implications that may attend the use of a mat, it is important that unless vital, a nose up attitude is not adopted close to the ground, since this will increase recirculation effects and may reduce the rate of climb or in the limit induce a no-go.

(ii) If possible the efflux from the engine and the reaction controls should be kept within the confines of the mat until 25 to 30 ft has been attained to avoid the risk of loosening the mat-to-ground attachments or

c. Sloping Ground VTO

VTO from ground with a lateral slope should be avoided when possible since the aircraft will tend to skip and skid down the slope during engine acceleration, because of the side component of lift thrust relative to the true vertical. It will not be possible to level the wings and prevent the slide until outrigger freedom is obtained and this occurs only after a level of thrust is reached that exceeds that at which skip and skid will start. Tests are not yet complete, provisionally the lateral slope limit should be taken as 4° maximum. If the aircraft is positioned pointing up or down the slope then the nozzles may be adjusted away from the hover stop by an angle equal to the slope, so that they are truly vertical and a clean unstick can then be made. It is preferable that the aircraft points up the slope since in this case there is no theoretical limit to the angle that can be accepted and in addition the disadvantages of recirculation and reingestion due to the braking nozzle angle which would be needed when pointing down a slope, are avoided.

d. Effects of Wind and Turbulence

(i) Control Effects

Because the engine intakes are ahead of the centre of gravity, intake momentum drag will turn the aircraft out of wind during a VTO if the rudder is not used to oppose the movement. Rudder must be used much more coarsely than the stick for precise control. In all other respects the effects on control of surface wind and turbulence during a VTO are negligible since the jet velocities used for lift and control are large compared with the wind/turbulence velocities, and the aircraft is very dense.

(ii) Performance Effects

Performance deteriorates slightly in cross winds and significantly when tail to wind. With the tail to wind, intake efficiency is reduced, recirculation is increased, and wing lift is negative.

Hovering

10. a. Leave the undercarriage down while hovering and check the RPM and JPT are within the planned limits. The view from the cockpit is adequate though it is progressively impaired as the nose is raised.

b. Control height while jetborne by natural manipulation of the throttle as a thrust control, using the handrest if desired to assist in making precise throttle movements. Judge rates of ascent and descent by looking out and around in the normal manner. Throttle sensitivity in the hover range is much reduced, compared to use in the lower RPM range, and is approximately 2½% RPM per inch of hand movement. Height control is therefore not a matter of small force changes on the throttle but significant hand movements of the order of ½ an inch. A suitable hovering height is about 50 ft and this will tend to be selected automatically. It is well above all ground effects and yet not so high as to impair judgement, and therefore control, of height. For gentle manoeuvres in free air, the hovering weight should be chosen to give a thrust/weight ratio of 1·08 minimum in the chosen JPT range, increasing to 1·10 for more energetic manoeuvres. These margins represent approximately 3% RPM and 4% RPM. Relative wind effects should be borne in mind constantly, since performance deteriorates slightly, cross wind and significantly when tail to wind. On no account should large reductions in power be made while jetborne, as it is easy to set up rates of descent which cannot quickly be stopped with the limited thrust/weight ratios likely to be available. In particular, any instinctive desire to throttle back in an emergency must be firmly resisted.

c. Control of position over the ground is normally achieved by leaving the nozzles at the hover stop and tilting the whole aircraft to achieve the desired horizontal component of lift thrust. Quite high speeds can be attained in any direction for small tilt angles. Stabilised conditions are about 10 kt per degree of tilt. The controls are sensitive laterally, fairly sensitive in pitch and sluggish in yaw. The aircraft is directionally unstable (see para. 9. d. (i)) and neutrally stable in roll and pitch. The reaction controls are acceleration demand controls as opposed to the rate demand control of aerodynamic surfaces in conventional flight. This difference calls for no conscious change of pilot technique but can lead to slight overcontrol until experience is gained.

d. Forward and backward translations in the hover may also be achieved by small movements of the nozzle control lever (10 kt per degree of nozzle angle), instead of tilting the whole aircraft.

Accelerating Transition

11. a. To achieve a transition from hovering to conventional flight, leave the throttle at the balanced hovering position, or as set for any desired rate of climb, and progressively move the nozzle lever forward. The aircraft will accelerate smoothly and gain aerodynamic lift to compensate for the decreasing vertical thrust component. The simplest transition is obtained by holding the aircraft attitude constant, and keeping the flight path parallel with the ground by adjusting the nozzle lever rate of movement as necessary. If this movement is too slow the aircraft will climb and if it is too fast it will sink. The constant attitude technique eliminates the need to monitor ADD. At mid transition speeds there is a slight nose up trim change and as the nozzles approach the fully aft position there is a marked nose down trim change together with a significant increase of buffet due to jet efflux excitation of the airframe.

b. The undercarriage may be selected up whenever convenient during the transition. Retraction takes 6 to 8 seconds and if done with significant IAS gives a transient small nose before selecting undercarriage up or rudder demands may hold the nosewheel off centre and prevent retraction. It is recommended that flap is left down until after the nozzles are fully aft to improve the initial wingborne handling characteristics especially at high all up weights. Flap retraction gives a small nose down trim change.

c. If a rapid level transition, or a climbing flight path, is required, the ADD must be monitored. An ADD of 12 units should be aimed for and the limit of 15 units should not be exceeded.

d. Whilst turning manoeuvres are permitted above 90 kt (Part 2, Chap. 2), it is recommended that turns are normally only carried out above 120 kt to reduce pilot workload, since great care is needed to prevent sideslip developing during manoeuvres.

e. If a crosswind transition is carried out, care should be taken to minimise sideslip (see para. 8).

f. Due to the pitch reaction control demands needed to trim during the transition, an increase in JPT is inevitable over that associated with hover or take-off prior to the transition (see para. 6. d. (i)). It is therefore essential that JPT is monitored and kept within the planned limits. It will be possible to throttle back, to control JPT, once some wing lift has been obtained, providing nozzle rotation has not been so fast that maximum allowable ADD has already been reached in order to prevent the aircraft sinking. However, a progressive reduction in throttle cannot be carried out simultaneously with selection of the nozzle lever and one or more step reductions in RPM may be necessary during the transition. In general any transition can be carried out at fixed throttle, provided that the preceding hover or climb from VTO has been carried out at a planned thrust/weight ratio which allows the transition rise in JPT to be added to the original JPT without the desired JPT limit being exceeded. A climbing transition

Rolling Vertical Take-off (RVTO)

12. a. An RVTO should be carried out:

(i) Where it is desired to lift off the maximum possible weight from a restricted site which places limits of approximately 100 ft and 500 ft on the ground run and distance to 50 ft respectively.

(ii) Where the nature of the surface makes it inadvisable to carry out a VTO proper, but is good enough to require only a low translational speed over it to avoid surface break-up (and consequent debris ingestion) with nozzles deflected.

b. Having completed the Checks before Take-off hold the aircraft on the toe brakes and set 55% RPM with the nozzles aft: check IGVs move to about 18°. Lower the nozzles to 30° and, without delay, check that the duct pressure rises off the stop and that the RPM reduce slightly (up to 2%). Release the brakes and slam to full throttle or to the adjustable throttle stop setting preset. Immediately grasp the nozzle lever and as the RPM stabilise pull the nozzle lever rapidly aft to the STO stop preset to 70°. For max angle of climb adjust the thrust vector by means of pitch attitude to give a constant or slightly reducing ground speed.

NOTE: IAS will not normally be registering at this stage unless the surface wind is more than about 15 kt.

c. Continue with an accelerating transition (para. 11.).

d. The technique described will enable weights rather in excess of 500 lb over the Vertical Take-off weight to be lifted within the above limits (see ODM). Alternatively, it gives a slight increase in rate of climb close to the ground compared with a VTO at the same weight. It provides an unstick ground speed in the order of 20 kt, assuming normal engine acceleration time. An approximate increase of 10 kt in the ground speed at unstick will be obtained for each 1 second pause after engine acceleration, before the nozzles are lowered.

e. The use of the hover stop is not recommended for an RVTO as instances have occurred of wing drops in ground effects.

Short Take-off (STO)

13. a. General

(i) If the AUW is too high for a VTO, an STO should be made. Unstick speed and nozzle angle for STO is given in the ODM.

(ii) Having completed the Checks before Take-off hold the aircraft on the toe brakes and set 55% RPM with nozzles aft. Check IGVs move to about 18°. Briefly lower the nozzles to between 20° and 30° and check that the duct pressure rises off the stop and the RPM reduce slightly (up to 2%). Raise the nozzles to fully aft, engage the nosewheel steering, release the brakes and check that the brake pressure is exhausted (gauge has residual pressure of 50 PSI) or that the aircraft rolls. Open the throttle quickly to the planned adjustable full throttle stop setting. Immediately grasp the nozzle lever, monitor the ASI and also check the RPM and JPT if time permits, but not at the expense of missing the unstick speed. At the planned unstick speed move the nozzle lever quickly back to the preset STO stop. (See also sub-para. b.). The ground pitch attitude should be maintained after the nozzles are lowered; this will require a small aft stick movement to about 0° tail-plane whilst still in ground effect. After unstick monitor the ASI. Any reduction in speed should be countered with an immediate small forward nozzle lever movement to prevent loss of wing lift. For maximum angle of climb, pitch attitude should be increased to hold the ADD at 12 units. Pitch attitude control is sensitive at this stage and care must be taken not to exceed the limit of 15 units (see also para. 16. (ii)). Tailplane setting during the climb, when clear of ground effect, will be +4° to +5°. When comfortably clear of the ground complete the remainder of an accelerating transition to wingborne flight.

Warning 1

If the brakes fail to release, the aircraft's acceleration will still be high at take-off RPM. With the wheels locked, however, the aircraft is very unstable directionally and an uncontrollable swing could develop. Immediate selection of the nozzle lever to the hover stop offers the best chances of recovery in such circumstances as directional control through the reaction controls will become available, and at the same time the acceleration will be reduced more rapidly than would be possible by throttling back.

Warning 2

Should the ADD limits be exceeded during a short take-off the limit of control is likely to be full forward stick. The ADD at which this will occur will depend upon the stores configuration and the amount of aileron and rudder in use at the time (since, with aileron and rudder applied less reaction control bleed air will be left for the rear reaction control jet). Under the most adverse conditions yet encountered, the limiting ADD was approximately 18 to 19 units. Should control be lost and the aircraft pitch up, recovery action is to slam the nozzle lever forward to pitch the aircraft nose down and then immediately relower the nozzles to an intermediate angle to restore reaction control and jet lift, thus preventing a 'conventional' stall.

(iii) Undercarriage and flap should be selected as for a transition (para. 11. b.) but in the case of a high AUW STO it is particularly beneficial to delay retraction of flap until comfortably wingborne at 190 to 200 kt.

b. Use of the Preset STO Stop

The use of the preset STO stop is recommended during initial STO training to give confidence in avoiding any over selection of nozzle angle, and consequent reduction of airspeed. With a little experience it is easy to control the nozzle lever without the use of the stop. Use of the lever, and the results of mis-use, are directly analogous to the use of the longitudinal control of any aircraft on a conventional take-off. The main disadvantage of the STO stop is that, particularly in short field operations in a situation demanding an aborted take-off, the need to override it could hamper the rapid selection of a nozzle braking angle, which could be vital. Also, if it is incorrectly set at too small a nozzle angle, the aircraft will not unstick without a much increased ground roll. It also fosters the misleading concept of a nozzle angle change being just a configuration change, when it should more rightly be thought of, and treated as, a primary V/STOL flying control, second in importance only to the throttle.

c. Crosswind Operation

A yaw out of wind may occur after unstick, requiring coarse use of rudder to correct it. Coarse use of aileron may also be required.

d. Loose Surface or Grass Operation

Whilst the ground speed at unstick will prevent debris ingestion when the nozzles are lowered, it is important that the brakes are released before the aircraft moves, otherwise the ground surface may be broken by the skidding mainwheels and the resulting material ingested.

e. Very Low Surface Friction Operation

If a ground roll over snow, ice or wet grass is to be made when nosewheel steering control might not be adequate, the nozzles should be left at 20° before releasing the brakes. This will allow directional control through the reaction control system. If the surface is also loose, then it is important that the front reaction control valve is kept shut during the ground roll to avoid kicking up debris ahead of the intakes. For this reason the stick should not be pulled back from the trimmed position during the ground roll.

Conventional Take-off (CTO)

14. a. Check that the planned AUW is below that set by the tyre limiting speed.

b. Having completed the Checks before Take-off, hold the aircraft on the toe brakes and set 55% RPM with the nozzles aft. Check the IGVs move to about 18°. Engage the nosewheel steering, with the rudder bar centralised, release the wheel brakes, and check that the pressure is exhausted or that the aircraft rolls. Open the throttle to 97% RPM using the adjustable throttle stop and check engine indications. The rudder becomes effective at 80 to 100 kt. At 145 to 150 kt apply gentle back pressure to the stick, aiming to fly the aircraft off the ground at an ADD reading of 13 to 14 units. Unstick will occur at 165 kt at 17,300 lb AUW (speed variation 6 kt/1,000 lb).

c. It is important not to unstick late or the tyre limiting speed (180 kt) will be exceeded. This is more likely to occur at high AUW.

d. Retract the undercarriage when comfortably airborne. Release the nosewheel steering button before undercarriage selection.

Use of the Autostabiliser

15. The use of the autostabiliser during take-off and in the hover noticeably steadies the aircraft in roll. In particular, in the hover, it makes the roll and pitch sensitivities very similar. The effect of the autostabiliser in pitch is not usually noticeable in the hover, or during VTO, since it operates only on the rear reaction control valve which is shut at hover trim. The pitch channel has a slight steadying effect longitudinally during an accelerating transition or STO. Due to the low authority of the system, autostabiliser failures of both the hard over and oscillatory types are easily overridden by the pilot. In some stages of flight it may not be immediately obvious that a failure has taken place.

Effects of Stores

16. There are only small handling changes resulting from the carriage of stores during take-off.

a. VTO, Hover, RVTO

During a VTO a slight loss of performance, in ground effect, is obtained with some fuselage stores combinations (see ODM). There are no other significant handling effects.

b. STO

During an STO, heavy outboard pylon stores result in a decrease in longitudinal stability immediately post unstick in the ADD range 10 to 15 units. Under these conditions extra care is needed to ensure that the 15 units ADD limit is not exceeded. Ferry tips are beneficial in this respect since they increase the stability and noticeably steady the aircraft.

c. Accelerating Transition and CTO

The presence of stores, particularly on the inboard pylons, leads to a noticeable increase in the buffet experienced at the end of an accelerating transition or CTO.

Air to Air Refuelling Probe

17. During a conventional take-off, with a refuelling probe fitted, a distinct yaw and roll to starboard will be apparent. The effect is reduced during an STO.

Icing and Snow

18. a. The engine and airframe have no anti-ice system but the engine will operate satisfactorily under continuous maximum and intermittent maximum icing conditions. In flight therefore no action is required as shedding takes place spontaneously. At engine speeds in excess of 65% RPM, shedding is rapid. At lower speeds shedding takes longer and a greater build up can occur causing some vibration immediately prior to shedding. This vibration is not harmful to the engine, but, if required, shedding may be accelerated by opening up to 90% RPM for 30 seconds. Ground running for test purposes should be avoided as far as possible. A rough guide to icing conditions on the ground is humidity above 90% or visibility less than 500 yards, at air temperature below +3°C. If in doubt stop the engine and have the intake and fan blades inspected for ice deposit.

If it is essential to carry out a VTO from a snow covered surface, it is advisable beforehand to run the engine at high power with the nozzles lowered to melt/blow away the loose snow in the area of the aircraft. Failure to do this can lead to complete loss of visual cues at the point of unstick. In addition, massive snow ingestion can cause surge and flame-out. Less severe snow ingestion causes stagnation or slow engine acceleration.

c. The most likely general effect of operation in snow is that the retraction of the undercarriage may be affected. The closed nose and mainwheel main doors reduce the chance of this as far as possible.

Night Flying

19. a. No changes of take-off technique are needed for night operation.

b. If a VTO is carried out from a small site with limited lighting cues, it is important that the attitude and heading needed for the transition are selected before the transition is commenced and the lighting cues are left behind. In particular any rate of yaw on to heading should be stopped before accelerating away, to reduce the risk of sideslip developing in mid transition.

c. Due to the angles of the cockpit side consoles some reflections from these may occur. For this reason the level of illumination of these consoles is best kept low.

PART 3

CHAPTER 2—HANDLING IN CONVENTIONAL FLIGHT

Contents

Engine Handling

1. a. **PRL and JPTL Operative (nozzles aft)**

    (i) Below 5,000 ft slam and reslam accelerations up to maximum thrust are permitted at all flight speeds down to the 1g stall with no limit on ADD. Between 5,000 ft and 10,000 ft similar conditions apply but with a minimum speed of 200 kt. It is necessary for the pilot to limit the RPM to 97% either by the use of the adjustable full throttle stop preset to 97% or by reference to the RPM indicator. For steady state running the JPTL will maintain RPM below 97% by controlling at 580°C.

    (ii) Between 10,000 ft and 40,000 ft slam and reslam accelerations up to maximum thrust are permitted down to 200 kt with no limit on ADD. Between these

Nozzles Deflected

Above 2,000 ft the throttle should not be opened at a faster rate than that equivalent to moving from Idling to 80% (maximum allowed) in 3 seconds.

Above 15,000 ft and 0·95M

When flying above 15,000 ft and 0·95M the engine must be throttled back to 80% RPM. Failure to observe this limitation could result in mechanical engine failure.

...bing

...limb at 400 kt/0·8M.

...lity and Control

Longitudinal

(i) The aircraft is stable in all manoeuvring conditions. The stick forces vary from light at low speeds to heavy at high speeds. If q feel is switched off control is light over the whole speed range. With q feel off, care is needed to avoid overstressing the airframe and some slight overcontrol may occur when controlling height tightly as in low flying.

(ii) There is little trim change with speed and a typical tailplane position is 0 to —1°.

(iii) A nose up trim change occurs with increase of power. This is very marked at low speed and low altitude, but reduces to insignificant proportions at high speed and high altitude.

(iv) When pulling g during transonic dive recoveries there is a step increment of about ½g at constant stick position when the aircraft becomes subsonic.

(v) The increase in stability with a heavy centre line store and the reverse with an outboard store is small but noticeable.

heights it will still be necessary for the pilot to limit the RPM to 97% as in (i) above when the OAT is above —9°C at 200 kts and —25°C at 400 kt.

(iii) Above 40,000 ft the throttle should not be opened faster than a rate equivalent to moving from Idling to maximum thrust position in 3 seconds.

b. **PRL and JPTL Muted (nozzles aft)**

Slam accelerations are not to be carried out above 10,000 ft. RPM must be limited by the pilot so that the non-dimensional fan speed does not exceed 101%. See Chap. 1 para. 6. e. (This value can be as low as 88% under the worst likely conditions and will normally be about 92% at 40,000 ft). If this value of RPM is exceeded the engine surge margin will be reduced. At all times the pilot may have to reduce RPM to prevent the JPT exceeding 580°C.

b. **Lateral and Directional**

(i) The ailerons are light and powerful and can produce high rates of roll.

(ii) The rudder is powerful. It is light at low speeds and very heavy at high speeds. Due to the high foot forces involved the aircraft is unlikely to be overstressed in a steady sideslip. However, cyclic use of the rudder during an oscillation could lead to large sideslip angles with only moderate foot forces and should be avoided.

(iii) Damping of the dutch roll mode decreases with altitude but is quite adequate for normal flight purposes.

Noise and Buffet

4. a. In general, roughness and buffet is present under most conditions of flight. The cockpit is noisy due to the size and location of the engine air intakes and the large engine. There is significant buffet when throttled back at high speed, due to intake spillage.

    b. The presence of inboard stores other than bombs noticeably increases the 1g buffet level especially at high power and low speed.

Straight Stalling

5. a. **Undercarriage and Flaps Up (nozzles aft)**

    (i) As speed is reduced buffet onset occurs at 10 to 12 ADD. This buffet increases progressively to become moderate at 17 to 18 ADD with the stick fully back. As the speed reduction continues some lateral twitches will occur which can be controlled with aileron. Occasionally a wing heavy tendency may be superimposed on the lateral twitches. With the stick fully back some directional 'untidiness' is likely to occur. Full stall investigation should be carried out with caution, a high rate of speed reduction should be

avoided and the height should be 15 to 20,000 ft. High rates of sink can develop leading to large height losses. Recovery is immediate on relaxing the back stick.

(ii) Stalling with external stores is not permitted. With stores the stalling characteristics are as described but are more pronounced, and a pitching motion may develop at high ADD.

b. **Undercarriage and Flaps Down**

Stalling with undercarriage and flaps down is not permitted. The behaviour of the aircraft is basically similar in nature to that during the clean stall but the characteristics are more pronounced about all axes. The lateral and directional motions in particular may combine into a dutch rolling motion which normally makes further back stick movements inadvisable.

g Stalling

6. a. At low Mach number the g stalling characteristics are similar to those obtained in the straight stall. As Mach number is increased the ADD for buffet onset reduces to 7 to 8 units at 0·9M. In general the lateral behaviour becomes more ragged and may involve lateral out of trims. In deep buffet a pitching oscillation may also occur. These characteristics may prevent stick hard back conditions being obtained.

    b. Stores in general do not introduce new stalling characteristics but rather change the emphasis on whether the rolling or yawing behaviour becomes the limiting characteristic. In general, with the larger and more destabilising outer stores, a directional trim change leading to lateral out of trim is more likely to be the limiting factor, whereas with fuselage or inboard stores, a wing rock is likely to be limiting. In all cases, some slight reduction of the maximum ADD obtainable without stores is likely to occur. Tightening or pitch-up does not occur.

    (i) Throttle back and check for engine surge. If this has occurred, stop-cock the engine immediately.

    (ii) Apply full rudder to oppose the direction of yaw as observed visually and relax the stick to the neutral position.

    (iii) If the spin shows no sign of stopping within two turns move the control column fully in the observed direction of roll. At the same time pull it fully **back** in the case of an **erect** spin or push it fully forward in the case of an inverted spin.

    (iv) Jettison external stores if carried.

    (v) If the spin has not stopped by 10,000 ft abandon the aircraft.

Rolling

8. a. Rapid rolling and rolling pull outs are permitted within the limitations of Part 2.

    b. If the rolling limitations are inadvertently exceeded inertia cross coupling effects may induce severe loads in the fin and front fuselage structure. If the limitations are exceeded by overriding the aileron spring stop the very high rate of roll will be obvious, and if maintained, will result in an increase in sideslip giving noticeable side force on the pilot. In addition, in the case of rolls at less than 1g, fluctuation in the normal g will be experienced. Airframe fatigue life will be adversely affected by any rolling exceeding the limitations, and an extreme case could cause loss of control or structural failure during the manoeuvre.

    c. The worst stores configuration for exciting inertia cross coupling effects is a heavy centre line store combined with empty 100 gallon drop tanks.

Aerobatics

9. a. In common with other aircraft which have a high wing loading, looping plane manoeuvres should be approached

Spinning

7. a. **Erect Spin**

    Generally speaking the aircraft is most reluctant to enter and maintain a spin. However, should it do so, it is most likely that the engine will surge and under this condition a spin which is very oscillatory in pitch and roll, may develop, involving an angle of attack of 60 to 70°. The roll rate is likely to oscillate between 0 and 150°/sec every turn, superimposed on a relatively steady yaw rate of 70 to 100°/sec, giving a time per turn of about 3 seconds. The symptoms of engine surge in a spin are slight vibration, coupled with falling RPM and rising JPT, possibly preceded by one or more pops. These symptoms could easily pass unnoticed and must therefore be looked for specifically, immediately any inadvertent spin commences. It is imperative that the engine is stop-cocked without delay, in the event of surge, to avoid damaging it. Recovery from a fully developed spin may be slow and is likely to require the full consolidated spin recovery action recommended below.

    b. **Inverted Spin**

    Specific inverted spinning trials have not yet been carried out. However, a few inverted spins have been entered accidentally following erect spinning attempts. These have been relatively smooth and have involved a negative angle of attack of around 30° and a time per turn of around 3 seconds. They have not so far been allowed to develop beyond 2 to 3 turns and recovery has always been prompt. Nevertheless, pending full trials, it must be assumed that the aircraft is capable of a more resolute spin from which the full consolidated recovery action recommended below, may be required.

    c. **Consolidated Recovery Action**

    In the case of any incipient spin all controls should be centralised, in the first instance. Should an actual spin develop, the following action should be taken:

changes can occur when recovering from an unsatisfactory manoeuvre.

b. The jet efflux induced buffet level becomes more noticeable as speed is reduced, but reference to the ADD assists in differentiating it from stall warning buffet. At the top of loops there will be a nose up trim change at high power as the speed reduces and a push force will be needed. Holding 10 to 12 ADD is recommended to give an adequate margin from wing stall effects.

c. Until experience is gained a loop should be started at 8 to 10,000 ft AGL and 450 kt, using 90% RPM. Power should be increased if necessary to maintain speed at 200 to 220 kt minimum over the top.

d. For initial rolling manoeuvres 300 to 350 kt is a comfortable speed range. At all times close regard must be paid to the rolling limitations in Part 2.

General Performance

10. The maximum level speed of the aircraft varies from 0·87M to 0·94M depending upon stores and height. There are no Mach number or airspeed limitations. The maximum speed achievable in a dive from 45,000 ft is about 1·25M. A sonic boom is generated at about 0·98M.

Stores Carriage and Release

11. a. **General**

    Apart from the increased AUW and drag due to carrying stores the general handling characteristics of the aircraft are little changed. The only exceptions are in respect of buffet (para. 4.) and g stalling (para. 6.)

    b. **Jettison and Release**

    With jettison or release of a wing-mounted store the aircraft rolls gently away from that store. This also applies to firing a single rocket pod. Symmetrical firing of rocket amplitude while the rockets are leaving the pods. The firing of an ERU produces a noticeable "bonk" through the airframe.

c. Asymmetric Carriage

Directional trim changes are small and easily held or trimmed. Lateral trim changes with g are large especially at maximum g. Roll control power is completely adequate for a 1,000 lb store on an inboard pylon at maximum g, but during variations of g, the control of bank angle may be erratic until the aileron co-ordination necessary has been practiced.

Thrust Vectoring

12. a. Thrust vectoring in conventional flight may be used within the limits of Part 2. Its main use is as an exceptionally effective airbrake. A slight increase in normal g (up to ½g) is also obtained, although at the expense of a very rapid reduction in airspeed.

b. Full stalling and manoeuvring trials have yet to be carried out with the nozzles in the braking position and max allowable RPM (80%). Trials to date indicate that whilst max g can be pulled with max thrust vectoring applied, the stick force per g is very low and this, combined with a nose up trim change as the nozzles are lowered, could easily lead to the aircraft being overstressed. In addition, the rate of speed reduction is very high indeed, 25 to 30 kt per second; this could lead to excessive speed reduction and loss of control. Pending further trials it is recommended that application of g during maximum thrust vectoring is limited to 2 to 3g.

c. Longitudinal control is degraded with the nozzles deflected, and the value of vectored thrust during attack is doubtful unless it is important to achieve a very steep dive angle without the speed increasing rapidly.

d. Great care must be taken not to exceed the RPM/Speed limitations when using the system as considerable fatigue

... this occurs.

e. In general a rapid speed reduction is best obtained by coarse use of nozzle at the existing or maximum allowed RPM, followed if applicable, by an increase of RPM to the limit to achieve maximum reverse thrust. The natural tendency to throttle back to Idle before deflecting the nozzles produces less deceleration.

Airbrake

13. There is no speed limitation on the use of the airbrake. When extended it gives a small nose up trim change. The onset of the trim change is quick and may cause a small overcorrection in pitch, by the pilot.

Flaps

14. a. No speed restriction is imposed on the operation of the flaps. There is a small nose up trim change when they are lowered. The angle achieved depends upon the IAS. Full flap is only available at low speed and the flaps progressively blow up to about 6° at max IAS. Approx 30° is available at 350 kt.

b. Below 400 kt/0·8M there is a negligible speed reduction at fixed RPM when mid flap is used. Above this speed a slight deceleration results.

c. In general the use of mid flap increases the maximum g available (½g at 400 kt) and results in a lower nose attitude of 1½ to 2° reflected in a corresponding change of ADD for a given g.

Ram Air Turbine

15. Extension of the RAT does not affect handling characteristics.

Instrument Flying

16. Instrument flying, using the HUD, requires scan techniques similar to those used with conventional head down instruments. Less concentration is required in cloud than in visual conditions as the absence of a moving background reduces possible distractions. The layout of the standby head down instruments is a compromise and it is important to maintain a good scan for accurate flying. In particular, the trim changes associated with large and sudden RPM changes can result in height excursions, especially when turning, because the pitch attitude reference of the attitude indicator is degraded with bank applied.

Air to Air Refuelling Probe

17. Due to the aerofoil shape of the probe root fairing it has an effect on lateral and directional trim. This trim change varies in both magnitude and direction with ADD. In normal level flight the authorities of the aileron and rudder trims are quite adequate. At high speeds and low ADD the directional trim change is to port. At high ADD the aircraft yaws and rolls strongly to starboard and care should be taken when manoeuvring.

Air to Air Refuelling

18. a. Before making contact select **Tank depress** so that this does not have to be done during close formation flying.

b. The aircraft should be flown to a position where the probe tip is about 2 to 5 ft behind the centre of the drogue. At this stage the aircraft should be trimmed: this requires practically neutral rudder and aileron trim, on the centre drogue, and some outboard rudder and aileron trim, on the wing stations. The proximity of a Harrier has very little effect on the position and stability of the drogue.

c. In formation with the tanker at low altitude, especially during manoeuvres, care should be taken with RPM changes as the throttle is sensitive and large speed changes can quickly occur. In addition, there is a strong nose up trim change with RPM at low speeds.

d. The aircraft should then be moved forward by opening the throttle gently and contact should be made with a closing speed of 1 to 2 kt. If the drogue is missed throttle back immediately and move directly astern. The aircraft should not be allowed to overrun the drogue by more than about 3 ft. If the overtake rate is too high, a dangerously long overrun can occur, and the drogue can disappear aft when subsequent damage to the aircraft or probe is possible.

e. Contacts on the parachute edge of the drogue are normally called 'rim' contacts. On wing drogues these normally resolve themselves quickly by the probe sliding into the drogue, or bouncing outwards off the rim. On early versions of the centre drogue, rim contacts can be damaging as the rim has a wide and 'soft' parachute edging, consisting of several annular strips which can be pierced and damaged by the probe tip. A Mk 2 "high speed" drogue has a much narrower and stiffer rim consisting of a single piece of nylon material. This design is much less susceptible to damage, and presents a larger target diameter within the rim for successful contacts. If the drogue is pierced, every effort should be made to withdraw directly astern. A high, low, or lateral withdrawal may cause undue loads on the probe and/or tear off the parachute edging.

f. Occasionally a 'soft' contact may occur, in which the probe tip fails to mate properly with the hose coupling and fuel may stream from the hose. This is often attributed to too low an overtake speed on making contact, so if this is considered to have been a likely cause, a slightly higher closure speed should be used next time.

g. Once in proper contact with the drogue the receiver should move forward until the middle of the orange section is approximately in its tunnel entrance. However, quite a lot of freedom in all directions is acceptable. When in contact, from 2 to 5% higher RPM will be required (than in free flight) because the receiver is carrying the drag of the drogue. The asymmetric drag causes a directional out of trim which is of no consequence to aircraft handling, but can be trimmed out if required. If movement aft exceeds 5 ft/sec the hose drum brake will operate automatically and disconnection will occur. The tanker will then have to retrail to full length before contact can be remade.

... the fuel contents indication of the fuel gauges should be monitored.

j. If the PWP **T.O.P.** warning appears during refuelling, the fuel flow should be stopped at once, by breaking contact. After a **T.O.P.** warning there is no restriction on further dry contacts, and further wet contacts can be attempted providing fuel flow is again stopped immediately any **T.O.P.** warning recurs.

k. TRANSfer warnings are likely to occur during air to air refuelling, particularly when the tanks are full or nearly full, and fuel flow has been stopped. The TRANSfer warnings will disappear soon after the tank depress switch is selected off. When a TRANSfer warning appears, the associated fuel contents gauge will drop to 300 lb. In spite of this the total internal contents (2,500 lb per side) should be available, but a steady or flashing fuel low level light must be taken as indicating the actual fuel available.

l. At high altitudes and weights the starboard wing station should be used when possible to minimise height loss during refuelling, since this station requires least extra RPM for contact.

m. Notes on Tanker Aircraft Installations

(i) Two hose drum units (HDU), the Mk 17 and Mk 20B are currently in use on RAF/RN tanker aircraft. All tankers are fitted with the Mk 20B refuelling pod, but the Victor has a Mk 20B pod on each wing and a Mk 17 unit on the centre line. The following description of the Victor therefore covers all RAF/RN tankers.

(ii) The wing HDUs each have a red, orange, and green light, and the centre HDU has two sets of red, orange, and green lights, one set on each side of the HDU tunnel.

... until the hose and drogue are trailed to their full length, and the hose winding motor has automatically changed from low to high gear. When this has been done, the red light goes out and the orange light appears, indicating that the tanker is ready for the receiver to make contact.

(iv) The centre hose is 80 ft long and the wing hoses are 51 ft long. On each hose there is an orange coloured section which on the centre hose is 10 ft long and starts 25 ft back from the aft end of the HDU tunnel. On the wing hoses the orange section is 6 ft long and starts 5 ft from the aft end of the tunnel. The coloured band, and some additional marks which may be painted on the hose, assist the receiver pilot in appreciating fore and aft velocity and position. Generally the receiver's position is satisfactory if some part of the orange band is in the entrance to the HDU tunnel.

(v) After the receiver has made contact with the drogue, the receiver must move forward at least 5 to 7 ft (all HDUs) in order to open the refuelling valve in the tanker. When this valve opens it operates a switch which changes the HDU indicator light from orange to green. Fuel will flow providing the tanker's pumps are on, which may be manually or automatically operated, and the receiver's system is ready to accept fuel. The Victor has a fuel totaliser to show the total fuel delivered. It also has a HDU footage indicator to show how much hose is out. The Victor may be fitted with a periscope through which an observer can watch the receiver aircraft.

Formation Flying

19. The aircraft is pleasant to fly in close formation. The deceleration afforded by thrust vectoring is very useful for coarse speed control when initially joining formation, but the associated trim changes make its use undesirable once in close formation.

Night Flying

20. The sloping side consoles produce reflections and their lighting strips are normally best set at low intensity. The bright-up facility is useful for making a specific check of the consoles. The HUD is especially valuable at night, because it is easily scanned against a dark background.

PART 3

CHAPTER 3—CIRCUIT PROCEDURE AND LANDING

Contents

Circuit Fuel Allowance

1. It is recommended that the circuit is joined with a minimum of 400/400 lb fuel remaining.

Checks Before Landing

2. a. Complete the Flight Reference Cards Landing Check.

b. Undercarriage lowering takes approximately 7·5 seconds. During lowering a transient small nose up trim change occurs. There is a slight increase in buffet with the undercarriage down.

c. Full flap lowering takes approximately 10 seconds. Full flap gives a small nose up trim change.

d. If the ADD is suspect it may be checked in straight and level flight. Undercarriage and flaps up, nozzles aft, no stores, 500/500 lb fuel, 250 kt, should give 4·8 units (±1 unit), plus 0·4 units/1,000 lb extra fuel or stores.

Engine Handling During Landing

Warning

A failure to understand the characteristics of the engine can easily result in the engine being overtemperatured and rejected.

3. a. Correct engine handling technique when landing is important for the same technical reasons as on take-off (Chapter 1, para. 6.). However, when landing, unlike taking off, it is not usually possible to throttle back as the manoeuvre progresses. This must be kept in mind during an approach, to avoid a period in excess of the planned JPT limit becoming necessary to ensure a safe landing.

b. A further difference between landing and taking off is that it is not normally possible to plan a landing in short lift rating. It is unlikely that a landing can be guaranteed within the short lift rating limit because the 15 second period will be reduced by the lack of thermal soak effects since engine acceleration will take place from a higher power setting than ground Idle. In consequence it is usual for the short lift rating to be kept in hand as a margin for normal lift rating operations.

c. Note on JPTL During Landing

If the JPTL is invoked when landing, the thrust will not increase further even if the throttle is opened more. This situation may first be noticed by the lack of aircraft response to throttle movement but it can be avoided by monitoring JPT during the approach. When landing it must be remembered that the JPT should not normally be anywhere near as high as the JPTL operating temperature if economic usage of engine life is to be maintained.

Use of Water Injection on Landing

4. a. If it is required, the water injection system can be armed during the checks before landing. However, in some circumstances it may be that the water endurance will be marginal if it is armed early at low RPM since it starts flowing at 94% RPM. Then it should be switched on, using the arming switch, later in the landing sequence.

b. The use of water does not change engine handling techniques but the following points should be noted.

(i) When the system is armed the RPM rise should be checked. If the rise does not occur, do not attempt to use the system, as the presence of water without the extra fuel flow from the bypass solenoid could lead to reduced engine acceleration times or even reduced RPM, should water flow.

(ii) If the green light does not appear above approximately 94 to 96% RPM, water is not flowing and care should be taken with throttle movements as the extra fuel supplied by the bypass solenoid, in the absence of water, could lead to surge. Return the arming switch to OFF whenever possible.

(iii) If water contents become exhausted there will be a rapid rise in JPT, although no loss of thrust, unless the engine is throttled back.

Sideslip in Jetborne and Partially Jetborne Flight

5. Reference should be made to Part 3, Chapter 1, para. 8. It should be noted that there is more likelihood of errors in this matter occurring during landing rather than during take-off, since greater concentration can be expected on achieving a particular flight path which leads to the touchdown point. There may also be more tendency to rudder the aircraft round to align it with the touchdown surface, without due regard being paid to the direction of the relative airflow.

Decelerating Transition

6. a. Complete the Flight Reference Cards Landing Check.

b. The simplest transition from conventional flight to hovering flight is commenced by positioning the aircraft wingborne into wind, at 8 units ADD (160 kt at 500/500 lb basic configuration, increase speed 6 kt/1000 lb), and about 1,000 yd from the desired hover point, at 50 to 100 ft. At this point leave the throttle as set (about 60%) and move the nozzle lever positively to the braking position. When this is done there is an abrupt longitudinal deceleration of about $\frac{1}{2}$g and a moderate nose up trim change. As the speed reduces and aerodynamic lift decreases, increase power to hold height, making sure that throttle is applied generously in the 110 to 90 kt region to prevent any sink occurring. Use the stick to hold the aircraft attitude steady and the rudder to keep the heading constant (i.e. the controls are used as in the hover, once the nozzles are deflected). When the hover is reached return the nozzle lever from braking to the hovering position. This selection is not critical but if it is done early the final deceleration will be low and if it is done late, after the hover is established, then the aircraft will need a nose low attitude until the nozzles are moved, to prevent it from moving backwards.

c. If the aircraft does not slow down as expected, during a decelerating transition, it will be because the nozzle angle is not correctly set. Check in particular that the STO stop has been cleared fully aft.

d. Once experience has been gained using the simple transition described in b. above, speed and flight path control can be carried out, to give the more usual descending approach path to a precise spot.

(i) Speed control is achieved by varying the nozzle angle relative to the ground and hence the horizontal thrust component. This can be done within the ADD limits by pitching the aircraft (15 units max, above 50 kt), or the aircraft attitude can be held steady and the nozzle lever moved. (Varying the thrust vector $\pm 14{\cdot}5°$ either side of the vertical gives 0·25g longitudinally if thrust = weight). If attitude is used to achieve speed control, some co-ordination with the throttle may be necessary to counter the associated wing lift changes.

(ii) Pilot judgement of the aircraft's deceleration performance towards the desired hover point is acquired with practice. Initially there tends to be a pronounced tendency to undershoot. To assist judgement when approaching a restricted site, it is often useful to have a period of slow approach where the speed is reduced to about 120 kt in good time, the remainder of the transition being carried out later. At this lower ground speed much more time is available to assess the remaining distance to run, and this allied to only approximately 600 yd being needed to decelerate from 120 kt to the hover, makes the task much easier. For details of slow approach technique see para. 9.

e. If maximum deceleration is not required, the transition may be carried out with the nozzles at the hovering position. In this case only shallow glide path angles can be used and deceleration is very small below 50 kt.

f. It is possible to overshoot and re-accelerate at any point in a decelerating transition merely by moving the nozzle lever forward as in a normal accelerating transition. This should be the usual reaction to a poorly judged approach which looks like producing a large overshoot, or an approach where the JPT and RPM do not remain inside the planned limits. In general less bleed life will be consumed by taking overshoot action early (reducing RPM once a speed increase is obtained) and doing a second approach at lighter weight, than will be consumed by continuing with as quick a VL as possible, at the excessive JPT. The more demanding the VL site is, the longer the positioning period is likely to be; thus the more important it is to overshoot should the JPT exceed the planned limit.

g. Where a deceleration is being made to a restricted site, a hover should be established, before descending below the level of obstacles in the overshoot path, to avoid the situation where insufficient power is available to decelerate further and yet a level overshoot cannot be carried out.

Vertical Landing (VL)

7. a. Solid Surface VL

(i) Ensure that the landing area is suitable and that there are no loose items liable to be blown about.

(ii) Check that the JPT and RPM are within the planned limits and confirm that the nozzle angle set is correct for landing, by observing that the hovering attitude is normal, then set up a medium rate of descent, aiming to achieve 3 to 5 ft/sec passing through 15 ft. At this height above the ground some turbulent effects are felt, similar to driving a car over cobblestones and the size of the stick movements to hold the desired attitude will start to increase. At about 10 ft a nose down trim change may be noticed. As the ground is approached the disturbances increase and coarse and frequent control movements are needed to control the attitude. Just before touchdown there may be a tendency to creep forward. Except with certain stores configurations (see para. 12.) no significant change of power is required in ground effect. When the wheels touch the ground and in no circumstances before, throttle back to Idling. Due to the oleo characteristics there may be a tendency to bounce, and it is therefore essential that the initial reduction in power is small and tentative until it is certain that the wheels are firmly on the ground. In order to minimise heating effects on the undercarriage and the ground surface, the toe brakes should be applied and the nozzles selected aft, immediately upon throttling back after touchdown. Where space permits it is good practice to taxy forward a few feet after landing to avoid any chance of the tyres becoming heated by the landing surface.

(iii) Once confidence in judgement of the correct rate of descent has been built up, do not attempt to cushion the touchdown. This is to save the increase in JPT that will necessarily occur during a gentle landing, due to the combination of increased RPM to check the rate of descent, extra bleed usage to stabilise the aircraft for a longer time in the turbulent ground effects and the increased exposure to recirculation. In addition there may be marked ambient temperature increases in the last few feet of descent, depending on weather and landing surface characteristics, which will lead to further increases of JPT if the aircraft is held in a low hover.

b. Mat VL

The normal solid surface VL techniques of para. a. are unchanged but care should be taken not to cross the edge of the mat below 25 to 30 ft (see Mat VTO Chapter 1, para. 9.b. (ii)). The view from the cockpit in the normal landing attitude is such that with the aircraft positioned over the centre of a 50 ft × 50 ft mat the front corners of the mat only are visible and these not from above 10 ft. Thus markers should be used to assess the correct hovering position before final let down. These markers may be natural features or objects near the mat. In the absence of suitable cues it is also possible to manoeuvre the aircraft to the desired spot with the nozzles in the braking position, thereby greatly improving the forward and downward view, and then re-adjust the nozzle angle and pitch attitude to the normal hovering values before the final let down. If this technique is used, great care must be taken not to mishandle the nozzle and throttle levers and it is recommended that the procedure is first practiced well clear of obstacles.

Rolling Vertical Landing (RVL)

8. a. When a VL would be possible from a performance consideration, but unwise from a debris ingestion aspect, a rolling VL should be carried out. Ground speed needed at touchdown to give the desired protection will vary according to the surface but is likely to be in the 30 to 50 kt range. Forward speed on touchdown may also be used to protect a landing surface (see sub-para. e.).

b. A hover should be established at a height of 50 ft, and short of the desired touchdown point. When ready to accelerate and descend, the nozzle lever should be moved forward slightly to give a nozzle angle of about 75°. (This movement is not critical and ± 1 to 2° is acceptable.) The nose should then be lowered to assist in accelerating to the desired ground speed. Height and rate of descent are controlled by the throttle in the normal hovering manner to achieve the desired touchdown point. The aircraft should be flared prior to touchdown to the normal hovering attitude, but never more nose up, or debris ingestion will occur even at quite high ground speeds due to the resulting forward vector of the exhaust nozzles.

c. The throttle should be put to Idle, the toe brakes applied and the nozzles selected fully aft as soon as possible after touchdown.

d. With experience, larger movements of the nozzle angle in the hover to 65 to 70° are practical and result in a much more positive acceleration towards the required ground speed, as well as initiating the necessary rate of descent, This results in shorter distances from 50 ft to touchdown. which may be important in some small sites.

e. With a smooth debris-free surface that might be damaged by a prolonged vertical landing 5 to 10 kt of forward translation will suffice to prevent the local heating from building up. Such a technique may be used on tarmac surfaces and require only the normal vertical landing techniques of para. 7., except that the aircraft is allowed to drift forward slightly when below 20 ft.

Slow Approach and Landing (SL)

9. a. General

If the AUW is too high for a VL, a partially jetborne slow approach and landing is carried out. The approach speed obtained depends upon the aircraft weight and the RPM used. The higher the RPM the slower the approach speed for a given weight. The maximum RPM available for use is dictated by either engine life or power reserve considerations. Performance charts are not required and the weight of the aircraft does not need to be known, in order to set up an optimum slow approach.

b. Engine Consideration

Keeping 5% below full throttle leaves sufficient reserve of thrust to allow a late overshoot to be made or a bad misjudgement to be corrected, but use of such high RPM may, under some ambient conditions, result in uneconomically high JPTs. Somewhat lower JPTs are desirable during a slow landing, compared with JPTs during a take-off, since the manoeuvre takes longer and so consumes more engine life for a given JPT. In general engine life consumption is insignificant below 600°C JPT but increases rapidly above 640°C. In order to keep within these JPTs the RPM range used is normally 90 to 95% unless it is important to reduce landing speed to a minimum, when higher RPM may be used.

c. Slow Approach

(i) Complete the Flight Reference Cards Landing Checks.

(ii) Position the aircraft wingborne at 8 units ADD (160 kt at 500/500 lb basic configuration, increase speed 6 kt/1,000 lb) and 2,000 to 3,000 yd from touchdown. Lower the nozzles to between 40° and 60° and increase RPM to the desired figure. Leaving the throttle fixed and controlling the flight path with the stick, use the nozzle lever to slow the aircraft down until 8 units ADD is reached. Note the speed and move the nozzle lever forward as required to maintain this speed. Continue the approach in this way using the stick to control the glide path, allowing transient changes of ± 2 units ADD, but maintaining the mean ADD at 8 units with the nozzle lever. Minimise sideslip by reference to the sideslip vane. The angle of approach should not exceed 5°, to avoid exceeding flare capability.

d. The following points should be borne in mind concerning this mixed jet and wing lift approach.

(i) The jet lift component of the total lift should be considered as constant at fixed RPM. The wing is optimised by setting a mean ADD of 8 units and thus, if insufficient lift is available from a small (up to 2 units) increase of ADD and the aircraft is sinking, speed must be increased to increase wing lift, hence the nozzle lever must be moved forward. Similarly if too much lift exists the aircraft must be slowed down in order to continue at constant ADD.

(ii) The sense of operation and co-ordination of the nozzle lever and stick is the same as that of the throttle lever and stick during a wingborne approach. In particular, when coming out of a turn or when increasing the glide path angle the nozzle lever will have to be moved aft and the nozzle angle increased. Similarly, when entering a turn or reducing the glide path angle, the nozzle lever must be moved forward and the nozzle angle reduced.

braking should be used as in para. 9.f. (ii). If this is not available a ground roll of 2,000 yd should be expected with wheel brakes alone.

(ideal) changeover speed will be reduced according to circumstances and in the limit would be zero.

(ii) Unprepared Surfaces

Since these surfaces are likely to have less friction than prepared surfaces, it is advantageous to use powered nozzle braking down to lower speeds on unprepared surfaces. However, due to their nature, unprepared surfaces are likely to include loose debris which can easily be ingested into the engine in low forward speed, high RPM, nozzle braking conditions. On unprepared surfaces it is therefore recommended that powered nozzle braking should not be used below 80 kt unless it is needed to avoid an overrun: in this case the engine will be put at risk.

Conventional Approach and Landing (CL)

10. a. Carry out the Flight Reference Cards Checks before Landing.

b. Make the final approach with flaps fully down at an ADD of 8 to 9 units (155 kt at 500/500 lb basic configuration, increase speed 6 kt/1,000 lb). Typical RPM will be 56%. The approach angle should not exceed 3° or sufficient flare capability may not be available. Flare normally, aiming to touch down 10 kt below final approach speed. A nose down trim change is apparent just prior to touchdown and full back stick may occur at touchdown. Do not throttle back sharply before touchdown or this will increase the nose down trim change. If the touchdown ADD is lower than 11 units then a mild porpoising motion will occur after touchdown, due to the nosewheel touching before main wheel reaction occurs. If porpoising occurs it will damp out as the aircraft slows down.

c. Other than for training, a conventional landing should only be carried out if the serviceability of the engine, nozzles or reaction controls is in doubt, or, if hydraulic supply is dependent on the RAT. In general, powered nozzle

Use of the Autostabiliser

11. The use of the autostabiliser during approach and landing noticeably steadies the aircraft in roll. The effect of the autostabiliser in pitch is mainly noticeable during a slow approach, or at the high speed end of a decelerating transition, when the aircraft is steadied longitudinally by its effect on the tailplane and rear reaction control valve. As during take-off, due to the low authority of the system, autostabiliser failures of both the hard over and oscillatory types are easily overridden by the pilot. Landings with all types have been carried out with failures, still switched in, although, when possible, AUTO STAB ENGAGE should be switched off following failure.

Effects of Stores

12. Apart from the effects on AUW, the only significant handling change when landing with symmetric stores is that during a VL or RVL with some fuselage store combinations, a small negative ground cushion is detectable.

NOTE: Pending further trials it is possible that lateral disturbances may be encountered just prior to touchdown if a float occurs when carrying Sidewinders and 100 gallon drop tanks on a slow landing.

Night Lighting

13. When making a VL at night with restricted lighting cues, there is a tendency to establish the hover at lower heights than by day. This could lead to damage to the landing area and its surroundings, depending on the circumstances. The use of a landing lamp or specially designed lighting patterns will reduce the risk of this happening.

(iii) It will be necessary to increase speed when entering a turn and reduce speed when leaving a turn if the ADD is to be kept constant.

(iv) When over 90% RPM are used the nozzle angles are typically 60° and above, so small changes of nozzle angle produce relatively large changes of horizontal thrust but only small changes of vertical thrust, as in the hover or early stages of accelerating transition. The higher the RPM the larger the nozzle angle needed and the more marked is this effect.

(v) An overshoot may be carried out, without increasing power, by easing the nozzle lever forward and maintaining constant ADD with the stick. There will be a slight tendency to sink initially unless RPM can be increased to compensate. In an emergency, increasing RPM will at once reduce ADD, increase speed and reduce rate of descent.

(vi) In the high power nozzles deflected configuration the aircraft is sensitive in pitch and care must be taken not to exceed the 15 units ADD limit. It is for this reason that the recommended mean ADD is 8 units. Under good conditions and with experience, the mean ADD can be increased to 10 units. When manoeuvring, at constant RPM, by variations in wing lift it should be appreciated that the wing is only supplying a small proportion of the total lift (typically 20 to 25%) so the manoeuvrability typically experienced for a small change in ADD when fully wingborne will no longer be obtained for the same ADD change.

(vii) It is important to minimise sideslip when manoeuvring below 120 kt. The directional stability of the aircraft decreases steadily with increasing RPM and reducing airspeed. (See also para. 6.c.)

(viii) If the airbrake is lowered a lateral and directional oscillation may occur during a slow approach. This can be controlled with aileron. (The airbrake exten-

reduction (2 to 5%) may be needed to ensure that the aircraft remains positively settled on the ground. Do not engage nosewheel steering before touchdown.

f. The following points should be borne in mind concerning a slow landing:

---

sion facility is lost with the use of the emergency undercarriage lowering system).

(ix) If minimum touchdown speed is required, engine life can be conserved by making the final power increase and speed reduction at a late stage of the approach. This is especially important if water injection is to be used, due to the limited duration of the system.

(x) In general, slow approach speeds of the order of 90 kt and above are needed to land a significant load in excess of that which can be landed vertically. However, circumstances can arise where, with only a small increase of AUW above VL capability, only a slow speed of 50 to 60 kt is needed. In this case, once the approach is established, it is easier to leave the nozzle angle fixed (it will be very close to the hovering position) and use the stick to control the ADD and the throttle to control the glide path. This is because, at the low speed, the wing lift becomes very small and unsuitable to use as a flight path control. The final approach and landing in this case becomes a question of "hovering" the aircraft on to the ground at a forward speed.

e. Landing

As the touchdown point is approached (i.e. 10 ft above the ground for every 1° glide path angle), reduce the rate of descent by increasing ADD, up to 12 units if required. Care must be taken not to exceed the limit of 15 units. The normal hover attitude should be adopted prior to touchdown. When ground effect is felt (5 to 10 ft), the nozzles should be moved to the hover position. This causes a further reduction in the rate of descent and also ensures that the aircraft is decelerating from the earliest possible moment. If necessary, RPM may be increased or reduced to make the final adjustment to the rate of descent at touchdown. The left hand must always be on the throttle as the throttle is the prime RPM control. At touchdown a small RPM

(i) The minimum distance from 50 ft to touchdown will be achieved with the steepest possible approach and the latest possible initiation of the flare consistent with not exceeding the undercarriage limit of 12 ft/sec. To achieve this, considerable judgement is called for and the throttle will have to be moved slowly and progressively, first to the hover and then to maximum to cushion the touchdown. Great care must be exercised in working up to this standard. In particular, any attempt to steepen the final stages of an approach in order to achieve an early and precise touchdown point can easily result in a heavy landing.

(ii) The minimum ground roll is achieved by moving the nozzles to the braking position as soon as possible and by using the highest RPM consistent with keeping the aircraft on the ground with the nozzles in this position. At normal landing weights, the braking position may be selected during the final stages of the landing. At weights above normal, larger nozzle angle changes will be required and the nozzles should be moved slowly and progressively, first to the hover and then to the braking position during the final stages of landing. This should prevent large sink rates from developing. Again, the left hand must be on the throttle at touchdown. A small number of instances of surge on touchdown have occurred and, pending further trials,

---

it is considered that the airborne use of nozzle braking in ground effect may have been a factor in causing these surges.

(iii) Until experience is gained the nozzles may be left at the final approach position for the landing.

(iv) Should the aircraft bounce during a slow landing, a nose up trim change may subsequently occur and full forward control column movement may be insufficient to correct it quickly. This trim change will vary with many conditions, e.g. nozzle angle, CG, type of store carried, speed and undercarriage reaction. If a nose up trim change is experienced at touchdown, the best method for recovery is to move the control column fully forward and reduce power to settle the aircraft on the ground.

g. Crosswind Operation

A wing down technique is not recommended as it conflicts with the requirements to minimise sideslip and could lead to overstressing an outrigger if the wings are not level at touchdown. Do not engage nosewheel steering before touchdown; the nosewheel can then castor initially and reduce the destabilising effects of touching down with a slip angle on the ground.

h. Braking Technique

(i) Prepared Surfaces

On dry prepared surfaces at speeds above 80 kt, maximum deceleration is obtained by using powered nozzle braking. With the nozzles at the braking position the throttle should be opened as far as possible without lifting the aircraft from the ground. Below 80 kt, normal use of the wheel brakes should be made with the throttle at Idling and the nozzles at the braking position. To avoid unloading the wheels and bursting the tyres, a mixture of powered nozzle braking and wheel braking should never be used. If the surface has low surface friction then the 80 kt

A Harrier GR9 pictured in a hard turn during a low-level training sortie. As part of Joint Harrier Forces routine operations, training exercises regularly saw Harriers at low level in many parts of the UK (particularly in Wales and Scotland), conducting training exercises at the minimum permissible peacetime altitude of 250 feet, and providing crews with realistic training experience, the local farmers and residents with a sporadic noise nuisance, and aviation enthusiasts with a magnificent spectacle. (Photo: Gareth Brown)

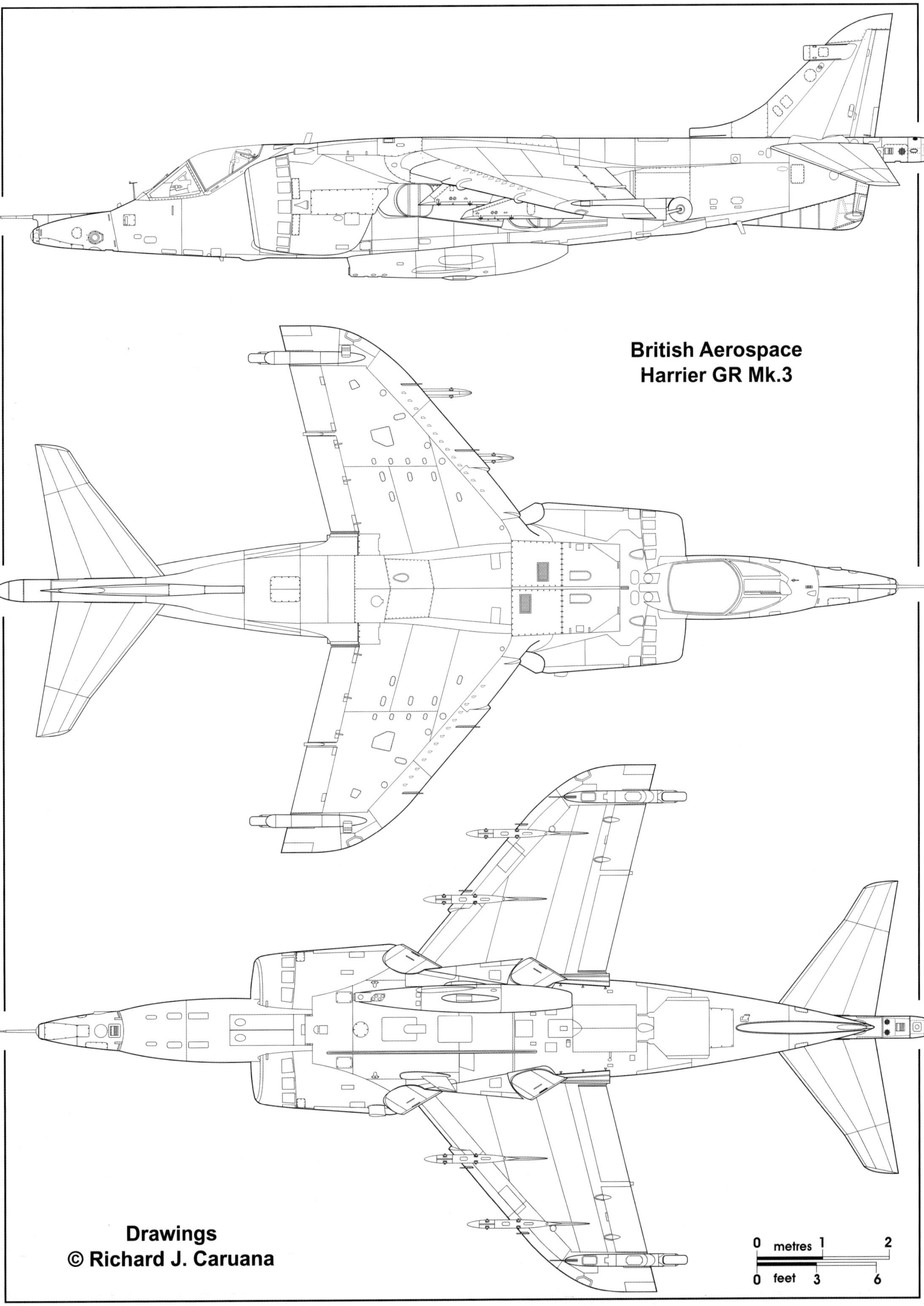

**British Aerospace
Harrier GR Mk.3**

**Drawings
© Richard J. Caruana**

0 metres 1 2

0 feet 3 6

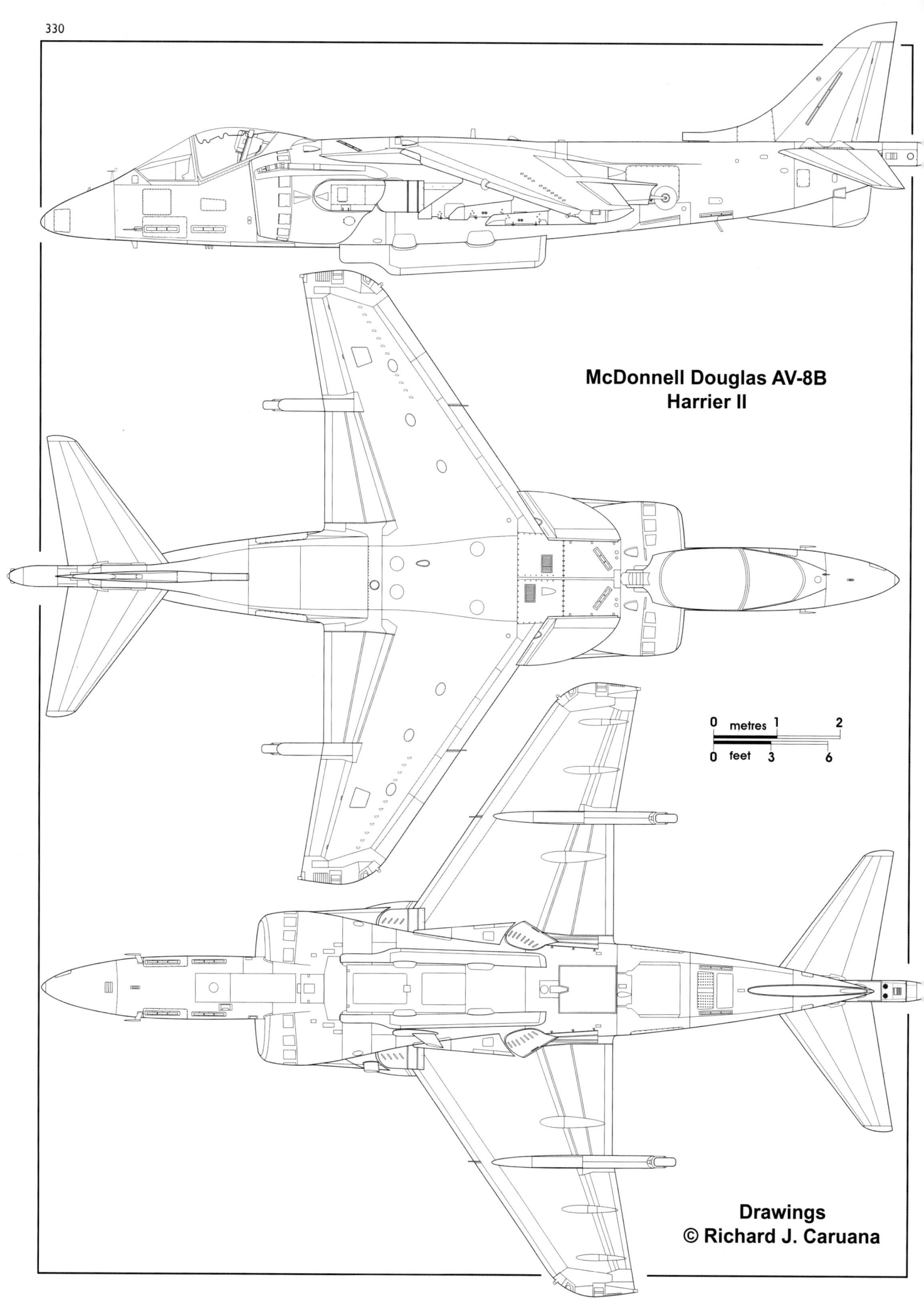

**McDonnell Douglas AV-8B
Harrier II**

0 metres 1 2
0 feet 3 6

**Drawings
© Richard J. Caruana**

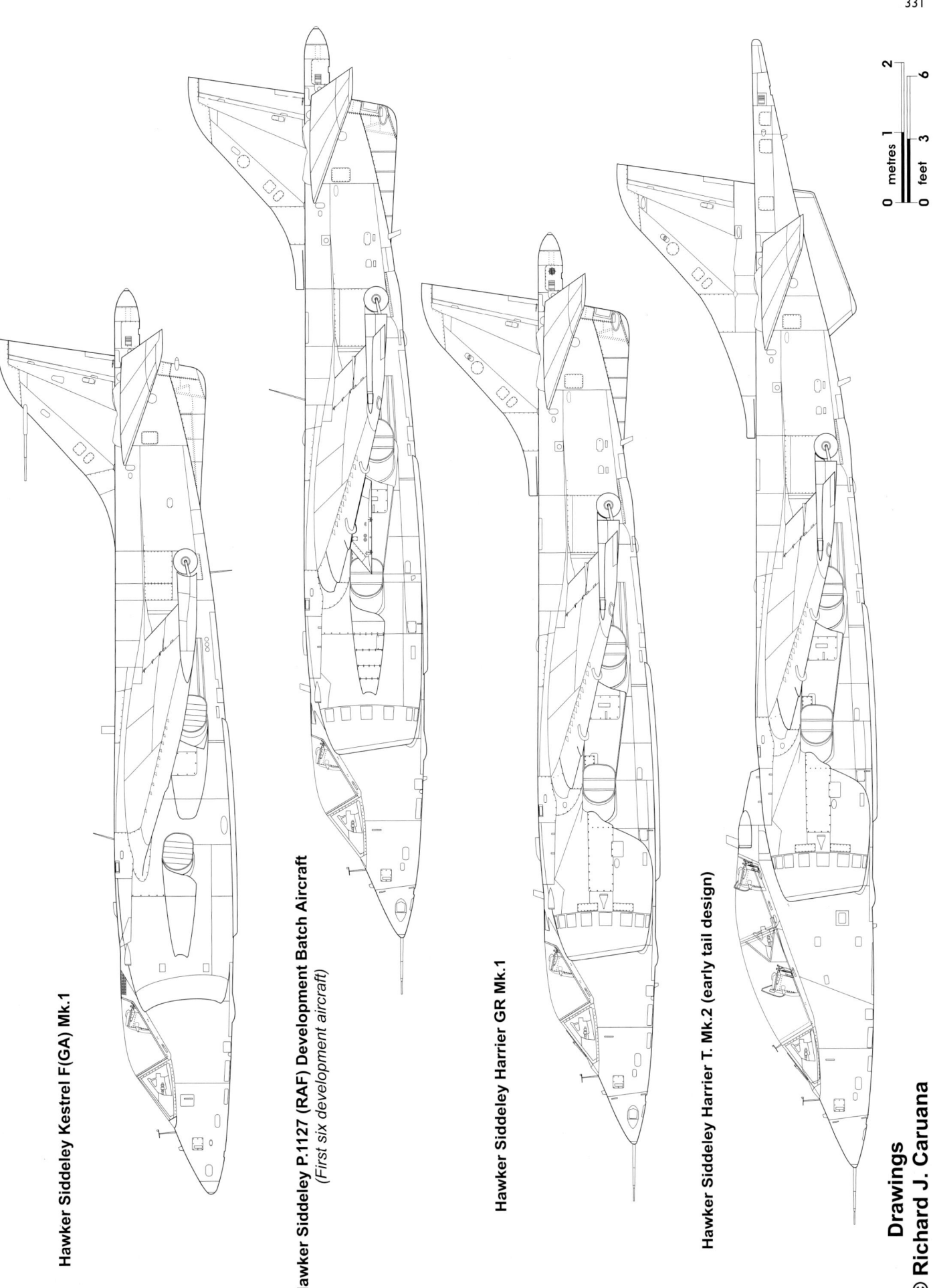

Hawker Siddeley Kestrel F(GA) Mk.1

Hawker Siddeley P.1127 (RAF) Development Batch Aircraft
(First six development aircraft)

Hawker Siddeley Harrier GR Mk.1

Hawker Siddeley Harrier T. Mk.2 (early tail design)

331

0 metres 1 2

0 feet 3 6

Drawings
© Richard J. Caruana

Hawker Siddeley Harrier T. Mk.2 (later tail design)

Hawker Siddeley Harrier GR Mk.3
(late configuration)

Hawker Siddeley Harrier T. Mk.4

Drawings
© Richard J. Caruana

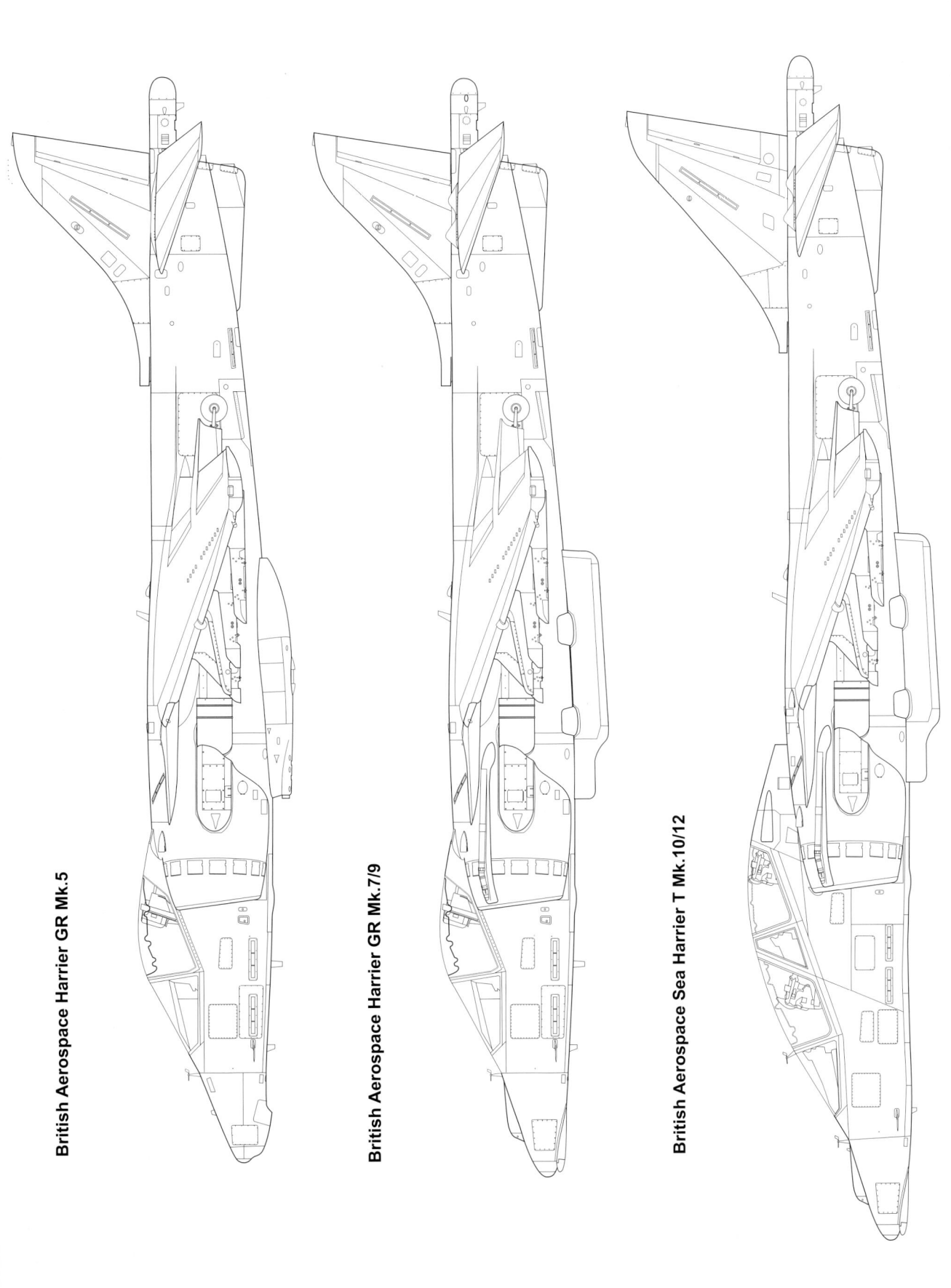

British Aerospace Harrier GR Mk.5

British Aerospace Harrier GR Mk.7/9

British Aerospace Sea Harrier T Mk.10/12

Drawings
© Richard J. Caruana

0 metres 1 2

0 feet 3 6

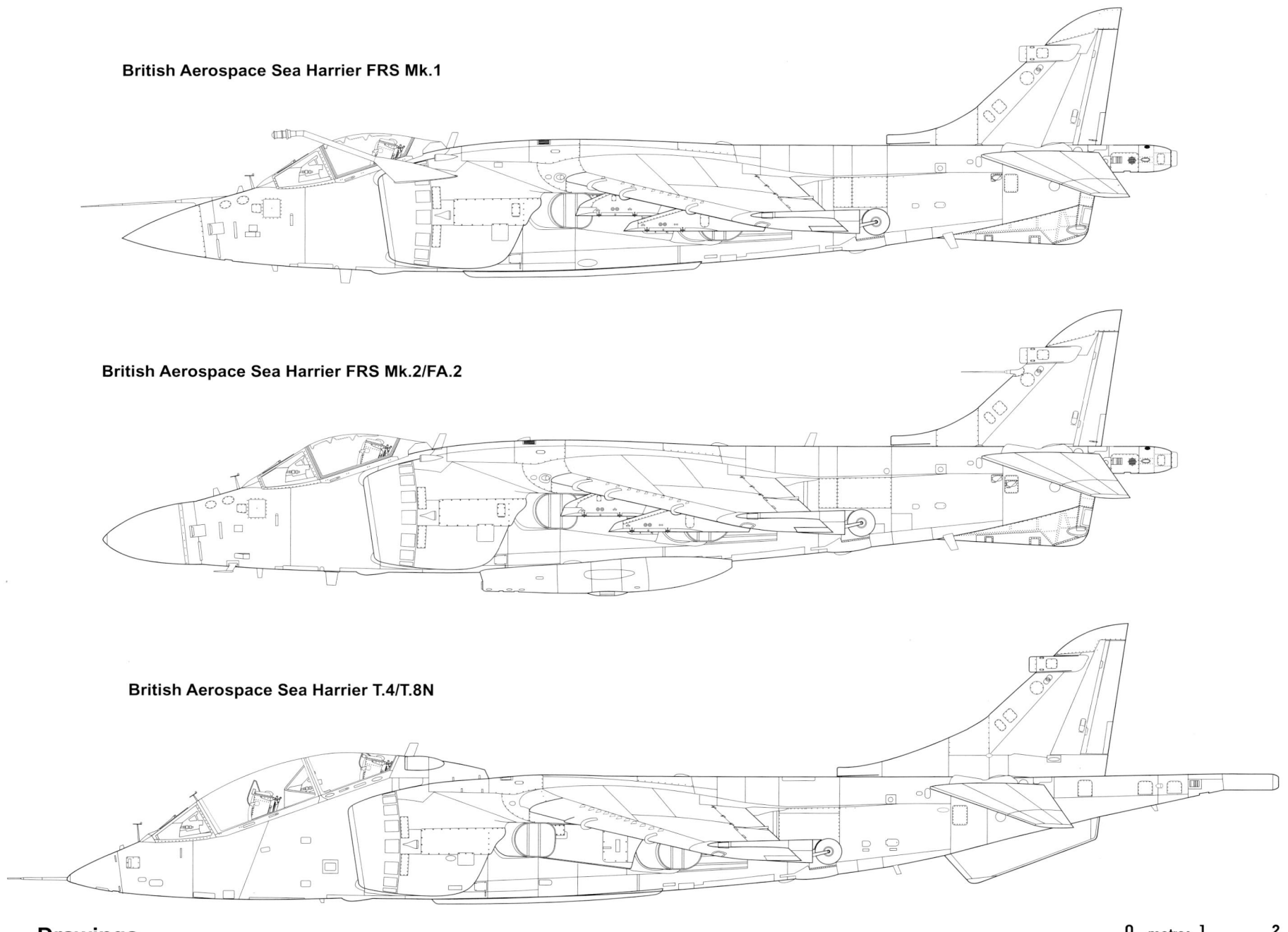

British Aerospace Sea Harrier FRS Mk.1

British Aerospace Sea Harrier FRS Mk.2/FA.2

British Aerospace Sea Harrier T.4/T.8N

Drawings
© Richard J. Caruana

0 metres 1 2

0 feet 3 6

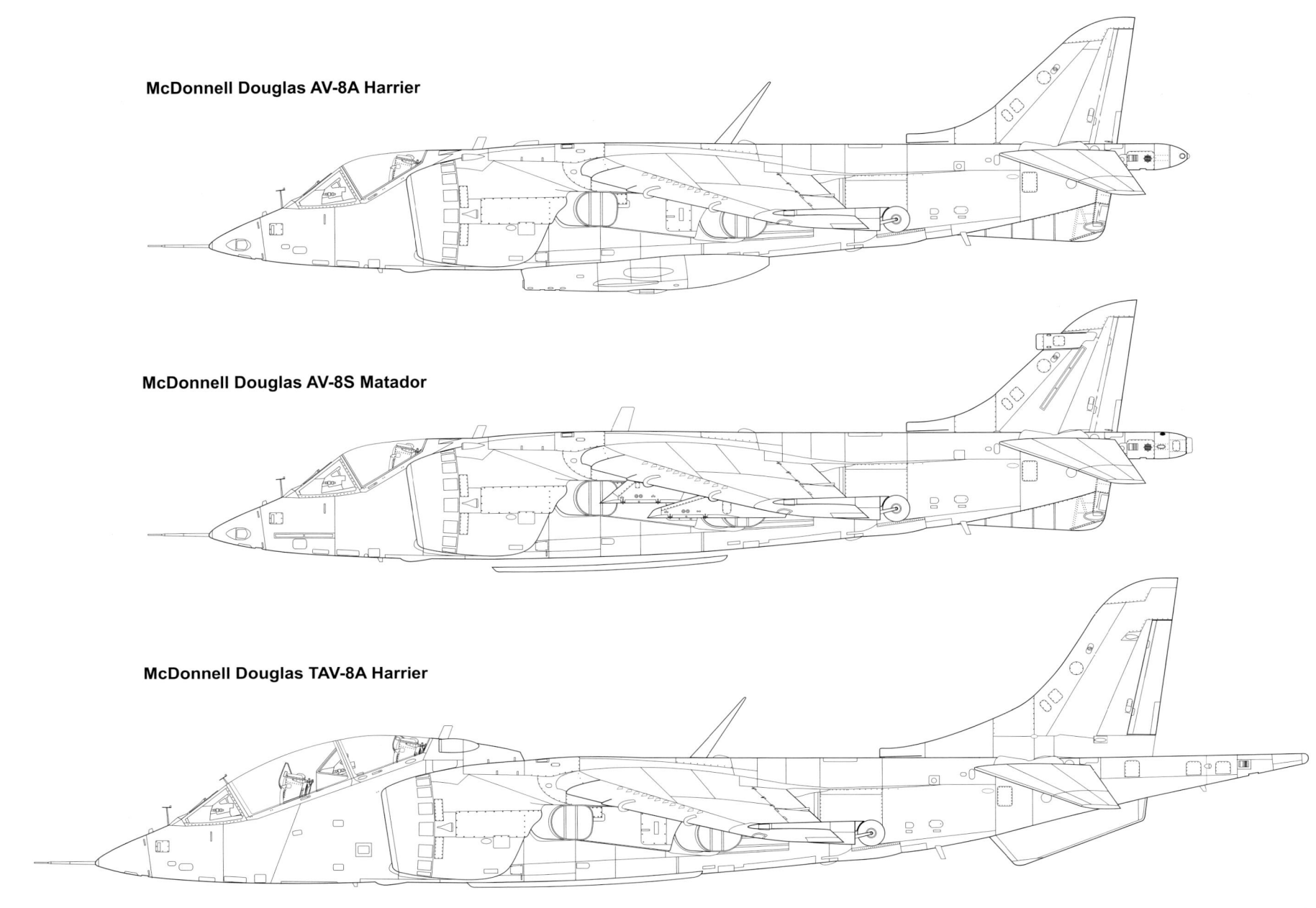

McDonnell Douglas AV-8A Harrier

McDonnell Douglas AV-8S Matador

McDonnell Douglas TAV-8A Harrier

Drawings
© Richard J. Caruana

0 metres 1 2
0 feet 3 6

McDonnell Douglas AV-8B Harrier II

McDonnell Douglas AV-8B Harrier II Plus

McDonnell Douglas TAV-8B Harrier II

0 metres 1 2
0 feet 3 6

Drawings
© Richard J. Caruana